UNFAIR TO GENIUS

UNFAIR TO GENIUS

THE STRANGE AND LITIGIOUS CAREER
OF IRA B. ARNSTEIN

DISCARD

GARY A. ROSEN

OXFORD
UNIVERSITY PRESS

OXFORD
UNIVERSITY PRESS

Oxford University Press, Inc., publishes works that further
Oxford University's objective of excellence
in research, scholarship, and education.

Oxford   New York
Auckland   Cape Town   Dar es Salaam   Hong Kong   Karachi
Kuala Lumpur   Madrid   Melbourne   Mexico City   Nairobi
New Delhi   Shanghai   Taipei   Toronto

With offices in
Argentina   Austria   Brazil   Chile Czech   Republic France   Greece
Guatemala   Hungary   Italy   Japan   Poland   Portugal   Singapore
South Korea   Switzerland   Thailand   Turkey   Ukraine   Vietnam

Published by Oxford University Press, Inc.
198 Madison Avenue, New York, New York 10016

www.oup.com

Oxford is a registered trademark of Oxford University Press

Library of Congress Cataloging-in-Publication Data
Rosen, Gary A.
Unfair to genius : the strange and litigious career of Ira B. Arnstein / Gary A. Rosen.
p.   cm.
Includes bibliographical references and index.
ISBN 978-0-19-973348-4
1. Arnstein, Ira B.—Trials, litigation, etc. 2. Copyright—Music—United States
3. Copyright infringement—United States 4. Fair use (Copyright)—United States. I. Title.
KF228.A76R67   2012
346.7304′82—dc23   2011042941

1 3 5 7 9 8 6 4 2

Printed in the United States of America
on acid-free paper

For Mom, Dad, Uncle Irv, and Aunt Esther

Our songs and cities are the best things about us. Songs and cities are so indispensable. Even if we go into darkness, the time will come when people will want to know how these ruins were made—the essence of the life we made.
—Jane Jacobs

CONTENTS

PROLOGUE

There is a fine line between genius and insanity, and I have erased that line.
—*Oscar Levant*

In September 1948 it fell to Francis Gilbert, Irving Berlin's longtime attorney, to inform his sometimes prickly client that he had just been sued, "along with pretty nearly everybody else in the industry," by that "perennial plaintiff in plagiarism suits," Ira B. Arnstein. Although their offices were only a few blocks apart, Gilbert chose to break this bit of unwelcome news by letter, sheepishly explaining that he was only telling Berlin "so that if you hear it talked about on Broadway, you will know something about it."[1] Berlin was sixty then, at peace in his domestic life and enjoying a spell as productive and lucrative as any in his long career. *Annie Get Your Gun* was in the third year of its original Broadway run; *Blue Skies* and *Easter Parade*, jukebox movie musicals that coasted on the strength of tunes from his back catalog, had been enormous postwar hits. Berlin accepted Gilbert's news with uncharacteristic equanimity, writing back: "I suppose we have to take the bad with the good in our system which gives everyone a chance to have their day in court." "Of course," he added puckishly, "Arnstein is stretching his day in court into a lifetime."[2]

One of the heroic archetypes in the annals of American jurisprudence is the bedraggled, unschooled litigant, armed only with a thirst for justice and a righteous determination to see it done, doing battle against entrenched and well-heeled interests, prevailing, and leaving a lasting mark in the life of the law. Ira B. Arnstein occupies a special place on the margins of that tradition. He never won a case, but over a thirty-year period he repeatedly went toe-to-toe with the popular music establishment of his day, leaving an enduring imprint merely by getting his days in court and, Rocky Balboa–like, going the distance. Lawyers will recognize this as no small accomplishment. A judge can do more to frustrate the intent of the law, and do it more efficiently, by blocking litigants at the courthouse door, or tossing them out of court prematurely on nice points of punctilio, than by laboriously adjudicating their cases on the merits. Even while asserting claims that strained credulity, Arnstein had a gift for posing conundrums that engaged some of the finest legal minds of his era, forcing them to refine and sharpen their doctrines.

In his losing causes, Arnstein established rules of procedure and evidence— "adjective law," in old-fashioned but still useful terminology—that have secured a day in court for many a worthier claimant, giving fresh force to the substantive law of music copyright. The claim that Michael Bolton's "Love Is a Wonderful Thing" infringed the Isley Brothers' song of the same title, or the claim that George Harrison's "My Sweet Lord" was a "subconscious" plagiarism of the Chiffons' "He's So Fine," might never have gone to trial, much less resulted in multi-million dollar judgments, without the legal foundation laid by Arnstein.[3] When Morris Albert's treacly "Feelings" was adjudged so "strikingly similar" to Louis Gaste's earlier *Pour Toi* as to justify an inference of deliberate copying, the court began and ended its legal analysis with reference to decades-old *Arnstein* precedents.[4] When avatars of rhythm and blues, or at least their estates and distant heirs, have obtained long overdue credit and compensation for their essential contributions to rock and roll, they too owe a hat tip to their quixotic forebear, Ira B. Arnstein.

Like many lawyers doing music copyright work, I first chanced upon Arnstein in the ordinary course of business. And like many others who share my taste for the absurd, the audacious, and the anarchic, I found the reports of his cases a hoot. Even in the dry prose of judges steeped in Edwardian mores and manners, Arnstein came across as equal parts Groucho, Harpo, and Chico. It was easy to envision the Marx Brothers having some fun with their early Broadway audiences, taking turns in the role of the eccentric and seditious Professor Arnstein (his preferred, though entirely self-conferred, honorific), or to imagine S. J. Perelman riffing on one of the jokey newspaper headlines that Arnstein's cases inspired, perhaps the *New York American*'s alliterative "Humming Held Prejudiced in Suit over Song—Defense Witness Denies His Da-Da's Were Unfair," or *Variety*'s snarky "Cole Porter Is Just a Guy Named Arnstein."

There is no reason to revisit or to doubt the conclusions of Arnstein's contemporaries that Alberto Dominguez's eminently danceable mambo hit "Perfidia" was not copied from Arnstein's dark, foreboding meditation on the Jewish Sabbath prayer *V'Shomru*, that Cole Porter did not in fact hire stooges to break into Arnstein's lodgings and steal his manuscripts, that the American Society of Composers, Authors and Publishers (ASCAP) did not bribe police officers to kidnap and silence him—to mention just a few of his more risible claims—or that Arnstein suffered from, in the quaint diagnostic vocabulary of his day, a persecution complex. It can be stipulated that Arnstein was, not to put too fine a point on it, a crank, a *noodnik*, and a loser, rank roadkill along the side of what Paul Goldstein has called "Copyright's Highway." But long before he became a recurring character in the law reports and in urban legend, Arnstein had led an accomplished, professional musical life. When it came to the intersection of art, commerce, and law, he could be an astute observer and trenchant scold. "He undoubtedly has some mentality," one judge, channeling Polonius, observed, "but I am afraid it is warped in some respects."[5] Instinctively, Arnstein was a legal realist and a behavioral economist before such schools of thought had names, and he possessed a comedian's knack for deflating pretension and snobbery. He was a provocateur who gave voice and drew attention to the plight of many other music industry outsiders, even if his personal grievances seemed delusional. From Arnstein's perspective, one may glean an utterly unromantic appreciation of a cultural milieu—whether referred to as "Tin Pan Alley," "The Golden Age of American Popular Song," or, as I suggest here, "The Age of the Songwriter"—that was shrouded, even before it was over, in a nearly impenetrable layer of nostalgia and hagiography.

Arnstein's career coincided with a fascinating and tumultuous period in American popular music, bookended by the World's Columbian Exposition of 1893 and Elvis Presley's first appearance on the *Ed Sullivan Show* in 1956. It began when "the music business" still referred to the manufacture and sale of instruments, a piano was an "indispensable piece of furniture for any household with even modest pretensions to culture,"[6] and the press covered pianists and piano makers with the same intensity that would later be devoted to movie stars and their studios. It spanned the birth and early maturity of popular music as a publishing specialty; the advent of radio broadcasting, talking pictures, and the modern recording industry; the creation and growth of performing rights organizations; and landmark expansions of legal protections for the intangible assets of these burgeoning enterprises. The parallels between the battles over control and distribution of creative wealth back then (when copyright memes were so pervasive they could be found in popular songs and screwball comedies) and those in our era of digital media and the internet are as striking as they are instructive. Time and again, laws and technologies "designed to enable the new" have been, in Lawrence Lessig's words, "transformed to protect the old."[7] A pattern of ebb and flow that began in the nineteenth century and continues into the twenty-first—as periods of artistic ferment and freedom alternate with periods of wealth concentration and creative hegemony—took some of its most dramatic turns in the years between the two world wars. Arnstein's journey through these legal and technological shoals provides occasion to consider some of the fundamental issues of public policy that dog all intellectual property law. What constitutes a creative contribution worthy of proprietary status? How can economic incentives intended to promote progress in science and the useful arts be vouchsafed to the writers and inventors, and not dissipated on the commercial overhead of big media and big science? How can we maintain a playing field that is not unfair to genius? "People are wrong," the documentarian Errol Morris recently observed, "if they think the profound and ridiculous are incompatible."[8]

Arnstein's is a human story of manifold layers—the amusing, the poignant, and the repellant always in close proximity. The biopic might be pitched as "Leonard Bernstein meets P. D. Q. Bach." A musically gifted boy from a family of laborers, Arnstein came to the United States in the first wave of Jewish exodus from the Russian Pale of Settlement. His youth was marked by precocious accomplishment, and he was a busy music teacher and productive composer through much of his adulthood. But Arnstein's thorough immersion in the common musical practice and culture of the nineteenth century left him ill-prepared for the artistic and technological upheavals of the twentieth, as new rules and new media wreaked havoc on the old ways. His midlife slide into destitution and madness—it is not clear if one preceded the other and, if so, which—was cinematic in its mix of pathos and bathos. There is an affecting, shabby dignity, part Leopold Bloom, part Chaplin's Tramp, to his perseverance in the face of near-universal scorn and ridicule.

Popular songs are the amber in which the DNA of a cultural moment is preserved. "We require arts which specifically refer to our moment, which create the image of our lives,"[9] wrote Gilbert Seldes in 1924, at the very dawn of the Age of the Songwriter. Following Arnstein's travails entails telling (and sometimes debunking) stories about some wonderful popular songs, about their creators, and about sixty years in the musical life of the city, New York, where their production was a major industry. Arnstein had a Zelig-like ability to insert himself into the orbit of important musical and legal figures whose names and accomplishments, though justly celebrated in their time, may barely elicit a glimmer of recognition today. Within a few degrees of separation from Arnstein one finds "Madame" Eugenie Lineff, Xaver Scharwenka, Yossele Rosenblatt, Nathaniel Shilkret, Edward B. Marks, L. Wolfe Gilbert, Charles Tuttle, Nathan Burkan, Arthur Garfield Hays, Sholom Secunda, and, above all, Sigmund Spaeth, a radio personality and popular writer on music who, for decades, was Arnstein's bête noire. And much as encounters between familiar celebrities and the brilliant Sacha Baron Cohen's obtuse alter ego Ali G can be unpredictably revelatory, the best known and most thoroughly documented personages in this story—Irving Berlin, Cole Porter, Jerome Frank, Learned Hand—can yield up fresh insights as they grapple with Ira B. Arnstein.

What follows is not biography—of which Arnstein's life is hardly the stuff—but a narrative romp across six decades of understudied legal and cultural history. Alighting just at those episodes and characters to which we are led by Arnstein Agonistes provides, for the general reader, a self-contained and accessible overview, and for the specialist an entertaining and informative complement to more comprehensive histories and scholarly monographs. The viewpoint is from the bottom up, a perspective that is seldom as well-preserved as it is in this instance, thanks to Arnstein's maddening devotion to that most persistent and least selective of all media, court papers. It harkens, as did Scott Sandage's recent *Born Losers*, to Mrs. Willy Loman's plea that attention must be paid. "By paying attention," Sandage showed, "we can learn a great deal about our culture and about ourselves from the stories of Americans who failed."[10] Now there's an apropos segue to the strange and litigious career of Ira B. Arnstein in the Age of the Songwriter.

UNFAIR TO GENIUS

1

LOONY TUNES, SCHMALTZY MELODIES

One thing about this peanut vendor song, it's popular, but you don't know how it goes till you hear it. Nobody can whistle it, that's what makes it the greatest bit of music during our time.
—Will Rogers

For a filmmaker trying to evoke a sense of the excitement surrounding Franklin D. Roosevelt's 1932 election campaign, the hope generated by the "First 100 Days" of New Deal legislation the following spring, or the catharsis unleashed by the repeal of Prohibition in December 1933, the musical cue of choice is "Happy Days Are Here Again." The chorus is an audio icon, what neurologist Oliver Sacks has called a "Proustian mnemonic,"[1] hardwired into the psyches of even those born generations later, and capable of stirring emotions and associations easily mistaken for actual memories. But lost in the haze of nostalgia surrounding "Happy Days" is the mordant humor that fueled its initial rise to popularity in the immediate aftermath of the stock market crash of October 1929, along with nearly all recollection of the songs that would make up a historically correct sound track to the not-so-happy days of 1932 and 1933 that proved to be the nadir of the Great Depression.

"Happy Days" was not inspired by Roosevelt or by any of the events for which it now serves as incidental music de rigueur. Nor was it Roosevelt's campaign song. FDR had wanted to use "Anchors Aweigh" as a none-too-subtle reminder that he had served as assistant secretary of the navy many years earlier—a civilian position, but still a reasonable proxy for the military credentials he lacked. The Democratic Party overruled him, selecting the only punningly nautical "Row, Row, Row with Roosevelt," a grating, oom-pah march that would stir more aural fatigue than political fervor: *"He's honest, he's strong, he's stead-ee/A chip off the block that gave us Tedd-ee/Row, row, row with Roosevelt/On the good ship U-S-A."* But "Row, Row, Row's" composers, J. Fred Coots and Eddie Dowling, were loyal Democrats, and they had given their little ditty a decisive edge by dedicating the song's roy-alties to the party treasury.[2]

There was little about the provenance of "Happy Days," on the other hand, that would have commended it to Roosevelt or the Democratic Party had anyone actually suggested that it would make a good campaign song. Milton Ager and Jack Yellen, composer and lyricist respectively, were Republicans. They had written "Happy Days" in 1929 as a "whoopee, hurrah song" for a scene in an early MGM backstage musical called *Chasing Rain-bows* in which the cast of the show-within-the-movie celebrates the armistice ending World War I,[3] a war and a peace that had been political kryptonite for the Democrats throughout the 1920s. Worse still, the subsequent suc-cess of "Happy Days" had been driven by a force deemed lethal in all con-ventional political wisdom—irony.

While *Chasing Rainbows* moldered, unreleased, on MGM's shelf, Ager and Yellen exercised their option to publish the songs they had written for it, just as the stock market crash of October 1929 was igniting a bull market in black humor. *Caught Short!*, Eddie Cantor's instant collection of lame one-liners ("I promised my wife a rope of pearls. I can't get the pearls but I have the rope—and I'm thinking of using it myself"), sold out three quick printings.[4] Even the genial Will Rogers turned dark: "When Wall Street took that tail spin, you had to stand in line to get a window to jump out of and speculators were selling space for bodies in the East River."[5] The sunny, guileless "whoopee, hurrah song" acquired a new layer of meaning. "It got the reputation of being 'the jumping song,'" as Yellen later recalled the joke, "if a fellow wanted to jump out a window, he sang a chorus of 'Happy Days Are Here Again' and then jumped."[6] As a musical accompaniment to Wall

Street's humbling takedown, the repercussions of which were not yet being felt by many outside of the investor class, "Happy Days" was a hit. In keeping with the practice of the time—when it was the song, not the performer, that sold records, and the distinction between "original" and "cover" had no meaning—each of the major record labels released at least one version featuring its own talent. The song's stand-alone success finally prompted MGM to release *Chasing Rainbows* in 1930, after interpolating some additional choruses of "Happy Days" into a grand Technicolor finale.[7]

How "Happy Days" came to be performed when Roosevelt's name was placed in nomination at the Democratic National Convention in Chicago two years later, and thereafter came to be indelibly associated with him and the party, is the subject of a body of apocrypha that is still growing, promulgated by serious journalists and historians, eighty years after the event. Recent literature has credited this stroke of political genius to a delegate who remembered the song from a cigarette ad,[8] and to Roosevelt aides who thought "Anchors Aweigh" sounded like a funeral march and wanted to use something "peppy" instead.[9] Writing in the *New York Times*, Milton Ager's daughter, the journalist Shana Alexander, at once authoritative, detailed, and surpassingly credulous, attributed it to an employee of the Ager, Yellen & Bornstein publishing house, specifically an industrious song plugger named Tubby Garen. At the very moment Roosevelt's name was being placed in nomination, according to Alexander's account, Tubby "wormed his way backstage, burst into the trailer where FDR was waiting to go on and shouted: 'Mr. President, have I got a song for you!'"[10]

The actual whereabouts of Tubby Garen on the day of Roosevelt's nomination are undocumented, but it can be readily verified that Governor Roosevelt was still in Albany, New York,[11] and that Chicago Stadium's house organist, Al Melgard, already had "Happy Days" in his working repertoire. Melgard, who had mastered the art of impromptu music programming as an accompanist for silent movies,[12] had been playing "Happy Days" on his mighty Barton organ just two weeks earlier for the Republicans, when their convention re-nominated President Herbert Hoover in the same hall,[13] and before that in the course of his regular duties entertaining Chicago Blackhawks hockey fans. "Happy Days" would continue to be played at Hoover rallies during the fall campaign,[14] a tone-deaf musical complement to his clueless slogan, "prosperity is just around the corner." The Democrats' territorial rights to the tune, and all its attendant emotions and associations, wouldn't vest until the election was decided, and apparently not for quite some time after that. The Ager, Yellen & Bornstein catalog boasted what was to become the quintessential Roosevelt song, but for the inaugural celebrations of March 1933 the firm was instead promoting "There's a New Day Comin,'" a pallid, labored, and quickly forgotten sequel composed by Ager specially for the occasion.[15]

Politics and popular music in the United States had been mixing since colonial times. "President Cleveland's Wedding March," a song dashed off by a teenage Isidore Witmark in 1886 on the mere rumor of impending White House nuptials, is often credited with putting Tin Pan Alley, popular music's factory village during the four decades that followed, on the map. The serendipitous, irrepressible success of "Happy Days," and Ager, Yellen's inability to manufacture a hit with "New Day Comin,'" were both emblematic of another round of big changes afoot in the music business.

By the time of Roosevelt's inauguration, economic misery had spread far beyond Wall Street and suicide rates were rising nationally. A good defenestration joke no longer needed a New York setting, as in a 1933 George S. Kaufman–Morrie Ryskind radio routine about a businessman in Cleveland who jumped out a twelfth-story window. "Was he killed?" Ryskind asked. "Worse than that," deadpanned Kaufman, "he fell into the hands of receivers."[16]

Outside the bubble of the political campaigns, popular music was dripping in pathos and sentimentality. A pseudonymous, operatically trained tenor—"The Street Singer"—briefly garnered a spot in the pantheon of network radio stars with a nightly fifteen-minute show on CBS. The Street Singer accompanied himself on the accordion, his voice and instrument blending to produce an ineffably mournful timbre, in a repertoire that spanned the small space between the maudlin and the lachrymose. Two decades earlier, Al Jolson had risen to fame as the "Mammy Singer" performing, in blackface redolent of an unreconstructed southern past, music that was neither jazz nor blues but nonetheless some indigenous American idiom that had absorbed and sanitized elements of both, through the filter of Ashkenazic cantillation. The Street Singer, later billed as Arthur Tracy, was Jolson's photo negative, a "Mother Singer" of pre-fascist central European sensibility, his small discography weighted heavily toward such weepers as "I'll Have the Last Waltz with Mother," "It's My Mother's Birthday Today," and "To Mother, with Love." The Street Singer's recipe for success was straightforward: "I always put all the schmaltz I had into my songs."[17] His unabashed sentimentalism resonated with a large and appreciative audience as the Great Depression was bottoming out.

Schmaltz was central to the musical vocabulary of the day. In early Depression-era America—a brief, unlamented musical interregnum between the end of F. Scott Fitzgerald's Jazz Age and the rise of swing bands and Fred Astaire, representing an idealized, aspirational "culture of elegance."[18] Foxtrots gave way to waltzes, and lyrics, ribald and sassy in the Roaring Twenties, turned wistful and chaste. "In a Shanty in Old Shanty Town" and "Lullaby of the Leaves" were typical hits. Gus Kahn, lately the lyricist for "Makin' Whoopee" and "Ain't We Got Fun," made the transition from the raffish to the mawkish with his 1933 hit, "Hi-Ho Lack-A-Day, What Have We Got to Lose?" "The very misery of the melody proved its appeal."[19] Of the more durable standards that came out of those years ("As Time Goes By," "Night and Day," and "April in Paris" among them), only one was as instant a sensation with the broad public as it was with the elite who could frequent Broadway shows and ritzy nightclubs—"Stormy Weather."

A period filmmaker will go to great pains to make sure that the visual artifacts of popular culture—fashions, furnishings, and other ephemera—are historically correct, and an army of vigilante film buffs stands ready to expose the most inconsequential of anachronisms. No such scruple applies to musical cues. The sound track speaks less to the intellect than to an innate and unchanging emotional grammar, making it less useful than, say, a Model T or a Nehru shirt for date-stamping a scene. Were it otherwise, "Play, Fiddle, Play" would be today a recognizable leitmotif for heralding the arrival of the New Deal. Although not overtly topical in the manner of "In a Shanty in Old Shanty Town" or "What Have We Got to Lose?," the song invokes an archetypal Depression image, the itinerant gypsy. A minor key "valse moderato," sprinkled with augmented intervals in the gypsy mode, and usually arranged to feature a wailing violin and castanets, "Play, Fiddle, Play" does not stint on the schmaltz in music or lyric:

The campfires are gleaming,
As red as the sun,
And my heart keeps dreaming,
Just dreaming of one,
So softly croon,
While the moon,
Weaves our two hearts in harmony,
Play, fiddle, play, to my love.

Though not suited for mellow crooners like Rudy Vallée or Bing Crosby, or for belters like Jolson and Kate Smith, this was manna from heaven for sob singers like Arthur Tracy, his natural vocal vibrato rendering strings all but superfluous. His female counterpart, Ruth Etting, the reigning queen of the sad song—"none chants more plaintively than she the agonies of the torch song's unrequited love"[20]—added it to her repertoire, as did the "Irish Thrush" Morton Downey, giving the gypsy love song an incongruous Celtic lilt. For Harry Horlick and His A&P Gypsies—the first commercially sponsored musical act on radio in the early 1920s—"Play, Fiddle, Play" was a chance to freshen up a gypsy conceit that had grown a little threadbare. And the song helped to launch Phil Spitalny's newly formed All-Girl Orchestra, which adopted it as a showpiece for its featured player, the classically trained Mrs. Spitalny, known well into the 1950s to a large and admiring public as "Evelyn and Her Magic Violin." The major record labels gave "Play, Fiddle, Play" to their A-list bandleaders, including George Olsen and Ted Lewis. Highbrow artists, or at least high middlebrow, jumped on the bandwagon. Russian violinist David Rubinoff played it on Eddie Cantor's *Chase and Sanborn Show*. Morton Gould, then a staff pianist at Radio City Music Hall and NBC, created a concert transcription for two pianos.

The "charts," such as they were in the early 1930s, relied on industry self-reporting and lacked even a veneer of statistical rigor. Any claim that a song "charted" in those years ought to be viewed with some skepticism, and specific assertions that a song "reached number two" discounted entirely. But by all available metrics, "Play, Fiddle, Play" was a palpable hit, a top seller in both sheet music and on phonograph records. That it was, at least for several years, something more, a song that managed to worm its way into the collective subconscious, is best evidenced by its cameo role in George Cukor's urbane adaptation of Edna Ferber and George S. Kaufman's stage play, *Dinner at Eight*, which opened in the summer of 1933. The movie version was a star-studded MGM vehicle with John and Lionel Barrymore, Marie Dressler, Wallace Beery, Jean Harlow, and Billie Burke. The interlocking plotlines revolve around Burke's frenetic attempts to give a formal dinner party on short notice, mixing guests from society, commerce, and show business, while her family and the invited guests cope, in the space of one afternoon, with doomed love affairs, financial ruin, terminal illness, and suicide. (The movies, like popular music, were slow to embrace unbridled escapism as an antidote to the still worsening Depression.)

Dinner at Eight is rife with sly allusions to the popular culture of the moment. The matronly Dressler character, for instance, calls her pet Pekingese, who fouls the carpets of a swank hotel, "Tarzan," the first *Tarzan* movie having preceded *Dinner at Eight* in the theaters by only a few months. And as Burke's surviving and still-ambulatory guests arrive for dinner, the musicians she has hired for the swank affair can be heard in the background. It is not "Happy Days Are Here Again" they are playing, although the jumping song might have been a droll touch given all that the guests had endured that day; it is "Play, Fiddle, Play." The Edward B. Marks Music Corporation's advertisements were touting that "Play, Fiddle, Play," was "in the air, here, there, everywhere."[21] The claim, it would seem, was not outrageously hyperbolic.

The Edward B. Marks publishing house was the marketing engine powering the success of "Play, Fiddle, Play." It was also, by the early 1930s, one of the last authentic vestiges of what can properly be called "Tin Pan Alley." "Like 'Hollywood,'" music industry historian David Suisman has observed, "'Tin Pan Alley' became a metonym for a place, an industry, and a mode of production."[22] It connotes, first and foremost, a business paradigm created and perfected by the first generation of music publishers to specialize in American popular songs. The geographical alley, the half-block of West 28th Street lying between Broadway and Sixth Avenue in New York City, was only briefly home to just a few of the Tin Pan Alley publishers. It was a way station, situated at approximately the midpoint of a migration route that began at Union Square in the 1890s—where burlesque houses, beer halls, and the fountainhead of vaudeville, Tony Pastor's, were then the city's main performance venues for popular music—and continued uptown as movie palaces and "legitimate" theaters opened in and around Times Square, where only a handful of Tin Pan Alley publishers still survived in any recognizable form by 1930.

Much like the movie studios that emerged a short time later, the new music publishing houses of the 1890s were mostly the creations of eagerly assimilating Jews—Charles K. Harris, Harry von Tilzer, the team of Joseph W. Stern and Edward B. Marks, the Witmark brothers, Jerome Remick, and Leo Feist, to name a few of the most prominent. Unlike the original Hollywood moguls, who had entered the movie business and made considerable fortunes as exhibitors and distributors before buying up distressed studios, the music publishers built their businesses from scratch, which they could do with virtually no capital—their "most complex technology was a metronome."[23] While still working day jobs, sales being the common denominator, the founders of Tin Pan Alley wrote the songs that would, when materialized in the form of printed sheet music, constitute their initial inventory. As creative artists *cum* salesmen, they were peculiarly well qualified to begin building a new kind of industry, one in which economic viability depended upon legal protection for intangible, intellectual property.

Copyright, at its core, is the lever by which the creators and distributors of a creative work extract its economic value from consumers. To lawyers, it is a generic term, covering not one but a whole panoply of rights—the exclusive right to make and distribute copies, of course, but also in the case of a musical work the exclusive rights to adapt it, to arrange it, to record it mechanically, to perform it publicly, and to use it in a synchronized video sound track. Absent copyright, it is difficult to imagine how the *creation* of popular songs—short, simple permutations of a limited number of tones, easily reproducible ad infinitum with the readily available technologies of the human ear and voice—could be a profitable enterprise. Before the twentieth century, examples of fortunes, or even nice livings, being made by composers of popular music are hard to find. The short lives and impoverished deaths of Stephen Foster and James Bland were more typical. Quite possibly, such cautionary tales were what Richard Rodgers's grandfather was thinking of when, in his dotage, he would advise young Richard against pursuing a career as a composer, ceaselessly perseverating that "even if you're successful, they'll never pay you."[24] With economic barriers to entry virtually nonexistent and nary a touch of genius required, *publishing* popular music would surely be a losing economic proposition without a robust copyright regime. It is no coincidence that the vicissitudes of the music business have closely tracked the development of copyright law, sometimes following changes in the law, and sometimes driving them.

Tin Pan Alley emerged in the immediate aftermath of one such legal development. Until the 1890s, music publishers in the United States had depended upon religious works, instructional materials, and reprints of European music. Instructional books were in steady demand at a time when music-making was the main form of home entertainment, had the virtue of being relatively immune to changing tastes and fads, and could be assembled from old material for which any copyrights had expired. Foreign music had no copyright protection at all in the United States, so even new works could be reprinted and sold without incurring any financial obligation to their creators or original publishers. In a small, geographically segmented market, free content was more highly valued than exclusive content, and the economic case for publishing new American popular songs was not compelling. Publishers treated them as a speculative sideline at best until the International Copyright Law of 1891 extended copyright to works first published abroad. This was tantamount to a protective tariff, creating more opportunities for domestic product.

Established music publishers, then as likely to be based in Boston, Philadelphia, or Cincinnati as in New York, adjusted slowly, but a few upstarts were quick to take full advantage of new legal landscape. A watershed moment came in 1892, when Charles K. Harris self-published his sentimental ballad "After the Ball," promoted it with energy and imagination (especially at the 1893 World's Columbian Exposition in Chicago, where it became so ubiquitous that few of the 28 million visitors could have avoided hearing it), and, by all accounts, sold multimillions of copies. For a generation of aspiring songwriters, gifted with more nerve and commercial acumen than musical talent, Harris's success with "After the Ball" was epiphanous. They swiftly adopted and elaborated upon Harris's model.

Tin Pan Alley's contributions to the cultural commons were not artistic— the commodification of popular music was its signal achievement. The target consumers were modestly skilled, often self-taught, home musicians who played the parlor piano and sang barbershop harmonies for their own entertainment. Conformity and simplicity were valued over originality. A successful Tin Pan Alley song drew from a common body of melodic, harmonic, and rhythmic material that gave it the virtue of "instant familiarity."[25] Even the best—"In the Good Old Summertime," "The Sidewalks of New York," and "Bird in a Gilded Cage" are exemplary—were harmonically simple, easy to learn and remember, and required no great vocal or instrumental sophistication to perform satisfactorily. Rhythm and tempo were dictated by the dance craze du jour. Theodore Dreiser, whose Falstaffian older brother Paul Dresser was one of the Alley's earliest and most successful songwriters ("My Gal Sal," "On the Banks of the Wabash, Far Away"), thought his brother's lyrics "mere bits and scraps of sentiment and melodrama in story form, most asinine sighings over home and mother and lost sweethearts and dead heroes such as never were in real life."[26] Although their catalogs would eventually contain numerous "rag" and "blues" titles, little that was genuine, important, or innovative in either genre was published by Tin Pan Alley firms, and no mislabeling law regulated such adulterations as Irving Berlin's "Yiddle on Your Fiddle, Play Some Ragtime" or Harry von Tilzer's "The Ghost of the Terrible Blues."

With a voracious appetite for new material and ever-churning wheels of mass production, there was no mistaking Tin Pan Alley for an artists' colony. It could have been situated in Dickens's London or Hugo's Paris, an industrial slum populated by rapacious publishers and mostly impecunious songwriters who suffered ghastly rates of morbidity and mortality, often parting outright with their best creations for a pittance, and dying, in the tradition of the sainted Stephen Foster, penniless, perchance in a proverbial flophouse. In an era when notions of "liberty of contract" could trump even the most minimal regulation of factory wages or child labor, Tin Pan Alley publishers managed to draw up contracts with songwriters that were "so inequitable" and "palpably disproportioned" that even turn-of-the-century courts balked at enforcing their terms.[27]

It never had offices on or near West 28th Street, yet the Edward B. Marks Music Corporation (known as Joseph W. Stern & Co. until Marks bought out his partner in 1920) epitomized Tin Pan Alley. Stern and Marks were traveling salesmen when they met in 1894 and decided to go into the publishing business together. Marks had been selling notions and Stern neckties, but they both had carried sheet music in their sample cases and were well acquainted with the music dealers in their territories. Marks had a flair for light verse; Stern could play a little piano. To launch their catalog, they composed their own sentimental ballads, including best sellers "The Little Lost Child" and "My Mother Was a Lady." The pump thusly primed, they soon had the wherewithal to start acquiring songs from others and to turn them into hits by applying the simple lesson of "After the Ball"—that demand for a popular song could be created by aggressive plugging.

Marks provided a colorful and revealing portrait of Tin Pan Alley in his 1934 memoir, *They All Sang*, ghostwritten by a young newspaperman who was then going by "Abbott J." Liebling. Liebling, whose prowess as a gourmand would become legendary (nobody has "written more accurately or more lovingly about food than Liebling," one of his colleagues at the *New Yorker* later wrote, nor "eaten more of it"[28]), spent his evenings at Marks's home working on the book, nearly emptying the icebox by the end of every session.[29] His services were well worth the cost of the groceries. Liebling produced the most readable of Tin Pan Alley's first-person histories while preserving Marks's seminal contributions for posterity, exactly as Marks wanted them to be remembered.

In the beginning, Stern and Marks did their own song plugging. In its earliest form, that meant visiting beer gardens and saloons, sometimes with a whistler who could help teach a drunken crowd a new song. "There was no surer way of starting a song off to popularity," Marks and Liebling wrote, "than to get it sung as loudly as possible in the city's lowest dives."[30] The object was to get the attention of variety hall and burlesque performers who might be out trolling for new material for their acts—their plugs were highly coveted and crucial to launching a song in New York City. Outside of New York, the most efficient medium for plugging songs, as had been true since Stephen Foster's day, was the minstrel show. Marks would spend part of every year traveling with minstrels, taking part in their legendary debauchery, stocking local stores with sheet music, and splitting the receipts with the producers in exchange for plugs. Marks fondly recalled his minstrel days as "idylls of profit and delight."[31]

As the entertainment business matured in the mostly prosperous early years of the twentieth century, Tin Pan Alley gradually developed a patina of gentility and more refined methods of plugging. Performers started to call directly on the publishers, where "professional departments" employed staff pianists to demonstrate new songs and arrangers to provide custom orchestrations. As vaudeville supplanted minstrelsy in the hinterlands, publishers opened branch offices in the biggest cities along the circuits. Stooges were planted in audiences to gin up participation in sing-alongs. Marks, and then others, provided stereopticon lantern slides illustrating their songs; these became popular attractions in themselves as the smaller variety theaters evolved into picture shows. (One scholar has recently suggested that Marks's innovative slide shows, expensive advertising for the publisher but cheap content for the exhibitor, "made their most significant contribution not to Tin Pan Alley but to the burgeoning moving picture industry."[32]) Department stores and five-and-dimes, mainly Woolworth and Kresge, became the largest retail music outlets, with Tin Pan Alley providing singers and pianists to demonstrate new numbers at the point of sale. Until the arrival of commercial radio and talking pictures in the 1920s, Tin Pan Alley's marketing apparatus remained quaintly low-tech, as did its undercurrent of petty criminality. Even as they moved further uptown, the youthful incorrigibility of the publishers was never entirely extinguished. Throughout its history, price fixing, group boycotts, and the unmentionable "evil" much later to be known as "payola" kept Tin Pan Alley in the crosshairs of law enforcement and just on the wrong side of savory in the public eye.

As long as its revenue came mostly from sales of printed sheet music, its market was a public that played the parlor piano and sang for amusement at home, and the primary vehicles for advertising its wares were free-form theatrical productions that allowed performers and producers to interpolate random songs without much regard for plot, character, or setting—minstrel shows, vaudeville, burlesque, revues, "extravaganzas," and "other loose variety shows"[33]—the Tin Pan Alley model was an economic no-brainer. The vertical integration of the Tin Pan Alley publishers, in which they controlled the means of production and distribution for popular music in its most tangible, merchantable form, printed sheet music, as well as the collection of all revenues and the calculation and disbursement of all royalties, meant that all but the very few name-brand songwriters who became publishers themselves were at their mercy. By the mid-1920s, however, the economic tectonics were shifting beneath Tin Pan Alley's feet, its stranglehold over the market for popular music was slipping, and the teeter-totter on which songwriters and publishers vied for power was tipping perceptibly in the direction of the songwriters.

Radios and phonographs were supplanting pianos as the principal source of music in the home. Along with movies, they were also taking a huge bite out of the market for live musical entertainment. If the only impact of these new media had been to diminish sheet music sales, Tin Pan Alley could have offset the loss with the new sources of revenue that they provided. In the Copyright Act of 1909, Congress had expanded the copyright in musical compositions to include the exclusive right to make "mechanical" reproductions. This nullified a U.S. Supreme Court decision from the year before, *White-Smith Music Publishing Co. v. Apollo Co.*, which held that the copyright in a musical composition extended only to a tangible reproduction from which the music could be "seen and read" by humans. "In no sense," the unanimous Court ruled, "can musical sounds which reach us through the sense of hearing be said to be copies."[34] Ironically, this had limited copyright protection to reproductions of music in a form "which appeals to the eye" rather than the ear, and therefore not to the player-piano rolls made by Apollo or, by implication, phonograph records. Royalties of two cents per copy per song from licensing of records and piano rolls—a rate set by Congress—became a second income stream for publishers, mailbox money that arrived without incurring any increased cost or risk. Songwriters, under the leadership of Victor Herbert and his attorney, Nathan Burkan, had lobbied hard for the mechanical right, and the apparatus they set up to spearhead this effort became, in 1914, the nucleus of the American Society of Composers, Authors and Publishers (ASCAP).

It was ASCAP that rescued another one of the exclusive rights granted to copyright holders, the right of "public performance for profit" of musical compositions, from a state of desuetude. Although the public performance right had been first recognized in an 1897 Copyright Act, the logistical difficulties inherent in monitoring thousands of "ephemeral, fleeting and fugitive"[35] performances of copyrighted music in venues scattered throughout the country, and collecting royalties for them, had rendered it ineffectual. ASCAP took on this task with Prussian efficiency, especially after Justice Oliver Wendell Holmes, writing in 1917 for a unanimous Supreme Court in *Herbert v. Shanley Co.*, held that "public performance for profit" is not limited to concerts or shows where music is the main attraction and admission is charged to hear it; it includes the more widespread incidental use of ambient music in public accommodations such as restaurants and hotels.

Burkan and Herbert had brought this as a test case against Shanley's Restaurant, a Times Square establishment that was offering patrons a form of entertainment then new to the United States, cabaret. Being "caterers rather than impresarios, the proprietors developed the practice of taking whatever numbers they like from current Broadway hits,"[36] including songs from Herbert's *Sweethearts*, while it was still running at the New Amsterdam Theatre only a block away. Holding that "if the rights under the copyright are infringed only by a performance where money is taken at the door, they are very imperfectly protected," Justice Holmes's reasoning was characteristically concise, penetrating, and pragmatic:

> It is true that the music is not the sole object, but neither is the food, which probably could be got cheaper elsewhere. The object is a repast in surroundings that to people having limited powers of conversation, or disliking the rival noise, give a luxurious pleasure not to be had from eating a silent meal. If music did not pay, it would be given up. If it pays, it pays out of the public's pocket. Whether it pays or not, the purpose of employing it is profit, and that is enough.[37]

Shanley was ASCAP's Magna Carta, its Declaration of Independence, and its Bill of Rights. Lower courts soon extended its reach to movie houses that provided incidental musical accompaniment for silent pictures and to commercial radio broadcasters. By the late 1920s, with the introduction of technologies for accompanying moving pictures with recorded music, there was barely a peep of resistance when the music industry asserted an exclusive "synchronization" right, similar in concept to the "mechanical" right, but unregulated by statutory royalty caps.

Each new source of revenue, however, entailed at least an equal and opposite loss of power and influence for Tin Pan Alley. A few national radio performances, or use as a movie theme, could "put a song over" to an enormous public within days. Neither the antiquated plugging apparatus of Tin Pan Alley nor its symbiotic relationship with the withering vaudeville circuits could add much value to the equation. Once ASCAP reached the stage, in 1921, where it could cover its administrative expenses, maintain an adequate reserve, and make distributions to its members, public performance royalties became the fastest growing piece of the music revenue pie. Edward B. Marks, for one, saw the writing on the wall: "So important are these moving pictures and radio rights now, that the day may come when publishers will not issue any sheet music for general sale, but will confine themselves to studio manuscripts and professional copies," thus becoming "a kind of authors' agents, placing the product and collecting for its use."[38] The gulf separating a vertically integrated empire sharing a small percentage of its revenues with creative talent, and a collection agent entitled to only a small share of its principal's earnings, is vast. The Tin Pan Alley publishers lost their place at the top of the music industry food chain with startling celerity.

Periodic bankruptcies and reorganizations had been a regular part of Tin Pan Alley's business cycle from the start, with publishers frequently failing and soon thereafter reappearing in an only slightly altered embodiment. In the late 1920s, some went down for the last time. The movie studios, using an ever-increasing amount of copyrighted music, were eager to acquire music publishers and their catalogs. Warner Brothers, in particular, went on an acquisition spree, snapping up publishers that represented as much as 40 percent of the active repertoire. MGM and Paramount followed suit, leading *Photoplay* magazine to ask in the fall of 1929: "Which has absorbed which? Is the motion picture industry a subsidiary of the music publishing business, or have film producers gone into the business of making songs?"[39] Among the few holdout publishers were Shapiro, Bernstein & Co., which remains independent and family-owned to this day, and Edward B. Marks.[40]

With the demise of Tin Pan Alley, the major economic stakeholders in the popular music business—songwriters, bandleaders, publishers, movie studios, theatrical producers, radio broadcasters, and record labels, in ever-shifting alliances—found themselves locked in battles that would outlast both the Great Depression and World War II. Songwriters and publishers (and by virtue of their publishing holdings, movie studios) uneasily made common cause in ASCAP, which in 1933 issued a pamphlet arguing that "radio 'kills' music" by reducing the lifespan of a hit from two or three years to a few months and that "as a result of this change, the sales of sheet music and of phonograph records have declined to practically nothing."[41] It was not a new accusation; ASCAP had been making it from the very beginning of the broadcast era, when radio stations were still relying on unpaid talent. "Do we hear Jolson, Belle Baker, Eddie Cantor, Will Rogers?" ASCAP's executive committee chairman E. Claude Mills asked, rhetorically, in 1924. "No, we hear Tillie Blatz, who has just graduated from some singing school, and this, that, or the other amateur individual or organization."[42] In contrast to the leisurely dissemination of a song across the country by skilled vaudevillians carefully selected and coached by the publishers, in circuits that might take a year or two to complete and leave a lingering demand for sheet music and records in their wake—the so-called long plug[43]—the ready availability of amateur performances of dubious quality at the turn of a dial could be hazardous to a song's health. When broadcasters insisted that publishers should be grateful for the free advertising they were providing, ASCAP meant it when it said, "Please don't do us favors."[44] But by the early 1930s, nearly every vaudeville notable had made the transition to radio, and publishers were ardently courting radio plugs. "If radio is the arch-enemy of music," the broadcasters asked in their own 1933 broadside, "why do representatives of publishers hang around the studios of networks and stations, slipping $10 bills and more to bandleaders to 'plug' their numbers?"[45]

To prevent the "promiscuous" radio play of its members' hottest properties, ASCAP—usually at the insistence of theatrical producers—designated certain numbers as "restricted" and required stations to obtain written permission before using them, giving rise to a steady flow of urgent telegram traffic between ASCAP headquarters in New York and broadcasters throughout the country, written in a vintage Western Union pidgin: "Permission Granted Stormy Weather Today," or "Permission Granted Easter Parade April First."[46] As a condition of these ad hoc licenses, station announcers were required to intone the words "by special permission of the copyright owners" whenever a restricted song was played, a bit of boilerplate so frequent and annoying it became an irresistible target for satire, as in one well-received number from a 1931 Broadway flop, *The Gang's All Here*:

> I asked your father, he said "O.K."
> I asked your mother, she said "Hoo-ray,"
> By special permission of the copyright owners, I love you.
> I asked your grandpa, he said "Why not?"
> I asked your grandma, she said "Get Hot!"
> By special permission of the copyright owners, I love you.

Something about this lawyerly intrusion into the still new and unregulated frontier of radio seemed to bring out the facetious wise guy in everyone who was forced to utter it, until finally, in a circular sent to all stations, ASCAP threatened that "if announcers and others are going to make a joke of this routine, the restriction upon reserved numbers is liable to be made absolute with no exceptions."[47]

Phonograph records in the early 1930s began carrying the warning "Not Licensed for Radio Broadcast," even though sound recordings were not protected works under the federal copyright laws (and would not be until the 1970s), and even though the right to perform the underlying compositions was being licensed to broadcasters by ASCAP. This was widely believed to be the doing of the Music Publishers Protective Association (MPPA), which was in the business of licensing its own electronic transcriptions of members' songs to smaller radio stations and wanted no competition from the recording companies. In fact, though, the record labels themselves were staking a claim to a common law property right arising from the investment, labor, and skill involved in "impressing upon our records, with an accuracy recognized by the public all over the world, high priced and famous artists and orchestras."[48] In this they had the full-throated support of some of these artists, led by bandleaders Paul Whiteman, Fred Waring, and Rudy Vallée, who believed that radio play of their recordings by "jerkwater broadcasters" in conjunction with "bush-league advertisers" would reduce demand for their live performances in theaters and over the radio networks.[49] The wrangling over broadcast rights helped to extend the glorious age of live radio music by at least a decade, until a landmark 1940 ruling by Judge Learned Hand of the U.S. Court of Appeals for the Second Circuit settled the issue in favor of the broadcasters.[50] Rudy Vallée was still bitter about this outcome in 1959, when he wrote to Judge Hand complaining that his decision had been responsible for creating "the disc jockey and the cacophony that floods the air waves of declining radio today."[51]

By then a long, lucrative, and thoroughgoingly corrupt *pax musica*, which would last until the dawn of the digital millennium, had descended upon the music industry. But it had taken many years for the dust to settle. In the meantime, through all the crossfire, the top songwriters had thrived as never before.

It is a commonplace that the mid-1920s witnessed a "great leap forward" in popular songwriting.[52] That was when Jerome Kern made his decisive break from what Alec Wilder called the "operetta world of dying subservience to European culture"[53] and created the revolutionary *Show Boat* with Oscar

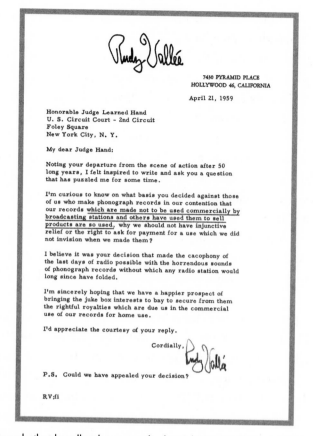

Rudy Vallée

7430 PYRAMID PLACE
HOLLYWOOD 46, CALIFORNIA

April 21, 1959

Honorable Judge Learned Hand
U. S. Circuit Court - 2nd Circuit
Foley Square
New York City, N. Y.

My dear Judge Hand:

Noting your departure from the scene of action after 50 long years, I felt inspired to write and ask you a question that has puzzled me for some time.

I'm curious to know on what basis you decided against those of us who make phonograph records in our contention that our records <u>which are made not to be used commercially by broadcasting stations and others have used them to sell products are so used</u>, why we should not have injunctive relief or the right to ask for payment for a use which we did not invision when we made them?

I believe it was your decision that made the cacophony of the last days of radio possible with the horrendous sounds of phonograph records without which any radio station would long since have folded.

I'm sincerely hoping that we have a happier prospect of bringing the juke box interests to bay to secure from them the rightful royalties which are due us in the commercial use of our records for home use.

I'd appreciate the courtesy of your reply.

Cordially,

Rudy Vallée

P.S. Could we have appealed your decision?

RV:fi

Rudy Vallée and other bandleaders waged a long, losing battle to restrict the use of their recordings on the air. (*Courtesy Historical & Special Collections—Harvard Law School Library and Eleanor Vallée*)

Hammerstein, George and Ira Gershwin collaborated on their first shows, and college buddies Rodgers and Hart emerged as a mature songwriting team with "Manhattan." Irving Berlin, though he had already achieved apotheosis as the personification of American music, was making his own leap forward with songs like "Always," "What'll I Do?," and "Blue Skies." Little of his earlier oeuvre sounds as fresh today, when it is heard at all. A new cohort—led by Cole Porter, Hoagy Carmichael, Vernon Duke, and Harold Arlen—was just arriving on the scene. Arlen was the first of this illustrious group to receive a nominal distribution of public performance royalties from ASCAP—$50—in 1930.[54]

So vast were the departures of these prodigious talents from the conventions of Tin Pan Alley, it is bracing to be reminded, a vocal segment of their contemporaries didn't get it at all. Writing in 1934, music editor Kenneth Clark confidently predicted that the popular songs written since 1925 would not last: "The trouble," as Clark saw it, "is that too many of the lads who now write songs really know something about music."[55] Others accused them of killing off melody in favor of primal rhythm, as in Douglas Gilbert's 1942 remembrance of George Gershwin. "The zenith of his talent was a death blow at melody," Gilbert wrote. "Its sentiment was pseudo, mocking, critical; its essence was mental; its technique, rhythm. It is robot music in relation to the pop-tune genre."[56]

The charge of melody-murder has long been a reflexive reaction to the shock of the new in music. Hadn't Beethoven beaten it senseless and Wagner administered the coup de grâce? How did it linger long enough for rock and roll to kill it all over again? What Gershwin and his peers brought to popular music were more complex, instrumentally conceived melodies that could survive and even flourish when divorced from their lyrics and context, melodies that contain surprises, providing possibilities for infinite jazz variations. The contrast with Tin Pan Alley's emphasis on instant familiarity could not have been more stark. Will Rogers's oxymoronic quip, the epigraph for this chapter, captures the subversive spirit of their accomplishment. You just don't know how these songs go until you hear them.

That the decline of Tin Pan Alley coincided with this Florentine artistic explosion is a circumstance worth pondering. Wilfred Sheed suggested that the very fact popular music had become largely a spectator sport might explain the great leap forward: "Simplicity might be good enough to sing, whistle and dance to, but listening might want a little something to think about as well."[57] The professionalization of music performance and the decline of home musicianship helped to create a market for more complex material. The contemporaneous introduction of the electronic microphone for recording and broadcasting, it is often observed, allowed for greater subtlety and nuance. Victor Herbert and other European-influenced light opera composers were passing from the scene, leaving the plotted, integrated musical comedy and the movie musical breathing room to develop as distinctly American art forms, calling for popular songs that aspired to express a greater range of moods and emotions. The sobering effect of Prohibition may have made audiences a bit more discerning. Attempting to sort out causes and effects in the midst of such crosscurrents is a futile exercise, but to disregard legal and economic factors would make no more sense than trying to explain the Renaissance without reference to the Church's influence or changing patterns of trade.

The Tin Pan Alley paradigm was inadequate to the task of supplying these more upscale goods. The Great American Songbook is largely the product of a different form of industrial organization, in which songwriters were no longer subsistence piece workers prized for their conformity to accepted norms, or for their ability to crank out knockoffs of the latest hit, or to cater to the latest dance craze. The important post–Tin Pan Alley songwriters were comparatively autonomous auteurs, free to make demands on the public, instead of kowtowing to its established preferences. Their theatrical scores were rewarded with shares of box office receipts, their split of the increasingly important performance and synchronization royalties was more lucrative than their share of sheet music sales had ever been, and movie studios offered the luxury of bountiful, dependable salaries. The formation, in 1931, of the Songwriters Protective Association (SPA, now the Songwriters Guild of America) as a counterweight to the MPPA gave the creative talent some institutional heft in their dealings with increasingly corporatized publishers, producers, record companies, and studios.

As much as any songwriter, publisher Max Dreyfus symbolized the new order. He was "the only man in the music publishing business of whom it may be said that he is also a musician," wrote S. N. Behrman in the *New Yorker*, "which enabled him to distill a profession from a racket."[58] The firms that Dreyfus presided over, first Harms, Inc. and later Chappell & Co., resembled literary salons. As David Ewen described the ambiance, the most important songwriters of the day, most of them Dreyfus protégés, "made it a habit to drop in at Harms during the noonday hour for some music, shop-talk, social palaver." In gestures that would have puzzled and dismayed the moguls of old Tin Pan Alley, "Dreyfus would then take a few of them out to lunch at the Hunting Room in the Hotel Astor where a special Dreyfus table was reserved for them,"[59] or he might invite them to spend a weekend at his country home.

In the canonical timeline of American popular music, Tin Pan Alley lasted until the arrival of rock and roll in the 1950s, when the "Brill Building" on Times Square became the geographical center and verbal shorthand for popular songwriting and publishing. In reality, by the time of "Play, Fiddle, Play," a quarter-century before rock and roll, Tin Pan Alley as properly understood had been relegated to history. For most baby boomers, and even the generation born just before World War II, if a genuine Tin Pan Alley tune is familiar at all it is probably from watching old cartoons on television— Bugs Bunny singing "The Daughter of Rosie O'Grady" or Betty Boop and the "bouncing ball" doing "Wait till the Sun Shines, Nellie." (Warner Brothers structured the Looney Tunes and Merrie Melodies animation series in the early 1930s to maximize exploitation of the Tin Pan Alley music catalogs it had recently acquired.[60]) The names of the great Tin Pan Alley songwriters, names like Billy Jerome, Paul Dresser, and Ernest Ball, are largely forgotten, their songs often misattributed to anonymous folk tradition.

The standards that make up the core of the vaunted Great American Songbook—the living repertoire launched by Fred Astaire, Bing Crosby, Ethels Waters and Merman, Frank Sinatra, Judy Garland, and Dinah Shore, and continually reinterpreted ever since by succeeding generations of artists in all genres—belong to their own era, extending roughly from the mid-1920s to the mid-1950s, richly deserving of a pithy sobriquet of its own. The clunky, anodyne "Golden Age of the American Popular Song" might serve, but it has been applied to so many different time brackets, without conveying the vaguest notion of what made them golden, as to be beyond redemption at this late date. If "Tin Pan Alley" denotes an era when music publishers dominated the popular music world, and "rock and roll" a time, apparently here to stay, defined by superstar performers and integrated big media companies, then the intervening period, when the composers and lyricists of the American popular art song reigned, was truly the "Age of the Songwriter."

In reaction to the artistic and financial emancipation of the songwriters, Edward B. Marks was comfortable playing the role of stubborn old cuss, railing against the tides of change and clinging as best he could to the ways of old. His partner, Joseph Stern, had retired from the business in 1920, no doubt figuring the best years were past. But Marks was soldiering on more than a decade later, approaching age seventy, commuting daily to Manhattan on the Long Island Railroad from his home in Great Neck, and enjoying far better economic times than many of the bankers, brokers, and chieftains of industry who were riding on the same train. As movie studios bought out his competitors, Marks remained resolutely independent. As his publishing brethren went to war with radio, Marks was making his own separate peace, openly importuning anyone with access to airtime for plugs, just as he had

Edward B. Marks, one of the last authentic vestiges of Tin Pan Alley, in his Rockefeller Center office in the 1930s. (*Courtesy E. K. Simon, Jr.*)

done with minstrels, beer hall singers, and variety house performers in his wayward younger years.[61] Unable to make much headway with the commercial musical theater, which now demanded integrated, plot-oriented musical scores instead of random, opportunistic interpolations, Marks ardently pursued opportunities to place his numbers in publicly subsidized productions, including those put on by the Works Progress Administration's Federal Theatre Project.[62]

Marks was not deaf to the refinement that the new generation of songwriters was bringing to popular music. But unlike a Max Dreyfus, he simply saw no percentage in the nursing of such high-priced, high-maintenance talents. He often bragged, without exaggeration, that his firm had published the earliest songs of Kern, Berlin, and Rodgers.[63] Those first songs, however, were also the last. Marks was more wryly wistful than bitter or remorseful about the ones that got away. He could well afford to be, as his company thrived commercially while keeping a studied distance from the artistic vanguard. Its back catalog contained many evergreen numbers—songs like "Parade of the Wooden Soldiers,"

"Sweet Rosie O'Grady," and "My Gal Sal"—that could be plumbed endlessly, rearranged, repurposed, and re-collected in new anthologies and in instructional books for all levels and instruments. The original twenty-eight-year copyright terms of early Tin Pan Alley songs were coming up for renewal, when by law rights that were once signed away reverted back to authors. Marks kept close tabs, pouncing on opportunities to pry copyrights from the grips of the unsophisticated heirs of long-dead songwriters with token payments. And to keep the catalog fresh, Marks was an adept bottom fisher, acquiring new songs from obscure sources on the cheap, demonstrating the same thrift and foresight as when he had hired the young and hungry A. J. Liebling, his son Herbert's college buddy, to ghostwrite his memoir. He purchased the rights to "El Manisero," a Cuban rumba composed by Moises Simons, had his in-house lyricist L. Wolfe Gilbert produce a "singable translation," and improbably published the first Latin hit in the United States, "The Peanut Vendor."[64]

Marks cultivated a mutually beneficial relationship with the Street Singer, Arthur Tracy, whose proudly retrograde repertoire didn't include much by Berlin, Kern, or Rodgers either. Marks allowed Tracy to use another Simons-Gilbert song, "Marta, Rambling Rose of the Wildwood," as his theme, in exchange for his plugging other tunes from the Marks catalog.[65] Marks's bargain-basement approach proved to be a great buffer against the economic headwinds that the music business was facing during the Great Depression. His ASCAP distributions nearly tripled from 1929 to 1933, far outpacing the growth of the blue-chip Harms and Irving Berlin publishing companies during those same years.[66]

"Play, Fiddle, Play" was another one of Marks's diamonds in the rough. The song came to Marks through Emery Deutsch, a Hungarian-born, Juilliard-educated violinist. Upon his graduation from Juilliard (then still known as Frank Damrosch's Institute of Musical Art), Deutsch had taken a job as music director of a local New York radio station that was, fortuitously, acquired shortly thereafter by William Paley as the flagship for his nascent CBS network. Only twenty-six years old in 1932, Deutsch already held the rather grand title of music director for CBS. His duties included selecting and conducing incidental music for dramatic productions, but much of his working day was devoted to leading a studio orchestra, "Emery Deutsch and His Gypsies," when it was called upon to fill short increments of dead airtime that were common in the early days of network radio. Deutsch

Emory Deutsch, music director for CBS, gave "Play, Fiddle, Play" its first radio plugs. (*Courtesy Carlin America, Inc.*)

played hundreds of these mini-concerts per year, and it was during one of them in the spring of 1932 that he gave "Play, Fiddle, Play" its first public performance. As an instrumental number, "Play, Fiddle, Play" was an ideal showcase for Deutsch's virtuosity, allowing him to carry the lyric melody on the violin and to improvise cadenzas and flourishes to fill whatever time was available. His captive audience took note; the cards and letters poured in, inquiring about the never-identified gypsy waltz. Deutsch had done much of the hard work of putting the song over before he approached Marks with "Play, Fiddle, Play." Though Deutsch was no big-time star, as the music director of CBS he was someone that Edward B. Marks was eager to do more business with. Marks took a flyer on the song.

For the sheet music cover, Marks used a gauzy publicity photo showing a deadly serious Deutsch with violin in hand, in an expression and pose that would have looked appropriate on a recital bill posted outside Carnegie Hall. (He put Arthur Tracy, who introduced the vocal version to the public, on an alternative edition.) Before long, Deutsch was being featured on scheduled CBS variety shows, leading the house orchestra at the Paramount Theatre on Broadway, and embarking upon a career playing dance auditoriums and recording as the "Gypsy Violinist." He gained a reputation, in the inimitable patois of *Variety*, as "an excellent stringer of the schmaltzy melodies, plus the long-hair stuff."[67]

Marks found a useful ally in radio star Arthur Tracy, the Street Singer. (*Courtesy Carlin America, Inc.*)

But only a few days after Marks had rushed off orchestrations of "Play, Fiddle, Play" to radio stations throughout the country in September 1932,[68] Deutsch's mail brought this discordant note:

Dear Sir

By taking my song "Where Are You Now" and turning it into "Play Fiddle Play" you made a great mistake.

A child can tell it is plagiarism. . . .

I am a peaceful man and am willing to settle this out of court.

I realize that if the management of your station will find out what is going on, it will not be so well, therefore I will wait three days for your answer and hope you will not listen to shrewd lawyers, who will advise you to fight it in court, because they wish to make a fat fee.

My intentions are not to make trouble for you if I can help it.

A word to the wise, e.t.c.

Sincerely yours,
IRA ARNSTEIN[69]

If Deutsch thought this message more than just a tad creepy, if not outright menacing, his concerns were not unfounded. "Play, Fiddle, Play" was suddenly "in the air, here, there, everywhere," and the emotions and associations that the tune set loose in Mr. Arnstein's mind were not a Proustian reverie, but a fevered rage straight out of Edgar Allan Poe. As Arnstein would later describe his mindset: "I was walking around the streets starving to death. I have nothing to eat and my music is played all over, wherever I turned." "I was so desperate," he told a court of law, "if I had a gun at that time I would have committed murder."[70]

A MOTHER'S PRAYER

The dream of all my life—my prayers—it's come! I knew it must be one of my children if I waited long enough—and prayed enough. A musician!
—*Fannie Hurst*

After a two-week sojourn in Chicago to explore the World's Columbian Exposition of 1893, Henry Adams pronounced it the "first expression of American thought as a unity."[1] There, Adams writes in his *Education*, he "found matter of study to fill a hundred years. . . . [W]hen one sought rest at Chicago, educational game started like rabbits from every building."[2] Adams's many gifts evidently included the ability to filter kitsch from his mass of apperception. Buffalo Bill Cody's Wild West Show, Little Egypt's belly dance, spectacularly oversized wheels of cheese, and Liberty Bell replicas sculpted from such diverse media as grains and citrus fruits were attractions that might have waylaid a lesser mind. But when observed through the prism of an intellect at once as discerning and as ethnocentric as Henry Adams's, the Exposition was a singular moment for the arts and sciences in America, when the United States demonstrated a thorough assimilation of its European cultural legacy, and emerged as the Old World's full-fledged partner in shaping modernity, neatly closing a loop that began with the very voyage of Columbus that the event was intended to commemorate.

Laid out by the great city planner Daniel Burnham (*Plan of Chicago*, 1909), on a landscape dredged from a marshy quagmire by Frederic Law Olmstead (*Central Park*, 1856), lit with the incandescent bulbs of Thomas Edison (*Talking Machine*, 1876) running on the tantalizing, but often-lethal, alternating current favored by his rival George Westinghouse (*Air Brake*, 1868), the White City was a stunning showcase for the artisans who would presently lead the "City Beautiful" movement, "an expression of a newly confident, ascendant America."[3] McKim, Mead & White (*Pennsylvania Station*, 1910) designed the Romanesque Agricultural Building, Adler & Sullivan (*Chicago Auditorium*, 1889) disrupted the Exposition's uniform palette and style with a multi-color, modernist Transportation Building, and Daniel Chester French (*Seated Lincoln*, 1909) created the monumental centerpiece sculpture, *The Republic*. The spectacle inspired the Emerald City as later conjured by one attendee, L. Frank Baum (*Wizard of Oz*, 1900), and the Japanese pavilions and gardens suggested some of the signature elements of the prairie architecture of Frank Lloyd Wright (*Taliesin*, 1911). The eyewitness accounts of construction crew member Elias Disney fired the imagination of the son born to him a few years later, Walter (*EPCOT Center*, 1982).

The Century World's Fair Book for Boys and Girls[4] tried to imagine the wonder of the White City through the adolescent eyes of two all-American boys, Harry and Philip, as they first gazed upon it:

> There was nothing to say; but each of them felt that the work of men's hands—of human imagination—had never come so near to rivaling Nature's inimitable glories. The full moon stood high above the buildings at their right, but even her serenity could not make the great White City seem petty.

At length the boys' tutor, Mr. Douglass, breaks the stunned silence:

> "At one time or another, each of us has tried to imagine what Heaven could be like. When we see this," and he looked reverently about him, "and remember that this is man's work, we can see how incapable we are of rising to a conception of what Heaven might be."

As media events go, the World's Columbian Exposition of 1893 surpassed anything that had preceded it, but the stories of the exotic peoples on exhibit there—the reindeer herders from Lapland, the Samoan warriors, the brightly costumed singers of Madame Lineff's Russian Peasant Choir—went largely unrecorded. It must have been a heady experience indeed for young Itzig Arenstein, a boy soprano touring with the Russian Peasant Choir, little more than a year removed from a shtetl in the Ukraine, a *Knaben Wunderhorn* of hot dogs, Coca-Cola and Cracker Jack, cowboys, electricity, fireworks, and—rising twenty-eight stories over it all—Charles Ferris's giant wheel, which received its initial passengers just as the Russian Peasant Choir was making its first appearance at the fair in June 1893.

When the Exposition had opened in May 1893, the reputation of Theodore Thomas, the director of its Bureau of Music, equaled or surpassed that of any of the other luminaries associated with its design, execution, and se-quelae. Neither his directorship nor his reputation survived intact to the closing ceremonies six months later.

His qualifications for the job had included no less than the invention of the American symphony orchestra. As a young violinist in 1860s New York, where his family had emigrated from Germany when he was a boy, Thomas found few satisfying opportunities to play the symphonic repertoire. Most orchestral concerts were one-off affairs, given by under-rehearsed, makeshift ensembles. The only orchestra with an institutional profile of any sort, the New York Phil-harmonic Society, was giving only half a dozen subscription concerts per year, using borrowed venues. Thomas formed his own orchestra and barnstormed the country with it for almost twenty years, insisting on high standards of art-istry and professionalism not seen before in the United States, and introducing some of the most important works of Brahms, Liszt, and Wagner. "It was the migratory Thomas, with the Thomas Orchestra, that whetted the appetite for disciplined performance in Boston, Philadelphia, Cincinnati, and Chicago."[5] In 1877, he was elected conductor of the New York Philharmonic Society as well. With the national celebrity he achieved, Thomas established the austere and authoritarian German *Kapellmeister* as the paradigmatic American orches-tra leader, a model that would still have dowagers sitting on orchestra boards swooning more than 100 years later. But neither the part-time Philharmonic nor the Thomas Orchestra, which needed to tour constantly to stay solvent, gave Thomas what he wanted—a full-time, resident orchestra that could be adequately rehearsed and financially self-sustaining in its own concert hall.[6]

In 1890, during the same wave of civic boosterism that brought the Columbian Exposition to Chicago and gave birth to the pejorative "Windy

City," some local movers and shakers formed an association to underwrite a new, year-round symphony orchestra. Thomas, declaring that he was ready to "go to hell if they gave me a permanent orchestra," accepted their invitation to lead an ensemble that would eventually become the Chicago Symphony Orchestra.[7] Once situated in Chicago, he was the obvious choice to head up the Bureau of Music for the upcoming Columbian Exposition as well.

Burnham's plan for the Exposition called for two elaborate and capacious concert halls, and the Bureau of Music was given a budget sufficient to support an orchestra of 114 musicians for the duration of its six-month run. This was abundance that Thomas—long admired for his "insolvent integrity"[8]—had never enjoyed before, and his ambition ran riot. At this world's fair, he decreed, music would be a full-fledged exhibit, equal in status to the other arts and sciences, not just an incidental amusement. The Bureau of Music's mission statement could not have been more sweeping:

I. To make a complete showing to the world of musical progress in this country in all grades and departments, from the lowest to the highest.

II. To bring before the people of the United States a full illustration of music in its highest forms, as exemplified by the most enlightened nations of the world.[9]

Despite these most worthy and catholic of intentions, in execution Thomas's programming for the Exposition adhered closely to a "two-pillar" formula that he had devised years earlier while touring with the Thomas Orchestra—open with Beethoven, end with Wagner, and fill the time in-between with other German pieces of appropriate length. As one critic complained, "an exposition which has fostered a national feeling, and begotten a national pride and confidence in our capabilities and possibilities in all other directions to an extent never before known in this country, has done little or nothing in advancing the interests of American creative musical art, nor has it called into being native musical compositions of a kind which the occasion might well have inspired."[10] Some influential new American music—Sousa's marches, Harris's "After the Ball," and the ragging of Scott Joplin and other itinerant pianists who had converged upon Chicago—did get exposure at the Exposition, but with little or no credit due the auspices of the Bureau of Music.

Thomas's artistic choices turned out to be the least of the complaints leveled against him. In a bit of unpleasantness known as the "Great Chicago

Piano War," his refusal to ban Steinway & Sons pianos from the concert stages in retaliation for Steinway's boycott of the Exposition's medal competition (New York-based Steinway believed the judging would be biased in favor of midwestern manufacturers) was portrayed as an affront "to Chicago, to its industries, to its people, and to its exposition," and as an unseemly quid pro quo for Steinway's longtime patronage of the Thomas Orchestra. He also came under fire for adopting a ticket pricing policy at odds with the Bureau of Music's stated educational mission—symphonic concerts were one dollar, twice the cost of admission to the Exposition itself, a "shortsighted policy" that "kept the price of tickets out of reach of the masses, with the result that many of the best entertainments were given before practically empty houses."[11] Halfway through the Exposition's run, after the press began questioning the Bureau of Music's expenditures—including Thomas's salary and the rental fee he was receiving for the use of his music library—Thomas tendered his resignation. Thomas's master plan was in shambles and the Exposition's official music program ground to a halt.

A distinct inverse proportionality can be detected in the music pages of the Chicago newspapers of 1893—the more closely a program was associated with Theodore Thomas, the more gleefully brutal were the reviews. It should not be surprising, then, that the highbrow musical sensation of the World's Columbian Exposition, the darling of audiences and the press alike, was a self-invited walk-on act that strode into the musical abyss by dint of its own industry and determination—Eugeniia Papritz-Lineva, "Madame Lineff," and her choir of Russian peasants.

Had Paul Robeson, Pete Seeger, and Alan Lomax been rolled into one, then American folk music might have had its own Madame Lineff. A native Muscovite, Lineva had a thriving career and an international reputation as an opera singer, choral director, and concert artist when she joined up with a small cadre of scholars and dilettantes who were working feverishly in the 1880s to preserve Russian folk music in its authentic, primitive form. Their sense of urgency stemmed from the effects of creeping industrialization on folk performance traditions, and from the ethno-musicological malpractice of their well-intentioned predecessors, who had sought to conform the archaic intervals and rustic polyphony of ancient folk songs to the strictures of modern modes and Western tonal harmony. Lineva began spending her summers in the countryside among the peasantry, traveling with religious pilgrims, systematically studying and recording regional variations in folk performance practice along the way.[12] Her passionate interest in the music and folk rituals of the rural proletariat was of a piece with her political ideology; Lineva and her husband, Aleksandr, an electrical engineer, corresponded with Marx and Engels and were among the early, illicit translators of their works in Russia.[13]

The Linevas were married in 1890 in England, where Aleksandr had formed the "Lineff Electric Traction and Lighting Syndicate" to promote his patented system for powering streetcars through an electrical conductor buried beneath the roadway surface. To what extent the Linevas were political exiles, and to what extent on an entrepreneurial mission, is not entirely clear. It was in London, as a recital encore, that Lineva first performed a traditional Russian folk song—"Lootschina" ("The Birchwood Splinter"), a new bride's lament over the tyranny of her in-laws—for a Western audience: "The effect produced by the song was striking; she was surrounded by people eager to know the name of the composer and the author of the words."[14] She resolved then to serve her country by using her time abroad to "make propaganda of Russian Folk-Music."[15] When the couple moved to New York two years later, the resources that she needed were readily at hand—a large population of recently arrived Russian and Ukrainian peasants from which a choir could be recruited and rehearsed (though not to so fine a polish as to sacrifice a rough-hewn authenticity), and an influential music critic, H. E. Krehbiel of the New York Tribune, who shared Lineva's keen interest in folklore.

In December 1892, Krehbiel and Madame Lineff's Russian Peasant Choir, then numbering sixty voices, including Lineva and a few other trained soloists, gave two concert-lectures in the main auditorium at Carnegie Hall, to enthusiastic audiences and to mostly rhapsodic reviews. The program, a commercially necessary abridgment of what Lineva had ambitiously conceived as three separate concerts, contained a sampling of social, labor, humorous, religious, and recruiting songs, and some operatic music—including selections from Eugene Onegin and Khovanshchina—that demonstrated the influence of the folk songs on Russia's most famous modern composers. The Times lauded the programs as "the most remarkable, interesting, and instructive musical entertainments given in the city this season," and as "a marvelously eloquent exposition of the spiritual life of a people of whom we know altogether too little."[16]

Lineva and Krehbiel repeated the concert-lectures at the Brooklyn Institute of Arts and Sciences and at Boston's Chickering Hall during the winter of 1893. In late March 1893, the Russian Choir appeared again at Carnegie Hall, this time as guest artists on a New York Symphony program conducted by Walter Damrosch, performing some of the same folk and operatic selections with full orchestral accompaniment. One "very diligent attendant" at the New York programs was Charles R. Crane, a plumbing fixture magnate from Chicago and perhaps the country's preeminent Russophile.[17] It is not clear whether the idea for an engagement at the Chicago Columbian Exposition originated with Crane, Lineva, or elsewhere, but it is certain that Thomas's Bureau of Music played no significant role, and that not one penny of its generous budget was allocated to the expense of transporting the reduced force of thirty singers, their sets, and their costumes to Chicago, or to publicizing the four performances that were scheduled for the first week of June 1893. Quite the contrary, it appears that the Exposition insisted upon and secured a rather favorable split of the receipts in exchange for giving the Russian Peasant Choir some midday, midweek slots in one of its two underused concert halls. Crane promised to arrange for a loan of $1,000 against the choir's expected share, though that too was thrown into doubt at the eleventh hour, when a panic roiled the Chicago financial markets just as the Exposition was opening in May.[18]

The money did come through in time—Lineva always believed that Crane had used his personal funds, though Crane always denied it—and on June 5, 1893, the Exposition's first Russian music concert was given at the Music Hall, a 2,500-seat Beaux-Art palace that faced the Grand Basin, the formal centerpiece to Olmstead's landscape design, adjacent to the Peristyle, which served as the ceremonial entrance to the fairgrounds for visitors arriving by boat on Lake Michigan. The local press had provided some helpful advance notices in the Sunday editions, and Lineva had shrewdly set the admission at fifty cents, half the price of Thomas's concerts in the same hall, factors that combined to roust a large crowd for a Monday at noon. The Exposition Orchestra of 114, under the direction of guest conductor V. J. Hlavac of St. Petersburg, opened the concert with the Chicago premiere of Tchaikovsky's "1812 Overture." Madame Lineff's Russian Peasant Choir followed with selections from the Orthodox Church liturgy. After an orchestral entr'acte, the choir returned to perform its core folk repertoire, including Lineva's solo, "Lootschina," and "Ay, Ouchnem" ("Heave Ho"), a song which would become

Madame Lineff's Russian Peasant Choir was the unlikely musical sensation of the 1893 World's Columbian Exposition in Chicago. Boy soprano Itzig Arenstein sits at the feet of Eugeniia Papritz-Lineva, center. (*Courtesy Philadelphia Free Library*)

familiar to generations of Americans, and recorded by artists as diverse as Glenn Miller and Feodor Chaliapin, as "The Song of the Volga Boatmen." In Madame Lineff's crowd-pleasing arrangement, the choir built slowly to a crescendo, and then gradually diminished to pianissimo, simulating the Doppler effect of a passing barge.

The audience responded enthusiastically, demanding encores of several numbers. The original four-concert engagement was extended to eight, and a special evening performance, without the participation of the Exposition Orchestra, was added. The local press heaped effusive praise on the Russian Peasant Choir without worry that Thomas or his Bureau of Music might bask in any reflected glory. Lineff was complimented for selecting "good natural vocalists" while avoiding "all schooling that would tend to eliminate from their singing any elements that are peculiarly characteristic of it in its original condition."[19] "Their singing, although showing the results of careful training, had about it a certain naturalness and homeliness that caused it to seem as more of the field and hut than of the concert-room."[20] For the *Evening Post*, the Lineff troupe was a welcome antidote to the Exposition's Hootchy-Kootchy brand of cross-culturalism:

> As a representation of Russian songs and costumes the choir might well be retained at the fair as a much more dignified and reputable addition to

the department of ethnography than much of that modern commingling of bowery, Babylon and Coney Island to be found along the retreat for skin games known as the Midway plaisance.[21]

The *Post* also had praise for V. J. Hlavac's "spirited" and "magnetic" conducting, and suggested that he, too, ought to be retained, so that perhaps "he might spur Theodore Thomas into an occasional symptom of life."[22]

For a farewell performance on the evening of June 13, the choir boarded Venetian gondolas and sang from the middle of the naturalistic lagoon that Frederic Law Olmstead had created for the fair, surrounded by a small armada of watercraft that Olmstead had personally selected for their visual effect.[23] Olmstead had chafed under the neoclassicism and dreary formality of the Exposition—his intent, as always, had been to create an integrated environment where education, aesthetics, and harmless amusement could co-exist in harmony. The evening hours, after the main buildings were closed, were the most conducive to realizing Olmstead's vision: "Men who have journeyed to every part of the world," the *Chicago Herald* observed, "who care nothing for ordinary architectural beauties and are blasé on the subject of landscape effects, have experienced, in viewing the White City by moonlight, a new and delightful sensation over which they wax as enthusiastic as a young woman at her first grand ball."[24] The Russian Peasant Choir's concert on the water, under the glow of the fully illuminated White City and a crescent moon, should have gladdened the heart of the elderly and ailing Olmstead.

The choir returned for a second engagement that lasted almost the entire month of October, the final month of the fair. Over the summer, Lineva had created a new, more theatrical program to be introduced at the Exposition and then taken on the road—"The Russian Peasant Wedding," a two-act, semi-staged oratorio. The choir's acting had the same natural, unpolished appeal as its singing. "The simple directness of the actors in their portrayal of this picture of Russian life gains both strength and charm through the characteristic qualities of the music."[25] Lineva's tacit commentary on Russian society was not lost in translation:

The sense of oppression and of unalterable destiny is also there as well as the shadow of a cheerless winter-time. There are moments of merriment seemingly the madder because of rareness, but even then the sunshine and the vodka seem equal sources of inspiration, a kind of assisted spontaneity, as it were.[26]

With the help of an overall bump in Exposition attendance as it drew to a close, admiring reviews, the dearth of music on the main fairgrounds, and Lineva's savvy decision to admit children for free—an un-Thomas-like gesture lauded by the press as "a real gift of generosity on the part of Mme. Lineff to education" that "Chicago will not forget"[27]—attendance was sufficient to make the costly production very nearly a breakeven proposition. The program book that Lineva prepared for these performances, with an explanation of the wedding rituals, annotated translations of the choir's repertoire, and an interpretive essay by Krehbiel, is an anomaly in the realm of world's fair collectibles, more readily found today in academic libraries than in curio shops or on eBay.[28]

The artistic and commercial success of the Russian Peasant Choir's daily performances during the final, musically barren month of the Exposition notwithstanding, the opposing factions in the music wars still could not find common ground. When Thomas's friend and biographer, George P. Upton, wrote his memoir fifteen years later, it was his very selective and bitter recollection that the Russian Peasant Choir's October engagement consisted of but "one funereal concert, October 11, to a handful of people which put an end to the musical muddle . . . a finale not worth a doxology."[29]

The choir's boy sopranos were singled out by critics for their exceptional voices and for the strange and pleasing qualities that their "piping treble" brought to its harmonies.[30] Itzig Arenstein was about twelve years old, although at various times he gave his year of birth as being as early as 1876 and as late as 1883. Spending two months in Chicago, with only one performance per day on his schedule, he had more time to explore the Exposition's wonders and absorb its vision of ascendant America than did his more privileged contemporaries Harry and Philip of *The Century World's Fair Book*, even if he lacked the expository services of a private tutor. And the Chicago engagements were just one leg of a whirlwind journey that would take young Itzig, in the short time before puberty ended his days as a boy soprano, to Carnegie Hall and to concert stages in "every principal city of the United States."[31]

He had arrived at Castle Garden in New York in December 1891, aboard the steamship *Bohemia* sailing from Hamburg, in the care of his older brother Aaron. Itzig's mother, Sophie, older sister Manya (known as Mae), and younger brother Jacob made the trek from Europe separately. The family hailed from the Letichev District in the southwest of the Czarist Ukraine. *Landsleit* from this area take justifiable pride in its status as a center of Jewish culture, with an outsized influence relative to the small population and short history of its Jewish community.[32] It was shtetl living with a cosmopolitan twist, at the crossroads of the Yiddish, Russian, and Ottoman worlds, "a fertile seedbed that encouraged new social and spiritual conceptions to germinate and take root."[33] Most significantly for Jewish music and philosophy, this was the birthplace of Chassidism—the Baal Shem Tov's synagogue and tomb in the village of Medzibahz remain venerated destinations for religious pilgrims. The Chassidim's ecstatic form of worship revolutionized Jewish music—with melody and rhythm triumphing over logogenic, or word-based, synagogue chant. The rebbes, wrote musicologist Irene Heskes, "encouraged their followers to join together in song and even in dance, so that music might blend with holy thoughts and enhance concentration upon communion with God." "Hasidic wordless song—melody intoned without text—was felt to attain for the singer what might not be reached by words, a vocal mediation in partnership with mystical thought."[34] The region has produced some of Judaism's greatest cantors.

Music and religion, as vital as oxygen in the ambient air, were not Arenstein family vocations. It does not appear that the Arensteins were any more than ordinarily observant or spiritually minded Jews, or that their lives and social status in the old country were other than provincial, secular, and quotidian. It is improbable that they owned property, or that they would have possessed the means to spare their three young boys from the hardships of military conscription. They would have witnessed, after the assassination of Czar Alexander II in 1881, some particularly violent pogroms against the Jews of the Letichev District. With little to lose and seemingly a world to gain, the Arensteins fit Irving Howe's description of those who came in the early wave of emigration from the Russian Pale of Settlement to the United States, before the "idea of America as a possible locale for collective renewal"[35] had gained much intellectual traction among religious and political leaders—they were "*folksmasn* who responded more to the urgencies of their experience than to any fixed ideas."[36]

All that can be said with certainty about Itzig's father, Ber Arenstein, is that his marriage to Sophie was not his first. It was only after their wedding, according to family lore, that Ber began to introduce Sophie, one at a time, to the issue of his first marriage. One of those half-siblings, Alexander, some ten years older than the eldest of Sophie's children, was the first family member to immigrate to the United States, arriving in 1886 and settling in Philadelphia, where he worked as a cabinet-maker until his death in 1897 at age thirty-three, leaving behind a widow and four children under the age of eight. Mae was one of the tens of thousands of new arrivals from Eastern Europe who went into the needle trades, where the German Jews who had come a generation earlier were happy to hire greenhorns whom "they could exploit with familial rapacity."[37] Mae was a savvy money manager who lived well during her long marriage to a machinist named Sherry, and even better during her widowhood in the 1940s and 1950s, though her peasant tastes and manners remained decidedly unrefined to the end of her life. Jacob, never married, drifted from job to job—electrician, traveling salesman, jeweler—reputedly working just enough to support a gambling habit until he, too, died prematurely in 1934.

Itzig and Aaron were singers, gifted enough to be enrolled in a conservatory, probably in Kiev, in their earliest youth. The genetic source of their talent is unknown, but Sophie, surely, was the source of their higher aspirations. A strong-willed, chain-smoking woman, Sophie was the gravitational center of her sons' lives until her death in 1919. Her mother was a Rapaport, a member of one of the Letichev District's most prominent families, a dynasty that included the most admired of its non-Chassidic rabbis and scholars.[38] Sending Itzig off on the road with Madame Lineff's choir was hardly the act of a *yiddishe momme*. There was more than age and vocal register separating Itzig Arenstein from the "wild creature[s] of the steppes that some of her singers appear to be."[39] As a Jew and a Ukrainian, Itzig was a foreigner traveling among foreigners harboring ancient enmities in a land foreign to all of them, singing Orthodox Church hymns and acting out rituals dating from pagan times in costumes rich with Christian symbols. Had most any other cheder-aged Jewish boy on the Lower East Side run away from home to join such a troupe, his vagrancy would have been cause for donning sackcloth and chanting lamentations.

After the Columbian Exposition, Lineva began retooling "The Russian Peasant Wedding" to moderate the pervasive sense of melancholy that the

Chicago critics had uniformly remarked upon, for the sake of workaday audiences whose thirst for edification had not been stoked by the excitement of attending a world's fair. The later versions dwelled less on the plight of the bride, who will go to live with her mother-in-law and become "the family drudge,"[40] and more on the hilarious antics of the *svat* and the *svakha*—the male and female matchmakers—with an enhanced role for the boy soprano playing the bride's obstreperous younger brother.[41] In February 1894, before embarking on a tour of the South, the choir again took to the stage of Carnegie Hall to unveil a rewrite that would have done Louis B. Mayer proud. It added two new characters—a bumbling, wisecracking American newspaper reporter (wearing western evening dress) and an English-speaking Russian peasant ingénue who could, conveniently, explain the pantomimed action and Russian dialogue. The couple provided some clash-of-cultures comedy and a wholesome romantic subplot as a "a pleasing *obbligato* to the chief romance of the piece."[42] Eventually, all the principal roles of the "Russian Peasant Wedding" were given to English-speaking actors, with the Russian choir reduced to serving as a Greek chorus.

Lineva remained in the United States for a few more years, but her choir's novelty waned. In 1896, after putting the choir's lavish and much-admired costumes up for sale, Lineva returned to Russia to resume her ethnological expeditions with funds provided by Crane, this time equipped with what she considered "an astonishingly useful notebook"—a recording phonograph.[43] Between 1904 and 1909 she published three volumes of transcriptions made from her phonograms, which are generally acknowledged to be major milestones in the study of Russian national music. When Stravinsky was working in Paris on the last of his "Russian" ballets, *Les Noces* (1923), his own peasant wedding setting, he had Lineva's first volume at hand, and wrote to his mother asking for the others. Shostakovich drew upon Lineva's work in his *Ten Russian Folk Songs* of 1951, which includes a lovely setting, for contralto, mixed choir, and piano, of Lineva's signature solo, "Lootschina," usually translated in that context as "The Match."

Itzig Arenstein's apprenticeship with Madame Lineff's Russian Peasant Choir was the first act in an adolescence marked by precocious musical accomplishments and proximity to several of the more celebrated musical figures to pass through fin de siècle New York City. When the time came for Itzig—no longer a boy soprano, but not yet a mature tenor—to resume his formal musical education, New York had hundreds of private music teachers whose ads filled multiple column inches of every newspaper. But the European-style conservatory had yet to take hold. "New York City at the turn of the century was strewn with failed conservatories that had been stricken by decades of sharp competition and mounting debt."[44] In his chauvinistic polemic of 1893, *Triumphant Democracy: 60 Years' March of the Republic*, Andrew Carnegie could name only two schools in New York, both recent startups, where an American could "receive as high musical instruction as in any of the foreign conservatories": the National Conservatory of Music and the Scharwenka Conservatory of Music.[45] The National Conservatory, where Antonin Dvorak served as director from 1892 to 1895, was a philanthropic endeavor established in 1885 with the patronage of the city's high society and classical music establishment. It should have been an attractive option for Itzig Arenstein—as a talented lad from a family of limited means, he might have attended tuition-free. Instead, he enrolled in the Scharwenka Conservatory, a proprietary venture founded by the composer and pianist Xaver Scharwenka in 1891. It was a choice that spoke volumes about the blend of New World ambitions and Old World sensibilities that, for better or worse, would determine the trajectory of Arenstein's life for many years to come.

"Now There's a Forgotten Composer for You" was the apt title of Harold Schonberg's 1968 appreciation of Scharwenka.[46] A few years later, another critic wrote with evident disdain that "a boom is apparently building for such forgotten nineteenth-century figures as Xaver Scharwenka."[47] This fear proved unfounded; "Scharwenka" and "forgotten" remain virtually synonymous. Schonberg's was just one in a long line of calls, so far unheeded, for a reconsideration and revival of his music. But when romanticism was in its final throes, Scharwenka was one of its most respected and popular practitioners. For a serious student turning his attention to composition and piano in the 1890s, to be a pupil of Scharwenka was a coveted credential.

Scharwenka, an ethnic Pole, was born in Prussia in 1850. When he was a teenager his family moved to Berlin, where he received his earliest formal musical training at Theodor Kullak's Academy, eventually joining the faculty there. Amy Fay, a talented American pianist and the sister-in-law of Theodore Thomas, encountered the young Scharwenka at the Kullak Academy. Her account, a veritable bodice-ripper, is found in her collected letters, *Music-Study in Germany*, first published in 1872 and in print ever since. "He has a delightful serenity of manner," Fay wrote, "and sits there with quiet dignity, his back to the windows, and the light striking through his fluffy hair."

> He is a Pole, and is very proud of his nationality. And, indeed, there *is* something interesting and romantic about being a Pole. The very name conjures up thoughts of revolutions, conspiracies, bloody executions, masked balls, and of course, grace, wit, and beauty! Scharwenka certainly sustains the tradition of his race as far as the latter qualification is concerned.[48]

Scharwenka's career took off after an 1870 pilgrimage to Weimar, where he received the blessing of Franz Liszt. In 1881, he opened his own conservatory in Berlin. Known as the Klindworth-Scharwenka Conservatory for most of its long existence, it was for many years one of the most prestigious in Germany, attracting a diverse faculty and students from across Europe and the United States, Jean Sibelius and Otto Klemperer among them.

Scharwenka arrived in New York in January 1891 to launch a four-month American concert tour sponsored by Behr Brothers. A new player in the cutthroat piano market, Behr was eager to have a celebrity virtuoso demonstrate its instrument on major concert stages. But it was a reputation as a composer, not as a performer, that preceded Scharwenka. The German conductors who presided over New York musical life Theodore Thomas, the Damrosches, and Anton Seidl—had all programmed Scharwenka's major orchestral works, as Mahler would later do during his brief tenure with the Philharmonic. Overshadowing Scharwenka's mature work, which included two piano concertos and symphony, was his youthful opus 3, number 1, the *Polish Dance in E Flat Minor* for solo piano, the calling card that had earned him his audience with Liszt. The persistent popularity of this slight piece, little more than a student's characteristic exercise composed when he was nineteen, was an everlasting source of chagrin for Scharwenka. He liked to regale his students with a story of him being driven to assault a hurdy gurdy man who was playing the *Polish Dance*, only to repair to a church where it was being played on the pipe organ.[49] A barber whom Scharwenka patronized in Philadelphia, during a pleasure trip to the United States in the summer of 1890, told reporters that he had nearly cut the throat of an excitable "Dutchman" who had jumped out of his chair upon hearing a band outside strike up the *Polish Dance*.[50]

In toasting Scharwenka's arrival in New York, Philharmonic conductor Anton Seidl suggested that an especially warm welcome was in order because the Polish maestro had not come in a quest for "American dollars."[51] This was a questionable assumption, and it was certainly true that America owed Scharwenka. Unauthorized copies and dubious arrangements of his *Polish Dance*, like the one for brass band that interrupted his shave in Philadelphia, circulated widely in the years before the International Copyright Law of 1891. When one of the most prolific of the offenders, publisher Gustav Schirmer, gave Scharwenka a VIP tour of his New York offices, the composer cheekily asked to be shown the firm's "reprint shop."[52]

The middle-aged artist that American audiences came to know bore little resemblance to the swashbuckler of Amy Fay's idylls. By the 1890s, Scharwenka's hair was thin, and he carried "flesh enough to show that he likes a good dinner.... [E]xcept for his hands, he appears more like a prosperous flour merchant than an artist."[53] His lack of affectation and pretense, in his personal bearing and his playing, was widely remarked upon.[54] "He is vastly different from the average pianoforte celebrity. He never strives for sensational effect, but is always the legitimate artist."[55] "He plays with delicacy rather than with ponderous effects, and deals with music as a matter of beauty and grace rather than of sublimity. He is by no means an egotistical artist."[56] When Paderewski made his debut in the United States a few months later, comparisons were inevitable, and not necessarily to Scharwenka's disadvantage. Though "Scharwenka has little of the spiritual magnetism of Paderewski," one critic wrote, he is "satisfactory for the opposite fact of his quietude, elegance, and dignity.... [T]o express the soul which Paderewski does with his whole body, he had but to indicate his feeling without outward effort to the muscles of his wrists and fingers."[57] Scharwenka's reviews, unlike Paderewski's, seldom dwelled on his appearance, his offstage exploits, or his box office receipts.

Scharwenka's tour succeeded in making the case for inclusion of his *Piano Concerto No. 1 in B Flat Minor* in the standard repertory, where it would remain—admired for its rich melodies, taut and carefully crafted orchestration, and dazzling piano technique in three relentless movements, all marked allegro—until fashions changed and Rachmaninoff's concertos supplanted it after World War I. The other compositions he performed and conducted, including his second piano concerto and excerpts from a work-in-progress,

Polish composer and piano virtuoso Xaver Scharwenka operated a prestigious conservatory in New York City during the 1890s, a "counterpart in every particular" of his "famous Berlin Conservatorium."

Mataswintha, an opera of Wagnerian scope dramatizing the fall of the Ostrogothic kingdom, were also well received. In remarkably short order, in the estimation of the critics, Scharwenka had "blotted out completely the one-sided reputation he used to have, in the popular mind at least, as a salon composer and ingenious follower in the footsteps of Chopin."[58]

Posterity's verdict has remanded Scharwenka back to the ranks of the lightweight, the "trashy," and the derivative, with even the *Polish Dance*'s stature much diminished by too close an association with Liberace. But his bond with the American audiences and musical oligarchy of his day was instant and mutual, and he found the lifestyle available to an acclaimed European piano hero in 1890s New York City much to his liking. Before his first concert tour had ended in April 1891, he had decided to relocate to the United States and had made plans to open a New York branch of the Scharwenka Conservatory, intended to be "conducted upon the principles that have made [his] Berlin conservatorium world famous."[59] It was reported that financial backers raised $200,000 in seed money, enough to recruit a faculty of international standing. Behr Brothers provided luxurious space in its headquarters building, a palatial edifice on lower Fifth Avenue near the heart of a piano district that surrounded Union Square, replete with statuary, ornate ceilings, marble floors, velvet carpets, and sixty instructional and practice rooms. There was also a 1,000-seat auditorium—known for what turned out to be the short duration of the company's leasehold as "Behr Brothers Hall"—a prestigious amenity that could be matched only by the company's most elite competitors. In addition to their regular lessons, under the well-honed Scharwenka system, students were required to attend supplemental lectures on the history of music; "lessons in fencing and other physical exercises" were also compulsory.[60]

Such opulent facilities and rigorous, Teutonic discipline came at a price. Depending on a student's level and course selections, tuition for a ten-week quarter could run $40 or more, a significant stretch for immigrant families, like the Arensteins, whose wage earners typically made less than $10 per week. But the Conservatory's catalog promised that the returns on the investment would be more than hedonic:

> The possibilities of music, as a profession and as a means of gaining a livelihood, have not, however, been sufficiently presented to enable the public to appreciate the importance of the subject in all its vast details. The future will prove that many, who are now wasting their talents and energies in pursuits which are as unprofitable as they are tiresome, will turn their attention to the practical advantages accruing from a thorough musical education.[61]

The Scharwenka Conservatory offered aspiring music professionals training squarely within the mainstream of late nineteenth-century musical practice. With that tradition about to come under assault from every direction, such an education may have been a mixed blessing. But no such reservations apply to the artistic ethos that Scharwenka exemplified—his lack of affectation, his craftsmanship in performance and composition, his burning desire to please audiences, and his generous and sincere commitment to pedagogy. The musical world abounded with less desirable role models—all manner of enfants terribles, poseurs, and prima donnas—that a young Itzig Arenstein might have chosen to emulate.

By the time Arenstein enrolled, the Scharwenka Conservatory had moved uptown to new quarters in the East 60s. Its tenancy at the magnificent Behr Brothers building had, in fact, lasted only one academic year. If Scharwenka's 1891 concert tour succeeded in calling attention to Behr Brothers' wares, it was attention of a sort that both the artist and the manufacturer could have done without. The reviews of its top-of-the-line concert instrument were so poor that Behr Brothers was forced to scale back its ambitions and terminate its association with Scharwenka by mutual consent. Henry T. Finck of the *New York Evening Post*, reviewing Scharwenka's American debut in January 1891, was particularly withering. The *Piano Concerto*, Finck wrote,

> was utterly marred by the wretched Behr piano on which he played. According to the program Herr Scharwenka has given his testimonial that this piano "answers every requirement in regard to tone and touch as fully as can possibly be expected of an instrument constructed in the year A.D. 1890." . . . Either he has not the power of getting a good tone out of a piano, or that he does not know when a piano is poor, for the one he played on Saturday was beyond comparison the most deficient in tonal resonance and sustaining power that we ever heard in all our critical experience.[62]

For his 1892 concert tour, Scharwenka "insisted upon a Knabe piano," and before long he was an exclusive Steinway artist and the Scharwenka Conservatory another Steinway redoubt.

Arenstein remained at the Scharwenka Conservatory after its namesake returned permanently to Berlin in 1898, continuing his studies in piano and composition with the new director, Richard Burmeister, formerly of the Peabody Institute, one of Liszt's last students and an active concert soloist. In 1899, the Arenstein family's investment and financial sacrifice began to yield dividends. Itzig accepted his first professional engagement, as a pianist for the Charles A. Ellis Opera Company, where he again had the opportunity to tour the country in the company of important visiting artists. Ellis, the founding manager of the Boston Symphony, was also the agent for the Australian soprano Nellie Melba, the most celebrated diva of her era, a client who gave Ellis considerable clout in the opera world. Ellis's company, formed after Melba had a falling-out with the Metropolitan Opera, brought fully staged productions of French and Italian repertoire to the provinces. Melba's drawing power was such that Ellis could go first class all the way—surrounding Melba with top-notch casts and letting her travel in "her own private rolling palace Pullman rail car . . . with her own private chef and waiter."[63] In San Francisco, it was reported, more than a hundred people waited in line all night for the box office to open, but "fortunately, the night was soft and warm, and there is not likely to be the consequence that followed the four days wait in Boston, where several messenger boys died of pneumonia as a result of the cold and exposure."[64] The *Los Angeles Times*

The "captivating sweet" theme of Arenstein's opus number one, "A Mother's Prayer."

expected that the Ellis Company's two-day engagement would be "unquestionably the greatest operatic event in the musical history of Los Angeles."[65]

Shortly after the 1899 Ellis Opera tour, Arenstein self-published his first piece for solo piano, "A Mother's Prayer." Arenstein might have dreamt that this would be his *Polish Dance*, and parallels are not hard to find. Each work served as a career springboard for a teenage composer who saw little direct profit from it, and both were sources of lifelong torment for their creators, stemming from piracies, real or imagined.

Musically—though closer in spirit and rhythm to a dirge than a dance, and harmonically elementary—"A Mother's Prayer" displays some of the compositional watermarks of Scharwenka's early keyboard works, sharing the teacher's strong "inclination towards overall symmetry and regularity of phrase length."[66] The piece starts with a four-measure introduction built from octaves in both hands, followed without pause by eight delicate, lyrical measures that state a "captivating sweet" theme in two antecedent-consequent phrases of equal length, each phrase resolving on the tonic A, as does every other important subdivision of the piece. At the melody's core are three descending adjacent notes, transposed up and down the scale each time they reappear.

A repetition of that melody is followed by a second theme, a pulsating eight-bar bridge, and finally, increasingly energetic and dissonant variations on the original theme. With its minor key and diminished intervals, "A Mother's Prayer" has an unmistakably Eastern flavor, surely influenced by the Russian folk music that Arenstein was singing with Madame Lineff's choir a few years earlier. It is captivatingly sweet as advertised, but not without emotional bite.

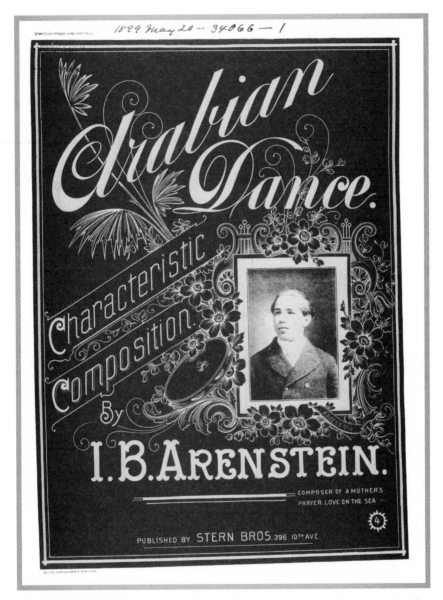

1899 May 20 — 34066 — 1

One of many characteristic piano pieces published by Arenstein before he reached the age of twenty-five. (*Library of Congress, Music Division*)

In 1900, Arenstein sold his copyright outright for $75 to Theodore Lohr, a piano-seller and publisher who specialized in Yiddish songs. "A Mother's Prayer" went on to have an unusually long and varied commercial life. An advertisement run by Lohr in 1907 claimed that more than 50,000 copies had been sold by then. Lohr and various successors-in-interest kept the original edition of "A

Mother's Prayer" in print continuously for decades. The Hebrew Publishing Company included it in an early twentieth-century collection of *Jiddische Lieder*, with music of the patriarchs of Yiddish musical theater Abraham Goldfaden and Joseph Rumshinsky. The Victor Military Band recorded it, under the German title "Der Mutter Gebet," as part of a medley with the Zionist hymn and future Israeli national anthem "Hatikva" in 1913.[67] Well into the 1930s, "A Mother's Prayer" was available in arrangements for violin and piano, for orchestra and other ensembles, and vocal versions in several languages. In 1968, after the original piano arrangement had passed into the public domain, it found its way into a popular folio of the *World's Favorite Piano Solos*, alongside Brahms's *Hungarian Dance* and Chopin's *Minute Waltz*.[68] Whether or not sales of "A Mother's Prayer," in all of its many manifestations, ever reached one million, as its composer would often claim, it was a remarkable achievement by any standard for a teenage boy's opus number one.

SOLDIERS OF ZION

Cantor Josef Rosenblatt may go vaude again.... Depression has hit the synagogues, too, according to authorities who know all about it, with high priced cantors now a thing of the past.
—Variety

The Arenstein family moved uptown before the turn of the century, fleeing the suffocating density of the Lower East Side for the relatively airy confines of Harlem, where a German-Jewish bourgeoisie had been prospering for a generation. Eastern European immigrants of a certain aspirational bent, like the family of eight-year-old Ira Stegman, author Henry Roth's alter ego, were heading there in large numbers, seeking to separate themselves from the "crude, embarrassing uncouth greenhorns" of Eldridge Street, with their "impenetrable Yiddish."[1] It was a six-mile trolley ride that entailed a cultural transformation in some ways as profound as the 5,000-mile journey from the Letichev District to the Lower East Side a few years earlier.

In the blocks between Park and Fifth avenues, bordered by the green wards of Central Park to the south and Mount Morris Park to the north, where the Arensteins made their new home, refugees from the Lower East Side lived in tenement buildings that offered them conditions and amenities not appreciably better than those they had just left behind. "More immigrants moved to Harlem in the hope of financial success than as a sign that they had already achieved this success."[2] Just to the west, between Fifth and Seventh avenues, was the "aristocratic Jewish neighborhood of New York, where most of the well-to-do Jews resided"[3] in row upon row of dignified brownstones. Although these early settlers had built a Jewish infrastructure of synagogues, cheders, and fraternal societies, their lifestyle was secular. In Jewish Harlem, the pace of assimilation of Eastern Europeans quickened, hurried along by the influence of the already acculturated German-Jews and the nearby Irish and Italian communities, and unimpeded by disapproving stares and gossip of the stubbornly orthodox.

A shtetl name like Itzig Arenstein would hardly do for an aspiring artist who was attending an upscale, Berlin-on-the-Hudson conservatory and living next door to some of the city's toniest Jews. He began to tinker with it while still a teenager. He could not have avoided learning, perhaps painfully, that among the Germans "Itzig" was a diminutive freighted with some nasty cultural baggage. In its most innocuous form, Itzig was a stock character of Jewish humor, an impish simpleton serving roughly the same role as the obtuse Ole of Norwegian jokes, as in one of Sigmund Freud's favorite stories:

> The boy Itzig is asked in grammar school: "Who was Moses?" and answers, "Moses was the son of an Egyptian princess."
>
> "That's not true," says the teacher. "Moses was the son of a Hebrew mother. The Egyptian princess found the baby in a casket."
>
> But Itzig answers: "Says she!"[4]

More perniciously, in anti-Semitic German literature the name "Itzig" was often reserved for the most repugnant Jewish characters. It became a generic pejorative for Jews, and part of the vernacular of Jewish self-loathing. "Börne, Heine, and the young Marx had imbibed the ugly language in which 'Itzig' . . . stands for everybody who talks with his hands."[5]

On his 1899 copyright registration for "A Mother's Prayer," Arenstein replaced Itzig with its cognate, Isaac. "Isaac Arenstein" was a name well suited to an important twentieth-century career in music, just long enough and just European-sounding enough to give it lilt and heft. Igor Stravinsky, Aaron Copeland, Isaac Arenstein, Karlheinz Stockhausen—the name is not the least jarring to the ear when included in such a litany. He would have done very well to stop there. But then Isaac Arenstein adopted the middle initial "B.," maybe in homage to his father, Ber, or perhaps just to impart a little gravitas to a very young man who possessed no degrees or titles. For a music teacher, "Isaac B. Arenstein" or "I. B. Arenstein," as he sometimes identified himself, was more than serviceable, but in the wake of his early successes he could have set his sights higher. The middle initial connoted "bourgeois," not "bohemian."

Within a few years Isaac was Ira, and Arenstein became Arnstein. If his purpose was to de-Russify, to cross Fifth Avenue symbolically by affecting a Germanic identity at a time when "Russian" was still a nasty smear, even inside the Jewish community, then "Ira B. Arnstein" made perfect sense, and that may have trumped all other considerations at the moment. But by removing that one vowel from his surname, he consigned the "r" that preceded it to oblivion in the dialect of New Yorkers, a sound—as in "Mis-tah Ahn-steen"—that would come to be perceived as more grating and déclassé with each passing decade. (That it was also the surname of a soon-to-be-notorious swindler, Nicky, was an added misfortune.) In a milieu where Jewish immigrants from Eastern Europe were changing their names "as easily as shirts,"[6] and where most of his family had opted for a sturdy Anglo-Saxon surname—Austin—"Ira B. Arnstein" was an unforced error.

In the spring of 1907, the Carl Fischer Company, then as now a leading purveyor of standard music in the United States, published "Farewell," a romance for solo piano by Ira B. Arnstein. Fischer marked the occasion with a flattering profile of the composer in its house organ, the *Musical Observer*. "At present," according to the *Observer*,

> Mr. Arnstein has installed himself in New York as one of our very busiest and most successful of local pianoforte teachers. His success has been attained through conscientious enthusiasm for the cause of artistic instruction and the inevitable results have been manifesting themselves in an ever-increasing class of earnest and hard-working pupils. . . . As a composer Mr. Arnstein has distinguished himself in many ways, having achieved unusual success with a number of piano solos which reveal remarkable talent for pleasing and melodious compositions.[7]

A formal photograph accompanied the *Musical Observer* article. Swarthy, resplendent in concert tails, a luxuriant head of hair swept back in a

IRA B. ARNSTEIN.

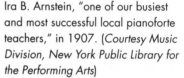

Ira B. Arnstein, "one of our busiest and most successful local pianoforte teachers," in 1907. (*Courtesy Music Division, New York Public Library for the Performing Arts*)

pompadour, a penetrating stare reminiscent of the young Picasso's contemporaneous self-portrait, the twenty-something Arnstein of 1907 cut an impressive figure. It is every bit a portrait of the young man as an artist. His jutting mandible, a pronounced feature that appears alternately pugnacious and baleful in other photographs, in this one seems benign, accenting an intense, even virile, countenance.

Fischer's imprimatur was prestigious, a considerable step up from the Yiddish vernacular publishers of his earlier works, and with it Arnstein—Harlem-based, young, male, and thoroughly Americanized—had another basis to distinguish himself among New York's overabundance of voice and piano teachers. His newspaper ads projected vigor and inclusiveness that would appeal to pupils who might have been put off by the stodgy Old World airs and Carnegie Hall addresses of a Signor Pizzarello or a Madame De Weinzkowska: "I want to make a singer out of you! Anybody! Everybody! I'll convince you that every human being has a singing voice if properly instructed."[8] His teaching philosophy emphasized anatomy over talent: "There is one position in everybody's mouth which when found by a singer, makes his tones come out beautiful, musical, and enjoyable to listeners."[9]

For twenty years, Arnstein maintained studio-residences in some of the modestly upscale apartment buildings that dotted Jewish Harlem, built in anticipation of a real estate boom that never came, and bearing such high-flown names as the "Gainsborough" and the "Victor Hugo"—busy, noisy ateliers in a neighborhood of working immigrants, far removed from the city's cultural infrastructure and the camaraderie that might have nourished artistic growth. Only one oasis of culture, "Arison's Music House," a music store and authorized Victor Talking Machine dealership on West 116th Street, reputed to have one of the city's best inventories of "high-class" music,[10] provided a haven for Arnstein, a place to meet other musicians, see his own publications on the racks, and listen to new recordings by Enrico Caruso and other Victor Red Seal stars. The proprietor was a fellow Russian immigrant, Theodore Arison, whose uncompromising musical standards and left-wing political sympathies infused his business philosophy, expressed in the store's idealistic slogan: "Everything that is Good in Music, PROFIT OR NO PROFIT." Arison's tastes, however, were decidedly revanchist—to the degree that he disposed of his own family's piano rather than let his daughter play jazz on it. News from music's cutting edge, word of romanticism's imminent demise, would be slow to reach his clientele.

With the perennially popular "A Mother's Prayer" on his résumé, Arnstein had no trouble finding publishers for the characteristic piano pieces at which he was particularly adept. (Arnstein designated a mazurka published in 1914 as his "Opus 80," implying a rate of five to six new pieces per year.) All demonstrated his talent for the pleasing and melodious, but none could be considered a significant artistic advance over "A Mother's Prayer," or approached its popular success. He made a sideline for himself as a supplier of piano transcriptions for publishers looking to expand their instructional catalogs—for Saul Schenker he arranged "La Donna è Mobile," "O Mari," and the sextet from *Lucia di Lammermoor*, among other songs and arias. Arison, who had been a printer before opening his store, brought out Arnstein's piano transcriptions of such popular violin pieces as César Cui's "Orientale" and Fabian Rehfeld's "Danse Espagnole" through his in-house imprint. In 1912, Mason & Hamlin named Arnstein in a year-end announcement of the "the most critical and discriminating artists" who had purchased a Mason & Hamlin piano that year, an imposing roster that also included Victor Herbert and Reginald De Koven.[11] Arnstein the young adult was burnishing his credentials at a markedly slower pace than he had as a teenager, but still he was living the type of productive, remunerative musical life that had been promised him in the Scharwenka Conservatory catalog, and earning his livelihood without resort to "more tiresome pursuits."

World War I disrupted this comfortable status quo. As a war economy diverted students and resources from private music study, Arnstein was forced for the first time to look elsewhere to supplement his income, leading to his earliest forays into the realm of popular culture. He self-published a song in the popular verse-and-chorus style, "Light My Life with Love," and took a job as a pianist at William Fox's Nemo Theatre, a silent-movie house at Broadway and 110th Street, where he would have accompanied Fox pictures ranging from Tom Mix serials to Frank Lloyd's *Les Misérables*. Although the allure of popular music and the movies would beckon again, leading Arnstein to his ultimate ruin, this early dalliance was cut short by a religious awakening, of sorts.

If Jewish culture or religious practice had played any meaningful role in Arnstein's life before World War I, it certainly left no discernible trace in his music. Though it was not hard to recognize Eastern European influences in Arnstein's compositions, there was nothing overtly religious or Jewish about them. But during the waning days of the war, Arnstein discovered in his faith and ethnicity a new energy and direction for his career. His conversion came in the wake of the emergence of Harlem's first musical superstar, an artist who shared Arnstein's roots in the southern Ukraine and his early exposure to Chassidism, but who wore those influences as comfortably as a second skin. The commercial triumph of Cantor Josef "Yossele" Rosenblatt showed Arnstein that there could be fame and modest fortune in the marriage of serious musical ambitions with unadulterated *Yiddishkeit*.

Few individual acts of religious scruple have been the subject of more rabbinic, journalistic, and parental sermonizing than Sandy Koufax's decision to forego his scheduled start in the first game of the 1965 World Series, when it fell on Yom Kippur. Instantly, Koufax was transfigured from mere sports star to Jewish saint, his images and relics becoming objects of veneration with magical powers to raise large sums for Jewish causes.[12]

Koufax, who spent that Day of Atonement in his hotel room, still managed to make three starts in the 1965 series, collected his full winner's share of $10,300, and took home a Corvette as the series' Most Valuable Player. Yet Koufax's gesture was undeniably powerful, if not as an exemplar of religious observance, then as a reminder, timed so as to be as impossible to overlook as the color of Joe Louis's skin had been a generation earlier, that one of the most dominant professional athletes of the time was a Jew. But as conscientious objections go, Sandy Koufax's day off was chopped liver next to Cantor Rosenblatt's lifetime of stubborn piety and self-abnegation in the face of the blandishments of mainstream celebrity.

"As Singular to See as to Hear" was the caption accompanying the oddly composed, full-length photograph of Cantor Rosenblatt that appeared in the *Boston Evening Transcript* late in 1918, on the occasion of his first concert appearance in that city. His top hat, frock coat, and awkward pose—a walking stick in one hand, the other hand thrust into a trouser pocket, casting a tiny stump of a shadow onto the clapboard wall behind him—all serve to accentuate Rosenblatt's diminutive stature, as does his beard, which, in impossibly literal compliance with Leviticus 19:27, sports four perfect, hospital corners.[13] After a quick glance at this bespectacled, hirsute dandy, a reader of the *Transcript* might have made a double-take, and wondered for a fleeting instant if President Wilson hadn't abandoned the Presbyterian Church.

The "Jewish Caruso," Cantor Josef "Yossele" Rosenblatt, successfully crossed over to concert hall, vaudeville, and movies without compromising his religious orthodoxy. (*Library of Congress George Grantham Bain Collection*)

Rosenblatt was born in Byelaya Tzerkov, fifty miles south of Kiev, in 1882. His vocal gifts were recognized early on. From the age of eight until his marriage at eighteen he traveled across the Austro-Hungarian Empire with his father, also a cantor—*chazzanut*'s answer to Leopold and Wolfgang Mozart. A series of prestigious synagogue positions followed, culminating with his appointment in 1906 as chief cantor of the central synagogue in Hamburg. Even there his salary was dwarfed by financial obligations that included support of his elderly parents and seven children, as well as providing dowries for eight older sisters. He was in no position to refuse the overture that he received in 1912 from New York's First Hungarian Congregation Ohab Zedek, a prosperous synagogue that had recently relocated from the Lower East Side to West 116th Street in Harlem. Ohab Zedek, which was seeking a new chief cantor, offered Rosenblatt $400 and travel expenses to officiate at two Sabbath services. The audition was a success, and Rosenblatt accepted a then-unprecedented annual salary of $2,400 for the permanent appointment. By the end of 1912, the extended Rosenblatt family had relocated from Hamburg to a tenement flat at 119th Street and Fifth Avenue.

Ohab Zedek's investment was recouped many times over. Cantor Rosenblatt proved to be a tremendous draw. "Every performance of his was a sacred concert, a most elevating religious experience, as soul-filling and satisfying as the finest symphony," his son Samuel later recalled. "He sang with such ease that it was hard to tell where the notes came from and whence the tones derived their power."[14] Nominally a tenor, his recordings and countless reviews confirm that Cantor Rosenblatt was endowed with a vocal instrument of exceptional range and purity that could move effortlessly and with perfect pitch from baritone to falsetto, a span of 3-1/2 octaves.[15] "Cantor Rosenblatt's voice is like the Old Testament itself translated into tone. . . . The range of Mr. Rosenblatt's tones is said to run from a subterranean B flat to the high C's. . . . Doubtless he could sing the whole score of the *Barber of Seville* all by himself."[16] "In the lower range, his tones are large, warm and full, of clear baritone quality. In the middle range, they are the tones of a thinner-voiced and dryer tenor; while higher still, they become a falsetto as piping as the voice of a bird and quite as agile."[17]

Rosenblatt's reputation spread quickly in the Jewish-American community, helped along by a growing discography and occasional appearances at synagogues outside of New York. A Yossele Rosenblatt 78 became as essential an accoutrement to a proper Jewish home as bottled seltzer and a Manischewitz recipe book. Every Jew could get the premise behind the classic Rosenblatt shtick:

A young cantor billed himself as "The Third Yossele Rosenblatt."
"And who," he was asked, "was the Second Yossele Rosenblatt?"
"Feh!" he replied in disgust, "Everyone knows there could be no *Second* Yossele Rosenblatt!"

But more than four years after his arrival in the United States, few Gentiles had heard of even the first Yossele Rosenblatt. That began to change in 1917, after he hired a manager, M. H. Hanson, a dapper, aggressive, and well-connected New York impresario. Rosenblatt gave Hanson exclusive control of his "artistic services outside of officiating at the Services of the Congregation Ohab Zedek."[18] Hanson, recognizing that this particular property called for special handling, astutely offered Rosenblatt's artistic services to the Central Committee for the Relief of Jews Suffering through the War, for what would become a nearly yearlong tour of thirty cities in the United States and Canada. Hanson knew that local relief committees would be happy to do much of the work and pick up much of the expense that usually falls to a concert promoter, while sharing the ticket receipts with him. Hanson assured organizers that ticket sales would be "but a drop in the bucket," compared to the money that would be raised by passing the hat at the concert. "Once within the hearing of Rosenblatt's voice, backed up by the strongest kinds of appeals, money is freely raised," he promised. "Not only did people give money and checks liberally, but stripped jewelry from off their person and threw it into the collection baskets."[19] Although Hanson had no direct financial interest in the donations, he was keen to draw the type of upscale audience that could later sustain the concert career that he envisioned in Rosenblatt's future. As he told Mrs. Samuel Untermyer, one of the doyennes of German-Jewish society: "I am very anxious to have at these concerts the best class of Jews, not only the immigrants from Russia and their immediate descendants . . . eventually, I hope to draw upon music lovers of the Gentiles as well."[20]

The voice of Cantor Rosenblatt was the drawing card, but the events were reported as fundraisers and society affairs, not concerts. After recounting some of the exhortatory speeches and itemizing some of the pledges made at the opening concert at the Hippodrome in May 1917, the *New York Times* had little to add about the headline performer: "The cantor is a singer of natural powers and moving eloquence. His voice is high in range and of peculiar quality, suited to the texts of prayers and chants familiar to most of his hearers. The audience listened with uncovered heads."[21]

It was at the tour's final stop, Chicago's Auditorium Theatre, in March 1918 that Rosenblatt's career took a decisive turn, vindicating Hanson's marketing strategy. Adler & Sullivan's 4,000-seat masterpiece was packed, and a thousand more were turned away at the door.[22] The Sunday afternoon audience included Cleofonte Campanini, the artistic director of the Chicago Grand Opera. Campanini pounced, approaching Rosenblatt with an offer that demonstrated his immediate grasp of Rosenblatt's commercial potential, as well as a thorough understanding of the constraints of his religious office. The role Campanini offered was that of Eléazar in Halévy's *La Juive*, a Jewish hero in an opera composed by a Jew, a role that would not require Rosenblatt to cut the beard that he had cultivated with bonsai-like patience and precision. Campanini promised there would be no rehearsals or performances on the Sabbath, and that he would cast a Jewish singer as Eléazar's daughter, Rachel. The concessions that Campanini made to Rosenblatt's orthodoxy were quickly forgotten, but the compensation he offered was not. Rosenblatt was, ever after, known as the cantor who rejected $1,000 per night to sing in opera. (Less well known was that Rosenblatt's fee per Central Relief Committee concert, each much less taxing than an opera performance, was $400.[23])

Rosenblatt led Campanini to believe that he would accept the offer subject only to the approval of Ohab Zedek's board. That condition was a pretext, a gentle rejection of a persistent suitor—Campanini could have offered to cast Mrs. Rosenblatt as Rachel, Yossele Rosenblatt still wasn't going to perform grand opera. "The opera," he felt, "was no place for a religious man. Too many women on stage, and the things an actor has to do!"[24] But playing coy turned out to be a public relations masterstroke. Campanini was forced to memorialize his offer in a letter to the president of Ohab Zedek, praising Rosenblatt's "voice and his art of singing" and adding that "I expect Mr. Rosenblatt to make a great success in opera, as he did in his concert appearance here." The short response of Ohab Zedek's board explained that "we feel that the Rev. Rosenblatt's sacred position in the synagogue does not permit him to enter the operatic stage," but the board had "no objections to his singing at concerts, whether sacred or otherwise." Both letters were released to the press (by whom it is unclear, but Hanson certainly possessed the motive and the savvy to do it) and were reprinted widely. In one fell swoop, Rosenblatt's artistry was validated without having to submit to the judgment of the musical press, his sacrifice on behalf of his faith and calling became a widespread source of Jewish pride, and his availability for concert engagements was made known to impresarios throughout the world, all without any taint of unseemly self-promotion.

On May 19, 1918, Rosenblatt launched his career as a concert artist, and made his debut before the music critics, at Carnegie Hall. The program established the eclectic template of "Russian, English, Jewish and Operatic Airs" that he would draw upon for the remainder of his life, ranging from his Hebrew and Yiddish specialties—including the indispensable "Eli, Eli"—and his own liturgical arrangements, to Verdi arias and Irish folk songs. Rosenblatt was happy to invite comparisons to Caruso and John McCormack, and his trills and coloratura reminded many of Nellie Melba and Amelita Galli-Curci. Critics agreed that his voice was astonishing, though they did not rush to second Campanini's appraisal of his artistry. Rosenblatt's vocal gymnastics, when applied to well-known operatic and art song repertoire, were deemed "a law unto itself."[25] "The tenor indulged in many a vocal stunt that in the art songs of Occidental civilization are considered bad taste."[26] But they also recognized that their reservations would do little to slow the Rosenblatt juggernaut. Although "traditions of style evidently mean little to him," one critic observed, "with his individual equipment, Cantor Rosenblatt may count upon pleasing his audience in practically every type of music."[27]

Audiences did adore Yossele Rosenblatt, and all the perquisites and burdens of celebrity descended upon the Rosenblatt family. Reporters came to their home to gather material for profiles, and the cantor obliged them with financial and domestic tidbits. An offer from a Philadelphia congregation to officiate at the High Holidays for $5,000 per service was national news—not even Caruso had received that for a single performance. And, in what might have been a fine conceit for a "Meet the Parents" comedy routine, the press widely and falsely reported that one of the Rosenblatt daughters was romantically linked with the world lightweight boxing champion, Benny "the Ghetto Wizard" Leonard.

Rosenblatt's fame and commitment to philanthropic causes also brought a constant stream of supplicants, to whom, it seems, he was constitutionally unable to say no. The Rosenblatt home, according to his son, was "looked upon as a paradise of *schnorrers* and my father as the redeeming angel of Jews in distress."[28] Tragically, when he was at the height of his fame in the early 1920s, he was persuaded to provide financial backing for a weekly, trilingual newspaper, the *Light of Israel*, which had been pitched to him as an instrument for preserving traditional, orthodox Judaism in America. After several years of funding tens of thousands of dollars of operating losses from his earnings, and guaranteeing the paper's debts to the tune of $200,000, Rosenblatt suffered the twin indignities of being charged with possession of a stolen car (a "gift" from his *Light of Israel* partners) and being forced to declare bankruptcy.

Though his responsibility for the *Light of Israel's* debts was legally discharged in the bankruptcy, Rosenblatt assumed a moral obligation to make its creditors whole. When it became clear that his income from the pulpit, concert stage, and recording studio, combined, would not be sufficient to do that in his lifetime, the much more lucrative sirens of vaudeville and Hollywood called. To a remarkable degree, Rosenblatt answered without compromising the integrity of his well-established brand, deftly adding another chapter to a personal narrative that he had been cultivating since his prodigal childhood.

It seems inevitable, in an "only in America" way, that Rosenblatt, the dutiful cantor's son and paragon of Jewish piety, and Al Jolson, the cantor's son who went into show business and buried his Jewish identity under a layer of burnt cork, would cross paths, even if the harmonic convergence was fictional.[29] In a pivotal scene from *The Jazz Singer*, Jolson's Jack Robin character attends a Rosenblatt concert in Chicago—"Sacred Songs, Popular Prices" says the sign outside the theater. As Rosenblatt's voice transports the hardboiled Robin, his image dissolves into that of Robin's father, Cantor Rabinowitz, chanting *Kol Nidre*. It is the first crack in Robin's otherwise emphatic rejection of his father for a career in show business, foreshadowing their final reconciliation. Rosenblatt received star billing for his cameo appearance. For him it was an *apologia pro vita sua*, proof that his musical activities outside the synagogue could serve a spiritually meaningful purpose. Inevitably, it was rumored that he had turned down the larger, more remunerative role of Cantor Rabinowitz, on religious grounds.[30]

Rosenblatt made his vaudeville debut at the Fox Theatre in Philadelphia, where he was paid $2,500 for the week (with Friday evening and Saturday off), and drew lines that stretched for blocks. The act that he took on the road was as Halachic as his High Holiday services. It was vividly recalled decades later by Louise Hovick, a young Gentile girl who once appeared on the same bill while a member of a vaudeville troupe called the "Dainty June Company." The austerity of his stagecraft broke with every convention of vaudeville. He came on stage in a cheap coat, the house lights on, without entrance music. "Then suddenly, almost frighteningly, one note broke through the silence. It was a high, piercing sound like a wail. There was a sadness in it that choked me," wrote Hovick. "He had the clearest, purest voice I had ever heard. There was a gentleness and strength and warmth in it. I felt that if God were to sing to us, this is how His voice would sound."

When his brief turn, three or four songs, was over, he left the stage "without a nod or a bow" and headed straight out to the street (he had no dressing room). When the cantor couldn't be found to give the encore that the audience was demanding, a near riot ensued. Louise's mother, Rose Hovick, had initially been annoyed that Rosenblatt was getting top billing—"religion or no religion, he is going to have one hell of a time following us"—but after witnessing similar frenzies at every show, she allowed that Rosenblatt could be the biggest thing in vaudeville, "if he'd just dress up the act a little."[31] Louise was even more deeply impressed, and a bit of the spirit of the cantor in the drab garb came to inhabit her later incarnation as Gypsy Rose Lee, in which she, too, used a parsimonious blend of exotic mystery, partial revelation, and ultimate denial, transcending the conventions of her genre and driving audiences into paroxysms of unconsummated adulation.

Cantor Rosenblatt's success paved the way for a steady migration of recognizable, uncoded Jewish memes into the American lively arts. In 1920, Caruso sang Eléazar, the heroic Jewish role that Rosenblatt had passed on, as his last at the Metropolitan Opera, where La Juive remained a repertory staple until well into the 1930s. Cantors could find stardom, first on records and in concert halls, later in radio, movies, and finally—with Richard Tucker in the 1940s—the grand opera stage, without being accused of apostasy. Yiddish theater in the United States, known theretofore mostly for its high-volume histrionics and lowbrow *shund*, lurched toward the mainstream in 1918 when actor-director Maurice Schwartz founded the Yiddish Art Theatre, where he "replaced traditional Yiddish acting with Stanislavsky's psychological re-alism."[32] At the same time, Fannie Hurst was emerging as the first Jewish writer to "tap significantly into the mass-American fiction market"[33] with her naturalistic stories of Jewish immigrant life. A 1920 film adaptation of her short story "Humoresque," in which a ghetto violin prodigy out-Rosenblatts Rosenblatt—turning his back on $2,000 per concert to enlist for combat in the Great War—was one of the biggest hits of the silent era.

And in a timely act of personal reinvention as he approached the age of forty, Ira B. Arnstein, classically educated American composer of standard music, became Ira B. Arnstein, composer of Jewish music, his sights trained on writing for Jewish music's greatest living expositor. Though Cantor Rosenblatt's Hebrew and Yiddish repertoire was vast, comprising hundreds of his own arrangements of prayers and traditional folk songs, he would on occasion employ his newfound celebrity to promote contemporary Jewish music, with the result that "Jewish songwriters of every description flocked to him."[34] The odds were stacked heavily against Arnstein.

Fortuitously, though, Rosenblatt was another habitué of Arison's Music House, which was located just a few doors down West 116th Street from Ohab Zedek. Arison, brusque and exacting in his appraisals of vocal talent, as in all matters musical, had advised Rosenblatt to obtain professional coaching before performing classical repertoire publicly, and then was dis-missive of the results—even walking out on one of the cantor's concerts. Despite this harsh judgment, or possibly as a result, Rosenblatt had the high-est regard for Arison. "Mr. Arison," he wrote in a testimonial, "is highly mu-sical, has an exceptionally deep knowledge of the Victor and the music business, and, what is of great importance, is a man with soul. He is in every respect reliable and trustworthy." Arison had published an original work by Arnstein, "La Prière," which had been transcribed for violin and piano by a teenage violinist who had recently arrived from Philadelphia, Sascha Jacob-son. Any musicians good enough for Mr. Arison were good enough for Cantor Rosenblatt—he engaged the young Jacobson as his accompanist for the Central Relief Committee concerts, and he gave Arnstein his chance to plug a tune.

The publication of Campanini's letter in April 1918 had coincided with the "Third Liberty Loan" campaign, a war bond sales drive. New York City was awash in makeshift performance venues—"Liberty Land" at the 69th Regiment Armory on Lexington Avenue, and the "Liberty Theatre" erected on the steps of the 42nd Street Public Library, among others—where organizations, trades, and the city's various immigrant communities were competing to hold the most boisterous rallies and put up the showiest subscription numbers. Cantor Rosenblatt, at that moment the object of intense public curiosity, emerged as the headliner for the Jewish rallies, leapfrogging over such proven draws as Al Jolson and Nora Bayes. By their very nature, these al fresco affairs called for rousing, nationalistic, stand-up-and-pass-the-hat numbers, in contrast to the liturgical music that had been so effective at the minyan-like Central Relief Committee concerts. Arnstein provided Rosenblatt with exactly what these events, coming not long after the Balfour Declaration, called for—a Jewish national anthem, "Zelner fun Tsion" ("Soldiers of Zion").

For his text, Arnstein adapted a poem by Morris Rosenfeld. While still working as a sewing machine operator on the Lower East Side twenty years earlier, Rosenfeld had gained fame as the best of a growing cadre of Yiddish "sweatshop poets." An 1898 collection of his poems, *Songs from the Ghetto*, was translated into numerous languages and was the first Yiddish literary work to receive significant critical attention in the United States. The simple rhyming patterns of Rosenfeld's stanzas and their march-like cadences made them naturals for musical setting; Rosenfeld would often sing them at his poetry recitals. "Soldiers of Zion" was a later and lesser work, representing intensely nationalistic feelings that Rosenfeld had long harbored but which had seldom seen print during his prime, before he suffered a debilitating stroke in 1906 and before the rise of political Zionism.

Taking only minor liberties with Rosenfeld's refrain, Arnstein rendered "Soldiers of Zion" as a Yiddish "Marseillaise," the kind of exhilarating, patriotic crowd-pleaser that Rosenblatt needed to open up Jewish wallets at his Liberty Loan programs. In the summer of 1918 Rosenblatt recorded it for the Columbia Graphophone Company. With a Sousa-esque tempo and major key verses and chorus, the frequently reissued "Soldiers of Zion" is a one-of-a-kind entry in the Rosenblatt discography, a rare opportunity for the modern, secular ear to hear his crystalline voice, an instrument seemingly on loan from Yahweh Himself, at the peak of its power and shorn of the falsetto and sobs of his synagogue *nusach*, faithfully hitting freshly written, unornamented notes exactly as they had only recently been set down on paper by a corporeal author.[35]

Sophie Arenstein died in 1919, succumbing in one of the last waves of the Spanish flu pandemic, and Arnstein soon joined thousands of other Jewish Harlemites in moving on to their next stop on the Diaspora trail, in his case the Upper West Side, where he would live a peripatetic existence for the rest of his life. By then the decline of Jewish Harlem was irreversible. Within a few years Ohab Zedek had moved to its present location on West 95th Street, and in 1929 Theodore Arison sold his Music House to a Spaniard, Daniel Castellanos, who operated it as one of New York's first Hispanic music stores, a cultural pillar of the emerging Spanish Harlem.

During his Harlem years, Arnstein had been an attentive son and doting bachelor uncle. He gave piano lessons to his half-brother Alexander's talented daughter Eva, who rode up from Philadelphia by train to see him, with a note for the Traveler's Aid Society pinned to her coat in case she got lost, and to his older sister Mae's less talented son Joseph, to whom Arnstein had dedicated a 1902 capriccio for piano, "Forest Nymphs." He had two more nieces by his brother Aaron, who sang under the name Harry Austin in the Metropolitan Opera's chorus. But once he left Harlem, hearth and home were all but absent from Arnstein's life.

Artistically, however, the move was rejuvenating, and the next few years were the most fruitful period of his career. A musical prologue that he composed for *Humoresque* was widely used in the Loew's theater chain throughout the movie's long run in 1920. In 1922, he published "V'Shomru," a dark meditation on Exodus 31:16–17, a mainstay of the Jewish liturgy that celebrates the Sabbath as a symbol of God's covenant with the Israelites. In Arnstein's Yiddish reworking, the weary children of Israel implore God to live up to His side of the covenant:

V'shomru b'nai Yisroel	*The children of Israel shall observe,*
Noch wie lang, is dein ferlang	*But for how long do you wish*
Dein folk tzu shtrofen	*To punish your people,*
Dein folk tzu shtrofen.	*To punish your people.*
Doch gloiben mir, nor in dir	*Still, we believe only in you,*
In ein Got, in dein gebot	*In one God, in your commandments,*
Hair dos beten fun dein folk	*Hear this prayer of your people,*
Dein elend folk.	*Your lonely people.*

The Victor Talking Machine Company and Columbia Graphophone Company were competing furiously for Jewish talent, Jewish content, and Jewish customers in the 1910s and 1920s. (Rosenblatt, characteristically, played one against the other to maximize his advances and royalties; Victor was usually the high bidder.) Both labels released recordings of Arnstein's "V'Shomru" in 1922. Columbia's version was performed by Shloimele Rothstein, a fine pulpit *chazzan* from Brooklyn. Victor's version featured William "Wee Willie" Robyn, a young tenor whose dreams of becoming a cantor were, in a reversal of *The Jazz Singer* scenario, deferred for years as he pursued an exceptionally varied career in show business.

Robyn had led prayer services as a boy in his native Latvia. When he came to New York as a teenager in 1913, he wandered the streets of Harlem looking for Cantor Rosenblatt's apartment, hoping for an audition. Rosenblatt was taken with Robyn's voice, but couldn't offer him a paying job. It was Ohab Zedek's loss. Two of New York's best vocal coaches, Jerome Hayes and Frank De Forge, soon took Robyn on as their pupil and ward, providing for his room and board on speculation against future earnings, and giving him a rigorous education in conventional classical vocal technique while he, unlike Rosenblatt, was still young enough and pliable enough for the training to take hold.

Robyn was living in a cheap room over a tailor's shop on West 55th Street when Lou Silvers, "Jolson's music man," there to pick up a pair of trousers, overheard him practicing "La Donna è Mobile." That happenstance led to three years on the B. F. Keith vaudeville circuit, followed by a long tenure as a featured soloist at New York's Capitol Theatre, the laboratory where a group of entertainment visionaries in the early 1920s retooled vaudeville for the age of mass media. Edward "Major" Bowes was the director, Samuel "Roxy" Rothafel the producer, Ernö Rapée the house orchestra's conductor, and Eugene Ormandy its concertmaster. A typical show at the Capitol might include "a concert from the house orchestra, a ballet number, some interpolated singers, a newsreel, a short . . . perhaps a historical recitation with accompanying staged tableaux, and then the feature film," much the same formula that Rothafel and Rapée would later bring to Radio City Music Hall.[36] In November 1922, when Rothafel brought his "divertissements" to radio as the *Capitol Theatre Family* program on American Telephone & Telegraph's WEAF in New York, Robyn was a charter member and star of the cast known as "Roxy's Gang." Over the next several years, as AT&T fed the show to more and more stations in a makeshift hook-up over its long distance lines, the improbable, far-flung success of a five-foot-tall singer with a pronounced Latvian accent was an early indication of the potential of network radio.

On the Keith circuit, where he had been billed as "Wolf Scarpioff," Robyn was presented as an exotic Russian act, but his big numbers—"At Dawning" and "The Sunshine of Your Smile"—were drearily familiar Tin Pan Alley fare. As a concert artist (he debuted to excellent reviews at Carnegie Hall in 1920 and continued to give serious recitals well into the 1930s) his repertoire included Schubert lieder and lyric tenor arias. At the Capitol Theatre he performed in abridged opera productions and original musicals, learning a new role every week. His recordings are as varied as the more than fifty pseudonyms that he recorded under, leaving behind a nightmarish task for archivists and discographers.[37] From 1920 to 1923, he recorded exclusively for Victor, the Tiffany of labels, doing popular songs passed over by its bigger stars until he was reassigned to the Foreign Department, where he recorded "V'Shomru" among many other Russian and Yiddish songs. He then moved on to the down-market Cameo label, where he was treated as a star and given choicer repertoire, including Irving Berlin hits like "Blue Skies" and "What'll I Do."

Missing from Robyn's professional résumé, however, was Jewish liturgical music. When his career stalled during the Depression and he decided to return to the cantorate, he faced considerable resistance. His trophy recording for Cameo, "Ave Maria," with violin obbligato by Eugene Ormandy, would have only raised eyebrows on synagogue ritual committees that were predisposed to assume, as Robyn recalled when looking back on his career at the age of one hundred in 1995, "because he was in show business he's no good. Period."[38] Robyn's recording of Arnstein's "V'Shomru," in which he deftly imparts the soul of a venerable synagogue chant to a brand new song, should have assuaged their concerns.[39]

Arnstein followed up on the success of "V'Shomru" with arrangements of traditional Yiddish folk songs and an original piece for piano and violin, "At the Wailing Wall." The growing market for serious Jewish-themed music now emboldened him to undertake his first large-scale work, a "biblical opera" based on the story of David. The material he needed for a serviceable libretto was readily at hand—the two Books of Samuel combined with wholesale appropriations from the Book of Psalms. In May 1925, at the 1,100-seat Aeolian Hall (the site of Paul Whiteman's "Experiment in Modern Music" concert a year earlier), Arnstein conducted a cast and chorus of fifty, accompanied by string quartet, organ, and piano, in a Sunday evening concert performance of his work in progress, *The Song of David*. In a casting coup, the role of David was sung by Mordecai Hershman, one of the many European cantors who had followed Rosenblatt to the United States and to the concert stage, and considered by many to be Rosenblatt's only true rival.

Though the score performed that night does not survive, it was well received by the audience and the critics. "The chief merit of Mr. Arnstein's music consists in its use of Hebraic melodic elements," *Musical America* wrote. "The typical descending cadences of synagogue plaints are at times very beautifully employed. Undoubtedly there is a great deal of talent displayed in the score, the themes being clearly defined and for most part marked by vigor and melodic effectiveness." It also detected "more than a tincture of modern jazz."[40] The *Telegram*, while criticizing the theatrical qualities—"a succession of set pieces that are hardly conceived in the operatic idiom or dramatic in quality"—found "a good deal of fluent, effective music in the score, including some very effective choral writing."[41] The *Times* agreed that the "choruses were among the best written and the most animated parts" and noted that the ballet music, "with its Oriental atmosphere," had to be repeated.[42] Virtually all agreed that much of the music was more reminiscent of such models as *Aida* and *Samson & Delilah* than original.[43] For a stripped-down performance of an unfinished work, the notices were reasonably encouraging and blurb-friendly.[44]

The success of the concert presentation of *The Song of David* led to a series of assignments for the Yiddish Art Theatre, providing incidental music and songs for plays by Shalom Asch and Harry Sackler, and a score for Maurice Schwartz's first photoplay, *Broken Hearts*. With the original twenty-eight-year copyright term on "A Mother's Prayer" coming to an end, Arnstein sold his interest in the renewal to Albert Teres, another major Yiddish music publisher, for $3,000— more than $37,000 in 2012 dollars—a handsome sum for a generation-old parlor piece. As a teacher, Arnstein was comfortably ensconced in a studio at the Metropolitan Opera House. Arnstein's growing stature was validated with an entry in the first edition of the Jewish Biographical Bureau's *Who's Who in American Jewry*, published in 1926.[45] Just shy of fifty years old, Arnstein had reached what turned out to be the short-lived pinnacle of his career.

UNMOVED MOVER OF MELODY

Amid the multitude of tawdry musical compositions which pour out so plentifully, it is not surprising that there should be similarity between pieces for two or three bars. No one can sit very long in this court without being aware that the amount of originality displayed in this kind of production is at the minimum.
—Judge Learned Hand

The hero of Frank Loesser's 1961 musical, the portentously and preposterously named J. Pierrepont Finch, window-washer and archetypal postwar striver, keeps a slim paperback in his back pocket—the eponymous *How to Succeed in Business Without Really Trying*. Oblivious to its snark and sarcasm, Finch slavishly follows the author's breezy aphorisms, charting a meteoric rise from the mailroom to the executive suite of World Wide Wicket, all before intermission. Had he been born a generation earlier, Finch might have carried around a dog-eared copy of another pocket-sized guidebook, *Inside Stuff on How to Write Popular Songs* (1927), written by the music critic and future editor of *Variety*, Abel Green. The proto-Finch would have ditched any thoughts of Wall Street in a New York second (and not a moment too soon, with the crash of 1929 looming) upon learning of the riches that success on Tin Pan Alley could bestow. "The venerable masters' works are preserved in ancient tomes, gathering venerable dust," Green taught, "whereas the modern songwriter lives in the present and knows that by syncopating and embellishing an intriguing melody it will fetch him beaucoup royalties."[1] His admonition that "the tyro should search about for new ideas"[2] might have seemed daunting at first, but in the end Green was reassuring—searching about for new ideas is, after all, infinitely easier than actually thinking them up. "On the matter of popular song technique, no amount of exposition will serve the purpose as well as an assortment of the current hit songs you have on your piano. Study those."[3]

With unschooled amateurs being encouraged to believe that the rich but rare jackpots of popular songwriting were plausibly within their reach—and judging by the prevalence of song-sharking rackets, vanity music publishers that preyed upon a credulous public by taking large fees for arranging a tune or setting lyrics to music, that belief was rather widespread—then Ira B. Arnstein, a conservatory-trained pianist and singer, an oft-published composer of pleasing and melodious piano solos, art songs, and serious theatrical music, could certainly be excused for thinking that a comfortable sinecure was his for the taking. No one, after all, was earning more writing popular music than Irving Berlin, the erstwhile Izzy Baline, whose family had arrived from Russia around the same time as the Arensteins, and who—the whole world knew—couldn't read music and could only pick out his tunes on the black keys of a transposing piano. At the age when Itzig Arenstein had been performing operatic choruses of Mussorgsky and Tchaikovsky in America's leading concert halls, Izzy Baline was plying his reedy soprano in some of the Bowery's worst dives, singing ribald parodies of Tin Pan Alley hits for tossed pennies. And if Arnstein lacked Irving Berlin's ear for the American vernacular and gift for insouciant rhymes and patter, the ability to write, as Alexander Woollcott described Berlin's lyrics, "ornery conversations written to music,"[4] that was no disqualifier. The "formulaic model of saying 'I Love You' in thirty-two bars" was by then well established.[5] Given just eight catchy measures, a Tin Pan Alley publisher could have its staff flesh out the rest of the chorus in the paradigmatic AABA form and dub in the "I Love You."

Arnstein had the necessary skills and the money was enticing. The professional recognition that had come his way in midlife, albeit gratifying, was not putting food on the table. With the assignment of his copyright renewal in "A Mother's Prayer" in 1926, he had wrung out the last dollars he would ever see from his one enduring hit. Writing incidental music for the prestigious dramas of the Yiddish Art Theatre, productions intended to run for maybe a week, provided only a meager return on the time invested. Speculative work on his magnum opus, *The Song of David*, was a costly diversion from more reliably profitable endeavors. Teaching no longer paid the rent. His recent taste of success as a composer had probably led him to neglect his teaching franchise, and the arrival of radio and consequent decline of home musicianship were no help. "Music teachers," Edward B. Marks wrote, "learned the meaning of unemployment long before the market crash of late 1929."[6] So, in 1927, at an age when the most protean of musical talents have left the hard work of doing something new to the young, Arnstein attempted yet another transformation. He set about writing AABA-I-Love-You songs, and began shopping them around latter-day Tin Pan Alley.

Of one of Arnstein's earliest efforts in this genre, "Alone," nothing survives. It might be surmised that it was in waltz time, perhaps with the unusual combination of a major key verse and a minor refrain, and that it may have employed dissonances and intervals vaguely reminiscent of the Russian folk harmonies he had sung in his youth with Madame Lineff's choir. It may, indeed, have resembled a similarly titled Russian folk song, the melancholy "Alone I Go Strolling" ("Vyhazhu odin ya na dorogu"), which he had recently arranged for publisher Saul Schenker. In any or all of these respects, it might have been uncannily similar to Irving Berlin's 1927 hit, "A Russian Lullaby."

The Copyright Act of 1976 provides that copyright protection "subsists" in "original" works of authorship "fixed in any tangible medium of expression." "Subsists" is an odd verb to find in an Act of Congress—it appears in no other context in the massive U.S. Code. Statutes positively decree norms and the penalties for violating them, or they grant benefits and set forth the conditions attached to them; it is not usually their province to acknowledge that which simply is. "Subsists" smacks of natural law, misleadingly suggesting that the intellectual rationale for copyright law is to be found in morality or teleology, rather than utilitarian economics. But our founders spelled out with unusual particularity in Article I, Section 8, of the Constitution that copyrights and patents were meant as carrots that Congress could hold out "to promote Progress in Science and the useful Arts." (Only the Second Amendment, with its Delphic "a well-regulated militia being necessary for the security of a free state," contains a similar mini-statement of purpose.) "The immediate effect of our copyright law is to secure a fair return for an 'author's' creative labor," wrote Supreme Court justice Potter Stewart, "but the ultimate aim is, by this incentive, to stimulate artistic creativity for the general public good."[7]

Yet this archaic-sounding verbal formulation conveys an important attribute of copyright. Unlike other forms of governmental largesse such as patents, broadcast licenses, or procurement contracts, which can be extraordinarily costly and laborious to obtain, copyright protection simply "subsists" in original works of authorship fixed in a tangible means of expression—a doodle, a snapshot, or a Tweet can be enough—and is therefore the most egalitarian of all forms of property, accessible to feckless slackers, idle daydreamers, and kitchen-table cleffers. Nor has the requirement that the work must be "original" proven to be a substantial barrier to copyright proprietorship. "Original means only that the work was independently created by the author," the Supreme Court has held, "the requisite level of creativity is extremely low; even a slight amount will suffice."[8]

The ease of obtaining copyright protection and the rather small set of shared materials available for constructing simple melodies with instant and widespread appeal ("we have," as composers and publishers are fond of quoting Sir Arthur Sullivan, "only eight notes between us") combined to form the very primordial ooze from which Tin Pan Alley materialized. They are also the conditions that have incubated what is commonly referred to as music "plagiarism" litigation. True plagiarism, as Professor Paul Goldstein has explained, "is an ethical, not a legal, offense and is enforceable by academic authorities, not courts."[9] Nonetheless, the term plagiarism persists in the legal literature and is a useful shorthand for one way that a music copyright can be infringed—by copying the protected expression of another and passing it off as one's own. Other forms of copyright infringement include the most morally culpable and sometimes criminal offenses—counterfeiting or bootlegging, that is, making copies that deceptively appear to *be* the original. At the other extreme, and typically the least blameworthy form of infringement, is a fully acknowledged use of an original that exceeds the scope of one's authorization, perhaps based on an ASCAP license to publicly perform music, or on the amorphous legal doctrine of "fair use." Each form of infringement raises its own set of legal and conceptual difficulties.

The chronicles of the popular music business teem with examples of costly struggles against easily made but difficult-to-refute allegations in the nature of plagiarism, asserted in the most famous instances by industry outsiders, some of them innocently deluded, others harboring extortion in their hearts. (An excellent, interactive website created by musician and lawyer Charles Cronin, the UCLA Music Copyright Infringement Resource, provides a comprehensive survey with musical samples.[10]) It is, in the view of popular music publishers, a plague that has been visited upon them with especial virulence. But these dreamers and schemers are just following a trail that was blazed by the publishers themselves. Internecine copyright infringement litigation was an accepted, if ultimately self-defeating method of doing business in Tin Pan Alley, where a Runyonesque ethos of "sue me" prevailed, and the moral code dictated only that "if a song writer is ethical, he will not cop a tune within three years of its publication."[11]

The rules of engagement were hashed out in an early line of cases, mostly brought by one publisher against another, with a disproportionate number of them decided by one judge, Learned Hand of the U.S. District Court in Manhattan. To Hand, as he made little effort to conceal in opinions that veritably gurgled with dyspepsia, Tin Pan Alley's internal warfare was "scarcely more than irritation, involving no substantial interest" and "a waste of time for everyone concerned."[12] In a 1910 suit by Edward Marks and Joseph Stern against Jerome Remick, Hand, then an unjaded new appointee to the federal trial court bench, ruled that "publication," a requirement for federal copyright protection that was not abolished until the 1976 act (before that unpublished works were protected, if at all, under parallel state regimes of "common law" copyright), could be met by the formality of a single token sale of a song, or by depositing two copies with the Library of Congress.[13] In 1915, Charles Boosey, an old-line British publisher, brought suit against Empire Music, accusing "Tennessee, I Hear You Calling Me," a syncopated Al Jolson number, of infringing "I Hear You Calling Me," a lamentation sung to a deceased love, first popularized by John McCormack, the Irish Yossele Rosenblatt. The case established that a single common phrase in two otherwise vastly dissimilar songs could give rise to liability.[14]

When Edward B. Marks tested the limits of *Boosey v. Empire Music* in a suit against Leo Feist over six measures from the 1921 hit song "Swanee River Moon," claiming they were extracted from a 450-bar instrumental number, the "Wedding Dance Waltz," Judge Hand drew a line, ruling that there must be proof of actual copying, and that "chance similarities are not actionable." The Second Circuit Court of Appeals, to which Hand would soon be appointed, unhelpfully added in its affirmance the multiply-redundant requirement that there must be "substantial copying of a substantial and material part."[15] But copying, as Judge Hand had held in an earlier case involving the 1915 anti-interventionist anthem, "I Didn't Raise My Boy to Be a Soldier," did not need to be proven by direct evidence, nor was it necessary to prove directly that the accused infringer was familiar with the copyrighted work—it was permissible to infer copying from circumstantial evidence of uncanny similarity to the copyrighted work together with proof of the alleged infringer's "access" to it.[16]

It was in his swan song as a trial court judge, a 1924 clash of songwriting titans, that Hand gave future copyright infringement plaintiffs their greatest reason to take heart. Fred Fisher accused Jerome Kern of copying the famous ostinato bass accompaniment from Fisher's "Dardanella," a huge hit in 1920, and using it to identical effect in "Ka-lu-a," which Kern had written for a 1921 Broadway show, *Good Morning, Dearie*. Hand ruled that the accompaniment, though not "at all as important to the success of 'Dardanella' as the plaintiff would ask me to believe," was nonetheless an element protected by the copyright on the piece. Hand went on to rule that Kern could not attack the validity of Fisher's copyright on the ground that "the precise work has independently appeared before it and is in the public domain," and was therefore not "original," in the absence of any evidence that Fisher had in fact copied from such a source.

Judge Learned Hand was Tin Pan Alley's reluctant lawgiver. (*Library of Congress George Grantham Bain Collection*)

On the issue of liability for infringement, it did not matter whether Kern's copying was conscious or deliberate—"it is no excuse," Hand said, "that in so doing his memory has played him a trick." Though Hand deemed Kern's denial of deliberate copying credible and acknowledged that Kern, with "an established place among composers of light opera," would have no motive to copy, he concluded that "everything registers somewhere in our memories, and no one can tell what may evoke it. . . . I cannot really see how else to account for a similarity which amounts to identity."[17] (Recent scholarship has turned up an early *Good Morning, Dearie* manuscript showing that Kern's quotation of "Dardanella" was likely conscious and deliberate, having started out as one of the score's many musical nods to dance crazes of the day.[18]) In the end, Kern's stellar reputation left him no better off in Hand's estimation than the somewhat disreputable composer of "I Didn't Raise My Boy to Be a Soldier," Al Piantadosi, an in-house tunesmith at Leo Feist whom Hand had condemned as having "small knowledge of musical notation and small skill in playing" and a well-known habit of borrowing themes from others.[19] In both cases, Hand registered his overall low regard for Tin Pan Alley and the litigation it spawned by awarding the statutory minimum damages of $250. "Such victories," he said, "I may properly enough make a luxury to the winner."[20]

Irving Berlin's proud lack of musical learning (an admiring musicologist, Allen Forte, calls him a "cultivated musical illiterate"[21]) and richer-than-God public profile made him an inviting target for copyright infringement charges, but his preternatural musical gifts and methodical work habits rendered him all but impervious to such claims, eliminating copying, even subconscious copying, as a plausible explanation for any similarity to music written by another.

In his classic study of the *American Popular Song*, Alec Wilder, after "searching assiduously for stylistic characteristics in Berlin," despaired of finding any, ultimately resorting to a mere listing of more than a dozen template songs that exhibited distinct, nonoverlapping "stylistic points of view."[22] Wilder conceded that his analysis suffered from the subject's refusal to allow his music to be quoted.[23] (Berlin considered his good friends Harold Arlen and Richard Rodgers "dumb schmucks" for cooperating with Wilder and, after reading an advance draft of the chapter devoted to his songs, he expressed his dismay that Oxford University Press would publish "such a piece of shit."[24]) More fundamentally, though, Wilder's search for a unifying style was frustrated by the stubborn resistance of Berlin's songs— with their seamless blending of words, melodies, and harmonies—to any kind of intellectual parsing. Though it was well-known that Berlin relied on his musical secretaries to harmonize his songs, Wilder found that Berlin had a "natural, intuitive harmonic sense at work in his head," making it "nearly impossible, upon hearing some of these melodies, to believe that every chord was not an integral part of the tune."[25] "The same goes for the lyrics," adds Wilfred Sheed, "which seem not so much brilliant as inevitable. They simply come with the notes."[26]

To show that a Berlin song used a stolen accompaniment, or that it borrowed a few measures of melody from an instrumental piece, that it hadn't simply emerged as a fully formed organic whole from the head of Zeus, was no less a challenge than splitting the atom. In one of the rare copyright infringement cases against Berlin to go to trial, a dispute over the intricately contrapuntal duet "You're Just in Love" from his 1950 score for *Call Me Madam*, witnesses for both sides attested to Berlin's singular gift:

> Two men, distinguished in the world of music, were called as experts: Abram Chasins, a noted pianist and composer, for the plaintiff; and John Tasker Howard, composer, author and curator of the Americana Music Collection, for the defendants. Mr. Chasins stated that Mr. Berlin was internationally recognized for his unique genius in the complete blending of lyrics and music. Mr. Howard testified that there is such a "perfect wedding of words and music" that they seem to be conceived together. There was unanimity that "You're Just in Love" was a combination of lyrics and music typical of the distinctive style and virtuosity of Irving Berlin.[27]

Plaintiff Alfred Smith, a gold and leather craftsman, must have found it deflating to listen to the testimony of the experts, including his own, knowing there was no similarity whatever between his lyrics and Berlin's, and there- fore no reason for anyone to believe that his music was the prototype for Berlin's. Smith, however, was among the more successful of Berlin accusers; few others ever got their day in court. At the first hint of an impending infringement case, a well-oiled defense apparatus would be mobilized under the personal command of Berlin himself, for whom such accusations trig-gered two deep-seated but conflicting emotions: a phobic distaste for having his music dissected and an overweening urge to sell his wares and propagate his legend through any and every available medium of publicity.

Berlin's aversion to musicological dissection of his songs was not born of fear of being exposed, but rather of his fear, and the fear of those around him, that once genius as mysterious as his was taken apart for inspection, it could never be reassembled. These anxieties can be heard in his border-line hysterical reaction to Alec Wilder's book, and in the timid, hesitant tone of his most trusted musical secretary, Helmy Kresa, upon being asked to evaluate an infringement accusation that Berlin was finding par-ticularly worrisome. Berlin's song and the accuser's shared *two* uncanny similarities. Kresa had some promising ideas for the defense, having to do with Berlin's song breaking one of the rules of strict counterpoint and using the subdominant key as a contrast, but he discouraged Berlin from concerning himself with the technical details: "This might all sound very involved and complicated, but anybody who has studied composition will verify my statements."[28] Music theory was not a subject the boss should be encumbered with; whether he was breaking established rules or adhering to them, nothing but trouble could come from making him conscious of it.

Yet every copyright claim presented an opportunity too. After learning that he was being sued over "Here I Am but Where Are You?," a torch song performed by Harriet Nelson in the 1936 Astaire-Rogers picture *Follow the Fleet*, Berlin told his attorney Francis Gilbert that although he was worried about the lawsuit, "if we were positive of winning the case I would welcome it as it would serve as invaluable good publicity" for his next project.[29] Once it became apparent to Berlin that Alfred Smith's "cockamamie allegations could not possibly threaten his eminence,"[30] he went on the offensive, taking the stand in a tour de force that included a summary of his career from "Alexander's Ragtime Band" to *Call Me Madam* – abjuring any false modesty – a demonstration of his compositional technique by striking "dif-ferent pieces of a near-by wooden shelf as though he were picking keys labo-riously," and finally a performance of "You're Just in Love," competently accompanying himself on a spinet piano. "The myth that Irving Berlin is a one-finger piano player," the *Times* reported, "was exploded yesterday in Supreme Court."[31]

Berlin's disciplined and methodical approach to the job of songwriting guaranteed that he would never find himself vulnerable in the way Jerome Kern had been in the "Dardanella" case, without an alibi, unable to provide an exculpatory story for every musical idea he used. His Calvinist work habits, photographic memory, pack-rat compulsiveness, industrial delegation of labor, and need for constant feedback all meant that there was a meticulous audit trail for every song, and it was always circular, leading right back to Irving Berlin. There was no need to hunt for earlier third-party uses of a phrase; it could always be found in an earlier draft or an earlier song of Berlin's own that predated whatever song he was being accused of copying, sometimes unpublished but carefully filed away in the back closet of his office. There were always witnesses of unimpeachable integrity to swear that Berlin had played the tune for them long before one of his secretaries took it down in final form, while Berlin was still working out the basic melody. "The old impulse of the busker is so strong within him," wrote Alexander Woollcott, "that his friends are likely to hear the shifting forms of a new melody as it takes shape during a year of experiment."[32] When a plagiarism case against "Pack up Your Sins and Go to the Devil" went to trial, Jascha Heifetz was one of the witnesses who appeared to swear to the priority of Berlin's creation.

All that Francis Gilbert had to do was ask, and Berlin could provide a detailed, verifiable genealogy. "Just a Little While," published in 1930? It started out along the lines of "What'll I Do?" "Somewhere there must be either a lead sheet or a piano copy," Berlin assured Gilbert. "I can easily prove through several people who heard the song that I wrote it at least three years ago. I set the tune to the title."[33] "Here I Am but Where Are You?" of 1938? The original version was written in 1927; the manuscript is lost, but no need to worry. Having that tune in mind at the time, Berlin had used six bars of the original eight in the opening chorus of the *Ziegfeld Follies of 1927*, and some other parts of it almost note-for-note in another number he wrote for the same show. "Then when I went out to California right after that show was produced, I wrote a ballad called 'I Can't Do Without You' and I again used 6 of the original 8 bars in that song."[34]

And verily did some such chain of begats—every link the work of the past master himself, the unmoved mover of melody—lead inexorably from the accused song in its final form back to a fully witnessed and copiously documented immaculate conception. Anyone thinking of challenging the primogeniture of an Irving Berlin tune could count on being met with a stout and well-funded legal defense fueled by the self-righteous indignation of one mightily ticked-off American icon.

Though later eclipsed by the contemporaneous "Blue Skies," in its day "A Russian Lullaby" was the bigger hit—the only Berlin song to be named in a 1933 survey of orchestra leaders as one of the top-ten numbers of the preceding decade.[35] A suit against Irving Berlin over one of his biggest hits might seem like an inauspicious way for Ira B. Arnstein to begin what would be a nearly three-decade-long career as a copyright litigant, but on Valentine's Day 1928 he swore out a complaint in the Supreme Court for the State and County of New York, alleging that the "musical composition 'A Russian Lullaby,' and in particular the musical portion thereof, substantially imitates and simulates the musical composition 'Alone' owned by plaintiff."[36]

Francis Gilbert and Berlin's other surrogates could counter with an especially convincing and affecting narrative of Berlin's independent creation of "A Russian Lullaby" during the weeks immediately following the birth of his first child, Mary Ellin. The real-life *Abie's Irish Rose* soap opera of Berlin and his Irish Catholic second wife, Ellin, had been fodder for the New York tabloids for several years. Berlin's patrician father-in-law, Clarence Mackay, had objected to his daughter's marriage to the dark Russian "jazz composer," and a bitter estrangement had followed the couple's elopement. Many New Yorkers were hoping vainly that the arrival of the blue-eyed Mary Ellin might prompt a reconciliation. Though not normally introspective, Berlin turned inward for musical inspiration, to painful memories of his immigrant childhood. "A Russian Lullaby" was the result. In addition to the formidable weapons Berlin brought to every copyright fight, in this one he presented a sympathetic human face.

Equally problematic for Arnstein was the issue of access. As Berlin's lawyers were quick to point out, the complaint contained no allegation of how Berlin could have seen or heard "Alone." According to the complaint it "was never published, nor were any copies of the same ever sold or offered for sale, nor was same ever copyrighted under the laws of the United States, or of any other country, nor was the same ever dedicated to the public, but the said composition remained in manuscript form."[37] (Arnstein's state-court case was based on common law copyright.) An amended complaint sought to remedy this defect, alleging that "prior to the commencement of this action" Arnstein "at defendants' request privately exhibited the original of his said manuscript to them."[38]

Mr. and Mrs. Irving Berlin. (*Library of Congress George Grantham Bain Collection*)

"Prior to the commencement of this action" was a rather flaccid little dodge. Nearly a year had passed between the first public performance of "A Russian Lullaby" and the "commencement of this action." A private audition in the interim, a loophole left open by the language of Arnstein's amended complaint, would not support any inference of copying.

The issue of access had not been much discussed in earlier music copyright cases, in most of which one publisher was suing another and the song that was allegedly copied may have been as well or better known than the accused song. But when individual, unpublished outsiders began suing—and Arnstein was at the vanguard of this new breed of plaintiff—it became a central issue. The difficulty that Arnstein confronted in the *Berlin* case establishing access, one of the crucial elements, along with similarity, needed to make out a circumstantial case of copying, would be a perennial challenge, played out in case after case. In the years to come Arnstein's signal contributions to copyright law and lore would come from his increasingly fantastic theories of similarity and access.

Arnstein's attorneys meekly threw in the towel and allowed the case to be dismissed before trial in October 1928, becoming just another notch in Berlin's cudgel. And Berlin *was* keeping score, convinced that "every one of these that fall through helps our cause in any future law suit; at least they make me less afraid."[39] Though for Arnstein this was just a starter lawsuit, ill conceived and quickly abandoned, from which he gained nothing, learned little, and made no lasting contribution to copyright law, some of the hallmarks of his more mature, better-known work were already apparent in *Arnstein v. Berlin.* Above all, it was clear that he was not afraid to punch way above his weight, and even after having butted his head against the Berlin Wall to no avail, he never picked on a target that would be easy to roll. "No one," wrote lawyer Alexander Lindey, "can accuse Arnstein of courting feeble opposition."[40]

Arnstein spoiled for a rematch with Berlin. He would, we shall see, spoil for a rematch with everyone. In the near term, however, he turned his attention away from this infuriatingly elusive autodidact of bottomless and inexplicable genius, and directed his energies toward an impeccably credentialed, well-schooled musician, a mere but essential mortal who toiled in relative obscurity among the demigods of the Age of the Songwriter—Nathaniel Shilkret, the hardest-working man in the music business.

ARRANGER ON A TRAIN

He's a human oscillator, vibrating on high frequency between the radio, recording, and talkie studios. Think how often his name flashes up on the screen—"Musical Score by Nat Shilkret." Think how many of your new records bear the legend "Nat Shilkret and his Orchestra." Think how often your radio says "and now, under the direction of Nat Shilkret." So he earns his title, the Napoleon of Music.
—Brooklyn Eagle

At the age of seven, Nathaniel Shilkret was touring the country as the principal clarinetist in the New York Boys' Orchestra. As a teenager he studied on a scholarship at the National Conservatory of Music, summered with Victor Herbert's orchestra in Saratoga Springs, toured with Walter Damrosch's Oratorio Society, and was much in demand for recording sessions and hotel dates. In his early twenties, he was a member of the wind section of Mahler's New York Philharmonic and studied piano with Charles Hambitzer, George Gershwin's mentor. In 1914, at age twenty-five, married, a new father, with ambitions of becoming a conductor, it was time to get a day job with a steady income and better prospects for advancement.

He took a salaried position as a staff arranger and conductor with the Victor Talking Machine Company. He was assigned to the Foreign Department, which produced records in thirty-two languages. "Engaging talent, picking the music, orchestrating, recording, listening to masters and picking the best rendition, translating the title and write-ups for the catalogues, and contracting each artist became my full-time occupation," Shilkret later remembered. "There were twelve dates a week—forty-eight separate titles and about two hundred records per month to be filled out."[1]

Shilkret's output during his ten years in Victor's Foreign Department was staggering in its quantity and variety, an education that supplemented his already vast knowledge of the standard symphonic repertoire with the folk and popular music of virtually the entire Western world. During the spring of 1921 alone, by no measure an atypical period, Shilkret recorded Neapolitan songs with Beniamino Gigli (fresh off his debut at the Metropolitan Opera), Swedish Christmas carols and folk tunes with bass Gustav Holmquist, Yiddish *nigunim* and Hebrew *piyyutim* with Yossele Rosenblatt, Mordecai Hershman, and William Robyn, and numerous Lithuanian and Czech numbers. His workload was back-breaking, made bearable only by his unflagging energy, minimal need for sleep, and seemingly limitless capacity for multitasking. Robyn recalled that when traveling by rail from New York to Victor's Camden, New Jersey, recording studios, Shilkret would work out his orchestrations and arrangements en route, while simultaneously carrying on animated conversations with his companions.[2]

Shilkret's responsibilities gradually expanded to include Victor's Export, Race, and Hillbilly departments. He worked in relative obscurity, and apparently without complaint, until 1924, when Vernon Dalhart, a singer of light opera and popular songs, persuaded Shilkret to let him record a folk song then very much in vogue—"The Wreck of the Old '97"—for the Hillbilly Department. According to Shilkret, he instructed Dalhart to find a song for the "B" side: "Dalhart said he had at home a manuscript of a song written by a cousin of his which might do. . . . A day or two later he showed up with some penciled notes but no music. The manuscript, as he submitted it, was a mess. It was only long enough to fill about half a record." Shilkret wrote some additional verses and "ground out a simple, mournful tune to fit the words."[3]

That "B"-side track was "The Prisoner's Song," with Dalhart accompanied by Carson Robison on guitar and—in a classy and nuanced touch that had Shilkret's fingerprints all over it—a viola obbligato instead of the obligatory country fiddle. It became the first multimillion-seller in the hillbilly genre. Some months later, Shilkret was dismayed to learn that the song had been published by Shapiro, Bernstein and that Dalhart's cousin, Guy Massey, was being credited with both the words and music under an agreement that reputedly assigned 95 percent of his royalties to Dalhart. And Shilkret was infuriated when Victor, which owned his copyrights under the terms of his employment contract, declined to fight for his songwriting credit or a share of the royalties, while Dalhart went on to re-record the song more than a dozen times for competing labels.

Massey's disputed authorship of "The Prisoner's Song" has long fascinated country music historians (Shilkret is only one of many competing claimants),[4] and Shilkret's grievance was one that festered for the rest of his life.[5] The incident served as a wake-up call for Shilkret, prompting the dutiful company man to start looking out for himself. He renegotiated his arrangements with Victor to obtain ownership of his compositions, a promotion from staff conductor to featured artist, and the freedom to pursue broadcast engagements. Over the next few years he made astute use of his newly won rights, becoming one of the top name brands in music.

Shilkret's earliest label credits came as the director of a popular music ensemble, the Victor Salon Orchestra, which he formed to play distinctive, concert-like arrangements that set it apart from dance bands like Paul Whiteman's. "Shilkret reasoned that there was a large public which was interested in light music, not done in dance tempi, but arranged for the ultimate in melodic effect."[6] The lush, string-dominated recordings of the Salon Orchestra, which also featured some of the earliest uses of the vibraphone, were, as Abel Green observed in *Variety*, "just as appealing for straight hear as hoof stuff."[7] Many remained in the Victor catalog long after the renditions of Shilkret's competitors, and the dance fads they catered to, had disappeared. By the time that Victor reunited George Gershwin and the Paul Whiteman Orchestra in 1927 to do an electronic remake of their original 1924 acoustic recording of *Rhapsody in Blue*, Whiteman had been custom tailoring the piece to the tastes of dance hall audiences for so long, Gershwin insisted that Shilkret conduct the recording session.

At the other end of the popular spectrum, Shilkret recorded hot jazz records with an "All Star Orchestra," which included, in one 1928 iteration, three future swing bandleaders—Benny Goodman on clarinet, Tommy Dorsey and Glenn Miller on trombone. Around this same time, Shilkret also began recording regularly for the upscale Red Seal Department, conducting the Victor Symphony in major orchestral works and accompanying many of the leading classical singers and instrumentalists of the day.

It was on the new medium of radio that Shilkret made his biggest splash. Bandleaders who were making their living on the dance hall circuit were reluctant to perform on radio, and in some cases were contractually prohibited from doing so, for fear of cannibalizing their own box office. But Shilkret, almost strictly a studio musician, had no such worries. On New Year's Day 1925, he and the Victor Salon Orchestra were selected to accompany singers John McCormack and Lucrezia Bori for a live radio concert, one of the first-ever by major musical talents, in an experiment to see whether radio could "create a demand for their Victor 'cannings.'"[8] The response to the program, carried over a small national hook-up, was impressive. McCormack sang a new Irving Berlin song that he had just recorded, "All Alone," and demand for both his record and the sheet music surged. (Music publishers' general suspicion of radio persisted. They credited the success of the broadcast to McCormack's unique appeal, and continued to insist that "radio alone, through mediocre renditions, has proved far from beneficial."[9]) Shilkret's versatility and vast recording-studio experience, which gave him an early and easy mastery of the technical aspects of capturing music of all sorts with microphones, soon made him a constant presence on the air, "he and his orchestra the outstanding ensemble of the ether."[10]

Musical polymath Nathaniel Shilkret.
(*Library of Congress George Grantham Bain Collection*)

On any given week in the late 1920s, Shilkret, by his count, "had from six to fifteen sponsored broadcasts." His list of sponsors read like a blue-chip stock portfolio: Maxwell House Coffee, Hire's Root Beer, Eastman Kodak, Pennsylvania Railroad, Mobiloil, and General Electric. He was also closely associated with radio's earliest omnibus cultural series, the *Eveready Hour,* "arguably the most influential show on radio."[11] His contributions to the *Eveready Hour* included an original orchestral tone poem, *Skyward,* dedicated to Admiral Byrd, and a full program devoted to his arrangements of Stephen Foster's songs, a broadcast that coincided with Victor's release of Shilkret's five-disc Foster compilation, one of popular music's first "albums."

Once he had wrested the intellectual property rights to his compositions from Victor, Shilkret did what copyright theory predicts, for the first time in his career devoting a significant portion of his energy to composing original instrumental works and writing popular songs. Though he later undertook some ambitious projects on speculation, such as his *Concerto for Trombone* (1942) and a *Clarinet Quintet* (1939), in the 1920s he was enjoying the luxury of writing to order for monied patrons, including his radio sponsors (hence the "Eveready Battery Suite" and the "Electricity March"), Victor's recording stars (Shilkret's only standard, "The Lonesome Road," was a collaboration with one of the biggest, Gene Austin), and Warner Brothers, which commissioned theme songs and scores for some of its early Vitaphone features from Shilkret. Vitaphone was a primitive sound synchronization technology, championed by Sam Warner not initially with the thought of making talking pictures, but as a way to "bring orchestral accompaniment for silent films to even the smallest towns."[12] Movie theme songs were, very briefly, all the rage, and Shilkret's "Jeanine, I Dream of Lilac Time," for Gary Cooper's 1928 World War I adventure-romance, *Lilac Time,* written with lyricist L. Wolfe Gilbert and sung by John McCormack, lived on commercially long after the movie was forgotten.

Shilkret's work for Vitaphone on the East Coast in the late 1920s laid the foundation for a later sojourn in Hollywood. As music director for RKO in the 1930s, he conducted Jerome Kern's score for *Swing Time,* provided crucial support to the dying, but tragically undiagnosed, George Gershwin on *Shall We Dance,* and received an Oscar nomination for his original score to *Winterset.* First though, his Vitaphone work would lead him on a decidedly unglamorous rendezvous between his younger self—the workhorse of the

Foreign Department who had churned out *canzoni, tonadas,* and *volkslieder* by the bucket for niche markets—and Ira B. Arnstein, composer of "V'Shomru," a mournful Yiddish air that Shilkret had arranged for cello and orchestra, and recorded with tenor William Robyn, in 1922.

The Divine Lady, a silent picture based on the love affair of Admiral Nelson and Lady Hamilton, opened in March 1929 at the Vitaphone-equipped Warner's Theatre in New York, with a score and a theme song, "Lady Divine," composed by Nathaniel Shilkret. The *Times*'s screen critic, Mordaunt Hall, was unimpressed, complaining that director Frank Lloyd "had the men, the money and the ships, but the development of some of his episodes is frequently abrupt and other scenes are marred by the now inevitable theme song, which in this instance is called 'Lady Divine.'"[13] *The Jazz Singer,* two years earlier, had already made silent pictures with synchronized mood music seem rather antiquated, and their sappy theme songs, which the studios had "pitch-forked into every picture and every conceivable situation, whether suitable or not,"[14] had become the butt of numerous parodies. With the form already held in such low regard, there was no disgrace in having contributed an undistinguished theme song to *The Divine Lady.* Yet, on July 1, 1929, Nathaniel Shilkret learned that a federal grand jury, acting on information provided by one Ira B. Arnstein, had indicted him for it.

The wide chasm that separates criminal from civil penalties for law-breaking—between the indignity of incarceration and the opprobrium of being labeled a "convict," on the one hand, versus being declared indebted for a sum of money on the other—resulted in the evolution of two separate and profoundly different legal regimes, with those facing criminal punishment having the rights, among others, to counsel, to confront adverse witnesses, to a presumption of innocence rebuttable only by proof beyond a reasonable doubt, to conviction only by a unanimous jury of twelve, and to prosecutors who are not hired guns, but are sworn to discharge a public trust, "to seek justice, not merely to convict."[15] Criminal sanctions have traditionally been reserved for conduct calling for societal retribution over and beyond any private recompense due. For more than 100 years after passing the first Copyright Act in 1790, Congress hadn't thought that infringement of copyright met that test. The first criminal copyright penalty—a misdemeanor punishable by one year in prison—was enacted in 1897, in the same piece of legislation that created the exclusive right of public performance for profit of musical works.[16] The reach of the criminal sanction was limited to "willful" infringements of that right. It is not likely that Congress thought that infringement of the public performance right was morally more culpable than infringement of other exclusive rights; rather, it made the not unreasonable calculation that the evanescence of musical performances meant that the overwhelming majority would escape detection by the copyright holders, and money damages for the few that were detected would not be an effective deterrent.

By the time of the next comprehensive copyright law revision, the epochal 1909 Copyright Act, the political power of the copyright-based industries was on the rise, and the testimony of Mark Twain, appearing publicly for the first time in an all-white suit—"the uniform of the American Association of Purity and Perfection," he told reporters—helped to elevate copyright discourse from the dismal plane of economics to the rarified reaches of moral philosophy.[17] Under Section 28 of the new law, criminal penalties were expanded to cover "*any* person who willfully and for profit shall infringe *any* copyright secured by this Act."[18] For the next twenty years, little if any practical effect came of this. The U.S. Attorney's offices of that era were grossly understaffed, with only a few poorly paid attorneys to handle all of the federal government's legal business, civil and criminal. There were complex espionage and antitrust cases to prosecute, and in just the next ten years the White-Slave Traffic Act of 1910, the Revenue Act of 1913, the Narcotics Act of 1914, the Immigration Act of 1917, and the National Prohibition Act of 1919 all surpassed the Copyright Act of 1909 as law enforcement priorities. It would take a prosecutor with an idiosyncratic agenda of his own to rescue Section 28 from oblivion.

Charles H. Tuttle, a Republican Party stalwart appointed U.S. Attorney for the Southern District of New York by President Calvin Coolidge in 1927, was that prosecutor. His predecessor, Emory Buckner, a transplanted Nebraskan possessed of a monastic sense of duty, had been best known for his reluctant but energetic enforcement of Prohibition. Under Buckner's watch, beginning the day that he was sworn in, a special Prohibition section led by assistant U.S. attorney and future Supreme Court justice John Marshall Harlan conducted highly publicized "padlock drives" against New York City's nightclubs and speakeasies, earning Buckner the enmity of New York's wet majority, and making him a perfect foil for the *New Yorker* just as it debuted in 1925 as a sophisticated chronicler of urban pleasures.

"Mr. Buckner is rampaging again with the padlock," an early "Talk of the Town" piece reported, "armed further with the ability to take himself seriously."[19] The ambitious Tuttle hoped to maintain the high public profile of the office while sidestepping the political third rail of Prohibition.

Though Tuttle was a lay religious leader and a teetotaler, a Coolidge doppelgänger in his demure appearance and solemn disposition, upon taking office he immediately signaled his lack of enthusiasm for "dry law enforcement," and scored some early points by pursuing corruption in the New York City branch of the Prohibition Bureau. "A clever and aggressive press agent was hired so that the Tuttle ballyhoo is efficiently carried on in spite of the Tuttle reticence."[20] So efficient that even the disappearance of the Tuttle family's Persian cat made the papers, and Tuttle's fawning New Yorker profile was titled, without obvious irony, "Saint in Politics." Tuttle's reputation-maker, the prosecutorial crusade with that certain je ne sais quoi that made the public stand up and cheer the feds, and made U.S. Attorney Tuttle a plausible Governor Tuttle, focused on the flourishing entertainment business, and specifically the rampant price gouging of theater ticket brokers.

Ticket speculation was an old scourge by 1927, and the New York State Legislature thought it had sensibly addressed the problem with a law restricting brokers' mark-up to fifty cents over face value. But just as Tuttle assumed his office, the U.S. Supreme Court, in a 5–4 ruling, struck down the New York law as an unconstitutional impairment of private property rights.[21] The majority, anchored by four of the old men who would later inspire Franklin Roosevelt's court-packing plan after they had eviscerated vital New Deal legislation, ruled that amusements and sports events were not "clothed with a public interest" and that sales of tickets to them "bear no relation to the commerce of the country." "It may be true," wrote Justice George Sutherland for the Court majority, "that, among the Greeks, amusement and instruction of the people through the drama was one of the duties of government. But certainly no such duty devolves upon any American government." In dissent, Justice Holmes rejoined:

> It seems to me that theaters are as much devoted to public use as anything well can be. We have not that respect for art that is one of the glories of France. But to many people the superfluous is the necessary, and it seems to me that Government does not go beyond its sphere in attempting to make life livable for them.

Tuttle and his advisors recognized that a political gift had been handed them. He stepped into the regulatory breach with an imaginative—if in some respects legally questionable—display of prosecutorial muscle. Presaging the Treasury department's use of the Internal Revenue Code to bring down Al Capone a few years later, the proximate target of Tuttle's federal investigation was not price gouging, but failure to remit federal income taxes on the profits. Before going to a grand jury, Tuttle and his chief assistant, George S. Leisure, conducted several weeks of hearings that were followed avidly by a press and public that little cared what Tuttle's actual legal gravamen was. "Public Cheering Ticket Inquiry On," one headline read. "Tuttle's Mail Is Bulky with Letters of Approval from Victims of Gouging." Testimony from low-level workers at the brokers' offices easily established the extent of the tax evasion. (Marvelously, as admirers of Mel Brooks's *The Producers* will appreciate, at the center of the tax scam was an accountant named Bloom, who had developed a double-ledger system of bookkeeping that was used by all of the Bialystocks of the ticket graft.[22]) In the months that followed, Tuttle threatened jail and heavy fines to extract plea bargains from the brokers, in which they agreed to adhere to a fifty-cent cap on their mark-ups over box-office prices, accomplishing by criminal prosecution the very result that the Supreme Court had ruled could not be done legislatively. After a year of uniformly positive press coverage, Tuttle was being boomed for the 1928 Republican nomination for governor.

But the Tuttle boomlet died as it became apparent that the Democrats were likely to nominate Franklin Roosevelt rather than Herbert Lehman for governor, making the Jewish state attorney general, Albert Ottinger, seem a better demographic play for the Republicans than the WASP Tuttle. As Tuttle bided his time until the next gubernatorial election in 1930, the glow of the ticket investigation faded. Inevitably, he was sucked into the political cesspool of Prohibition enforcement, clashing with the "Prohibition Portia" in Washington, Assistant Attorney General Mabel Walker Willebrandt, who instituted a crackdown on New York City nightclubs while Tuttle was on summer vacation. It must have been a pleasant and intriguing diversion for Tuttle when Ira B. Arnstein came to his office in the spring of 1929 to lodge a complaint against one of the biggest stars on radio.

As true crime yarns go, the one that Arnstein offered up to Tuttle and his assistants was a rather bloodless affair. In 1922, after successfully pitching "V'Shomru" to Shilkret, Arnstein decided to press his luck. He offered

Shilkret a song that he had composed and self-published in 1915, "Light My Life with Love," the first that Arnstein had written in a popular idiom—specifically, the idiom of "The Sunshine of Your Smile," a big hit from that same year and still a vaudeville audience favorite in the 1920s. Shilkret, Arnstein claimed, had liked the last eight measures of the chorus (the part that went "*my soul is weary/come back to me dearie/and light my life with looooove*"), and he offered to buy just that snippet, eight bars being exactly the amount of genetic material needed to clone a passable Tin Pan Alley tune. It was an offer that Arnstein, in 1922, could still afford to find insulting. But when *The Divine Lady* opened in the spring of 1929, Arnstein discovered that Shilkret's theme song not only made repeated use of the eight measures that Shilkret had expressed interest in buying years before, but that of "Lady Divine's" fifty-six measures, fully twenty-four were "taken bodily" from "Light My Life," with "such minor variations that if the two choruses are played simultaneously, a perfect harmony is arrived at."[23]

One can only speculate why Tuttle, on nothing more than Arnstein's say-so, concluded that a crime had been committed at all, much less one worthy of presentation to a grand jury for indictment and prosecution by his overburdened office. Shilkret assumed that the indictment could only have been procured "by some cleverly played trick."[24] But Tuttle was no naïf—he knew how to scrutinize and debunk a plagiarism claim if motivated to do so. Shortly before his appointment as U.S. Attorney he had done that for playwright Richard Tully and producer Oliver Morosco, whom he represented in the appeal of one of the largest and most notorious copyright infringement judgments to that date, $781,000 in 1926 dollars, representing an accounting of their profits from a long-running 1912 show, *The Bird of Paradise*. The case had wended its way through the courts for more than a decade, halting productions of *The Bird of Paradise*, delaying a film version, and bankrupting Morosco while Tully, who could not afford to post an appeal bond, flirted with jail time for contempt of court.[25] It was an appeal brief that Tuttle wrote, painstakingly parsing the plaintiff's evidence of copying, that eventually persuaded the New York Court of Appeals to reverse outright and enter judgment for Morosco and Tully in a fascinating, scholarly opinion that implicitly accused the plaintiff of being the plagiarist.[26]

In prosecuting Shilkret, Tuttle was treading a fine line between misguided idealism and outright cynicism. The case presented another chance to use the criminal law to expose what he considered to be rot in the entertainment business, to prompt legislative action to address it, and—while at it—to settle an old score. The rot, in Tuttle's view, was the American Society of Composers, Authors and Publishers. As the lead attorney and lobbyist for the just-formed National Association of Broadcasters (NAB) in the early 1920s, Tuttle had fought unsuccessfully to have Congress legislatively over-rule early court decisions that had held radio broadcasts to be "public per-formances for profit," and thereby to spare the embryonic radio industry the cost of licensing copyrighted music through ASCAP. While the broadcasters argued that they were performing a service for the public and for the music business, Tuttle attacked the very foundations of ASCAP, charging that copyright in music was a bastard child of legislative compromise, that it was "not an invasion of any inherent right" to perform a composition, and that ASCAP was a criminal monopoly—a "trust octopus" he called it.[27]

Direct legal action against ASCAP was not an option for Tuttle's office; the Department of Justice had just cleared ASCAP in 1926 after a lengthy antitrust investigation, an investigation that Tuttle, as the NAB's attorney, had egged on. (This piece of music business history, and Tuttle's pivotal role in it, is taken up in greater detail in chapter 8.) But what better way to hoist ASCAP by its own petard, and to grab a few headlines in the process, than to threaten one of the society's best-known members with jail time for the theft of eight utterly pedestrian measures, under the authority of the very 1909 Copyright Act that ASCAP held so sacrosanct? Arnstein, in Tuttle's scheme of things, was just a useful idiot, and Shilkret an unfortunate collateral vic-tim.

ASCAP knew Tuttle well and knew where he was really aiming his fire. Within hours of the indictment, ASCAP's general manager, J. C. Rosenthal, summoned Shilkret to his office for a talk.[28] Rosenthal, ASCAP general counsel Nathan Burkan, and Francis Gilbert all urged Shilkret to turn his defense over to one of the "experienced lawyers of music copyright" who, they assured him, could quickly get the case dismissed.[29] But ASCAP had little influence over Shilkret, who to that point had earned little from com-posing—he hadn't bothered to join ASCAP until 1925, and his first distribution, for 1928, was only $20.[30] His principal loyalty was to Victor, which had been acquired by RCA a few months earlier. RCA's general coun-sel, I. E. Lambert, was advising Shilkret to hire lawyers with criminal law experience and political clout. On Lambert's recommendation, Shilkret retained two lawyers who, in that summer of 1929, were forming the nucleus

IN THE DISTRICT COURT OF THE UNITED STATES
FOR THE SOUTHERN DISTRICT OF NEW YORK.

Southern District of New York, ss: The grand jurors for the United States of America, duly empaneled and sworn in the District Court of the United States for the Southern District of New York and inquiring for that district, upon their oath present:

That heretofore, to wit, on or about the 26th day of February, 1929, at the Southern District of New York and within the jurisdiction of this Court, NATHANIEL SHILKRET, the defendant herein, did unlawfully, wilfully and for profit infringe a certain copyright secured by the Act of Congress approved March 4, 1909, entitled "An Act to Amend and Consolidate the Acts Respecting Copyright" as amended by the copyright Acts of Congress approved August 24, 1912, March 2, 1913, and March 28, 1914, that is to say, a copyright for a musical composition, entitled "Light My Life With Love", which said copyright had theretofore, to wit, on or about the 28th day of June, 1915, been obtained and secured for a period of twenty-eight (28) years from that date by one Ira B. Arnstein as the proprietor and owner of said musical composition; against the peace of the United States and their dignity and contrary to the form of the statute of the United States in such case made and provided. (Section 28, Copyright Act; Title 17, United States Code).

United States Attorney.

United States Attorney and gubernatorial hopeful Charles H. Tuttle indicted Nathaniel Shilkret for criminal copyright infringement on Arnstein's say-so.

of one of the great New York law firms of the twentieth century, later known as Donovan, Leisure, Newton, Lumbard & Irvine—William "Wild Bill" Donovan, the future founder of the Central Intelligence Agency, and George S. Leisure, Tuttle's right-hand man in the ticket broker investigation. It was Donovan who, a few years earlier, while an assistant attorney general in the Coolidge administration, had closed down the Justice Department's ASCAP antitrust investigation.

Their clout turned out to be of little use. Tuttle had quickly lost interest in a case that, whatever its significance to him personally, wasn't generating much press coverage and didn't appeal to any important political constituency. Shilkret's attorneys made periodic visits to the U.S. Attorney's office over a two-year period, where they were bounced from one noncommittal assistant to another in a bureaucratic runaround. Finally, in June 1931, long after Tuttle had resigned to challenge incumbent Governor Roosevelt in the 1930 election (a contest he lost in a landslide), his successor, George Medale, dropped the case. Medale stated that an investigation, conducted *after* the indictment, had disproved "various statements of the complainant," identified witnesses who would testify that "Lady Divine" was "written under circumstances that preclude the possibility of an unlawful infringement," and discovered that, though there were similarities between "Lady Divine" and "Light My Life with Love," a "playing of the two songs shows there is a considerable difference." "In view of the foregoing," Medale concluded, "I do not believe there is any likelihood of successfully presenting this case to a petit jury."[31] Six years would pass before a federal prosecutor would bring a successful criminal case under Section 28 of the 1909 Copyright Act for acts amounting to plagiarism. In October 1937, Groucho and Chico Marx were convicted by a jury in Los Angeles of plagiarizing a radio script that had been submitted to them, and were sentenced to pay the maximum fine of $1,000 each, although the court did spare them the "jail jolt" that Groucho had feared.[32]

For Shilkret, the satisfaction of exoneration was fleeting. Lambert forwarded Donovan and Leisure's legal bills to Shilkret, making it clear that he considered them to be Shilkret's personal responsibility.[33] Shilkret thought that the publisher of "Lady Divine," Witmark, and the label that released McCormack's recording of it, Victor, ought to contribute to a defense that had inured to the benefit of all. But in the two and a half years since he had done the score for *The Divine Lady*, Victor had been acquired by RCA and Witmark by Warner Brothers. Shilkret's pleas fell on deaf ears, an object lesson that under the domination of radio and the movies music was no longer a family business. Once he had resigned himself to footing the entire legal bill, Shilkret ventilated his anger in a letter to Lambert. After apologizing for any "embarrassment" that he had caused the company, Shilkret lamented that he had "served the company for many years (nearly fifteen) without a law suit in any of my departments, and worked an average of twenty hours a day including Sundays," and—still oblivious to his collateral role in the set piece that Tuttle had intended to stage—expressed continued bewilderment that the indictment had been issued in the first place. It was the bitter recrimination of a jilted middle manager, not the tantrum of a star maestro of the ether.[34]

With that, it seems, Shilkret was ready to put the matter behind him. But only days later, Groundhog Day 1932 as fate would have it, a U.S. marshal came calling on him with a summons and complaint in *Arnstein v. Shilkret*, a civil suit based on the very same allegations that the government's belated investigation had just declared unfounded, and bearing the imprimatur of yet another giant of the New York City bar, Arthur Garfield Hays.

Placated in the belief that in the government was tending to the Shilkret matter, Arnstein had concentrated on his music for two full years. Five years after the chamber-scale Aeolian Hall performance of *The Song of David*, he finished a full orchestral score and conducted the completed work at Town Hall on April 26, 1930, with a capable group of soloists and a chorus and orchestra of 100. Again, the audience responded favorably—despite being forced to wait outside the hall for a half hour while a last-minute rehearsal took place[35]—and the critics were respectful. *Musical America* found the score "appropriate, rich and comprehensible," and the performances "given with fine spirit. The audience displayed its pleasure and approval in enthusiastic applause."[36] "The performance had vitality," said the *Times*, and "whatever the lack in baton technic and routing of the composer, Mr. Arnstein, there was no question that he knew his own music score and what he was after."[37] Though the economics of the performance must have been rather dicey—the audience, at a dollar or two per head, probably did not outnumber the assembled performers and crew by very much—Arnstein was satisfied that he had proven his concept artistically and commercially, and he began readying his score for submission to the Metropolitan Opera.

Charles Tuttle's involvement in the Shilkret matter, and the presumption of propriety that came with it, gave Arnstein some cover but did not shield him entirely from economic fallout over his role in procuring the indictment. To most of ASCAP's publisher-members he was, if not yet radioactive, certainly an unwelcome specter. A notable exception was Edward B. Marks. Never one to let a show of solidarity with his publishing brethren stand in the way of the potential for a new royalty stream, Marks made it a point of pride to feast on the leavings of his competitors. Marks made a deal with Arnstein to retool his thirty-year-old warhorse, "A Mother's Prayer," as a popular song. With a suitably saccharine set of lyrics written by Marks's professional manager, L. Wolfe Gilbert, one of the truly outstanding Tin Pan Alley lyricists ("Waiting for the Robert E. Lee," "Ramona"), the song was plugged on the air by the Street Singer, Arthur Tracy, in time for Mother's Day 1931.[38]

After a decade of constant peregrination among rooming houses on the Upper West Side, Arnstein had settled into space on one of West End Avenue's most picturesque blocks, between 76th and 77th streets. His

SINGERS AND CONDUCTORS OF THE WANING SEASON

Mme. Schumann-Heink in recital at Town Hall Tuesday evening.

At top, to left—Ira B. Arnstein, conductor and composer of "The Song of David," at Town Hall next Saturday evening.

Arturo Toscanini, conductor of the Philharmonic-Symphony Orchestra, in last concert of the season at Carnegie Hall tomorrow afternoon.

At top, to right—Vanda Nomicas, soprano, in recital at Town Hall Tuesday evening next.

Arnstein's concert performances of his "biblical opera" *The Song of David* at Aeolian Hall and Town Hall received respectful reviews, but the Metropolitan Opera rejected it as "amateurish."

apartment, in an elegant, 1891 Lamb & Rich–designed house, had enough space to support a music school that Arnstein attempted to launch under the name "Musical Culture League of New York" (its ads listed a number of prominent instructors and directors, including, most improbably, Joseph Schillinger, as a teacher of "harmony and counterpoint") and to hold rehearsals with the twenty-five-member cast of his Russian-themed stage show, "Echoes of Moscow," which had a short run at the nearby Beacon Theatre in April 1932.[39]

The dismissal of the Shilkret indictment in June 1931 was a tipping point in Arnstein's life. Had he accepted it as meant to be, recognized that life was sometimes unfair, that the courts offered neither effective nor efficient means for redressing his every grievance, and resigned himself to playing the music game by rules that sometimes offended his sense of artistic integrity and natural justice, his career was still eminently salvageable. But at the very moment when Arnstein could have benefited mightily from advice to just let it go, he received reinforcement of his worst instincts, and began down the tortured path of the obsessive litigant, a tragic figure familiar to most lawyers and judges. From then on, every new setback would only provide additional confirmation of a confabulated worldview in which an ever-widening circle of malfeasors conspired against him, eventually encompassing his own attorneys, the judiciary, and officials in high places and dark corners of the executive branch.

The well-meaning soul who inadvertently set Arnstein on this course was Arthur Garfield Hays. His patrician-sounding name notwithstanding, Hays was a Jew from Rochester with no presidential lineage. He had built an eclectic and lucrative private practice in New York City, but it was his reputation as one of the bar's leading advocates for "the poor, the defenseless, and unpopular, always the dissenters and persecuted,"[40] the William Kunstler of his day, that attracted Arnstein to him. As general counsel to the American Civil Liberties Union he had served on the defense team for John Scopes in the "Monkey Trial," he had made a personal plea to the governor of Massachusetts for commutation of the death sentences of Sacco and Vanzetti, and he was, when Arnstein went to see him about the Shilkret case, working on an appeal for the Scottsboro Boys. Arnstein, no doubt, considered himself the victim of a miscarriage of justice of comparable magnitude. Far from disabusing him of the notion, Hays (who was no babe in the woods either—as counsel to the Dramatists' Guild he was personally familiar with the ruin that *The Bird of Paradise* case had wrought) met with Arnstein several times, declared that he was "very much impressed with the justice of your case," and agreed to try it.[41] No amount of discouragement over the remaining twenty-five years of Arnstein's life would erase the aura of self-righteousness that Hays's blessing had bestowed upon him. Retribution for his hubris came with the swiftness of a Greek tragedy.

Within days of the filing of the Shilkret civil suit in February 1932, Italian conductor Giuseppe Sturani, after reviewing the *Song of David* score that Arnstein had submitted to the Metropolitan Opera, delivered his verdict: "Amateurish music without any real character of opera."[42] It was a decisive blow to Arnstein's ego. Arnstein the accomplished music professional disappeared that day, subsumed from then on by Arnstein the batty litigant. He was suddenly hearing his music *everywhere*. Not just in "Lady Divine" and in "Play, Fiddle, Play," the new hit that was driving him to near-homicidal rage, but also in "My Wishing Song," "Isle of Capri," and "Boulevard of Broken Dreams."

The rapidly expanding list was a source of acute embarrassment for Arthur Hays. Not long after Hays had taken on Arnstein's case, Billy Rose approached him for assistance in forming a new trade organization for songwriters, the Songwriters Protective Association. In what would today almost certainly be considered a breach of professional responsibility, Hays abruptly fired his now very inconvenient client: "You have through your actions . . . come to be regarded as a person who makes pretty free claims about plagiarism of your material. In other words, you practically charge that people are continually thieving from you. Since I represent the Songwriters Protective Association I am not willing to represent one who expresses that point of view."[43]

Arnstein v. Shilkret was listed for trial in December 1933. Arnstein found new counsel, business attorneys of no particular distinction, who entered the case just in time for the bench trial before Federal District Judge Frank J. Coleman. Shilkret was represented by George Leisure—if nothing else, the civil case allowed Shilkret to salvage some of the legal work he had paid for in the criminal matter. No transcript was made of the two-day trial, nor did the newspapers cover it. Only Judge Coleman's damning decision, delivered from the bench on December 20, 1933, was transcribed; it is unclear at whose expense, but obviously for the purpose of hanging it around Arnstein's neck like a scarlet letter. For years, *samizdat* copies circulated around the copyright defense bar, to be handed over the transom to judges unfamiliar with Arnstein's history. "Every judge who ever tries a case of mine," Arnstein later complained, "receives a copy of said opinion on the smallest pretext."[44] The only similarity between "Light My Life with Love" and "Lady Divine" that Coleman could detect was in the last eight bars of the chorus, and to that he ascribed no significance whatever "except to carry out the cadence to the end of the piece":

> It is my belief that if in humming or whistling a chorus I had remembered the first twenty-four measures and did not remember the last eight, that even I would approximate what both these men did in their last eight measures . . . There was not sufficient originality in the plaintiff's eight measures to make it worthwhile for anyone to steal them.[45]

As to Arnstein's testimony that Shilkret had offered to buy those eight bars, Coleman scoffed that "the thing is so improbable as to be fantastic." More generally, he observed "[Arnstein's] credibility as a witness is of a low order . . . he is the type of mind that would never prompt me to place reliance upon his statements of fact." Coleman denied Shilkret's request for attorneys' fees because of Arnstein's distressed financial condition, and "because while I have the strongest feeling that the plaintiff ought not to continue to make a nuisance of himself, I do believe that he is convinced of the merit of his own contention."[46] Nothing Judge Coleman had to say could shatter those convictions. "I can only say that 'to err is human, to forgive divine,'" Arnstein later wrote. "Poor Judge Coleman was very ill and irritable. He died a few weeks later."[47]

The repeal of Prohibition had taken effect on December 5, 1933, when Utah ratified the Twenty-First Amendment. Shilkret and his defense team could toast their victory and the arrival of 1934 legally. One of Shilkret's expert witnesses, Dr. Sigmund Spaeth, himself partial to Manhattans garnished with extra maraschino cherries, took a few moments on that first wet New Year's Eve to mail off his bill for $100, together with an expansive, well-lubricated letter of congratulations. Spaeth urged Shilkret to press charges against Arnstein for "blackmail, extortion, and false arrest," and generously volunteered his services in such a cause. "You are in a position to put him in jail," he assured Shilkret, "if you once make an example of such a crook, it will keep a lot of other bugs from rushing into court with absurd cases."[48]

But Arnstein was just now getting the hang of this. His odyssey as a serial copyright litigant had barely begun, and Sigmund Spaeth would along for the rest of a very long journey.

THE TUNE DETECTIVE

Sig Spaeth can do more things at one time than any living person—and do them all well. He can bid six no trump, detect the origin of Yes, We Have No Bananas, lob a tennis ball over a net, organize a barber shop quartet and answer all the questions on a quiz program while filling a lecture engagement in Anchorage, Alaska.
—*Rube Goldberg*

Commercial radio broadcasting was barely a year old in the summer of 1923 when the new medium's first killer application arrived in the form of "Yes! We Have No Bananas," a novelty song lampooning the fractured syntax of a Greek greengrocer. Composed on a lark by two dance band musicians, Frank Silver and Irving Cohn, "it swept the land like a medieval calamity," according to Alexander Woollcott, and "crossed the Atlantic more rapidly than any airship."[1] Newspapers reported that the price of bananas skyrocketed as "many people who had almost never heard of bananas have become curious to know all about them."[2] Some of the song's more delirious enthusiasts found themselves charged by the authorities with disturbing the peace; others were assaulted by irate auditors who took the law into their own hands. In Seattle, "some unknown benefactor of the human race" silenced a music store phonograph that had been playing the song incessantly for several days "with a well-directed rifle bullet."[3] The international crime wave incited by "Bananas" culminated in a London courtroom scene that couldn't have been scripted any better by *Monty Python's Flying Circus*: "A badly bruised groceryman limped into a police court today and told a story which exasperated people have been expecting these many months," the *New York Times* reported. "Your worship, a customer came into my shop and asked for a banana. I replied, 'Yes, we have no bananas.' Then he struck me."[4]

Amidst all the pandemonium, America's newspaper of record devoted more than a full page to "a calm and deliberate, even a scientific inquiry into why 97.3 percent of the great American Nation, at the present advanced state of civilization, devotes itself zestfully and with unanimity to singing 'Yes! We Have No Bananas.'"[5] After surveying the opinions of "psychologists, neurologists, song market experts, musicians, specialists in folk songs and students of mass reactions," the *Times* still could not unlock the mystery. Will Rogers offered the most straightforward explanation: "Mother has been done to death in songs," he wrote, "conditions were just ripe for a good fruit song."[6]

Sheet music for "Yes! We Have No Bananas" sold at an unprecedented pace—2,000,000 copies in the first three months alone, and as many as 37,000 copies in a single day. The press reported that Silver and Cohn's first quarterly royalty payment was $69,000, and it was expected that they would make at least that much again before the fad had exhausted itself. "Bananas" was their band's ticket out of the kitschy Murray's Roman Gardens restaurant where they had first plugged the song, but neither Silver nor Cohn ever again attained such dizzying heights of success. Silver made no secret that he lost the small fortune he'd earned from "Bananas" in the crash of 1929. A much more enduring beneficiary of the "Yes! We Have No Bananas" craze was Sigmund Spaeth, Ph.D., a traveling spokesperson for the American Piano Company. Dr. Spaeth parlayed an amusing musical dissection of "Bananas" into a long career as America's favorite popularizer of classical music and classicizer of popular music, and into a lucrative sideline giving expert testimony in music plagiarism cases, in which he played a relentless Inspector Javert to Ira B. Arnstein's beleaguered Jean Valjean.

The musical sensibilities of Sigmund Gottfried Spaeth, born in Philadelphia in 1885, were nurtured in the warm embrace of home and church musicianship, far from the intellectual crucible of conservatories and universities. Though his formal musical education was limited to childhood violin lessons, Spaeth's life was thoroughly imbued with music from the cradle. His father, a Lutheran minister, composed church hymns, had an excellent tenor voice, and played clarinet, piano, and organ. His mother compiled a widely used Lutheran hymnal.

> I was naturally encouraged to develop my interest in music at an early age, and we regularly practiced music in the home during my boyhood. My father had eleven children altogether by the two marriages. There were never more than perhaps five or six of them in the house at one time, but we always had enough for a vocal quartet at least and for some sort of instrumental ensemble.[7]

Spaeth played Beethoven and Mozart sonatas as a young boy in the 1890s with his sister Carola, a fine pianist who in later life served as accompanist for another amateur violinist, Albert Einstein. "At the same time," he recalled, "we were very familiar with all the popular songs of the time—'A Little Lost Child,' 'After the Ball,' and so on."[8] Spaeth and his siblings grew up taking it for granted that anyone could sing and play by sight or by ear: "I don't remember when I learned to read notes anymore than I remember when I learned to read the letters of the alphabet."[9] The young Spaeth, however, harbored no illusions that he possessed the talent required for a career as a concert artist.

At the age of sixteen, Spaeth enrolled in Haverford College, a Quaker school with an all-male student body of 150. It was a felicitous choice. The strapping "Rab" Spaeth became a very big man on that small campus. The 1905 *Haverford Class Record*, for which Spaeth served as editor in chief, contains a staggering list of literary, athletic, and musical activities and achievements: senior class president; Mandolin Club leader; Glee Club leader; Banjo Club; Orchestra; editor in chief of the school magazine; cricket, soccer, tennis, debate, and chess teams; chairman of the junior play committee; winner of the systematic reading prize, and more. He had also established a reputation among his classmates as a writer, humorist, and omnivore. "His ability to eat cauliflower and drink salted milk is cited as sure proof of his genius. . . . The best efforts of the College failed to produce an article of food which Spaeth couldn't eat."

Spaeth's fastidious notes from the Quaker philosopher Rufus Jones's *Development of Christian Thought* class, preserved in Haverford's rare book collection, show that he took his academics seriously, while also

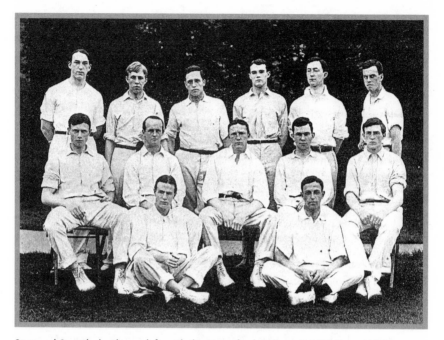

Sigmund Spaeth, back row left, with the Haverford College Cricket Team, 1905.

evidencing his lifelong fixation with sports—the results of tennis matches and sketches of buff athletes locked in various clinches and scrums fill the margins—as well as his lifelong weakness for excruciating puns. Somehow Spaeth was passed over in the voting for most likely to succeed, but he won the greatest honor a Haverford graduating class could bestow on one of its own—he was elected "Spoon Man," the senior most admired by his peers.

Spaeth stayed on at Haverford to earn a master's degree in English. Then, on the recommendation of his considerably older half-brother, John Duncan Spaeth, a member of Woodrow Wilson's faculty at Princeton, he was given a position teaching "baby German" to Princetonian jocks, for an annual salary of $1,000. After two years of this, having been advised that any further academic advancement would require a Ph.D., he entered Princeton's graduate school on a fellowship. He continued to participate in extracurricular musical activities while at Princeton (and served as an informal musical preceptor to the three Wilson daughters), but Spaeth's major field was English and his ambitions were literary. His dissertation topic, suggested by a professor who had been waiting for a doctoral candidate with some musical background to come along, was *Milton's Knowledge of Music*.

This page and next: Sigmund Spaeth's Development of Christian Thought class notes, circa 1904. (*Courtesy Haverford College, Quaker & Special Collections and Donald M. Spaeth*)

P. vigorously demanded freedom
for Gentile Christians & en-
dorsement of his work. P.
seems 2 have carried his point
with X "pillars" at least.

Pillows of the church

Outcome of meeting — a compromise, which really provided
4 2 kinds of Christianity.
P. & B. — Gentile preachers
Others — Jew "
2 kinds of Churches.

An exuberant little piece of scholarship, published in book form by Princeton in 1913 and reissued by the University of Michigan Press in 1963, it exhibits the wide-ranging knowledge that characterizes Spaeth's later commercial writings, together with an analytic rigor he never again aspired to or achieved. *Milton's Knowledge of Music* is primarily biographical, a musical life of the blind poet, but Spaeth the doctoral candidate was at his best and, he felt, most original in his extrapolation of an entire metaphysic of music from the poems, a combination of the Pythagorean notions of universal harmony and music of the spheres with Christian theology. In Milton's system, as Spaeth described it, "the universal harmony has as its object the praise of the Creator" and "the spheres join in some mysterious fashion with Christian spirits and angels to produce a complete concord, inaudible to man until he shall succeed in escaping from the bonds of sin."[10]

Spaeth completed his Ph.D. in 1910, but Princeton did not tender any promotion. He taught and coached sports at the Asheville School in North Carolina for a few years and then, after a summer of travel in Europe, moved to New York in the fall of 1912 to pursue his ambition to be a writer. He rented an apartment on Irving Place that, Spaeth had been told, O. Henry once occupied, "but it did me no good at all."[11] He sold some essays, short fiction, music reviews, and light extemporanea, but was unable to support himself as a freelance writer. He applied for a position as the humor columnist for the *New York Evening Mail*, a job left vacant when Franklin P. "FPA" Adams moved over to the *New York Tribune* in 1914. Spaeth did not get the Adams spot, and only reluctantly settled for another position that was opening up at the *Mail*—music critic, covering the New York City opera-concert-recital scene. In September 1914, Spaeth's career as a writer on musical subjects began in earnest.

Spaeth's quota of about 700 words allowed for reviews that were thoroughly professional but generic, almost blasé. The musical populist that lurked within Spaeth couldn't drum up much enthusiasm about world-class musicians performing in stuffy halls for well-heeled audiences. Only sporadically did his reviews demonstrate a distinctive point of view or voice, as in his pan of one diva's *Carmen*:

It is vulgar without being sensuous, substituting the slapstick horseplay of burlesque for comedy, and expressing its tragedy in howls of rage and terror. Mme. Gay is unquestionably the roughest prima donna on the stage today, as her colleagues know to their sorrow. She not only knocks off an occasional helmet herself, but she encourages her chorus girls to do the same. And how a stage helmet does bounce! Amid such general sacrifice of art, it would be vain to look for good singing.[12]

In 1916, the *Mail* introduced a twice-weekly "Music in the Home" page. This was a beat that could get Spaeth's juices flowing consistently, and his writing for this feature was infused with a utopian vision. A community chorus of 6,000 performing old songs in Central Park proved that "it is only in superficialities that people differ. Reality is the same in everybody."[13] A neighborhood symphony orchestra, with musicians representing seventeen nationalities, demonstrated the unique power of music to bridge religious and political differences.[14] He waxed enthusiastic over crackpot theories of all kinds: "Gadski Believes Music Will Eliminate War."[15] "The music of the future will be written in harmony with the speaking voice, not for definitely tuned instruments."[16] Spaeth used the Music for the Home forum to organize and raise funds for two of his pet projects: midday outdoor concerts for working people ("if noon-hour concerts become an American institution, the 'tired business man' may in time disappear altogether"[17]) and popularly priced "Home Symphony Concerts" at Carnegie Hall, with programs selected on the basis of reader input ("since it is obviously impossible to bring the orchestra to the home, the next best thing is to bring something of the intimacy of the home circle to the concert hall"[18]).

It was during this heady time that he took a wife, Katherine "Katie" Lane, a divorced, noncustodial mother of one son. Katie Lane worked in one of the roughest neighborhoods in early twentieth-century New York City, the South Street seaport, where she edited the newsletter of the Seamen's Church Institute and was at the frontlines of the battle to end shanghaiing and other forms of exploitation in the Port of New York. Self-taught, hardboiled, witty, and independent, Katie Lane proved to be a perfect complement and helpmate. Although the Spaeths' devotion to one another through fifty years of marriage was genuine, their frequent separations during the course of their childless union—and, upon closer consideration, Spaeth's student marginalia, his flamboyant skewering of the diva Maria Gay, and his infatuation with the operas of Wagner, cult favorites of German homosexuals[19]—at least suggest the possibility that Mrs. Spaeth was contentedly bearding for a compatible, but closeted, male companion.

Spaeth probably did not realize it at the time, but the Music for the Home page was his closest encounter yet with his ultimate calling as a writer and public figure. That destiny was deferred by the U.S. entry into World War I. The Spaeths made a job swap, with Sigmund, who wanted to make some sort of contribution to the war effort, going to work as a civilian morale officer organizing musical activities for sailors and factory workers, and Katie taking over his duties at the *Evening Mail*. When the war ended, the *Mail* did not take Spaeth back. His explanation was that Mrs. Spaeth had proved such a success as a music and feature writer (which indeed she had) the paper had no spot for him. More likely he was a victim of unfortunate external circumstances. In the waning days of the war the *Mail*'s publisher, Edward Rumely, had been arrested and indicted on charges of having concealed that his purchase of the paper in 1915, days after the sinking of the Lusitania, was financed by the imperial German government. With aspersions afoot that the paper must have served by "implied contract" as the Kaiser's propaganda vehicle[20]—and at a time when anti-German sentiment was still such that his beloved Wagner was banned from the Metropolitan Opera House—the name Sigmund Gottfried Spaeth was a distinct liability.

He landed briefly at the *New York Times*, with a vaguely defined position on "the sports staff." No Spaeth byline appeared in the *Times*, nor did his duties with the sports department prevent him from competing in tennis tournaments that the paper covered, or from occasionally reviewing New York concerts for the *Boston Transcript*. He appears to have been little more than a glorified stringer; one *Times* colleague delicately referred to this as a "chequered period of his career."[21] (He did, during this time, help to ease Wagner back into the Met repertory, with palatable English translations of *Lohengrin* and *Tristan* that he collaborated on.) With Katherine Lane Spaeth securely employed at the *Mail*, this was not an altogether unpleasant situation for a childless sports and music enthusiast in his early thirties. It likely took a push from Mrs. Spaeth ("if it were not for the sublime faith of my wife," he said later, "I would still be drawing down my forty dollars per week as a journalist"[22]) for him to accept a "real" job, in the fall of 1920, as the educational director of the American Piano Company. The position entailed traveling the length and breadth of the bourgeois America immortalized in Sinclair Lewis's *Babbitt*, demonstrating the Ampico "electronic re-producing piano" (a sophisticated player piano capable of reproducing the touch and dynamics of the recording artist) while lecturing on music appreciation before school groups, social clubs, and civic organizations, and over some of the very earliest broadcast stations, sometimes putting on as many as five programs in a single day.

The Ampico job gave Spaeth the opportunity to hone three personas that he would comfortably and profitably juggle for the remainder of his life—Pied Piper of music appreciation, cornball entertainer, and commercial huckster. With the security of a steady salary, he could "lecture to audiences of all kinds without having to worry about assembling them or getting a fee for it."[23] (Publicity surrounding the events, however, downplayed the employment relationship and seemed calculated to create the impression that he was endorsing the Ampico as an independent musical authority.) Sometimes he would team up with a noted pianist who had recorded rolls for Ampico in a "is it live or is it Ampico?" demonstration, and sometimes he appeared with singers or instrumentalists who would use the Ampico as an automated accompanist. But most often he was left to his own devices to entertain his audience while stimulating interest in the product. In a typical bit, he might play a few notes of a Rachmaninoff prelude,

> and then pretend to play while Rachmaninoff's record was turned on. Then at a certain point, where the music became faster, I would start to turn a page and purposely knock the music off the stand. While I scrambled after the music, the piano continued by itself, which of course brought a big laugh.[24]

Spaeth's most popular routine was one that he called "New Tunes for Old." He would play a familiar popular song to demonstrate that the Ampico worked well as an ordinary home piano, and then encourage his audience to listen closely as he pointed out common themes in a classical piece as it was reproduced on the Ampico from a recorded roll. "I'm Always Chasing Rainbows," with direct quotes of Chopin's *Fantasie Impromptu in C-sharp Minor*, was a famous example in the day. Spaeth, gifted with a prodigious musical memory, came up with dozens more. The act helped sell Ampicos, but Spaeth liked to claim it was part of a larger pedagogic program, "to give people something to listen for in music, to give them a reason for listening."[25] "The whole problem of making good music popular," he wrote, "is simply that of making it familiar."[26]

The "tune" was Spaeth's fundamental unit of musical analysis. Spaeth chided the public for "believing that classical music is tuneless while at the same time it goes into raptures glad or sad over modern strains which are purloined from the works of the greatest masters."[27] (As if to prove Spaeth's point, a civic booster advocating creation of a local symphony orchestra in the contemporaneous *Babbitt* admits that he'd "rather listen to a good jazz band any time than to some piece by Beethoven that hasn't any more tune to it than a bunch of fighting cats."[28]) If that misapprehension could be corrected, Spaeth argued, popular music could be "utilized as a means toward the end of appreciating the classics themselves."[29] Music theorist Kevin Korsyn suggests that Spaeth's stunts illustrated a "profound truth about musical analysis," which he dubbed "the Sigmund Spaeth principle." Just as a variegated theme may impart an identifiable internal coherence to a piece, it may also lead the mind elsewhere, "to wander, to summon up other contexts, to evoke . . . the already heard."[30]

When "Yes! We Have No Bananas" burst upon the world in 1923, Spaeth saw a chance to piggyback on a national craze and add a surefire crowd-pleaser to his programs. "The music," Douglas Gilbert wrote, "is as lovely a bit of bastardy as was ever seminated in the Alley."[31] Spaeth traced the "distinguished ancestry" of the chorus, "cheap and trivial as it appears,"[32] to Handel's "Hallelujah Chorus," "My Bonnie Lies over the Ocean," the folk tune "Seeing Nellie Home," Cole Porter's "An Old-Fashioned Garden" (Porter's one and only hit to that point), and the aria "I Dreamt I Dwelt in Marble Halls" from *The Bohemian Girl*. Spaeth was not the first to notice such parallels; John Philip Sousa had told the press that he thought these allusions might explain the song's immense popularity,[33] and the publisher—Shapiro, Bernstein—had gone to Max Dreyfus in advance for permission to use the Cole Porter phrase.[34] But Spaeth turned his dissection into an entertaining performance piece of its own that concluded with a rousing rendition in which he skillfully interpolated lyrics from the sources: "Hallelujah, Bananas! O bring back my Bonnie to me!"

"Hallelujah, Bananas!" became Spaeth's signature piece, an obligatory finale to his programs long after the "Yes! We Have No Bananas" craze had run its course. Soon it was Spaeth himself, not the Ampico or the professional musicians, who was drawing the audiences. "Dr. Spaeth's talks on music are quite different from any of the conventional performances of the lecture platform," one paper gushed. "His methods are entirely original and the effects he achieves are truly astonishing."[35]

The doctor does not attempt the well-nigh impossible feat of dragging his audiences up to high-brow attitudes. On the contrary, he has been showing club members and school children that music is not so hard as it is pictured. He is entertaining them and leading them, step by step, up to a comprehension of music.[36]

Disdain for highbrow affectation was central to the Spaeth credo. "Our well-intentioned guides have tried to pour music into the people from the top, instead of letting it grow normally from the ground up,"[37] as it had grown, Spaeth might have added, for himself. He decried the "fetish of exclusiveness" and the "delicate snobbery" of so-called connoisseurs, while praising the "honest appreciation of the comic strip, jazz, barber shop ballads, and vaudeville comedians."[38] Before the Iowa Federation of Women's Clubs, in May 1925, he gave his blessing to jazz, declaring it "good music, because its restless energy and blunt honesty is truly typical of this nation."[39] He extolled the virtues of amateur musicianship and excoriated music teachers for concentrating on the tiny minority of pupils who could hope to pursue professional careers. Into this mix of optimism and populism he threw in a dash of machismo, constantly reminding audiences and the press of his athleticism and love of sports. If he, a "real he-man," could find so much pleasure in making and listening to music, then clearly this was not just a pastime for women, children, and girly-guys. In an article for *The Rotarian*, "It Isn't Sissy to Like Music," Spaeth reeled off numerous examples of athletes, businessmen, and politicians who were music lovers, proving "that a man can do a respectable job and make a more than adequate living without giving up his private inclination toward something that represents permanence of beauty."[40]

Spaeth's message was perfectly attuned to what Professor Rebecca Bennett, in her study of the early twentieth century music appreciation "racket," has termed the "middlebrow fervor" of the times.[41] A large swath of the Prohibition-era American public was thirsting, like George F. Babbitt and his fellow members of the Zenith Boosters' Club, for respectable and conspicuous cultural attainment, and maybe a spot of fun to boot. During his stint with the American Piano Company, Spaeth laid the groundwork for turning his hobby into not just a vocation, but into a highly profitable omnimedia enterprise. He was, quite simply, an "exponent of everything that is good in music,"[42] and what could be bad about that?

Spaeth gave up the security of his American Piano salary in 1926 and embarked upon a freelance career. The Ampico programs had provided the foundation for Spaeth's first—and best—book for a general audience, *The Common Sense of Music* (1924), an idiosyncratic amalgam of nontechnical music theory, history, and rambling polemics. Spaeth believed that he was putting forth common sense, but the title also referred to "the sense of music that is common to everyone," which, he thought, "can be developed into an actual art of enjoyment through the simple process of listening."[43] *The Common Sense of Music* is truly the Spaeth urtext; virtually all his subsequent writings can be seen as further exegeses upon it, and all as part of the same overarching project, "to 'sell' good music to the public as a recreation, as a normal pleasure" sans "pontifical utterances" and "patronizing attitudes."[44] The books began pouring forth at a rate of more than one per year, a pace that Spaeth could maintain thanks to his encyclopedic command of factoids, whether they be true or not, which obviated the need for extensive research, and his proclivity for recycling and repurposing his ideas, often *in haec verba*, again and again.

The collegiate Spaeth—Haverford '05's indefatigable organizer, leader, and Spoon Man—resurfaced around the same time to become the animating force behind numerous organizations he saw as advancing his agenda: Community Concerts, Inc., the National Federation of Music Clubs, the National Association of Composers and Conductors, and, as near and dear to his heart as any, the mellifluously acronymed SPEBSQSA—the Society for the Preservation and Encouragement of Barbershop Quartet Singing in America. Sig Spaeth's presence on a nonprofit's letterhead was seldom honorary or ex officio; he could be depended upon to do his share of the heavy lifting and to be the life of any convention or chapter meeting, always ready to don an outlandish costume and perform one of his specialties, serve as a convivial toastmaster, or lead the gathered in an old-fashioned community sing.

While maintaining his grueling schedule of speaking appearances, Spaeth became a more frequent presence on radio, an early specimen of that mainstay of airwaves—the "personality." "With their place in the family circle, their voices speaking intimately to the individuals listening, their repeated presence," historian Michele Hilmes writes, early radio personalities "entered into an unprecedented relationship with the vast numbers of people who began to make up a new listening public."[45] Whether he was offering music reviews and commentary, recreating football games, announcing "synthetic prize fights," hosting on-air studio parties in which "celebrities of the music world gathered before the microphone in an informal fashion," or emceeing live performances, Spaeth tried to cultivate the easygoing, intimate style pioneered by his friend, Roxy Rothafel, on the *Capitol Theatre Family* program. The results were decidedly mixed. The erudite Spaeth's ad-libbing was as smooth as the typical personality's scripted speech, without the warmth or friendliness. His joke were poorly delivered and often had a nasty edge. "A Little Gypsy Tea Room," he quipped, would naturally contain "La Cucaracha." Why, he asked, would anyone in Depression-era America sing an ode to "A Little Shanty in Shantytown"? The song ought to be "A Penthouse on Park Avenue"—that would be something to be proud of! It was not his intent to belittle Tin Pan Alley songwriters, he assured his listeners; most of them are so short, to belittle them would be physically impossible. Listening to Spaeth's vaguely racist and classist banter, it is sometimes hard to believe this was a dyed-in-the-wool Wilson-Roosevelt (and later Kennedy) Democrat speaking. The hail fellowship and winning sense of humor that made him such a prolific collector of friends and admirers in life, and reportedly elicited "gales of laughter"[46] at his personal appearances, are little in evidence in the extant recordings of his broadcasts.

The core of the Spaeth franchise, in print, on radio, on stage and screen, was his trusty "Old Tunes for New" routine. Rechristened as "The Tune Detective," he outfitted himself for visual media with a constabulary moustache, magnifying glass, and Sherlock Holmes deerstalker cap and cape. (Through the magic of radio, the Tune Detective might make his entrance from the inside of a grand piano where he'd been "shadowing a couple of tunes.") In the early 1930s, when the act was at the height of its popularity, Spaeth was dissecting the current hits on two weekly NBC shows of his own, as a guest star on many others, in newspapers and magazines, and in one-reelers for Fox and Vitaphone. His job title, he told *Time* magazine in 1932, was "writer, broadcaster, lecturer, composer, arranger and general showman and entertainer."[47]

At their best, the Tune Detective routines were entertaining and edifying. On the great stage of Radio City Music Hall in the summer of 1933, the Tune Detective expounded upon Phil Baxter's "Going, Going, Gone," assisted by the resident orchestra and ballet, and a rather monolexic Dr. Watson. After first illustrating the song's debt to earlier blues numbers, including the "St. James Infirmary Blues," Spaeth continued:

Sigmund Spaeth poses in full Tune Detective regalia for a 1935 NBC publicity photograph. (*Music Division, New York Public Library for the Performing Arts, Astor, Lenox and Tilden Foundations*)

SPAETH: Aha! And the ancestor of all those blues was Willie the Weeper [plays and sings] . . . But let's follow the trail still further back. That whole gang started with the old oriental scale pattern [plays] and you'll find that pattern in every country of the world under a different name.

DR. WATSON: Marvelous.

SPAETH: Elementary, my dear Watson. Listen to Tchaikovsky's *Marche Slav*. [Orchestra plays twelve bars, as Russians march across circle.] And don't tell me the classic composers were not guilty. Cesar Cui has exactly the same melody in his *Orientale*. [Orchestra plays sixteen bars, as oriental dancers move across circle.] Aha!

DR. WATSON: Marvelous. [With special admiration of the dancers.]

SPAETH: The Negro version of that oriental scale [plays] is of course [sings] "Water Boy." And perhaps the most ancient and popular of them all is the Jewish "Mazzultoff." [plays]

DR. WATSON: Marvelous.

SPAETH: Elementary, my dear Watson.[48]

The Tune Detective came closest to repeating the success of "Hallelujah, Bananas!" in 1935, when "The Music Goes 'Round and Around" sparked a craze that rivaled "Yes! We Have No Bananas." Its "whoa-ho-ho-ho-ho-ho" refrain prompted a learned discourse from Spaeth on the history of musical nonsense syllables, and a burlesque of the song that shoehorned in a "hey nonny nonny," a "ta-ra-ra-boom-der-e," and a "boop-boop-a-doop." But by then the routine had grown a little tired, and the Tune Detective was soon relegated back to the rubber chicken speaking circuit. Spaeth's brief taste of big-time show business success, however, long lingered in his palate.

It's not easy for a twenty-first-century copyright litigator to fathom the thinking that preceded Spaeth's first engagement as an expert witness in a music copyright case. He had no academic training in music or musicology. To call him a "composer" or "arranger" was a stretch—he dissected popular songs for laughs and occasionally wrote lyrics, usually parodies or translations of existing material. He considered himself a showman and entertainer, and loved to wear silly costumes. His trail of published writings on music, much of it rather casually tossed-off, was a mile long. He carefully cultivated an image as a supercilious know-it-all. If such obvious and unassailable objections to the idea of using him as a courtroom expert were raised at all, his rightful claim to the title "Doctor," imposing physical presence, stentorian voice, and undeniable skill at speaking authoritatively while simultaneously illustrating his points on a piano must have prevailed. Spaeth not only made courtroom tune detection a regular sideline, he came to be viewed by some members of the copyright bar as a virtually indispensable fixture in music plagiarism cases.

The point is perhaps best illustrated by one of the few important music plagiarism cases of the 1930s and 1940s in which Spaeth did *not* testify, *Wilkie v. Santly Brothers.*[49] After a trial in November 1935, the court had held that Bernice Petkere's "Starlight" infringed the plaintiff Bud Wilkie's unpublished song "Confessing," entirely on the basis of strong melodic similarities, in particular an identity of eight bars, although there was no evidence of access whatever. The defendants' attorneys then petitioned for a retrial based on "newly discovered evidence":

> Up to the time of the trial the defendants had endeavored to find examples of the same combination of notes appearing in the entire eight bars constituting the theme. The defendants were advised the one man who could undoubtedly readily furnish this information was Sigmund Spaeth, but ascertained that he had left New York City the early part of October for an extended lecture tour of the Pacific Coast and that his services would not be available for some time to come.

Upon Spaeth's return to New York just before Christmas, he was given copies of the Court's opinion and the compositions at issue. "Later in the day," the petition continued, "Mr. Spaeth telephoned and advised that he had already succeeded in finding this theme in one musical composition."[50] Ergo, it could not be inferred that Petkere copied from Wilkie.

The petition for a new trial was denied. That one of the most prominent members of the New York copyright bar, Julian Abeles, could think for a moment that Spaeth's return from a West Coast speaking tour might be grounds for granting a new trial suggests that tune detection was no longer just an after-dinner diversion; it was recognized de jure as a learned profession, with Sigmund Spaeth its leading practitioner.

Spaeth was on the winning side in almost every case he appeared in, an enviable record that certainly contributed to his allure. It is unclear, though, whether his testimony was ever outcome-determinative or even especially influential. He usually appeared on behalf of defendants, who held most of the cards in such cases, and his testimony was usually corroborated by another, more conventionally credentialed expert. It was as though defendants had come to believe that Spaeth's mere absence would be grounds for some kind of adverse inference. The only case in which contemporary accounts suggest his testimony was decisive was not a music copyright case at all, but a celebrated defamation suit that arose from Republic Pictures' 1936 film *Frankie and Johnny*. Miss Frankie Baker, who operated a shoe-shine parlor in Portland, Oregon, claimed that both the bawdy song "Frankie and Johnny" and the movie based on it were salacious distortions of the facts surrounding an 1899 incident in St. Louis, in which she had killed her boyfriend in self-defense. Spaeth, the only witness for the studio, testified that this was impossible because the song pre-dated the Civil War and was most likely based on an incident that had occurred in North Carolina. Spaeth added that he had first heard the song as a college student in 1901. "I couldn't have heard it earlier," he joked, "because I was reared in a minister's home." Spaeth brushed aside cross-examination based on his 1926 book *Read 'Em and Weep*, in which he had placed the song's origins in St. Louis: "I've changed my mind since then."[51]

Spaeth's courtroom demeanor exuded cheeky self-confidence. Many opposing attorneys played on his inflated ego and pedantry, with varying degrees of success, but it was only Mr. Ira B. Arnstein, Spaeth once said, who "ever referred to me as a faker or a moron" in a court of law.[52]

SONG-LIFTING TRIAL GOES INTO AGITATO

The king of musical litigants is unquestionably Ira B. Arnstein, who has spent the greater part of his adult life in trying to prove that most of the hit songs of modern times have been stolen from him, attacking the biggest names in popular music and timing his activities with rare commercial perspicacity.
—*Sigmund Spaeth*

Just two days after Judge Coleman delivered his final decree in *Arnstein v. Shilkret* from a courtroom in the obsolete, crumbling U.S. Post Office in Lower Manhattan—a much-maligned eyesore in the French Second Empire style, razed shortly thereafter for an expansion of City Hall Park—the first sworn testimony in *Arnstein v. Edward B. Marks Music Corporation* was being taken in more stately surroundings. L. Wolfe Gilbert, who was living safely beyond the subpoena power of a federal court sitting in New York City while writing for Eddie Cantor's Hollywood-based radio show, was back in town for the holidays and staying at the St. Moritz Hotel, one of several sparkling new art deco skyscrapers lining Central Park South. On December 22, 1933, lawyers for Marks and Arnstein trooped uptown to the commodious

St. Moritz to take Gilbert's deposition *de bene esse*. (That is, to preserve his testimony for use in his absence at a later trial. The Federal Rules of Civil Procedure, which would make pretrial depositions for purposes of fact discovery a standard practice in civil litigation, were still five years in the future.)

Wolfe Gilbert had been one of the first Tin Pan Alley' old-timers to head west, recruited there by Fox Films on the strength of his 1928 hit theme songs for *Lilac Time* and *Ramona*. But by the time Gilbert arrived in Hollywood a glut of stinkers had already poisoned the box office for musicals, and their production was grinding to a halt. After two years of drawing handsome salaries from Fox, Paramount, and Warner Brothers, living in picturesque bungalows on studio lots while mostly working on his golf game, Gilbert's writing assignments dried up completely. He returned to New York in 1931, where he spent a few productive months as professional manager and in-house wordsmith for Edward B. Marks, modernizing the company's song-plugging operation and writing English lyrics for tunes that Marks had imported from Cuba. The result was a fresh string of hits that included "Marta," "The Peanut Vendor," and "Oh, Mama Inez." Gilbert's newly discovered affinity for things Hispanic earned him quick passage back to California, where a job writing songs for Fox's Spanish language division awaited. "The fact that I couldn't speak one word of Spanish," Gilbert wrote in his memoir, *Without Rhyme or Reason*, "didn't seem to make any difference."[1]

Gilbert's tenure with Marks was brief, but it overlapped rather precisely with the publisher's equally short-lived dalliance with Ira B. Arnstein. In the spring of 1931 Gilbert and Arnstein collaborated in reworking "A Mother's Prayer" as a popular song, with Gilbert contributing lyrics for both English and Yiddish editions. Arnstein became a rather persistent visitor to Gilbert's office, popping in every week or so to pitch something new that he was working on. Gilbert thought that at least one of Arnstein's offerings, a song called "I Love You Madly," had some possibilities, needing only a little musical revision and new lyrics to replace Arnstein's rather turgid monorhyme:

> Tell me you care, my feelings spare,
>   And we'll forever happiness share.
> Fine music entrancing will be our fare,
>   With exotic dancing in open air.

Gilbert testified that he kept Arnstein's manuscript for five months while waiting for an idea for a lyric to present itself, but that Arnstein took it back before he had done any work on it. Arnstein claimed that he made some musical revisions at Gilbert's suggestion, resulting in a simplified song called "Where Are You Now?" for which Gilbert had written a whole new set of words:

> *Where are you now? I long for you my gypsy sweetheart.*
> *You broke each vow, and still I'm true my gypsy sweetheart.*
> *Just let me know, no place on earth would be too far for me to go.*

This much, however, was undisputed: Arnstein's relations with Marks had soured when the vocal edition of "A Mother's Prayer" failed to catch on, prompting him to retrieve "I Love You Madly" from Gilbert in September 1931. There matters lay until September 1932, when Marks published a gypsy waltz in which the first four syllables of the chorus—"play, fiddle, play"—were set to the same sequence of tones in the key of D minor, A-F-G-A, as were "tell me you care" and "where are you now" in the two versions of Arnstein's song. Whether the similarities stopped there, or whether there were others that could justify the inference that "Play, Fiddle, Play" was derived from the manuscript that supposedly sat untouched in Wolfe Gilbert's desk drawer for five months, that is the stuff from which federal cases are made.

Even the mother song—"always a sure-fire idea and universally appealing," Abel Green advised aspiring songwriters[2]—was once something fresh and new. "The Old Arm Chair," published in 1840, was the first big mother hit:

> *'Tis past! 'Tis past! But I gaze on it now*
>   *With quivering breath and throbbing brow;*
> *'Twas there she nursed me, 'twas there she died;*
>   *And memory flows with lava tide.*
>   *Say it is folly, and deem me weak,*
> *While scalding drops start down my cheek;*
>   *But I love it, I love it, and cannot tear*
>   *My soul from a mother's old arm chair.*

In a rapidly industrializing antebellum America, "the timeless constancy of motherhood as it was imagined in 'The Old Arm Chair' and in similar songs stood in comforting contrast to the shifting patterns of social life."[3] It is unlikely that any such psycho-sociological insights occurred to publisher George P. Reed of Boston, but he was quick to grasp the opportunity for gray-market arbitrage that the 1831 extension of copyright to musical works had presented. He paired a popular poem by Eliza Cook, first published in England and therefore unprotected by copyright in the United States, with an ostensibly original, copyrightable tune. Samuel Carusi, another music publisher based in Baltimore, did the same. Legal contretemps ensued.

Charles Dickens was on a lecture tour of the United States when "The Old Arm Chair" was at the height of its popularity, using his platform as a beloved foreign author—and, by his reckoning, "the greatest loser by the existing Law alive"[4]—to campaign for a bilateral British-American copyright treaty. He might have appreciated the irony that lay at the core of *Reed v. Carusi*. Here were two international literary outlaws, equally deplorable in Dickens's eyes for their flagrant appropriations of Eliza Cook's words,

A jury found competing versions of "The Old Arm Chair" published by George P. Reed (above) and Samuel Carusi (next page) as alike as "Tweedledum and Tweedledee."

fighting over the rights to the most prosaic of melodies, and in the process creating a durable precedent for enforcement of musical copyrights.

Reed's edition of "The Old Arm Chair," by far the better seller, credited the music to Henry Russell, the Street Singer of his day. Russell was "primarily a showman" who, according to Sigmund Spaeth, "quickly grasped the American technique of hokum and staked everything on dramatic effects."[5] Carusi's edition purportedly re-used a tune, "New England" by I. T. Stoddard, that Carusi had previously published and copyrighted. In a writ filed in the U.S. Circuit Court for the District of Maryland in November 1844, Reed conceded that there were differences, but alleged that Carusi had simply varied the "main design" of Russell's music "with intent to evade the law."[6] Carusi defended, first, by invoking his right to use Stoddard's tune, second by attacking the validity of Reed's copyright—on the grounds that Russell's music was not "original," but itself copied from two older songs—and finally by arguing there was no actionable similarity between the two songs.[7]

Federal circuit courts of the nineteenth century were hybrids that both heard appeals from inferior district courts and exercised original trial jurisdiction over certain causes of action, including copyright cases. Justices

of the Supreme Court were obliged to "ride circuit," sitting twice yearly in each district within an assigned circuit. Thus it came to pass that *Reed v. Carusi*, a dispute over a few hundred copies of "The Old Arm Chair," with a statutory penalty of $1 per copy at stake, was tried in November 1845 before a jury in Baltimore, with the Chief Justice of the United States, Roger B. Taney, presiding.

Taney's memoir, compiled posthumously by his son-in-law, includes a letter from Carusi's attorney, William Frick,[8] with his recollections of the trial:

> The case was entirely novel in its features, and presented some very perplexing questions as to what constituted "originality" in musical composition, and as to the right of Mr. Russell to be considered the "author" of the air which had been copyrighted. There was a great deal of learned musical testimony and forensic discussion on these very important points.

On the issue of similarity, "the musical experts, proverbially discordant among themselves, differed widely in their testimony." Taney ruled that the best evidence would be for the jury to hear both songs performed. John Cole, "an old professional singer," was sworn in as an expert witness and "proceeded in the gravest manner, under the direction of the Chief Justice, to intone the two songs successively in open court."

Taney personally drafted jury instructions addressing the originality and similarity issues. His handwritten notes evidence that he grappled with the difficulty at the core of any copyright case involving popular music, that in setting the same bathetic couplets of Eliza Cook to music suitable for the parlor pianist and singer, Russell and Carusi had only eight notes between them. Taney articulated legal standards of originality and similarity that left ample breathing room for composers to draw upon the common musical vocabulary, though his formulations were hopelessly subjective: Mere correspondences or stylistic similarities with earlier works would not disprove Russell's original authorship and entitlement to copyright if, "in the main design," the song was "the effort of his own mind." Conversely, Carusi could not be liable for infringement even if his song was similar in its main design and in "its material and important parts" to Reed's if it was, nonetheless, the effort of *his* own mind, "or taken from an air composed by some other person, who was not a plagiarist from that of Russell."

The jury, Frick wrote, "made up their minds that there was only a difference in the songs between 'Tweedledum and Tweedledee,'" and rendered a verdict of $200 in favor of the plaintiff Reed. By statute, the penalty was to be divided equally between Reed and the United States, but on February 3, 1846, President James Polk intervened. Citing "the trifling value of the music, and the inconsiderable injury, if any, inflicted on Reed," President Polk granted a petition remitting Carusi's liability to the government.[9]

Twenty years later, Frick recalled the ludicrous sight and sounds of old John Cole: "Mr. Cole's emphatic rendering of the songs would, under any other circumstances, have created in the crowd of bystanders irresistible laughter and confusion. But the Chief Justice, with that power peculiarly his own, of restraining almost by a glance the slightest breach of decorum in his Court, overawed and repressed every demonstration of disrespect." Frick doubted that any other judge, presented with similar circumstances, could maintain order in the court. Rife with all manner of histrionics, tantrums, and puerile towel-snapping, the trial of *Arnstein v. Edward B. Marks Music Corporation*, ninety years later, would put Frick's prediction to the test.

JURIST FROM THE COW COUNTRY SITS IN ON TIN PAN ALLEY RUSTLING CASE
Fiddlers Aid Composer in Court

The repeal of Prohibition had done nothing to ease a chronic state of docket congestion in the U.S. District Court for the Southern District of New York. The void left when Volstead Act prosecutions ended was more than filled by complex corporate reorganization proceedings under Depression-era amendments to the Bankruptcy Act. Increasingly, the Southern District's routine matters were assigned to visiting judges from other districts who volunteered to help with the backlog. Much of the court's business was carried out in rented overflow space in the Woolworth Building, just across Broadway from the old Post Office, where some lucky judges and their tipstaff got the opportunity to acclimate to the charms and conveniences of a distinguished Cass Gilbert tower while awaiting completion of the new federal courthouse that Gilbert had designed for nearby Foley Square.

When *Arnstein v. Edward B. Marks Music Corporation* made its way onto the trial calendar in June 1935, a visiting judge from Denver, the

Honorable John Foster Symes, was assigned to hear it. Every hackneyed stereotype of the Frontier West seemed to spring, spontaneously and simultaneously, to the minds of the New Yorkers who would be trying the case or reporting on it. It didn't matter that Judge Symes had been educated at Yale and Columbia, or that he had begun his legal career in New York. The arrival of the laconic westerner disrupted the settled rhythms and expectations of the close circle of attorneys who sparred with each other regularly in music copyright cases and the journalists who covered the courthouse beat. They could hardly have been more perturbed if it had been Judge Roy Bean who strode into the makeshift courtroom on the twelfth floor of the Woolworth Building. Arnstein assumed that Marks's lawyers had pulled some strings to bring in a presumptive cultural illiterate.[10] "Stupid" and "phlegmatic" was his take on Symes.[11] The defense worried that this "corn-fed pontiff," presiding over his first music copyright case, would be intoxicated by the unaccustomed glamour and attention.[12] The bemusement was mutual. "Tin Pan Alley people," Symes told reporters after the trial ended, "are somewhat different in temperament from the kind of men one runs across in Colorado."[13]

"Play, Fiddle, Play" was three years old, well beyond the average life expectancy of a popular song, but still "in the air, here, there, everywhere," and showing signs that it might have the legs to become a standard. Only a few weeks earlier, the Radio City Music Hall Symphony Orchestra used it as the overture for a stage show called "Romany Airs"[14]—as if the gypsies had adopted an American pop tune as their national anthem. Its cachet was still such that the ravenous New York City press, ten major dailies in cutthroat competition, came out in full force to cover the trial. The principal players in the courtroom drama did not disappoint.

The case had been filed on Arnstein's behalf by John P. Chandler, a respected practitioner of patent, copyright, and trademark law, who told Arnstein when he accepted the case in February 1933 that he had investigated it "very thoroughly" and was "satisfied that you have a sound cause of action."[15] But not long after the *Shilkret* ruling came down late that year, Chandler and Arnstein parted company. Once again, Arnstein had to go to trial with a lawyer, in this case one Ralph Vatner, with no expertise in copyright law. But by now Arnstein was an experienced hand at this, and Vatner was, at least at first, content to let the client choreograph the show.

Arnstein had asked Leonard Liebling, the editor of the *Musical Courier* and a noted tune detective long before Sigmund Spaeth took up the trade, to serve as his expert witness. Although Liebling declined because of contractual restrictions against such work, he liked Arnstein's music and, after reviewing the evidence, told Arnstein, "you seem to have reason for complaint and sympathy."[16] With that modicum of encouragement, but friendless in the world of popular music ("my name is poison to all publishers," he said, "because I've got their number, and they know it"[17]), Arnstein worked up his own tune detective act, in which he traced thirty-four measures of "Play, Fiddle, Play" to "I Love You Madly."

When Arnstein took the stand to present his analysis, he was accompanied by two violinists, Aaron Fastovsky and Simon Mogiliansky, who illustrated his testimony by playing from a crib sheet that Arnstein had prepared. Fastovsky played the passages on the left and Mogiliansky, alternately, those on the right. The demonstration had proceeded only as far as the third stave before Marks's attorney, Theodore Richter, objected, complaining that

Arnstein brought two violinists to court to play passages that illustrated his theory of similarity.

Arnstein had cherry-picked arbitrary snippets of the two songs for comparison. "Why not play the whole thing?" Judge Symes asked, "wouldn't that give a better idea than just picking out excerpts?" Vatner, prudently, accepted the court's suggestion, but Arnstein sprang to his feet:

> MR. ARNSTEIN: I don't want to go on with this case. I want to prove what he stole and I don't want this.
>
> THE COURT: Just sit down.
>
> MR. ARNSTEIN: This is my place here to be understood. I do not want to go on with the case. I am not going on.
>
> THE COURT: Take this gentleman out of the courtroom.
>
> MR. ARNSTEIN: I am not going on with this case because I am not getting a chance in this court.
>
> THE COURT: Just a minute now. Take this gentleman out of the courtroom.
>
> (The plaintiff is removed from the courtroom.)

Arnstein later disputed the accuracy of the official transcript, insisting that he had stated that he would not go on with the case only once, not three times, and that he had not been "removed" from the courtroom, but had walked out voluntarily, followed by the bailiff. It would be fair to say that under either version, the plaintiff's case was not off to a promising start.

Once Arnstein had collected himself and returned to the courtroom, Judge Symes, "a bland sandy-haired man with a fatherly smile and unrimmed pince-nez,"[18] instructed Fastovsky and Mogiliansky to play each song once, straight through, in its entirety. "After that," Symes told Arnstein, "you can have them play anything you want." When they were finished, court was adjourned for the day. Leaving the Woolworth Building after listening to Mogiliansky's rendition of "Play, Fiddle, Play," Emery Deutsch told reporters that he was "itching to get hold of a fiddle" to show how it should be done. "This is something that might happen to anyone," Deutsch added, "there are only eight notes you know."[19]

CHOPIN DIRGE MADE
INTO JAZZ IN COURT
Composer Gives Tinpan Alley

Rendition to Show Tempo
Can Disguise Piece

When court reconvened the next morning, Vatner asserted control over the presentation of the case, and the plaintiff's side rallied. As Arnstein's testimony resumed, Vatner had Fastovsky and Mogiliansky sworn in as well. Gone for now was Arnstein's annotated crib sheet, although similar charts, ever more recondite and crammed with gratuitous invective, would be a fixture of every case to come. Vatner had the fiddlers two play straight from the copyrighted sheet music in evidence, calling first for two or three measures of "I Love You Madly," and then for two or three from "Play, Fiddle, Play." "Violins sobbed in Federal Court today," read the lead in the *Evening Journal*, "echoing the heartbreak which Ira B. Arnstein, a—or perhaps THE—composer declared was his over the alleged 'pirating' of a tune by the E. B. Marks Music Corporation."[20]

The demonstration was, on its face, pretty persuasive—the juxtaposed excerpts did strike the ear as similar. But its probative value ultimately depended on whether certain of Arnstein's musicological premises were to be indulged: that excerpts from two songs could be selected for comparison without regard to order, rhythmic grouping, or original phrasing; that notes from the principal melody of "I Love You Madly" and the accompaniment could be concatenated and compared to the principal melody line of "Play, Fiddle, Play" (resulting in the most striking similarity—the sixth line from the bottom of Arnstein's chart—a stretch of nine identical tones); that a difference of an octave between two sequences of notes, or a change in rhythm from common to waltz time, was not inconsistent with copying and, indeed, might be signs of conscious concealment. But with those caveats, even one member of the defense team had to agree: "It sounded exactly like our song!"[21]

Vatner skillfully guided Arnstein through his testimony, which anticipated many defense objections to his theory of the case and preemptively rebutted them. Illustrating some of his points with his well-trained tenor voice, and others on a spinet piano that had been brought to court, Arnstein acquitted himself reasonably well. He argued with some force that the notes he had extracted from the accompaniment of "I Love You Madly" were not harmony but counter-melody (an unusual ornament in a popular song) and, to the ear, just a continuation of the melody line though placed in a different instrumental part:

MR. ARNSTEIN: There is a sustained note in the top and the second part
   takes up the melody. The phrase is in the second violin.... They are in
   my score, in my music, and he uses the same notes in my music. What is
   the use whether he uses it on the top or the bottom, he continues the
   same melody. The melody continues from my notes. It makes no
   difference whether I have it in one part—
THE COURT: Just answer the question.

Arnstein was on shakier ground on the question of the rhythmic differences between the two songs. Conflating rhythm and tempo, he argued that
any plagiarism could be disguised to the layman's ear by simply speeding up
a song or slowing it down. His demonstration of the point—playing Chopin's *Funeral March*, first as "the slowest of movements," and then, without
altering a note, "as the wildest of dances"—all the newspapers agreed, was
one of the day's highlights.

Not so boffo was Arnstein's performance under Richter's cross-examination, a slow-motion train wreck, still cringe-inducing to read more than
seventy-five years after the event. Richter was determined to let Judge Symes
know "the type of man this is," and quickly went on the offensive.

Arnstein had testified that he had distributed professional copies of "I
Love You Madly" to various musicians, including Emery Deutsch and another man that he said he met at CBS, Arthur Altman, who was credited as
Deutsch's co-composer of "Play, Fiddle, Play." Building ineluctably to the
coup de grâce with ominous cadences, and deftly running the judge's stop
sign, Richter's cross-examination on this point was one for the trial practice
textbooks:

MR. RICHTER: And it is your claim that you personally delivered another
   photostat to Mr. Altman?
MR. ARNSTEIN: Absolutely.
Q: And that took place in June, 1931?
A: Yes.
Q: And you are absolutely positive of that?
A: Yes, about June.
Q: Do you know Arthur Altman?
A: Yes, I have seen him.
Q: Pick him out in court now, please.

A: In court?

Q: Yes.

A: I don't think he is in court. I don't know.

Q: Look well now.

A: This man there (indicating). Who sits next to Mr. Deutsch.

RICHTER: Will you state your name for the record, please?

A VOICE: Edward J. Eaugani.

THE COURT: I think we have had enough of this point. He has picked the wrong man.

RICHTER: Mr. Altman, will you please stand up?

ARNSTEIN: I apologize, it is another man. It wasn't Mr. Altman.

Richter then turned to a conversation that Arnstein had with Max Marks, Edward's brother, before he filed the lawsuit:

ARNSTEIN: I said, "I am very desperate and you can't tell what a desperate man does." I was at that time. I was so desperate, that I tell your Honor this is the truth, if I had a gun at that time I would have committed murder.

RICHTER: Isn't it a fact at that time you told Mr. Marks you had to have a thousand dollars even though you had to go to the electric chair for it?

ARNSTEIN: Yes, I told him, "If I cannot get any justice in the courts."

Richter's most devastating line of cross-examination was still to come. "Reading my testimony," Arnstein had to concede, "anyone would get an idea that the person testifying is of a disordered mind." As reported by the *Post*:

Mr. Arnstein, over strenuous objections of his lawyer, who obviously feared that his client would undermine his own credibility, swore that no fewer than fourteen song hits had been lifted from compositions of his. Among the fourteen was a piece called "My Yiddishe Mama." "What is a Yiddishe mama?" Judge Symes wanted to know.[22]

Arnstein's list of fourteen, starting with Irving Berlin's "A Russian Lullaby," had most recently grown to include Harry Warren's "Boulevard of Broken Dreams." When Richter was through, Vatner made one last attempt to close the Pandora's box that his client had opened:

MR. VATNER: If your Honor please, I make a motion to strike out all the testimony as irrelevant and immaterial to the issues before the Court.

THE COURT: The motion is denied because the witness refuses to answer questions properly and therefore has opened the door in spite of the admonitions of the Court.

By the time Arnstein stepped down, Richter could feel confident that Judge Symes would agree with Judge Coleman's assessment that Arnstein's "credibility as a witness is of a low order" and his mind of the "type that would never prompt me to place reliance upon his statements of fact." Yet Richter was uneasy. Symes was an impassive figure on the bench, and his comments and rulings bespoke an old jurisprude's penchant for focusing on the narrowest issues that he would need to decide, none of which would actually turn on Arnstein's personal credibility. Unlike the *Shilkret* case, in which the defendant swore that he never saw or heard "Light My Life with Love," here there was no dispute over the basic facts establishing access: that Arnstein and Gilbert had collaborated on "A Mother's Prayer," that Arnstein had played "I Love You Madly" for Gilbert while he was employed by Marks, that Gilbert had expressed genuine interest and held on to the manuscript for months, and that Gilbert was acquainted with Emery Deutsch. And when Richter's cross-examination had turned to matters musical, Arnstein had parried his thrusts with aplomb, standing his ground on the most material matters and conceding obvious points without undermining his credibility by sparring or quibbling.

Judge Symes's steady gaze and stoic demeanor throughout Arnstein's testimony was a nagging reminder to Richter that, in the eyes of the law, even a delusional, serial nuisance litigant with a habit of stretching the truth could have a meritorious case. As the press buzzed with the news that day three would feature the testimony of radio personality Sigmund Spaeth, a glowering courtroom presence and fastidious note taker throughout Arnstein's testimony, Richter had begun to doubt that the vaunted Tune Detective would impress this detached son of the Rocky Mountain West.

HARD TO STOP SPAETH'S SONG
Judge and Lawyer Unite
to Stem Melodic Flow

Spaeth, not one to be crippled by self-doubt, had been working the press corps energetically. "The tune detective plans to reveal some nice 'adaptations' from Brahms, Chopin and other classicists," the *Post* reported, "when he appears as a witness in a money dispute among songsmiths charging note thievery."[23] If Richter hoped that Spaeth could suppress his urge to ham it up, or that he could modulate the didactic hauteur that bowled over the men at Kiwanis dinners and the ladies at conventions of the National Federation of Music Clubs, he had to be disappointed with his expert's performance on the stand. In the give-and-take between Richter and Spaeth, it was clearly the witness who was in charge, with Richter reduced to being little more than an offstage prompter feeding cues to the star. Spaeth seized upon the narrowest of Richter's questions to launch into long discourses that displayed the breadth of his musical erudition, if not always precision of thought. Unaccustomed to the indignity of being interrupted or cut off when he was performing—as he was frequently, sometimes by Symes, sometimes by Richter—he mugged for the spectators, miming "gestures of helplessness when he was not allowed to intersperse his testimony with many technical explanations in musical terms"[24] and "regretful expressions"[25] when he was not permitted to sing.

Spaeth's complementary gifts for tune detection and for lecturing while playing the piano were on full display as he performed a medley of pieces containing the sequence A-F-G, which, in his analysis, was the only similarity between "I Love You Madly" and "Play, Fiddle, Play." As three contiguous notes on the D-minor scale, Spaeth opined, it is a pattern so basic it could not give rise to an inference of copying. Both songs actually featured the somewhat more distinctive sequence A-F-G-A, but Spaeth dismissed the second A as a mere repetition, a bit of ad hoc musical theorizing that left Arnstein sputtering. Long after the fact he came up with a stinging riposte: "If an expert in English were to state that the last two A's in charlatan do not count because there is already one A following the H," Arnstein asked, "would anyone think him an expert?"[26]

HUMMING HELD 'PREJUDICED'
IN SUIT OVER SONG
Spaeth, Defense Witness, Denies
His Da-Da's Were Unfair

N. Y. American Staff Photo.

HIST|—"Tune Detective" Sigmund Spaeth (right) tips Theodore B. Richter defense counsel, in court on "clues" in music sheet.

Arnstein v. Marks Music Corp. received blanket coverage in New York City's daily press.

Spaeth scored his best points in critiquing Arnstein's use of random fragments—"not in any case completed musical thoughts"—as the basis for comparison of the two songs:

> A writer may use the words "to be." I have often used the words "not to be." I have used the short sentence, "That is the question." Has Shakespeare stolen my work because he has written, "To be or not to be, that is the question"? That is an absolute analogy in literature.

He was at his weakest in disparaging the aural evidence of similarity that everyone in the courtroom had heard the day before, insisting that regardless of how a passage might sound to the ordinary listener, no parallel can be said to exist without "an absolute sequence note for note and identity of at least, we will say, five, six, eight or nine notes in a row—an absolute identity of melody." Richter sensed danger in this ad-libbed testimony, but his efforts to rein Spaeth back in only called more attention to it:

> RICHTER: I don't think I made myself very clear, apparently. Let us elimi-
> nate for a moment the notations as to what they say to the eye and tell us
> rather what they say to the ear.
> SPAETH: They would say the same thing to the ear. The note A—
> RICHTER: I ask you whether musically they tell the ear the same thing.
> SPAETH: They are not alike, because in the chorus you have—.
> RICHTER: Yes or no, please.
> SPAETH: They are not alike.

Vatner began his cross by tripping Spaeth up with one of the oldest tricks in the book:

> VATNER: I think you have told me you have read a number of books on
> theory and harmony?
> SPAETH: Yes.
> VATNER: Have you read a book by Hugh Clark on Theory, of the University
> of Pennsylvania?
> SPAETH: I know Mr. Clark, and I have lectured at the University of Pennsyl-
> vania. I will not say I have read all of it.
> VATNER: Do you know the book by Perdick on Theory?
> SPAETH: I know such a book.
> VATNER: Don't you know that there is no such book as Perdick on Theory?
> SPAETH: I am not sure.

Sensing that Spaeth had an unsung song in his heart, and that he would sooner try the patience of Judge Symes than let go of a nice theoretical point, Vatner decided to have some sport with him. He asked Spaeth to hum some of the passages in question:

> VATNER: Those tunes sound similar to you?
> SPAETH: The point is that I judge similarity by the written note.
> VATNER: Forgetting the written notes.
> SPAETH: I am not qualified to say. They sound differently because the notes
> are so obviously different.

VATNER: Do you feel you have given us a fair way of humming those two comparisons?

SPAETH: I have hummed exactly what is before me in the notes.

VATNER: There is no da, da, da before you. . . .

"Vatner, attorney for Mr. Arnstein," the *Times* reported, "complained that the witness killed the similarity of sound by humming one song and singing 'Da, Da, Da' in the other."[27] Spaeth's stubborn refusal to acknowledge the aural similarities, a point the defense could have cheerfully conceded without much risk to its case, exacted a price in lost credibility.

But Spaeth had surely succeeded in entertaining. The day's proceedings once again had reporters poring over their thesauruses for musical puns—"loud raps for order formed an obbligato"[28]—but it was the challenge of transcribing Spaeth's scat that separated the mere scriveners from the true writers. Where the official transcript states only "witness hums," Michel Mok of the *Post*—a stylish writer who later did the first English translations of Anne Frank's stories and essays—easily won the day with an onomatopoeia of Joycean proportions, "tee-taya-tee-taya-tee-tum-tum-tayada."[29]

DEUTSCH CALLED 'INSPIRATION'
FOR SONG IN TRIAL
'Play, Fiddle, Play' Not His in Note or Word,
Yet He Gets Credit, Court Hears

Richter's original trial strategy had figured on a TKO by this point, but Judge Symes—though he was becoming equally impatient and cantankerous with both sides—was showing no inclination to stop the fight. A mid-course correction was needed. As Jack Lawrence, the young songwriter credited with the lyrics to "Play, Fiddle, Play," recalled many years later:

> The reporters were having a field day with our saga and the courtroom filled with spectators. Finally, our attorneys called another meeting and announced that the situation looked bad. They had decided to put Arthur [Altman] and me on the stand to tell the truth, that Emery [Deutsch] had written not one note of our song.[30]

Such testimony would, of course, be rather embarrassed by the hundreds of thousands of copies of sheet music in circulation that identified Deutsch as the principal composer of "Play, Fiddle, Play"—in typeface nearly twice as large as the credits for Altman as co-writer of the music and Lawrence as lyricist—but it was the truth. Lawrence and Altman were still teenagers, with dreams of making careers as songwriters, when they were introduced to Emery Deutsch. Lawrence's older brother was dating a girl who knew Deutsch, and she was able to arrange an audition for them at CBS. After listening to a few of their numbers as a favor, Deutsch shooed the boys away, politely suggesting they come back if they ever wrote something he could use as a theme for his gypsy fiddler act.

A year or so earlier Altman and Lawrence had written a song called "What Can I Do?" based on a Ukrainian folk tune, "Viyut Vitry," that Lawrence's mother liked to hum. It had a gypsy flavor to it. That night Lawrence, who at his parents' insistence was studying to be a chiropodist, came up with a new title and new lyrics for "What Can I Do?" The next day he skipped an anatomy exam to finish off the song he now called "Play, Fiddle, Play" with Altman. They brought it to Deutsch who "thought it was swell" and began playing it on the air.

Altman was able to find undated manuscripts that documented the true provenance of "Play, Fiddle, Play," and his charming young wife was able to fill out the timeline to the complete satisfaction of a somewhat besotted Judge Symes:

> "I remember the song because it was very important to me at that time, when we were engaged," she said. "That's the experience of everybody," Judge Symes chuckled.[31]

It was an appealing story of youthful pluck and good fortune, and it virtually precluded any possibility that the song's creation could have been tainted by exposure to "I Love You Madly." Altman and Lawrence were ciphers; not even Ira B. Arnstein could find a way to besmirch them. The defense had sandbagged Arnstein with new information in a manner that would be virtually unthinkable under the pretrial discovery procedures adopted by the federal courts a few years later.

This might have been the knockout blow that Richter was looking for, but for his ham-fisted insistence on somehow justifying Deutsch's compositional credit. What Jack Lawrence called "the whole truth," that "Emery Deutsch was what is known in the music business as a 'cut-in,'"[32] a non-composer who was rewarded by Edward B. Marks with principal credit and the lion's share of the royalties for his role in plugging the song, never did come out. This was an issue tangential to the case at hand, but an especially sensitive subject for Edward B. Marks. He had been instrumental in the 1916 creation of the Music Publishers Protective Association, an organization originally formed to protect publishers from their own increasingly costly practice of paying singers and orchestra leaders for performing their songs, a practice then known as "the evil." "This expenditure brought no increase in the total number of plugs or the total sales of the industry," Marks explained, "publishers paid simply as a defensive measure against their competitors, who otherwise would monopolize the plugs."[33] The MPPA's bylaws "dictated that a publisher would be fined five thousand dollars for violating the no-payment pledge."[34] The inevitable workaround, cutting-in performers on compositional royalties, took root immediately. Jolson, for example, received his first copyrights in 1918, as the coauthor with Sigmund Romberg, Buddy De Sylva, and Gus Kahn of songs for his extravaganza *Sinbad*. "My collaborators are having their convention in Cleveland this week," was the rueful joke among real songwriters who were seeing their royalties diluted by cut-ins.

Altman and Lawrence, after first extracting an increase in their share of the royalties from Marks, agreed to play along. Their testimony vaguely adumbrated that Deutsch was their "inspiration" and that maybe he had provided the title or contributed to the verse. Deutsch's testimony was an elaborate fiction in which he claimed to have "played the violin for the boys and imbedded in their minds various gypsy themes of the kind that I would have liked to see in a gypsy song. . . . It is just like if I would give an order and if I make a draft, if I make a rough etching of something. I will give it to a man to make the finished product." Though their stories were inconsistent and the presentation of it maladroit, Richter succeeded in protecting his client— the arrangement came across as silly rather than corrupt. As the *Post's* Michel Mok wrote:

> In the last three days Federal Judge J. Foster Symes of Colorado, where there are canyons, ravines and gulches but no Tin Pan Alleys, has learned many strange things. . . . That if a popular comedian or musician tells a song writer "Turn me out something Mexican, something on the order of 'You Are My Hot Tamale Baby,'" he's known as a "collaborator" and his name appears as co-composer on the published music.[35]

Reviewing the record on appeal, even the normally savvy Judge Learned Hand was confused, finding Deutsch's contribution "very vague indeed" and naively guessing that it had been Altman and Lawrence's idea to give the better-known Deutsch credit.[36]

The sheer banality of the "Play, Fiddle, Play" backstory would have been nauseating enough for Arnstein—a couple of teenagers with no musical training, living with their parents, an audition arranged by a big brother's girlfriend, a chiropody student skipping his anatomy exam to write the verse. A chiropody student! But the revelation that Deutsch hadn't written a note was another watershed moment in Arnstein's decline and fall. Here was confirmation that the game was rigged, that popular music was a racket run by musical illiterates in which talent counted for nothing and true geniuses go hungry. The composer of "A Mother's Prayer" and *The Song of David* starves while a fraud like Emery Deutsch reaps fame and fortune. And what, for that matter, had Nathaniel Shilkret written since he was indicted for stealing from Arnstein? A most disturbing pattern was becoming apparent, an unsuspecting world needed to know, and steps would need to be taken.

SONG-LIFTING TRIAL GOES INTO
AGITATO WITH SOUR NOTES
Pianist in Tears,
'Tune Detective' Hisses

By the fourth and final day of the trial, emotions were raw and patience was wearing thin. "In a cacophony of sour fiddle notes, tinny piano sharps and flats and a babble of highly-excited foreign tongues, the Tin Pan Alley Plagiarism trial ended slightly off key."[37] The carping between Richter and Vatner had taken on a nasty, personal edge. Young Altman and Lawrence were feeling emboldened after facing down old man Marks. Sigmund Spaeth was still smarting over the aspersions cast upon his humming. Ungentlemanly and downright rude behavior of all sorts roiled the musty courtroom.

Three more witnesses, including two experts testifying on behalf of Arnstein—the organist from New York's Central Synagogue, Melchiorre Mauro-Cottone, and its cantor, Isador Weinstock—and Emery Deutsch himself, illustrated their testimony "with snatches of the two romantic pieces, which have been played so often during the trial that even the elevator operators are humming them."[38] Their performances elicited catcalls, heckling, and insults. Judge Symes, the *Sun* punned, was receiving "intensive instruction in everything except harmony."[39]

Mauro-Cottone, a Roman Catholic, held a Ph.D. from the University of Chicago and for ten years had been the house organist at Roxy's Capitol Theatre, where he had earned a reputation as "a supreme theater artist" with the "ability to improvise by the hour."[40] Reporters noted Altman and Lawrence's visible "discomforture"[41]—that they "blanched and their jaws dropped"[42]—when Richter asked Mauro-Cottone which of the two songs in suit had the greater artistic merit. After graciously demurring at least three times, creating considerable suspense, the witness finally answered:

MAURO-COTTONE: If you ask me about the artistic merits, I don't find any.
RICHTER: In either of them?
MAURO-COTTONE: In either of them. You just put me up against it and I must tell you.

Mauro-Cottone used the skills that he had honed at the Capitol to great advantage during his testimony. Sitting at the spinet piano, he was called upon to play the fox-trot "I Love You Madly" on the fly in three-quarter time, to play excerpts from each song with a different hand, and to manage an unruly audience:

In the midst of his rendition, Altman and Lawrence, young songwriters, cried out: "You're not playing it right."

Dr. Melchiorre Mauro-Cottone brought the song to an abrupt stop. He glanced frigidly at the interrupters.

"You're putting in some extra notes!" cried Dr. Sigmund Spaeth....

"Dr. Spaeth, I'll have to ask you to subside," excitedly demanded the defense lawyer, Theodore B. Richter.[43]

The plaintiff's side was just as vocal in its criticism of Deutsch's violin renditions, loudly accusing him of playing one number legato and the other staccato, and of adding unwritten grace notes to "Play, Fiddle, Play." Deutsch's playing brought tears to the eyes of some in the courtroom, but only "muttered imprecations from Arnstein."[44] When the last witness stood down and the attorneys completed their summations, Judge Symes "confessed to a headache and reserved decision."[45] The plaintiff was supremely confident of the eventual outcome. "For years Arnstein wore a hang-dog look," wrote a correspondent for Chicago's Jewish weekly, *The Sentinel*. "Now Arnstein has his chin up and his chest forward."[46]

NO SONG THEFT IS FOUND
Judge Rules Against Arnstein
In Plagiarism Suit

A week later, Symes issued a concise, surgical opinion dismissing Arnstein's complaint.[47] Symes evidently found Spaeth's testimony, which he did not mention, less persuasive than the plaintiff's repeated demonstrations of musical parallels—the judge was not inclined to disregard what his ears were telling him. There were, he wrote, "some rather striking similarities in the two pieces." The similarity was "not apparent upon the first rendering of the two pieces of music, but the listener does become conscious thereof after several playings of the same in whole or in part." The parallels, however, were not enough "to force the conclusion that one is a literal copying of the other or that the defendant's song 'Play, Fiddle, Play' was necessarily lifted entirely or in any major part from plaintiff's composition." With enough evidence of similarity to allow an inference of copying, but not enough to compel it, Altman and Lawrence's story of their independent creation of the song carried the day: "I am of the opinion that the authors of the defendant's song have, by original intellectual effort, produced a composition similar in some respects to the melody of the plaintiff's copyrighted song, without consciously copying the same." If any of the expert testimony had influenced Symes at all, it was Mauro-Cottone's: "Neither is a work of great merit, both being popular songs of the kind that have a limited vogue and soon pass to the great limbo of forgotten songs, never to be resurrected."

Theodore Richter was disappointed that Symes had treated Arnstein so "tenderly,"[48] but he was supremely confident that Arnstein would not be able to mount an appeal. He returned several key pieces of evidence, including the early "What Can I Do?" manuscripts, to Arthur Altman, convinced there would be no further need for them.

Richter had underestimated Arnstein's resolve and powers of persuasion. A very able appellate attorney, Sydney Krause, agreed to foot the considerable cost of transcribing and printing the record, and took Arnstein's case to the Second Circuit Court of Appeals on a contingent fee. Richter had also underestimated the extent of Altman and Lawrence's animosity toward Edward B. Marks. At that very moment, they were trying to escape a five-year exclusive contract they had signed with Marks, whom they now suspected was deliberately burying their songs out of pique. (Here was one thing on which Ira Arnstein and Jack Lawrence could agree: they both considered Marks a crook.[49]) Altman decided to hold the trial exhibits that Richter had returned to him hostage in the negotiations. Caught in the middle of the standoff, Richter had to defend Judge Symes's ruling on appeal without access to the most persuasive evidence of independent creation.

Richter was fortunate that the case was assigned to a panel that included Learned Hand who, after ten years on the appellate bench, had an unsurpassed reputation for diligence in mastering the factual and legal nuances of every appeal. Latter-day federal appellate lawyers, accustomed to rigidly scheduled oral arguments of twenty minutes to a half-hour, in the diminishing percentage of appeals where the court deigns to hear an oral argument at all, could scarcely imagine the flexibility of Judge Hand's Second Circuit, where cases were only very roughly calendared for argument, and the judges were able to devote more or less time to any given case as they pleased. After a formal courtroom argument on January 14, 1936, before the three-judge panel of Hand, Thomas Swan, and Harrie B. Chase, the litigants were summoned back the next day to Judge Hand's chambers for a private musical audition.

After hearing Arnstein demonstrate the musical parallels, all three judges indicated in internal memoranda that they detected significant similarities, although Judge Chase added that "unless someone pointed out parts that sounded alike, I could have heard the pieces played innumerable times without thinking one was like the other."[50] Judge Hand, convinced that the case turned on the issue of independent creation, let it be known that he would like to examine the missing "What Can I Do?" manuscripts. Backed by that impressive moral suasion, Richter convinced Altman to relent.

Judge Hand's opinion for a unanimous court of appeals panel, affirming the judgment of the district court, was issued in February 1936. Hand first seized upon the opportunity the case presented to clean up a bit of jurisprudential detritus that had long rankled him. A 1910 Second Circuit case, *Hein v. Harris*,[51] had held that the independent reproduction of a copyrighted work could constitute an infringement, distinguishing Chief Justice Taney's contrary ruling in *Reed v. Carusi* on the ground that the 1831 Copyright Act then in force imposed liability only where the infringer acted "with intent to evade the law," a requirement eliminated under later statutes. Hand had never followed the *Hein* precedent while sitting as a district court judge, having written as far back as 1922 that, while it was "embarrassing to be called upon to ignore such a decision," it was clearly "contrary to the whole theory of copyright which differs from patents in just this, that priority does not give monopoly."[52] (Translation: A patent is infringed even where an infringer conceives the invention independently; a copyright is infringed only where an infringer actually copies from an original work of authorship.) In private, Hand was even more dismissive. *Hein* was "just as wrong as a decision can possibly be in copyright," and it was inexplicable that his predecessors on the court "should have seen fit to overrule Taney by such an abysmally ignorant decision."[53] Nonetheless, it was the binding law of the Second Circuit. The *Marks* case provided the occasion for Hand to absolve himself of his long-standing violation of the doctrine of stare decisis by authoritatively overruling *Hein*.

He did not need to go much further. In finding that Lawrence and Altman's independent creation constituted a defense, Judge Symes had also ignored *Hein*, so the appeal came down to a factual issue that Symes had decided in the defense's favor based on his evaluations of witness credibility, findings that could be reversed on appeal only if "plainly wrong." Under that standard, Symes's opinion should have been affirmed summarily. But Hand thought, as he told his colleagues, that Symes had "written an opinion which shows about as little understanding of copyright as can be packed together in such small compass"[54]—a harsh appraisal that seems more a product of Hand's proprietary interest in copyright law and East Coast parochialism than of any real defect in Symes's legal craftsmanship. Hand took it upon himself to review the evidence *de novo* and show how a superior legal mind arrived at the same conclusion.[55]

Hand assumed, for the sake of argument, that the evidence of Altman and Lawrence's independent creation of "Play, Fiddle, Play" was not airtight and could indeed have been a complete fabrication. He proceeded to moot various alternative theories. It was possible, Hand allowed, that Wolfe Gilbert had given "I Love You Madly" to Deutsch, who copied it, but why then would Deutsch share credit for it with Altman and Lawrence?

> Altman was an entirely unknown person, a one-finger composer who had no reputation; the most he could do was contribute the simple themes

which by this hypothesis Deutsch intended to lift from the copyrighted song; that is to say, his only part could be just what Deutsch did not need, the melody. Lawrence could apparently write the kind of treacle which passes in a popular love song, but such mawkish verses are reeled off by hundreds of poetasters all over the country.

Deutsch, Hand concluded, "needed no help from either of these men." So he considered an alternative scenario: perhaps Altman received "I Love You Madly" from a third party and had then disguised it in the manner that Arnstein alleged.

A plagiarist might of course work in that way, seizing a sequence from the middle of a phrase in an accompaniment as a happy theme, but Altman was scarcely the man for that; his gifts were very limited, and to attribute to him the ingenuity and penetration so to truncate and modify, and thus really to create a melody out of other elements, is harder than to suppose that the extremely simple theme should have occurred to him out of his mind.

Finally, Hand rejected the contention that the similarities were so uncanny as to rule out any possibility that Altman and Lawrence came up with their melody independently. "The seven notes available do not admit of so many agreeable permutations that we need be amazed at the re-appearance of old themes, even though the identity extend through a sequence of twelve notes." Nothing that had occurred in the twelve years since he left the district court bench had led Hand to reconsider his low opinion of popular music. "Success in such music as this," he added, somewhat gratuitously, "is by no means a test of rarity or merit." Judge Learned Hand, for one, simply wasn't buying into any "golden age of American popular song" nonsense.

Notwithstanding the dismissive comments of Judges Symes and Hand, "Play, Fiddle, Play" never did pass into musical limbo—to the contrary, with recordings by Erroll Garner, Slam Stewart, Dizzy Gillespie, and Marian McPartland, among many others, it has stood the test of time as a jazz standard. Nor were Jack Lawrence and Arthur Altman one-hit wonders. They went on to collaborate on Frank Sinatra's first big hit, "All or Nothing at All," and then pursued separate hall-of-fame–caliber songwriting careers.

Any blow to Emery Deutsch's reputation was short-lived. He recorded prolifically and toured for many years, cultivating an über-romantic persona as the "Park Avenue Gypsy" playing his "Violin of Love," a 1704 Guarnerius. He had another hit with "When a Gypsy Makes His Violin Cry," which was published shortly after the *Marks* trial. Obviously emboldened after once dodging justice, Arnstein believed, this time Deutsch had infringed the crown jewel of his canon, "A Mother's Prayer." Arnstein found an attorney to put Deutsch's new publisher on notice. John Paine, then the head of the MPPA, responded on his member's behalf:

> Isn't this the same Mr. Arnstein who has so persistently made claims against the music publishing industry, and who has recently lost a case to the Edward B. Marks Corporation, and who has tried by criminal indictment to ruin the reputation of Mr. Nathaniel Shilkret, and who has claimed from time immemorial that every important musical composition published by any publisher anywhere, anytime, is an infringement of something which he has composed?[56]

Yes, Mr. Paine, that would seem to be the same Mr. Arnstein. But there is no need to exaggerate. This is only the fifteenth hit stolen from him—so far.

JUSTICE FOR GENIUS

It is your obligation as a music lover to support ASCAP in every way, should there ever be a local attack upon it. An attack never can mean anything but a high-handed effort to take away from creators what is legally and rightfully theirs.
—*The Etude*

While the attorneys were briefing his appeal of the *Marks* ruling, Arnstein exorcised his homicidal impulses with a foray into musical theater. The foreword to his script for *Broadway Music*, a "music drama in 10 scenes," promised an exposé of the music business, "authentic and not exaggerated, excepting the murder . . . which really was in the leading character's mind." A starving symphonic composer, Alfred Arno, brings an enchanting popular song, "Constantly I See Mari," to an unscrupulous publisher. The publisher has a couple of one-finger songwriters in his employ tweak a few notes and alter the rhythm to turn it into "Night and Day I Sigh for You," which becomes a number-one hit for radio bandleader "Jimmy Faike," a thinly fictionalized composite of Nathaniel Shilkret and Emery Deutsch. Faike, who has never written a note of music, receives the compositional credit.

Still desperate for money, Arno offers to sell Faike more songs that he can pass off as his own. Faike declines, but soon Arno hears one of those songs in a movie score, also credited to Jimmy Faike. In need of a continuous supply of hits to sustain the charade that he is a composer, Faike bribes Arno's landlady for access to his manuscripts. In all, fourteen of Arno's songs are purloined and become big hits credited to Faike and others.

Under the tutelage of a disillusioned radio singer, a comely exposition device named Rita Mansfield, Arno comes to realize that there is an "organized gang of racketeers" responsible for his predicament, a society called "Song Pirates, Inc." The society controls everything, she tells Arno, "all leaders, all programs, arrangers, all agents of sponsors . . . the only way to get anywhere is by plugging their songs." Hollywood is in its pocket too, obeying the society's orders to have leading men and women "endorse our songs and say something funny about old fogies who like classic music." It wields its power to squelch any music, old or new, that is not controlled by its members, especially Arno's. "All we have to do is pass the word 'Poison Ivy,'" they chortle, "and his songs will never see daylight." When Arno succeeds in getting Faike indicted, the Song Pirates employ the clout of a former attorney general to get it quashed. When the most admired and idealistic lawyer in New York agrees to represent Arno, the society co-opts him. Arno offers to assist the Department of Justice in an investigation of the society, but Rita warns that it is useless to fight them: "They collect about five million dollars a year royalties. While some of the hacks receive fabulous yearly incomes, the majority get very little. Think how much money they can spend to fight you." Finally, an enraged Arno bursts into Faike's office and bludgeons him with the bluntest symbolic object readily at hand, Faike's inkstand. After a climactic trial scene Arno is acquitted of murder—it is not clear whether on grounds of justifiable homicide or insanity—and his symphony is given a triumphal premiere at Carnegie Hall.

A Broadway audience of 1935 would have had no trouble recognizing the villains of Arnstein's piece. Among those outside of its elite membership, the epithet "racket" was almost synonymous with the American Society of Composers, Authors and Publishers. As Arnstein's life grew ever stranger and more isolated, his deep-seated antipathy toward ASCAP was a vestigial social grace.

The U.S. Department of Justice opened its investigation of ASCAP in 1923, in the waning days of the Harding administration. Over the next twenty years, the file passed through the hands of some legendary assistant attorneys general responsible for antitrust enforcement—most notably Wild Bill Donovan under Coolidge and Thurman Arnold under Roosevelt. A comprehensive 1941 consent decree brought no closure. It was just, as ASCAP's management soon realized, "a document by which the United States Government became a partner in our business."[1] To this day, the matter of *United States v. ASCAP* has never lain dormant for very long.

Upon its formation in 1914, ASCAP's stated objectives were mostly high-minded and beneficent: "to promote reforms in the law respecting literary property," "to promote and foster by all lawful means the interest of composers, authors and publishers of musical works," "to promote friendly intercourse and united action among composers, authors, publishers and producers." Barely noticeable amidst these soaring generalities was its true raison d'être, the hard-nosed economic function that made it more cartel than guild: "to grant licenses and collect royalties for the public representation of the works of its members . . . and to allot and distribute such royalties."[2]

The essence of ASCAP, as Nathan Burkan conceived it, following the model of France's Société des Auteurs, Compositeurs et Éditeurs de Musique (SACEM), was the pooling of copyrights. Members assigned their public performance rights to ASCAP and authorized it to issue licenses and institute copyright infringement suits in their names. The formation of the society in 1914 was a songwriter initiative, and from the outset there was tension between the two classes of members—songwriters who wished to monetize their previously unenforced exclusive right of public performance, and publishers who were long accustomed to paying for public performances, "plugs," to promote the sale of sheet music. Initially, the membership of the self-perpetuating board of directors and the division of royalties was stacked 2:1 in favor of songwriters over publishers, and members were free to withdraw their catalogs at any time. In 1920, in order to keep the major Tin Pan Alley publishers in the fold, the Articles of Association were amended to split board seats and royalties 50–50, and to require members to assign performing rights for five-year terms. (The knotty question whether it was songwriters or publishers who actually controlled those performance rights, we shall see, was deferred to a much later day.)

By the dawn of the Roaring Twenties, ASCAP exclusively licensed the performance rights to a formidable back catalog and to nearly every new mass-market hit—by its own reckoning, 90 percent "of the recognized, established, authors, composers, and publishers in the so-called 'popular' field."[3] An ASCAP licensee could use as many or as few of these songs as it wished, as often or as infrequently as it liked. ASCAP's product came in one size only, a "blanket license" to perform the entire repertoire for one fixed annual fee.

The directors of ASCAP made a fundamental choice at the outset—performers would neither be required nor permitted to take licenses. They were considered mere "servants for the people or establishments who engage them, and therefore should not be harassed in the earning of their livelihood by the imposition of any royalties."[4] ASCAP would only issue licenses to the operators of public performance venues. That was a limited market in the 1910s, when music was still enjoyed mostly in the home. Vaudeville was prospering, but by unwritten gentleman's agreement insisted upon by the publisher members, the major vaudeville circuits were never pressed to take licenses—it was too late in the day to reverse the direction in which money had always flowed between vaudeville and Tin Pan Alley.[5] Nor was the legitimate musical theater a potential market. The rights assigned to the society were limited to nondramatic performances of individual songs—so-called small rights. Producers of musical plays generally retained control of the

Founding members of ASCAP at the Hippodrome in 1916. From left: Gustave Kerker, Raymond Hubbell, Victor Herbert (seated), Harry Tierney, Louis A. Hirsch, Rudolf Friml, Robert Hood Bowers, Silvio Hein, A Baldwin Sloane, and Irving Berlin. (*Museum of the City of New York, White Studio*)

"grand rights." That left hotels and restaurants offering musical entertainment, including cabarets like Shanley's, dance halls, and—most promisingly—a rapidly growing population of motion picture theaters that would not think of exhibiting a silent picture without musical accompaniment, if not by an Al Melgard on organ, an Ira B. Arnstein on piano, or a symphony orchestra conducted by an Ernö Rapée, then at very least by some "amateur thumping a piano in a dark corner."[6]

Pricing was another novel problem. ASCAP had no established custom or economic model to draw upon, so it aimed low at first. Hotels and restaurants paid $5–$15 per month depending on the number of musicians employed and the type of entertainment provided. New York's Roseland Ballroom, "a dance hall with receipts of $4500 a day, paid a license fee of 50¢ a day," as did the Palais Royale, which at the time was paying Paul Whiteman's orchestra $3,600 per week. Movie theaters paid on average 10¢ per seat per year:

> The receipts of the Capitol Theatre, New York City, the leading moving picture house of America in 1922 were $58,000 a week, out of which they paid the American Society for their license $5.89 a week.... The 1922 net receipts of the moving picture industry of America, according to its own figures, were $520,000,000, from which the American Society received 1¢ out of every $20.[7]

That was a levy of .05 percent on movie exhibitors, for an admittedly indispensable accessory to their entertainments. ASCAP's directors figured that they would make up for these modest rates on volume, that music users would willingly pay a nominal price rather than bear the costs and risks of copyright infringement litigation. They miscalculated badly. By unilaterally imposing a tax on a business practice that had for long been carried on for free, ASCAP stirred up the strident rhetoric, paranoia, and concerted resistance typical of tax protests, to a degree grossly disproportionate to the dismal little millage that it was trying to extract.

After the Supreme Court ruled for ASCAP in *Herbert v. Shanley* in 1917, hotels and restaurants generally fell into line, but other music users remained recalcitrant. ASCAP hired musicians to ferret out infringements and appointed attorneys in every region of the country to deal with violators. The inspectors' lives were not "a bed of roses, for they not only in very many instances got cursed at, but in several instances have been kicked bodily out of the establishment which they visited by irate proprietors."[8] Nor did the regional attorneys, who received a quarter to a third of license fees collected in their territories, find the work lucrative:

> The persuading of establishments to take out licenses has been no easy job in the first place, entailing a great deal of correspondence, personal interviews and racing and chasing hither and thither, and in the second place, the ASCAP home office has been very easy on defendants even after judgment has been obtained against them, and has not permitted their local attorneys to insist upon the full payment of penalties prescribed by the Copyright Law.[9]

Only about a third of the 15,000 movie theaters in the United States agreed to take ASCAP licenses. The Motion Picture Theatre Owners of America encouraged this massive resistance by offering to defend any infringement suits brought against its members. In 1922, after a federal court in Philadelphia, which had sixty of those cases before it, rejected every defense to copyright infringement that its members had interposed,[10] the MPTOA brought its grievances against "the Music Trust" (or, more pointedly, "that select group of Jesse Jameses"[11] using "Shylock tactics,"[12] by whom the copyright law was "now being perverted into a legal blackjack"[13]) to the Federal Trade Commission and Attorney General Harry Daugherty. With its pooling of so many desirable copyrights, the theater owners argued, ASCAP possessed the ability to impose monopoly prices, to "take every dollar away from the public that they cared to."[14] They complained bitterly that representatives of ASCAP's publisher-members would importune them for plugs and provide complimentary sheet music, only to have ASCAP "turn around and sue us for back taxes in a very short time."[15] ASCAP inspectors, they claimed, would readily perjure themselves to prove up a copyright infringement:

> We absolutely refused to pay them blood money after our pianist assured us that she could play non-licensed music and keep away from music controlled by them. Then they notified us that on a western serial picture our pianist played "It's a Long Way to Tipperary." The accusation was so ridiculous that we took it as a joke, but when they seriously insisted, demanding $100.00 damages for infringement . . . we figured out that paying their license fee of $30.00 was the cheapest way out. What we would

like to know is: how can we escape similar proceedings? What's to prevent them from swearing that we played "The Holy City" in a Lloyd comedy?[16]

The FTC declined to intercede, finding that a claim for royalties, made in apparent good faith, was not "an unfair method of competition," because the parties were not in competition with each other and there was nothing unfair about the "assertion of a supposed legal right which is fully determinable by the Courts."[17] But at the Department of Justice, unfettered by the FTC's relatively narrow statutory mandate, the complaints were turned over to J. Edgar Hoover, who launched a full field investigation.

If the ASCAP of the early 1920s was, as its detractors claimed, a shakedown racket, it was a ludicrously inept one. Between the timid pricing of its licenses and the enormous expense involved in detecting infringements and taking hundreds of violators to court, to obtain damages that rarely exceeded the statutory minimum of $250, at the end of the day ASCAP's take was a pittance. It had no net revenue at all to distribute to members until 1921, when total royalty distributions were $112,000 and no songwriter received more than $742. (Even in 2012 dollars, still an underwhelming $8,000—this was Irving Berlin, after all.) The $72 that up-and-comers like Fred Ahlert and Irving Caesar were paid was closer to the mean.[18] A significant portion of the revenue pie was set aside for the relief of widows and orphans, and the "artificial respiration"[19] of unproductive but well-liked old-timers. A bootlegging operation so small-time wouldn't have been worth the Prohibition Bureau's bother. But for ASCAP's members these distributions were a welcome supplement to sheet music and mechanical royalties, which were, with the imminent arrival of radio broadcasting, about to see a severe decline.

The Bureau of Navigation, under the purview of Secretary of Commerce Herbert Hoover, had licensed the first thirty-one radio broadcast stations in 1921. Two hundred more licenses were issued in 1922, mostly to large commercial interests—radio equipment manufacturers, newspapers, hotels, department stores—looking to promote their primary businesses. In April 1922, ASCAP's directors received the opinion of their general counsel, Nathan Burkan, that commercial broadcasters' musical programs constituted public performances for profit under the copyright law.[20] A few weeks later, ASCAP sent all broadcast license holders a copy of Justice Holmes's opinion in *Herbert v. Shanley*, under cover of a disingenuously amicable letter:

Due to the unprecedented rapid development of "Radio" in its popular aspects, a situation has been created wherein authors, composers, and publishers, as copyright proprietors, are deprived of revenue and rights, through the infringement of their copyrights . . . but apparently in the very rapidity of this development the proprietors of broadcasting stations have in good faith overlooked the rights of these parties.

"The position of the composers, authors and publishers to 'Radio' is not a hostile or unfriendly one," the letter continued. "They realize the great potential service which it may render to the whole people, and they would not be disposed, even if they could, to hamper or retard its fullest development and service."[21] Notwithstanding its diplomatic tone, there was no mistaking the underlying threat: Awfully nice revolutionary new medium of mass communications you have there; it would be a shame if anything were to happen to it.

Among the letter's recipients was David Sarnoff, who had recently been promoted to general manager at the Radio Corporation of America, a cooperative venture of General Electric, Westinghouse, and American Telephone & Telegraph, the major patent holders in radio telephony. All four entities were ramping up to service a growing market for transmission and receiving equipment, demand that they expected to stoke through their own broadcasting operations. Even to Sarnoff's "lay mind" it was apparent that Justice Holmes's *Shanley* opinion was "rather sweeping."[22] RCA's counsel confirmed his fears: "I see no distinction between these cases and our own where we render our broadcast service to increase the sale of our receiving sets. That we do obtain an indirect profit is fully shown by the tremendous increase in orders that pour in as a result of the broadcasting."[23]

Sarnoff agreed with his attorneys that ASCAP's demand for royalties should be addressed simply as a business proposition, and that there was no "reason to be incensed by their attitude."[24] Nor was he offended by ASCAP's opening, highly negotiable demand, a fee schedule based on a station's power, beginning at $5 per day. But Sarnoff saw profound ramifications. Radio was relying on unpaid performers happy to work for the publicity; the talent would surely grow restive if songwriters were paid in cash. Nor did Sarnoff want to set any precedents that would come back to haunt him later when—as he then envisioned—he would be operating a small number of "super-stations" reaching tens of millions of receivers nationwide, and when, he hoped, many thousands of restaurants and other places of business would be using RCA

Radiola and Loud Speaker combinations to entertain their customers, in lieu of live entertainment. ASCAP could only have exacerbated Sarnoff's anxieties when it put forth an ill-considered proposal to collect a $5 annual fee from every home radio user.[25] Sarnoff put his stations on strict orders to avoid using ASCAP music while he played for time.

As with much else in the development of commercial broadcasting, Sarnoff was writing the playbook that others would follow. By the middle of 1924, ASCAP had licensed only thirty-six stations, at an average annual fee of $500, arrived at through laborious station-by-station dickering. "The broadcasters," one of ASCAP's regional attorneys complained, "have followed the proverbial ostrich with their heads in the sand."[26] And those were the more docile ones, those who like Sarnoff recognized ASCAP's rights and simply asked that it defer enforcing them until radio had matured, assuming it ever would, as a viable commercial proposition. Many others, including Sarnoff's counterpart at the Zenith Radio Corporation in Chicago, Eugene F. McDonald, were genuinely incensed by ASCAP's attitude and were ready, through their newly formed National Association of Broadcasters (NAB), to put up a fight—a "finish fight"[27]—with no acceptable outcome but the dissolution of the Music Trust.

The NAB conceded that the performing rights provisions of the copyright law, although conceived long before the advent of broadcasting, were at least "ambiguous" as applied to radio.[28] It had no interest in following the path of the motion picture theater owners in trying to wear down ASCAP by defending numerous infringement suits, and it rejected ASCAP's overtures that they contrive a single *Shanley*-like test case to settle the issue. The NAB chose, instead, to go on the offensive, launching an aggressive legal and public relations blitz calculated to gut the public performance right and destroy ASCAP.

It began, in the spring of 1924, with one of the first great demonstrations of the incipient power of broadcasting to mold public opinion, a propaganda campaign designed to drum up support for a "free radio music" bill that was pending in Congress. The bill, the product of intensive NAB lobbying, would have added a proviso to the 1909 Copyright Act that "copyright control shall not extend to public performances, whether for profit or without profit . . . by the use of the radio." NAB executive chairman Paul B. Klugh's radio address on behalf of the bill reached an audience of millions over a station hook-up provided by the NAB's most powerful member, AT&T, and no law or regulation required that the opposition be given equal time or, for that matter, any time at all. At the outset of hearings before the Senate Committee on Patents, Clarence Dill of Washington, the bill's sponsor, reported that "more telegrams have come in here on this bill than have ever come on any bill, except that for the declaration of war in 1917."[29]

David Sarnoff of RCA had told another congressional committee: "We broadcast primarily so that those who purchase our receiving devices may have something to feed those receiving instruments with. Without a broadcasting sending station, the broadcast receiver is just a refrigerator without any ice in it."[30] In sharp contrast, Eugene McDonald of Zenith tried to convince the Dill Committee that there was no money at all to be had in broadcasting. McDonald testified that Zenith's broadcasting activities had no effect on its sales of radio receivers, and that it broadcasted "simply because I have got that fever, the thrill of broadcasting. I love it."[31] Broadcasters could not convert their growing audiences into direct revenue, he said, because as soon as one "put obvious advertising on the air that station would be killed. The public would take care of that. There would be nobody listening."[32] Broadcasting, he insisted, was a public service. The NAB might just as well have brought a fife and drum corps to the hearing, so shamelessly did its witnesses wrap themselves in the flag. NAB director Klugh made an appeal on behalf of the "invalids, shut-ins, to whom radio certainly brings great relief from their physical and mental worries," "the blind, who are certainly much benefitted by hearing things going on in the world," and "deafened" people, who "can hear through radio what they cannot hear with even those devices provided for hearing."[33] The director of occupational therapy and recreation at Walter Reed Army Hospital appeared on the NAB's behalf, attesting to radio's therapeutic value in bringing "up-to-date" music to bedridden soldiers.[34]

When it was his turn to testify, E. Claude Mills, ASCAP's administrative committee chairman, made it clear he had heard his fill of NAB smarm:

> We think that radio is the greatest contribution that science has ever made to man, that it will bring about a universal language, that it will make wars impossible, that it will make the farmer happy, and that in general it will render the greatest service to humankind of anything that has ever been conceived.[35]

But "Over There," Mills reminded the senators, had been written by one of ASCAP's members, so the society would take a back seat to no one where service to country and support for our troops was concerned.

Mills's Tin Pan Alley-by-way-of-Texas sarcasm was lost on NAB's legal counsel, Charles H. Tuttle, the white shoe New York lawyer and devout Episcopal vestryman. Tuttle often quoted Mills's "greatest service to humankind" snark as though it had been the sincerest and highest encomium radio could possibly receive. The passion with which Tuttle spearheaded the NAB's anti-ASCAP initiatives, before the legislative, judicial, and executive branches, suggests that he may have considered it a gross understatement.

In a carefully choreographed move on the day before the Dill Committee hearings began, Tuttle had filed an antitrust lawsuit against ASCAP on behalf of one of its original and most important publisher-members, Waterson, Berlin & Snyder. A few months earlier, Henry Waterson (dubbed the "Judas Iscariot of the music business"[36] by ASCAP's colorful president, longtime *Ziegfeld Follies* lyricist Gene Buck) had allowed the NAB to disseminate publicly a letter in which he stated that his firm was seeking to withdraw from ASCAP because it was "not in sympathy" with its efforts to license broadcasting stations, hotels, and moving picture theaters, "agencies which we believe to be of distinct value to us in advertising our products."[37] There can be little doubt that both the lawsuit and the letter, which was read over the air by many stations, had been ginned up by the NAB. Tuttle laid out for the Senate Committee the gist of his antitrust theory, which stood for many years as the most nuanced analysis of the issue:

> They have the ability to fix the price and they exercise it. They have the ability to punish any recalcitrant member and they exercise it, and they have the ability to say to anybody, "You shall not put out a single piece of copyrighted music unless you buy from us wholesale," and they exercise that. I do not know what are the other indices of illegal monopoly. They are all there.[38]

He implored the committee not to be taken in by the modest fees ASCAP had imposed up to that point. "We are in the same position as the mouse who accepts the friendship of the cat's paw," Tuttle warned. "There will come a time when playing with us ceases, and there will be a time when mastication begins."[39]

The senators, however, expressed little interest in antitrust issues that were before the courts or under investigation by the Department of Justice. Tuttle was more effective when he turned to the NAB's public-interest arguments. Relying heavily on a Yoda-like pronouncement from a House committee report that accompanied the 1909 Copyright Act—"not primarily for the benefit of the author, but primarily for the benefit of the public, such rights are given"[40]—Tuttle provided some legal substance to go with the patriotic gore that the NAB's lay witnesses had served up:

> This is not an issue involving some inherent or natural right to property, it is a right which has been created by the public for the public interests solely, and the public has an entire right to hold that interest in accordance with new inventions and new circumstances for its own interest, without invading anybody's invested right at all. At common law there was no such thing.[41]

What Congress giveth, Tuttle was arguing, Congress is free to taketh away when the greater public good requires. And the public good served by radio broadcasting should trump any private rights improvidently granted to music copyright holders before its invention.

In the end, the NAB's public-interest theory proved too much; intellectual property protection by its nature and design restrains, "for limited times," the dissemination of beneficial products and services. Kentucky senator Augustus Stanley best illustrated the difficulty, with some gentle ridicule of Senator Dill: "I am in thorough harmony with your idea of giving the people all the music and all the eloquence and everything they want and give it to them free because the people like that and I like to please the people." Accordingly, suggested Stanley, why not broaden the bill to abrogate the patents that were driving up the price of radio apparatus? "It would help very much to make the air free."[42]

The free radio music bill died with the adjournment of the 68th Congress, in no small measure because, as Tuttle had presciently forewarned his clients,[43] the theater and hotel owners crashed the party, pleading that they too did their part for God and the commonweal, and therefore were entitled to free music as well.

Within a year, Eugene McDonald's prophecy that advertising would be radio's death knell had proved unequivocally wrong. Many stations were very profitably selling time to advertisers, following the "toll" broadcasting model pioneered by AT&T's station WEAF in New York, where sponsors bought blocks of time to present programming they produced themselves. The concept was so novel it required a clinically precise explanation: "The radio broadcaster renders entertainments varied unexpectedly from time to time with talks on where and when to buy commodities and commending such commodities. This advertising is paid for, yet those who listen do so mainly in expectation of more entertainment to follow."[44] Although some courts initially resisted the conclusion, holding that a public performance required "an audience congregated for the purpose of hearing that which transpires at the place of amusement,"[45] the receipt of direct advertising revenues soon put to rest any lingering doubt that *Shanley* would be applied to broadcasters.

Its hand strengthened considerably by the introduction of a direct source of profit into the broadcasting equation, ASCAP sent out license renewals that ratcheted up its base fees several-fold, with additional charges for each hour of sponsored programming. The broadcasters regrouped and returned to Congress with a new tack. Copyright owners, they now acknowledged, were entitled to compensation for over-the-air performances of their music, but the logical way to provide it would be to extend the compulsory licensing provisions of the 1909 Copyright Act that applied to recordings, thereby requiring copyright holders to offer licenses to broadcasters at royalty rates set by Congress. Compulsory licensing, as the NAB saw it, would have the twin virtues of providing predictability and rendering ASCAP superfluous. Senator Dill dutifully introduced a bill to implement this approach, and in April 1926 a familiar cast of characters—Tuttle and Klugh on one side, Mills, Buck, and Burkan on the other—reconvened for joint Senate–House hearings on the new Dill Bill. Once again, representatives of ASCAP and the NAB—two private, vested interests—discoursed at length on their competing views of the public interest, making these hearings a stark, early example of a persistent phenomenon in the legislative history of copyright law, the naive insistence of Congress that the interests of an unrepresented public can be, in the words of Professor Jessica Litman, "somehow approximated by the push and shove among opposing industry representatives."[46]

The highlight of the 1926 hearings was Burkan's magisterial presentation of the case against the constitutionality of compulsory licensing. Burkan—an up-by-his-bootstraps Jew, copyright scholar, hard-nosed "theatrical lawyer," soft-touch friend to starving artists, and Tammany Hall fixer—was Charles Tuttle's natural foil. He had long bristled over compulsory licensing, and the stingy two cents per song royalty set by Congress, as blights upon the 1909 Copyright Act's recognition of an exclusive mechanical reproduction right, Burkan's signature legislative victory. The NAB proposal provided a high-profile occasion to have Congress revisit the issue of compulsory licensing.

Charles H. Tuttle led the National Association of Broadcasters' campaign for free radio music before all three branches of government. (*Courtesy Charles H. Tuttle Literary Trust*)

Drawing upon a vast array of historical sources, Burkan argued that the constitutional power to secure for limited times "the exclusive right" to writings meant that Congress could do no more, and no less, than grant copyright holders "the power to exclude others from making any profitable use of the work during the term of the copyright." A compulsory license, he concluded, "is the antithesis of the exclusive right."[47]

Weary of playing the go-between in the troubled courtship of ASCAP and the NAB, Congress took no action on the compulsory licensing bill. In the fall of 1926, Senator Dill publicly expressed his hope that the NAB and ASCAP would reach an accommodation that would obviate the need for legislation. In the meantime, ASCAP had continued to best radio in a war of attrition. In August 1926, the Department of Justice announced that it would be taking no antitrust action against ASCAP. The department's lawyers concluded that licensing intangible rights to put on musical performances that were "entirely local in character" did not touch upon interstate "trade or commerce," and therefore was not subject to federal antitrust scrutiny.[48] (This generally followed the reasoning of an opinion by Justice Holmes in the famous *Baseball Case* of 1922,[49] considered one of Holmes's weakest efforts and an anomaly in the law of antitrust

ASCAP's founding spirit and legal mastermind, Nathan Burkan, repeatedly thwarted the NAB. (*Courtesy ASCAP*)

that the Supreme Court would never apply to anything but the national pastime.[50]) Broadcasters transmitting across state lines might stand on a different footing than theaters, hotels, and dance halls, but because the state of the law was "unsettled," the Justice Department deferred to Congress for clarification. Waterson, Berlin & Snyder abandoned its private antitrust suit and rejoined ASCAP. For Charles Tuttle, having failed to win relief for the broadcasters in any of the three branches of government, but with his political profile much enhanced by the exposure his role in the ASCAP-radio war provided, an impending vacancy in the U.S. Attorney's Office in Manhattan beckoned, with the Executive Mansion in Albany looming in the distance.

By the end of 1926, RCA had acquired AT&T's broadcasting operations and was preparing to launch the National Broadcasting Company "Red" and "Blue" networks, with top-drawer paid talent and advertising revenues conservatively projected to be $15,000,000 in the first year—"the biggest step so far in the history of broadcasting," *Variety* rightly declared.[51] David Sarnoff now concluded that a few thousand dollars per station per year for copyrighted music was an acceptable cost of doing business. The NAB, following Sarnoff's lead and taking Senator Dill's hint, reached a five-year agreement with ASCAP providing for gradually rising. By 1931, ASCAP was collecting an estimated $1 million annually from broadcasters.

Five years of relative peace and rising radio fees allowed ASCAP to lower its overhead costs from more than 65 percent to below 25 percent of revenues, and to increase its distributions from about $320,000 in 1925 to over $1.3 million in 1931, with the largest writers' shares quadrupling from $1,300 to $5,200.[52] Small rights were becoming big money; by 1934 they were "the principal source of income for both writer and publisher."[53] With its institutional future reasonably secure for the first time, ASCAP could turn its energies to the next big thing. On August 5, 1926, Warner Brothers had exhibited its first Vitaphone feature, *Don Juan*, with a synchronized score that included several pieces from the ASCAP catalog. Within days, ASCAP served notice of infringement, and soon Vitaphone had agreed to pay $100,000 annually for synchronization rights. Tin Pan Alley had grabbed Hollywood's attention. But the studios had learned an important lesson from the futile resistance of theater owners and broadcasters—if you can't beat 'em, join 'em.

By 1930, most commercial music users were locked into multiyear blanket licenses that provided unlimited access to the entire ASCAP repertoire for a flat fee—a strong disincentive from incurring the cost and administrative fuss of using any other copyrighted music. Membership in ASCAP had become more than a nice way to supplement one's income; it was a practical necessity for anyone hoping to have their music performed publicly and, if performed, to collect a royalty for it. "For publishers and composers, to be outside of ASCAP was to be a nonentity in the music business."[54]

When it first took on radio in 1922, ASCAP was a closed shop comprised of about 250 elite popular songwriters and a few dozen of their publishers, the vast majority of them based in New York City. A statistic being widely tossed about (bearing in mind that in the ASCAP–radio war, the tactic of "pulling numbers out of the air was used repeatedly"[55]) had it that there were more than 6,000 composers and authors of copyrighted music in the

United States. The NAB's propaganda campaigns, in which one-finger song-writers driving Rolls Royces and summering in Europe figured as promi-nently as the welfare queens in Cadillacs of a latter day, helped to swell those ranks further by leading the public to believe "here is a 'get-rich-quick' busi-ness for anyone."[56] Publicity surrounding ASCAP's growing revenues swelled the numbers applying for membership. Few of these applicants, however, could add marginal value to ASCAP's blanket license; most new members would simply dilute the distribution pool.

The original criteria for membership set out in ASCAP's Articles of Association were liberal: "Every composer of music and every author of musical works who regularly practices the profession of writing music or the text of lyrics of musical works shall be eligible."[57] Later, this was amended to also require that the applicant "have had not less than five works regularly published."[58] An unwritten rule required that an applica-tion be endorsed by two members. The membership committee, more-over, had discretion to reject applicants who met these objective requirements, and it frequently did so if it felt the published works were not "in vogue," that is, not "sufficiently popular to bring income to the Society."[59] Therein lay the catch. With ASCAP membership virtually a prerequisite to publication by a top firm, and to the public performances needed to establish "vogue," how could a newcomer qualify for member-ship in the first place?

Ira B. Arnstein first applied for ASCAP membership in March 1931. "The reason why for 17 years I did not apply," he explained, "is because I earned a good living composing and teaching. Unfortunately, things reversed, and I now find myself in very desperate circumstances." His appli-cation, duly proposed and seconded by two members in good standing, Edward B. Marks and L. Wolfe Gilbert, was supported by evidence of nu-merous publications and contained Arnstein's assurances that, contrary to a rumor being spread by some members who were irate over the still-pend-ing Shilkret indictment, he was not a Communist.[60] Whether Marks and Gilbert were genuinely enthused over Arnstein's commercial prospects as they worked with him in turning "A Mother's Prayer" into a popular song, or whether these gentlemen, both of whom had been slower than their peers to join ASCAP and who relished their images as gadflies, were just sticking a needle in the organization's eye, it cannot be determined at this far remove.

To ASCAP it was simply a case of someone who "refused to join the Society until he lost whatever talents he had theretofore had."[61] Arnstein's application languished for over a year in the membership committee, until it was finally decided:

> The applicant is not qualified as a composer. . . . His catalogue as listed could not possibly be considered as making a contribution to the earning capacity of the Society and it would be manifestly unjust to those members whose works do contribute to that purpose that their dividends should be reduced in order to make payments to a member whose works contribute nothing of value to the repertoire.[62]

Arnstein was at least in good company. The list of songwriters black-balled by ASCAP during the 1930s was a long and distinguished one. It included some major artists who worked in disfavored genres, hot jazz pioneer Jelly Roll Morton and singing cowboy Gene Autry being two famously egregious examples. ASCAP's restricted membership left room for a few small-niche performing rights organizations to spring up early in the decade. Paul Heinecke, the U.S. representative for such prestigious foreign publishers as Breitkopf & Hartel, formed the Society of European Stage Authors & Composers (SESAC), which early on added gospel, country, and polka music, all of which were shunned by ASCAP, to a core repertoire of European classical music. Yiddish theater composers led by Sholom Secunda and Joseph Rumshinsky founded the Society of Jewish Composers, Publishers and Songwriters to license their performing rights, primarily to a few Yiddish radio stations and Jewish resorts on the East Coast. The competition that these organizations provided was inconsequential, although their mere existence would be helpful to ASCAP when the government's attention returned, as it inevitably would, to the question of illegal monopoly.

Arnstein protested the rejection of his application in continuing correspondence with ASCAP officers over the course of several years. The inspiration for *Broadway Music* probably came in the wake of a particularly caustic exchange with E. Claude Mills in the fall of 1935, after Mills told him:

> The plain facts are, Mr. Arnstein, that your works are not sufficiently performed in establishments licensed by ASCAP to justify a membership

which would result in a participation by you in the earnings derived by ASCAP from such establishments and distributed amongst the members whose works are used in such performances. You are not "barred as a member from the society." When the records show that your works are reasonably active on the programs of establishments licensed by ASCAP, I am very sure the Membership Committee will give prompt and favorable consideration to your application. . . . I am sorry you feel so abused.[63]

"First of all, I must correct your impression that I desire to become a member of your society," Arnstein replied. "It is true that I applied for membership several years ago, but since I found out that the ASCAP is controlled by a handful of people having no knowledge of music, and no sense of truth or justice, I lost all desire to be one of them." And how, Arnstein asked, would it be possible for his works to become active on programs licensed by ASCAP?

Assuming I have ten songs now which would become international hits if I only had a chance to let the world hear them, how would you as a sincere and honest administrator suggest I go about it, when all avenues are closed to me? I doubt whether there is another man in N.Y. who knows as much about the workings of Tin Pan Alley as I do. So when you think that a few evasive words will convince me that your Society wishes to be just to me and everyone else I must close with an outburst of mirth. Ha Ha Ha . . .

Laughingly yours,
Ira B. Arnstein[64]

Arnstein's grievance was neither wholly imaginary nor unusual. The FTC and Department of Justice were hearing with increasing frequency from songwriters and independent publishers who had been rejected for membership and were, in fact, finding all avenues closed to them. The Allen & Harrison Music Company presented a well-documented complaint to the FTC in 1933, after ASCAP rejected its membership application for lack of the required two sponsors. "In view of the fact that every new member decreases the share of the existing members in the income of the Society, the rule amounts to practically a restraint because of the unwillingness of publishers to endorse a new applicant." With substantially all of radio under ASCAP blanket licenses, Allen & Harrison complained, "no radio station will permit a new song to be broadcast over their facilities, and especially will they not do so if they are obliged to pay for the privilege."[65] The CBS and NBC networks were particularly strict in rejecting any non-ASCAP music, even if offered royalty-free, creating a widespread impression that they were following an edict at least tacitly imposed by ASCAP. But in fact this was simply the pull of the "commercial force of gravity," an inherent consequence of blanket licensing, exactly as Charles Tuttle had theorized in his 1926 congressional testimony on behalf of the broadcasters. "Having committed ourselves to [ASCAP's] catalogue for a substantial sum," Tuttle hypothesized, before any broadcaster had actually done so, "it is perfectly obvious that the natural tendency will be to confine ourselves to that particular catalogue, with the result that the chance of relationship between the independents and the broadcasters is much lessened and the tendency to monopoly is increased."[66]

Far from being cathartic, the act of writing *Broadway Music* nourished Arnstein's inner demons, as though the fulminations emanating from his characters' mouths constituted proof corroborating his a priori theory of everything. As perceived slights and actual misfortunes piled up over the next several years, Arnstein's hold on reality only grew more tenuous.

A casual remark, almost certainly misheard, seems to have triggered the next leg down in Arnstein's psychological spiral. As he was leaving the old Post Office Building after the arguments in the *Marks* appeal, on a nasty January day in 1936, Arnstein spotted his attorney, Sydney Krause, huddled with Theodore Richter on the portico, conversing jocularly while they waited for a driving rain to subside. It was an ordinary moment of professional collegiality between adversaries, the type of respite from battle that lawyers require in order to sustain their mental health, but which never cease to leave their clients nonplussed. Arnstein was sure that he overheard Richter say to Krause, "We fooled him, didn't we?"

After chewing over that remark for many months, Arnstein wrote a letter to Judge Learned Hand accusing Richter of having submitted falsified exhibits and a doctored trial transcript to the court of appeals, with Krause's acquiescence.[67] At Hand's suggestion,[68] Arnstein filed a motion to set aside the judgment on the ground of fraud. For the first time, he drafted his own legal papers ("I am appealing to the Honorable Judges according to logic, rather than law; if the two have nothing in common, the fault is not mine"[69]) and represented himself *pro se* in a bizarre hearing before a Special Master appointed by the Second Circuit to investigate the charges. The proceeding devolved quickly into Arnstein's first attempt to lay out his bill of particulars against ASCAP. "The case of Ira Arnstein vs. E. B. Marks is so in name only," Arnstein asserted. "The actual fact is that it is the Tin Pan Alley Publishers vs. Arnstein."[70] The Special Master found no evidence to support the charge of tampering with evidence, and declined to pass upon any extraneous issues.[71]

Arnstein was scratching out a living with the help of two live-in voice students who shared the rent on his apartment on West 71st Street, a few steps from Central Park, and with wages from a job with the Federal Theatre Project of the Works Progress Administration. The Theatre Project had begun to put musicians on its payroll in May 1936, within weeks of beginning operations, after its original plan to requisition musicians from the Federal Music Project on an as-needed basis proved unworkable.[72] Arnstein, an early hire, became convinced that the musical directors for the Theatre Project's New York City unit were "tools" of ASCAP. He complained that they had fired one classically oriented conductor who did not want to plug popular songs, and that they had rejected Arnstein's score for another production so that ASCAP numbers could be used instead. He was dismissed from the Theatre Project in November 1936. His supervisors had concluded that he suffered from a "persecution mania," though Arnstein claimed that, too, was a slander being spread by ASCAP—perhaps as self-refuting an assertion as was ever made.

The only way to escape ASCAP's persecutions, Arnstein decided, was to get out of New York City altogether. So he took his pupils on a road trip. Their first stop was Washington, D.C. Upon learning that the Department of Justice had reopened its ASCAP antitrust investigation in 1934, Arnstein wrote to Attorney General Homer S. Cummings, volunteering to provide evidence of "dishonest acts too numerous to mention," including "a conspiracy among them to kill every song or musical composition not published by their group."[73] The assistant attorney general for antitrust, Harold M. Stephens, urged Arnstein to submit a detailed statement.[74] For once, Arnstein had the attention of authorities in high places who would be favorably disposed to investigate any plausible grievance. But by the time he appeared at the Justice Department for an interview on December 1, 1936, the events of the intervening two years had left him in far too

Ira B. Arnstein in 1936.

addled a mental state to be of any assistance to the government. Arnstein, the interview notes indicate, made no effort to "connect his troubles with the antitrust suit against ASCAP which is now pending." Instead, he offered up a tale ripped from the pages of *Broadway Music*:

> He has become convinced that music publishers and their organizations are engaged in a racket and conspiracy which includes stealing songs, reaping the rewards from them and "fixing" cases if need be in the Federal and other courts. . . . He is supposed to have been shadowed and had his rooms watched and entered in a search for new material.

Arnstein's debriefer then pressed him for more pertinent information:

> This irritated him and he said that if he presented 2,000 facts no one in the Government would be convinced and that I could not recognize "an open and shut case." . . . He left in evident disgust and with the announced

conviction that there was no justice, either in Washington or in New York, and did not see how there could be a Department of Justice.[75]

From the nation's capital, Arnstein and his students headed to the sun and fun capital of the world, Miami Beach, where the local press noted the arrival of this "interesting new-comer to Miami's art colony." Arnstein told the papers he had come for a winter vacation, but that he also hoped to mount a production of *The Song of David* before the season was over.[76] Whatever the original plan had been, Arnstein found a city flush with hotels in dire need of performers to provide the nonstop entertainment programs their snowbird guests had been promised. The brand new Shoreham Hotel, an art deco low-rise on South Beach designed by Lawrence Murray Dixon, hired the trio to give white-dinner-jacket concerts on its ocean-side "Tropical Patio." That, however, proved not to be the right setting or the right crowd for such Arnstein tunes as the funereal "Sadness Overwhelms My Soul," even when retrofitted with special lyrics and retitled "Sunshine on Miami Beach." The engagement ended prematurely, and the troupe returned home.

Arnstein was certain that ASCAP had something to do with his losing the Shoreham Hotel gig. Upon his return to New York in early 1937 he was determined to confront his tormentors head on. This he accomplished with a piece of street theater that would forever secure his place in urban legend. Arnstein donned homemade sandwich-board signs and picketed, five to seven hours per day for ten weeks, outside the Sixth Avenue entrance to ASCAP's new headquarters in Rockefeller Center's RCA Building. (ASCAP's decision to take a lease in the same premises occupied by NBC was consistent with its pattern of alpha-territorial behavior—its previous location was in the Paramount Building, on the very site where once stood the vanquished Shanley's Restaurant.)

The human billboard—"animated sandwiches," Dickens had called them a century earlier[77]—had been a visual cue that connoted "failure" since long before the Great Depression.[78] Still, "no matter how insignificant I am," Arnstein was convinced, "thousands of people who stop to read my signs do not know it."[79] As unwelcome, provocative, and lacking in self-awareness as Leopold Bloom in Barney Kiernan's Pub, Arnstein was met with a mix of hostility and condescension. While some ASCAP members took the time to chat civilly with him, others jeered and heckled him. The sight of the animated sandwich left a lasting impression on all of them, although their memories differed as to the actual content of Arnstein's signs. Sigmund Spaeth, perhaps thinking of Arnstein's courtroom exhibits, wrote that the sandwich boards displayed stolen musical notes.[80] Jack Lawrence, writing almost seventy years after the fact, recalled that Arnstein's sign read, front and back, "I, Ira Arnstein, Claim that my Songs have been Stolen by the Following ASCAP Writers," followed by a long list of names.[81] Nathaniel Shilkret's version, too elegant to possibly be true, nonetheless captures perfectly the essence of the protest. He recalled Arnstein carrying a spartan, sardonic send-up of ASCAP's *cri de guerre*—"Justice for Genius"—that read simply "UNFAIR TO GENIUS."[82]

The only reliable, contemporary account appeared in *Variety*, under the headline "For the Curious—That Picket is Mr. Arnstein":

> Fore card of his picketing sandwich reads: "I am protesting against the pirating of all my songs by the American Society of Composers, Authors and Publishers. They are making millions, while I am starving." On the rear card Arnstein has pasted sheet copies of tunes which he claims were lifted from manuscripts of his.[83]

When the weather started to turn cold, his picket having failed to get any discernable rise out of ASCAP management, Arnstein put away the signs and picked up his pen. In November 1937, acting as his own lawyer, and with leave of court to proceed *in forma pauperis* (excused from paying the usual fees and costs in light of his poverty), Arnstein filed what *Variety* dubbed the "MultiSuit," *Arnstein v. American Society of Composers, Authors and Publishers, et al.* There were twenty-three defendants in all, a rogue's gallery of those who had given Arnstein umbrage during the ten years since he first tried to find profit in writing popular music: ASCAP, the Music Publishers and Songwriters Protective Associations, the CBS and NBC radio networks, Warner Brothers Pictures, music publishers Witmark, Harms, Feist, Irving Berlin Inc., E. B. Marks, many individual officers and directors of these entities, and, for good measure, Nathaniel Shilkret and Emery Deutsch.

The MultiSuit complaint is what a decade's worth of spleen looks like. Arnstein alleged that he had "unintentionally aroused a bitter antagonism and hatred" among ASCAP's leaders. As a result, ASCAP had barred him from membership despite his meeting the society's formal criteria, "deprived him of all income and stamped him as an outcast to be shunned by all publishers, theatrical producers, motion picture producers, radio sponsors, etc.," and "encouraged all its members to plagiarize all his songs which he submitted to various publishers." Arnstein insisted that this was purely a conspiracy and not a copyright infringement case, but as evidence of ASCAP's "diabolical scheme" he cited numerous specific instances of piracy by its members, some old and familiar, some new. The conspirators had induced his students to become "stoolpigeons and spies," hired stooges to break into his lodgings, induced attorneys to drop his cases, and spread rumors that he was a lunatic to potential employers. In sum,

> all of the defendants have worked in harmony with each other, and have conspired with each other to rob the plaintiff of all his creative work, have agreed about their methods, have agreed about spreading lies about his character, his mental state, and his musical ability, and are using such malicious propaganda wherever he attempts to get employment.[84]

The MultiSuit was the closest thing to a full-scale production of *Broadway Music* that would ever be staged in New York City.

MY BEER IS A SHAME

*For a number of years, I and all other owners of dance halls have been forced
to pay tribute to these Jew racketeers. The Federal Govt. took Capone.
Can't it take the ASCAP?*
—Letter to Representative James Hughes (D-WI)

The songwriting team of Sammy Cahn and Saul Chaplin was an indigenous
product of the Age of the Songwriter, the two men having had only a passing
acquaintance with the Tin Pan Alley of old. They were both in their mid-
twenties in 1937, working in relative comfort as salaried employees of
Warner Brothers' New York-based music publishing and short subject divisions, when they conceived "Bei Mir Bist Du Schön (Means That You're
Grand)." Like their close contemporaries Jack Lawrence and Arthur Altman,
Cahn and Chaplin had the misfortune of running afoul of Ira B. Arnstein the
first time they hit one out of the park.

The sequence of events that led three Norwegian-American teenagers
from Minnesota, a discouraged sisters' act on the brink of disbanding, to
record this randy little Yinglish burlesque is another unlikely music business
tale that lies buried under layers of unnecessary embellishments. It is possible to piece together the most likely scenario with the help of contemporaneous legal documents. Cahn told Warner's attorneys that he and Chaplin

happened to be in a Harlem nightclub when they heard a Yiddish song performed "by two colored fellows—the reaction of the audience was so great we decided to make an English version."[1] The song, "Bei Mir Bistu Shein," had been written in 1933 by Sholom Secunda, the youngest and last of the great Yiddish Theatre composers, with lyricist Jacob Jacobs, for a romantic comedy that had a short run in Brooklyn. Cahn and Chaplin found a copy of the sheet music and approached the publishers, Jacob and Joseph Kammen, for permission to do an adaptation. The Kammens, it turned out, had printed the music for Secunda and Jacobs, but had not acquired any rights to the song. They acted immediately to tie up that loose end.

Secunda had just returned to New York after a summer-long stay in Hollywood, where he had tried vainly to assimilate to its culture—taking up golf, fishing, and going to the fights, learning the differences between the three branches of the Brown Derby, and studiously avoiding any schmoozing with other Yiddish theater types—while looking for a job with one of the studios. When he could no longer tolerate the frustration of interview appointments not kept by busy music directors, and the "anguish, anxiety, tenseness, and superhuman suspense" of waiting to hear back from those he had managed to see, he had come home to take the position of music director at Maurice Schwartz's Yiddish Art Theatre. Having abandoned any hopes of succeeding outside the "Jewish field," he considered his half share of the $30 that the Kammens offered for the "Bei Mir Bistu Shein" copyright found money.[2]

Without altering a note of Secunda's chorus and with only minor changes to the verse, Cahn and Chaplin were able to wring out "all the Jewish flourishes" and give the song a little more swing.[3] A boyhood friend of Cahn's, Lou Levy, an artists and repertoire man for Decca Records, matched the Cahn-Chaplin "Bei Mir" with the Andrews Sisters. Intended originally as a "B" side, its commercial potential must have been immediately apparent. Within days of the recording session, and well before its release during Christmas week 1937, Warner Brothers' Harms publishing subsidiary had made an arrangement with the Kammens for the rights to publish the English version. Warner's music department was soon busy placing the song in any and every plausible vehicle the studio had in production, including the screwball comedy *Love, Honor and Behave*—in which, among other incongruous cues, "Bei Mir Bist du Schön" serves as the musical backdrop for a Harvard-Yale tennis match. Benny Goodman added "Bei Mir" to the program for his path-breaking January 16, 1938 Carnegie Hall concert, with a solo by trumpeter Ziggy Elman that gloriously restores the "Jewish flourishes."

The title lyric, the only part of the original Yiddish preserved by Cahn, was a mondegreen waiting to happen—"My Mere Bits of Shame" and "My Beer, Mr. Shane" were among the earliest recorded mishearings—but the language barrier didn't impede the wheels of commerce. The *New York Post's* Michel Mok reported that "records of the ditty are selling like aspirin tablets at a legion convention . . . those in the know believe [the sheet music] is outselling 'Yes! We Have No Bananas' and 'The Music Goes 'Round and Around' when those hymns were at their height." Mok spoke to Secunda, who was remarkably good-humored and circumspect—the Kammens, he was sure, had acted in good faith and would do right by him; he was just grateful, thank God, to have a steady job, a family, and his health.[4]

Secunda possessed the instincts of a good press agent. The story of how he threw away a lifetime annuity for $15 was a nice bit of public relations, but in reality the Kammens had already agreed to give him a share of the royalties that it received from Harms. From a financial standpoint, Secunda's real albatross was his affiliation with the Society of Jewish Composers, which could pay him only a tiny fraction of the performance royalties that he would have earned as an ASCAP member.

Secunda's self-effacing tact didn't fool Ira B. Arnstein. Every single measure of "Bei Mir Bist Du Schön," Arnstein had already demonstrated to his own satisfaction, was copied from "A Mother's Prayer." Of much more interest to him was Mok's reportage that the first royalty distributions were expected to amount to "hundreds of thousands of dollars." Within days, Arnstein had filed a lawsuit against Warner Brothers and Harms in the Southern District of New York, the second *pro se* complaint he had filed there in a sixty-day span.

The earlier case, the MultiSuit, had already run into trouble. Arnstein's do-it-yourself complaint was not what lawyers would call an artful document. It had been met with motions to dismiss from every defendant, all of which were promptly granted. The court gave Arnstein leave to file an amended complaint, but strongly urged him to find an attorney: "The plaintiff has the legal right to represent himself in court. Nevertheless, no layman is capable of conducting a litigation of this kind. In consequence, if the plaintiff feels himself aggrieved, his first step should be engage counsel to represent him."[5]

It is surprising that some judges of the Southern District of New York were, by this time, still not sufficiently acquainted with Arnstein's history to realize the impracticability of this suggestion. By his own count, Arnstein had by then been through more than thirty lawyers. Whether one credited Arnstein's explanation that they had all been co-opted by ASCAP, or simply assumed that an impoverished, high-maintenance ingrate, whose credibility had been repeatedly disparaged in judicial opinions, had finally exhausted the trial bar's patience, there was no realistic prospect of Arnstein finding a lawyer willing to represent him in the MultiSuit.

Undaunted, Arnstein amended his complaint. He rectified the more glaring legal deficiencies of the original, in particular its failure to show any basis for federal court jurisdiction. (The alleged conspiracy was a tort actionable, if at all, only under state law.) By adding several claims under the Copyright Act he kept the MultiSuit in federal court, but at the cost of compromising his original strategy, which had been to focus on ASCAP as the center of a concerted scheme to deprive him of a livelihood, without having to laboriously prove up the technical elements of multiple copyright infringements. The amended complaint survived a second round of motions to dismiss. In November 1938, newly appointed Judge Edward Conger ruled that "the plaintiff should have his day in court. He does allege generally a conspiracy on the part of the various defendants to plagiarize his songs. . . . Under the circumstances his pleading should be given a liberal construction and should be construed so as to do substantial justice."[6] Arnstein's allegations regarding the conspiracy hadn't been beefed up in any substantive way that would account for this happier outcome. Rather, he was one of the earliest beneficiaries of the new Federal Rules of Civil Procedure, which had, fortuitously, been enacted only a few weeks earlier.

Litigators practicing in New York in the first third of the twentieth century could count themselves lucky. Long gone for them were the dark ages of common law pleading, the system that the colonies had inherited from pre-industrial England. "By the time of Edward I, it had become a science to be formulated and cultivated."[7] Common law pleading required the mastery of dozens of arcane writs with Latinate names, at pain of having rights irretrievably lost for the slightest technical lapse, perhaps bringing a writ sounding in *replevin* where only *assumpsit* would lie. The Field Code, one of the great law reforms of the nineteenth century, which governed both state and federal courts in New York, had abolished most such procedural twaddle. Any case could be commenced with "a plain and concise statement of the facts constituting the cause of action." Even that simple formulation, however, became riddled with traps and snares for the unwary. Facts, it turned out after generations of judicial exegesis, were "not such definite and certain things as the codifiers apparently believed."[8] The Federal Rules of Civil Procedure dispensed with the nettlesome word "facts," requiring instead that a complaint contain "a short and plain statement of the claim showing that the pleader is entitled to relief." Development of the "facts" would be left to a vastly expanded set of pretrial discovery tools. Early decisions were a mixed bag, with many judges resisting the idea of such barebones "notice" pleading. In time, though, the courts settled on the *pro se* plaintiff-friendly standard that Judge Conger implicitly applied to the MultiSuit's allegations of conspiracy: "A complaint should not be dismissed for failure to state a claim unless it appears beyond doubt that the plaintiff can prove no set of facts in support of his claim which would entitle him to relief."[9]

In Judge Conger, Arnstein had chanced upon an early and sincere advocate of the "liberal ethos"[10] of the new Federal Rules. Conger's reward for his forward thinking was the assignment to preside over what would assuredly be a messy trial in the MultiSuit, a trial—further complicated by consolidation with the "Bei Mir Bist du Schön" case—that his ruling had made possible.

ASCAP was pleased to see the focus of the MultiSuit shift to copyright infringement charges in which, institutionally, it had no direct stake. Its attorneys let the other defendants know that ASCAP intended to lie low at trial, doing only the bare minimum necessary to defend against the conspiracy count. ASCAP had more pressing legal problems to deal with and good reason to want to avoid attracting any unnecessary attention to itself in the MultiSuit.

With the Depression decimating all other sources of songwriter and publisher income in 1932, ASCAP, in a stunningly ill-timed move, had ended its five-year truce with radio. It forced through a three-year license that imposed a levy of 3–5 percent on advertising revenues over and above the flat "sustaining fees" already in place, with the result that for most stations total annual fees at least tripled. The NAB, which had been rather quiescent on the copyright front for several years while concentrating on the broadcast industry's own regulatory and antitrust issues, hired a full-time "Director of Copyright Activities," Oswald F. Schuette. At its convention in November 1932, the NAB resolved to protect radio, "by legislation, litigation, or otherwise," against "any organization which may undertake to levy an arbitrary and extortionate tribute upon the users of music under the pretense of a copyright monopoly."[11] Agitation by the NAB, together with an increasing number of complaints from independent songwriters and publishers over ASCAP's stranglehold on the music business, put ASCAP back in the sights of the federal government, just as New Dealers with a more expansive view of their jurisdiction and mandate were taking office.

On August 30, 1934, the Department of Justice filed a petition in the Southern District of New York under the Sherman Antitrust Act seeking the dissolution of ASCAP. Federal jurisdiction was proper, the petition alleged, because ASCAP's activities restrained interstate traffic in "energy, entertainment, and ideas" by "dictating the manner in which radio broadcasting stations may be operated" and "depriving those owners of copyrighted compositions who are not members of defendant Society the opportunity of transmitting their musical compositions to the ear of the purchasing public."[12]

This was the first time that ASCAP was forced to respond to a fully wrought theory of antitrust liability under the Sherman Act, although it was essentially the same theory Charles Tuttle had been whistling in the wind a decade earlier. The government's attack on ASCAP's central business practice, blanket licensing, went to the very heart of the enterprise. It argued that such pooling of individual copyrights was a form of price-fixing, that it restrained competition both among ASCAP's members and from non-members, and that it was therefore illegal "per se." If the court agreed, it would not matter whether ASCAP's intentions were laudable, whether the prices it demanded were objectively reasonable, or whether its blanket license was demonstrably more efficient than a system in which prices are individually negotiated with numerous copyright holders—all the virtues that ASCAP general counsel Nathan Burkan had touted for years and could easily prove.

On the eve of trial Burkan engaged as his co-counsel Thomas D. Thacher, a former federal judge and solicitor general of the United States, to provide the antitrust expertise that Burkan lacked. Thacher dressed up Burkan's practical, intuitive defense of blanket licensing with a fig leaf of antitrust law. He relied upon the Supreme Court's 1933 decision in *U.S. v. Appalachian Coal*, which held that an agreement that had the indirect effect of fixing prices was not per se illegal, but rather that "a close and objective scrutiny of particular conditions and purposes is necessary in each case. Realities must dominate the judgment."[13] Thacher argued that prior to the formation of ASCAP, there was no market for performing rights, and that individual negotiation with hundreds of copyright owners "is absurd, so absurd that nobody would attempt to do it. . . . So here the government is attacking as a restraint of trade an instrument of trade which is perfectly necessary and vital to the existence of the trade."[14]

The team of Burkan and Thacher ran roughshod over government lawyers who had relied excessively upon the NAB in preparing their case. When the case went to trial in June 1935, Burkan was at the height of his considerable powers as both an ASCAP apologist and as a celebrity trial lawyer. In just the preceding few years, Burkan had made headlines representing Mae West against indecency charges, Marlene Dietrich in an alienation of affections suit (brought by the wife of *The Blue Angel* director Josef von Sternberg), disgraced former Mayor Jimmy Walker in sundry matters of petty corruption, and Gloria Morgan Vanderbilt in her losing battle for custody of "Little Gloria." With so many years of tilting against ASCAP's enemies behind him, the savvy Burkan easily took control of the courtroom. One witness for the government after another, mostly radio industry lackeys, wilted under hours of his cross-examination. "What has impressed observers of the trial most," *Variety* reported, "has been the success Nathan Burkan has had in getting a wealth of the Society's side of the case into the record through the Government's own witnesses."[15]

The program director of one NBC-affiliated station, William Benning, testified as a witness for the government that he could not use public domain music as a substitute for ASCAP-controlled music because nearly all available arrangements and orchestrations of public domain pieces were published by ASCAP members. Burkan cross-examined Benning for two days, confronting him with a seemingly endless barrage of counterexamples, and finally touching upon the economic feasibility of the radio industry creating its own arrangements:

MR. BURKAN: You could engage a staff of arrangers to score for you and in
the form in which you required it, any work in the public domain
provided you are willing to pay the price?

MR. BENNING: If you can stand the expense and still operate.

MR. BURKAN: So what it gets down to is purely a question of expense,
that is true, isn't it?

MR. BENNING: Primarily, yes, sir. . . .

MR. BURKAN: The average arranger, how much a week does he get?

MR. BENNING: From $75–$100.[16]

Burkan had previously established that broadcasters' annual revenues
exceeded $100 million. It would have been fatuous to deny that the radio
industry could absorb the cost of a few $5,000-a-year arrangers as an alterna-
tive to the $3,000,000 it was then paying for ASCAP licenses. It was a
plausible alternative that at least cast some doubt on whether ASCAP
wielded sufficient market power to restrain trade.

Variety's headlines declared "U.S. Appears Shaky" and "Burkan Scores."
After seven days of trial, the government—which had initially succeeded in
having the case advanced on the Southern District of New York's congested
trial calendar in light of the imminent expiration of ASCAP's 1932 radio
licenses—pulled the plug, and was granted a four-month adjournment in
order to regroup. It was speculated in music circles that the trial would never
resume, government lawyers not being "in the habit of picking up a case that
has already been botched or proved a cropper."[17] Radio people had evidently
reached the same conclusion—by mid-summer of 1935 all but the most bel-
licose of station operators had resigned themselves to extending their
ASCAP licenses through 1940.

The hiatus eventually stretched to five years (not coincidentally, the duration of the ASCAP license extensions), but the case remained on the court's
docket, and the more antagonistic attitude that the Department of Justice
had assumed toward ASCAP was irreversible. A meaty antitrust issue had
been squarely joined and the feds would certainly be heard from again. And
while the federal case was in abeyance, the NAB waged a successful campaign against ASCAP at the state level. A number of state legislatures had
passed or were considering statutes that created a phalanx of taxes and regu-
lations, nominally directed at any performing rights organization, which
threatened ASCAP's very existence. (The NAB hired Andrew Bennett, the

government's lead trial counsel in the federal antitrust case, to coordinate this effort.) ASCAP called these state laws the "Snide Acts."[18] In a 1937 epistle to his counterparts in the European performing rights societies, ASCAP general manager John Paine wrote that the Snide Acts were "so onerous and so complicated and so impossible of compliance," that they would actually operate "as an absolute prohibitive against two or more copyright owners combining" to collect performance royalties. "ASCAP is being assailed on all sides," Paine added. "The fight at the present time is a bitter one, and a hard one and a costly one, and it looks as though it might also be a long one."[19] And it was a fight that ASCAP now had to carry on without its legal and strategic mastermind, Nathan Burkan, who had died suddenly at the age of 56 in the summer of 1936.

With its constitutional challenges to the Snide Acts that had been adopted in Florida, Nebraska, Washington, Montana, and Tennessee wending their way through the courts, and the federal antitrust action hanging over it like the Sword of Damocles, it was no time for ASCAP to risk handing its foes additional ammunition via a courtroom showdown with an unpredictable and cagey *pro se* litigant with a proven ability to attract attention from the press.

With ASCAP content to take a back seat, Warner Brothers, its publishing holdings, and their officers became the lead defendants in the MultiSuit by default. In addition to the "Bei Mir Bist Du Schön" infringement claim, they had to defend against the charge that Joe Burke's 1932 "My Wishing Song" was plagiarized from an unpublished number that Arnstein had allegedly submitted to its Witmark subsidiary. Further complicating Warner's task, two of its officers, Edwin Morris and Abraham Wattenberg, were singled out in the MultiSuit as having been instrumental in suppressing Arnstein's music, spreading the libels that he was a "pariah" and a "lunatic," tampering with his lawyers, and disrupting his picket of ASCAP, as Arnstein explained to Judge Conger through an awkward game of charades:

MR. ARNSTEIN: This Wattenberg, very often when I was walking up and
down, he says that to everybody [*gestures*], pointing to me, you know.
You know, pointing out like this [*gestures*].

THE COURT: Indicating that you were demented?

MR. ARNSTEIN: Yes. He was standing there laughing and jeering.

Upon being served with Arnstein's complaint, Wattenberg, an attorney, confirmed to his superiors at Warner Brothers his opinion that "the complainant is *non compos mentis*."[20] Despite that, Warner's decided to treat the case with the utmost seriousness. And showing the utmost seriousness, in matters such as these, meant paging Dr. Sigmund Spaeth.

The trial was a twelve-day free-for-all, pitting Ira B. Arnstein, appearing as his own attorney, against more than twenty of New York City's most prominent copyright litigators—*Mr. Deeds Goes to Town* as it might have been scripted by a well-liquored Algonquin Roundtable. The tone was set early, when Arnstein took the stand on his own behalf. "With the manners and appearance of an old-fashioned music teacher" and "a mop of graying hair hanging down on his forehead,"[21] Arnstein reveled in the freedom to pontificate before a captive audience, unconstrained by the usual protocols of courtroom examination. Judge Conger directed Arnstein to address the copyright infringement claims first, a task he undertook with a febrile pedagogic intensity that the music world would not see again until, perhaps, Leonard Bernstein's Norton Lectures at Harvard in the 1970s. "He sang most of his testimony in a clear, well-trained tenor voice. Occasionally he sat down at a small piano and played . . . When he was not singing or playing the piano he was writing notes on a blackboard."[22] Arnstein began his testimony on an ebulliently Bernsteinian trope:

> Now, your Honor, before I start in to show you the similarity of the music, I wish to call to your attention that music is also a language, like English or Latin. The only thing is that it is a language in sound [that] has an emotional and intellectual appeal.

One reporter's paraphrase of this introductory remark—"music is a language in sound like Latin or French"—was picked up by a wire service and quoted as column filler in newspapers nationwide. Although by all accounts Arnstein was in fine voice and there were no complaints about his piano playing, after a day or two of tedious, note-by-note dissection of the songs in issue, the press bailed out.

The courtroom, however, remained packed, and once Arnstein had gathered a head of steam, his testimony only became more gobsmackingly extravagant, severely testing the limits of judicial deadpan:

MR. ARNSTEIN: I want to prove something to your Honor that is the greatest evidence of plagiarism that was ever known in the history of stealing music from another composition.

THE COURT: That is a big statement.

Nor would Professor Arnstein brook any interruption from his adversaries at the defense table:

MR. ARNSTEIN: Your Honor, will you let that man sit down? I can't do anything. The man doesn't know anything, and he is only interrupting me.

THE COURT: You have to prove this case, and if I do not understand it, it is too bad for you. I may be thicker than he is.

MR. ARNSTEIN: The Judge is honest and says he doesn't understand, but this man says he knows.

AN ATTORNEY: You are not putting in the same notes Mr. Arnstein.

MR. ARNSTEIN: Will you please tell that man to sit down? I don't want that man to cross-examine me now.

With the experience of two copyright infringement trials behind him, Arnstein knew the routine for putting on a prima facie case. He brought in credible expert witnesses, including Eugene Plotnikoff, a conductor of the New York City Symphony and the WPA's Federal Symphony Orchestra, and David Sapiro, a busy piano teacher and concert recital accompanist. They, and more than a dozen other musicians of distinction, had signed a petition attesting to their support of Arnstein's claims. When it appeared that Arnstein intended to call every available signatory to the stand, the defendants prevailed upon Judge Conger to put an end to the filibuster.

It is not surprising that Arnstein would hear familiar strains in Secunda's music; the two men had been raised on similar musical palettes. Both were from the southern Ukraine, both had performed professionally as boy sopranos after coming to the United States, both composed for the Yiddish theater, and both had made serious study of piano and composition when their voices changed. (Secunda attended Damrosch's Institute of Musical Art and later studied with Ernest Bloch.) Each man had been frustrated by his failure to break into the popular mainstream.

WE THE UNDERSIGNED have examined the Songs mentioned below
and believe that the same were plagiarized from
Ira B. Arnstein's Songs and Instrumental Compositions.

	Arnstein
"The World Is Mine Tonight"	) "I Only Want To Prove") " Light My Life With Love"
"Be Still My Heart"	) Celestial Melodie) Ave Maria
"My Wishing Song"	) Whisper To Me
"Bei Mir Bist Du Schoen"	) "A Mother's Prayer"
"Take Me In Your Arms"	) "Where Are You Now"
"When A Gypsy Makes His Violin Cry"	) A Mother's Prayer
"Play Fiddle Play"	) Russian Gypsy Valse,) I Love You Medly.
"Lady Divine"	) Light My Life With Love.

Bitter experience had taught Arnstein that it would not be enough to show mere identities of tonal sequences. He was ready to offer, for each of the songs-in-suit, the greatest evidence that was ever known in the history of stealing music. For "Bei Mir Bist Du Schön," it was the introduction. "Anyone who writes or arranges songs for Tin Pan Alley," he pointed out, "knows that the introduction generally consists of a few measures of the chorus or sometimes the verse." The introduction to "Bei Mir" was based on nothing found in the verse or chorus, but with a little cutting and pasting, as shown in a juxtaposition of the two prepared by Arnstein, it could be traced to "A Mother's Prayer," leaving "no doubt" that it was copied.

Arnstein found scattered strains of "A Mother's Prayer" in the introduction to "Bei Mir Bist du Schön."

Moreover, Arnstein showed, the three adjacent, descending note motif of "A Mother's Prayer" (E-D-C in the "5th measure" on Arnstein's chart, C-B-A in the "4th") appears repeatedly in both the verse and chorus of "Bei Mir," nefariously concealed, of course, amidst rhythmic changes and alternative phrasings. Access was not an issue. "A Mother's Prayer" had been continuously in print, in numerous editions, for forty years. Secunda admitted to having heard it. But the elements of similarity that Arnstein's theory of infringement relied upon, Secunda argued, were common to "every Jewish *freylich*."[23]

Judge Conger never had to reach the merits of Arnstein's similarity argument. The claim against "Bei Mir" foundered on a threshold inquiry. Arnstein was unable to prove that he had regained ownership of the copyright on "A Mother's Prayer," and therefore standing to sue for its infringement, upon the death of Albert Teres, to whom he had sold the copyright renewal for $3,000 in 1926.

Arnstein's claim that Joe Burke's "My Wishing Song," a minor hit of 1932, was copied from "Whisper to Me," a self-published tune that Arnstein claimed to have once submitted to Witmark, required a more thorough examination. Burke was a Tin Pan Alley old-timer with hundreds of published songs to his credit, including "Tiptoe Through the Tulips," "Dancing with Tears in My Eyes," and "In a Little Gypsy Tea Room." Burke's hits were hardly on the cutting edge of popular music, but he was more than capable of turning out an old-fashioned waltz like "My Wishing Song" without help from Arnstein. Only an exceptionally strong similarity case could have overcome Burke's credible denial of access, but Arnstein at least made this one a contest worthy of the big guns that Warner had brought to bear on it.

Arnstein's argument centered on the first eight measures of each song's chorus—the most important and identifiable strain in any conventional popular song, and the most likely to be coveted by another composer. His theory involved no borrowing from the accompaniment, no truncating of measures, no scrambling of phrases. The comparison Arnstein put up on the chalkboard was not the least bit tricked-up—just two continuous treble staves, transposed to the common key of F, aligned one above the other in the missionary position:

This time it was Sigmund Spaeth who had to slice and dice. Demonstrating his proclivity for ad hoc music theorizing, Spaeth opined that it was really only the first *two* bars that mattered, "owing to the fact that every popular melody has to expose its character immediately in the first two measures." In those two he saw "not even a resemblance." Then, "for the sake of thorough analysis, which the case really does not deserve," he compared four measures at a time. Bringing the tools of tune detection to bear on the problem as thus framed, he could find no basis for inferring that the similarities resulted from Burke having copied Arnstein. The first four measures of "My Wishing Song" bore greater similarity in melody and rhythm to the 1927 Roy Turk-Lou Handman standard, "Are You Lonesome Tonight?" than to "Whisper to Me." The last four measures were a commonplace incomplete cadence, exactly as found in "My Country 'tis of Thee." As for a theme combining strains of "Are You Lonesome Tonight" (not nearly as familiar then as it became after Elvis Presley recorded it in 1960) with "My Country 'tis of Thee," Spaeth offered no antecedent.[24]

In the end, Judge Conger found that "there is a similarity in the melodic line, but not such a similarity as amounts to identity or to constitute copying."[25] His ruling relied heavily on the testimony of Warner's other expert, Kenneth Clark, a composer and music editor, whose musical expertise was conceded by Arnstein. His approach, quite different from Spaeth's tune detection, was to ask, "What gives each song its individuality?" In "Whisper to Me" it was a jumpy, syncopated four-note phrase; in "My Wishing Song" it was a four-note phrase using similar scale steps but with an "alternating of the long notes and the two short slurred notes, which gives it a very lilting waltz movement."[26] In Conger's detailed opinion, generally complimentary of the expert testimony on both sides, Spaeth barely rates a mention.

Spaeth had maintained a constant vigil in the front rows of the courtroom—installed there deliberately by the defendants, Arnstein believed, solely to heckle and rattle him. If that was indeed the plan, it worked. As Arnstein was singing the chorus of "My Wishing Song" for the court:

> Sigmund Spaeth, music expert, spoke to one of the defense witnesses at a counsel table, where they sat. Arnstein stopped and eyed him. "I don't want you to disturb me," he said sternly, "You're not a musician. You're a shoemaker."[27]

Why a "shoemaker" is anyone's guess. It is possible that the reporters misheard "faker," Arnstein's preferred epithet for Spaeth, whom he often referred to as the "notorious faker who studied music at the public library." Arnstein couldn't resist taking a swipe at Spaeth while he was down. Not long before, Dan Golenpaul, the creator of a new game show for NBC—*Information, Please!*—had tapped Spaeth to be one of his regular panelists. It was Golenpaul's then-radical idea to let Mr. and Mrs. America play along with members of the New York intelligentsia in a sophisticated party game. Listeners-in submitted the questions, with a $5 prize for stumping a four-member "board" of highbrows. The quiz, however, was secondary. "The questions were an intellectual exercise, something to get the talk rolling and the humor bubbling from within."[28] For example:

> Name four literary titles that sound as though they might be business terms.
> Quote a line of poetry that includes each of these words: (a) Cohorts; (b) Symmetry; (c) Native.
> Dress a man with song titles which mention articles of clothing.[29]

Golenpaul's casting of the *New Yorker*'s book critic, Clifton Fadiman, as the emcee, and newspaper columnists Franklin P. Adams and John Kieran as permanent panelists, inspired in retrospect, was considered a huge gamble at the time. With much more radio experience than all the other regulars combined, Spaeth was a reassuring choice for a network and a sponsor dubious about the whole concept. But when a standing commitment to teach at the University of Hawaii prevented Spaeth from participating in the first shows during the summer of 1938, Golenpaul substituted Oscar Levant, an obscure young pianist whom Michel Mok had recently anointed "the wag of Broadway" in the *New York Post*.[30] He quickly proved himself every bit the equal of the show's resident wits, and became an audience favorite. His store of musical, sports, and general knowledge was vast, but most striking was his incorrigible, edgy persona. "It soon became clear that he would say anything on the air."[31] A common household expression? "Are you going to stay in that bathroom all day?" A song with a zoo animal in the title? "Seal It with a Kiss." You go to the movies, don't you, Mr. Levant? "They come to me too."

Levant was a wholly new kind of radio personality as far as most Americans were concerned, an Oscar Wilde for the age of broadcasting, an "impudent, brilliant wise guy who seemed so New York, so cheeky, so smart."[32] Levant, his career tragically constricted by his inability to believe that he merited any success that came his way, marveled over the "accidental circumstance by which my impertinence had become a saleable product."[33]

By the time Spaeth reported for duty on the September 27, 1938 broadcast, with actor Basil Rathbone on hand as a guest panelist, Golenpaul's bold casting strokes had been vindicated and Spaeth, a throwback to an old radio order that *Information, Please!* had left behind, was eminently dispensable. His performance that night sealed his fate. In an ensemble that thrived on good-natured repartee and bonhomie, Spaeth's irrepressible know-it-all-ism was toxic, his attempts at humor unspeakably lame. "An uproarious error or a brilliant bit of irreverence," Kieran and the others understood, "rated far above any dull delivery of truth."[34] But Spaeth hadn't gotten the memo; he was accustomed to declaiming on the air, not bantering. A late arrival to a louche soirée, he was the worst kind of party-pooper, a sober bore. The normally unflappable Fadiman's impatience with Spaeth was most palpable and audible after he asked the panel to sing lines from four barbershop favorites in harmony. Spaeth insisted on bringing the festivities to a halt while he ascertained the vocal ranges of his fellow panelists and assigned the parts. (Spaeth: "Are you a bass, Frank?" Fadiman: "He's as base as can be, Mr. Spaeth . . . Make up your mind, *make . . . up . . . your . . . mind*.") It was, Spaeth was still grousing years afterward, the worst barbershop quartet he had ever heard.

This was Spaeth's first and only appearance on *Information, Please!* Though he thought it had gone very well (meaning, evidently, that he had answered so many questions correctly that only $10 in prize money had been given away), Golenpaul gave the music expert's seat permanently to Oscar Levant. Spaeth attributed Levant's popularity to a general coarsening of public taste, and for many years thereafter he continued to claim that pursuant to his agreement with Golenpaul, he was "technically and legally" the *Information, Please!* music expert. "Mr. Oscar Levant," he insisted, "has been my substitute all the way through."[35]

Information, Please! boosted many a career—most notably that of utility executive Wendell Wilkie, whose guest shots helped to position him as a contender for the 1940 Republican presidential nomination. Levant went on to parlay his quiz show heroics into a wide-ranging radio, movie, and television career. But for Spaeth it marked the beginning of a long decline. He soon found a more suitable berth on the Texaco Metropolitan Opera quiz, which borrowed its format from *Information, Please!* but could do with just an occasional *bon mot* from its panelists. Spaeth's days as a mainstream radio personality were over. Levant was now serious music's funny man, and Deems Taylor, another frequent guest panelist and Walt Disney's choice to narrate *Fantasia*, its avuncular public face. Though Spaeth was still in demand as an after-dinner speaker, Middle America had many more entertainment options open to it than back in the day when he was barnstorming the country for the American Piano Company.

His books continued to pour forth voluminously, as they grew ever more formulaic: *Stories Behind the World's Great Music, Music for Fun, The Art of Enjoying Music.* Two quirky exceptions were *Great Symphonies: How to Recognize and Remember Them,* and its sequel, *Great Program Music: How to Enjoy and Remember It.* Their conceit, or "heresy," as he put it, was vintage Spaeth, "to set words to symphonic melodies so that people could retain them in their memories and thus be able to follow the musical structure of a symphony from start to finish."[36] The opening to Beethoven's *Fifth Symphony* was rendered: "I am your fate; come let me in." The theme of Ravel's *Bolero*: "Dance, the Bolero with a firm triple beat, can't you feel it in your feet." Somehow the concept clicked. *Great Symphonies* became Spaeth's best seller, and some who were exposed to it in their youth (such as John Rockwell, who found the lyrics "gruesome," and Larry Rothe, to whom they were merely "ridiculous"[37]) grew up to be serious music writers with these obstinate little verses still swirling about in their heads.

Arnstein's long experience in copyright litigation did him little good when it came to putting on his conspiracy evidence. He wrongly assumed that he would be able to prove the conspiracy through the mouths of hostile music industry witnesses, and was left flatfooted when they didn't cooperate, as when Louis Bernstein of Shapiro, Bernstein, a named co-conspirator, simply denied Arnstein's claim that he had once agreed to publish "Light My Life with Love":

> If the man sits down and lies and says he never met me, your Honor, I have nothing more to question him about. These are all perjurors, liars, and crooks and they sit down there and deny facts which the whole world knows. This man has met me a hundred times and he had a quarrel with me in his office. He was going to publish this song and he denies here that he ever met me. What can I ask him, Your Honor?

Arnstein put Arthur Garfield Hays and other lawyers who had abandoned him over the years on the stand; each provided a perfectly innocent explanation for withdrawing, and Arnstein had no way to impeach their credibility. His own credibility took a hit when he flunked yet another courtroom identification test, unable to point out Edwin Morris, to whom he had supposedly submitted "Whisper to Me." When Arnstein was done, the defendants rested en masse without putting on any evidence to rebut the allegation of conspiracy. That was, of course, a show of considerable strength, but Arnstein didn't see it that way:

> What inference may, can and must be drawn from such refusal to come out in the open to oppose? To plaintiff it is an inference conclusive and uncontradictory of his charges. The purposeful simultaneity in resting is a matter of profound significance for your Honor to consider. . . . It makes plaintiff's evidence stand out like beacon lights in the distance.[38]

"It is academic to state," Judge Conger observed, "that plaintiff is wrong and unjustified in his inference."[39] Conger had been a model of judicial temperament throughout the trial, taking great pains and suffering much foolishness to ensure that Arnstein had his day in court. But his ruling, delivered four months after the conclusion of the trial and coming in at just under 9,000 well-chosen words, was unsparing in its methodical demolition of one Arnstein chimera after another:

> These things may have happened to the plaintiff or they may not, but assuming that they did happen, what do they prove against these defendants? Not one bit of proof that they had anything to do with it. He did not know who attacked him. He did not know who, if anyone, stole his letters or ransacked his rooms or stole his papers and yet, on such facts as these, he asked me to find as part of the conspiracy that the defendants had something to do with intercepting his mail; that they caused him to be beaten by two gorillas and that they caused his room to be ransacked and manuscripts and letters to be stolen.[40]

Perhaps Conger intended to administer some sort of judicial talking cure, to force Arnstein—who had appeared to him, over the course of a three-week trial, to be a man of intelligence and certainly no *raving* lunatic—to confront his own folly. But it was useless. Arnstein now inhabited a mental place that reason could not realistically hope to penetrate. Since returning from Miami two years earlier, Arnstein had moved from one Upper West Side rooming house to another with such frequency that the defendants were having difficulty finding him. Invariably, they would learn that he had been dispossessed for non-payment of rent, had left no forwarding address, and that his former landlords were relieved to be rid of him because "he was a trouble-maker and had threatened them with bodily harm."[41] The landlords, Arnstein believed, were allowing detectives and other stooges from Tin Pan Alley into his rooms. Secretaries, too, had now been drawn into the conspiracy. As he wrote in one of his many letters to Harry Warner:

> I don't know whether your secretary is in league with them to keep all my letters from you—not to let me see you whenever I phone and call personally, but I do know you as a courteous gentleman and I am sure that had you received any of my letters in the past, you would have answered. If I don't receive a reply, I will be certain and will surely make it my business to see you where there are no secretaries.[42]

To Arnstein, Judge Conger's ruling was just another in a long line of "frame-ups." He tried to take an appeal to the Second Circuit, but the court ruled that the appeal could not go forward without a complete transcript of the lengthy trial, an expense well beyond Arnstein's means. Being denied a judicial forum to air his grievances seem to anger him far more than Conger's opinion had. He let loose a jeremiad of seven single-spaced typed pages,[43] which he mimeographed and circulated widely to reporters and government officials, laying it all out for a benighted world:

> During the entire trial (March 6–29) a group of men, sometimes 12 sometimes 15 or more came and sat from the beginning to the end of each session. Some of them engaged me in conversation and even showed sympathy. I often asked them why they came every day, but they explained that they were unemployed and that my case interested them. I believed them until I saw that they all went up to the 29th floor of the Courthouse.

The New York office of the Federal Bureau of Investigation was on the twenty-ninth floor. The scales fell from Arnstein's eyes. "Everything became as clear as crystal." The FBI was behind all of it—the lost jobs, burglaries, intercepted mail, pupils who turned into stoolpigeons, authorities who ignored his complaints, lawyers who dropped his cases, people who missed appointments or otherwise treated him rudely. "Private detectives could not do such things. Only the magic of the FBI would frighten and intimidate people to do what they have done."

As for Judge Conger, he too was controlled by the monied interests and had acted throughout the trial as both their attorney and their witness. "After the Manton case," Arnstein wrote, alluding to Martin T. Manton, the senior judge of the Second Circuit who had recently been forced to resign and sentenced to two years in prison for accepting gifts and loans from litigants, "one would imagine there would be more justice, or at least an attempt to improve the outward appearance of justice." He concluded with a call for journalists to look into his charges, which "if properly investigated will remain an historic document of the corruption of the first half of the 20th Century." "Do it now," he implored, "because they are planning to *remove me from the scene.*"

ASCAP could not have asked for more emphatic language than that with which Judge Conger obliged it in categorically rejecting Arnstein's claim that he had been wrongfully denied membership:

I find that ASCAP is a private association; that its rules and by-laws define the manner and means upon which it admits composers to membership; that no one has an absolute right to be a member; that it has the sole power to say who shall belong and who shall not. That refusal to admit plaintiff to membership is not an invasion of his rights and gives him no right of action against ASCAP thereby.[44]

Unfortunately for ASCAP, this was not the final word on the subject. A legal dragnet was enveloping it, and Nathan Burkan was no longer around to execute an escape. By the time of Judge Conger's ruling, seven states had passed anti-ASCAP Snide Acts, and many more had such legislation under deliberation. Hostilities had escalated to the point where Gene Buck was arrested and briefly jailed in Arizona on a warrant issued out of Montana. ASCAP won a provisional victory in April 1939, when the U.S. Supreme Court upheld a preliminary injunction against enforcement of a Florida statute that prohibited any combination comprised of "a substantial number of the persons, firms or corporations" from fixing license fees for performing rights.[45] The Court did not pass upon the constitutionality of the statute, but simply held that the challenges raised by ASCAP were not frivolous and that allowing the law to be enforced while the lower court was considering the merits of the case would cause ASCAP's members irreparable harm. Justice Hugo Black's dissent, however, was an ominous portents of things to come:

> We have here a price fixing combination that actually wields the power of life and death over every business in Florida, and elsewhere, dependent upon copyrighted musical compositions for existence. Such a monopolistic combination's power to fix prices is the power to destroy. Should a Court of Equity grant this combination the privilege of violating a State anti-monopoly law?[46]

When a similar statute enacted by Washington came before a three-judge district court the following year, on ASCAP's request for a permanent injunction on a fully developed record, the lower court panel followed Justice Black's lead. It denied ASCAP any equitable relief on the ground that it did not come into court with "clean hands," that is, it had "acquired the power to fix the prices at which rights of a particular nature may be purchased by prospective users," and was therefore illegal per se under the

Sherman Act.[47] For the first time, a federal court had adjudicated ASCAP to be an unlawful trust.

In the meantime, Thurman Arnold, a Yale law professor and antitrust specialist, had taken charge of the Department of Justice's new Antitrust Division. Arnold's 1940 book, *The Bottlenecks of Business*, had laid out, in language accessible to the lay public, a sweeping agenda for vigorous enforcement of the Sherman Act. A scholar of formidable intellect, Arnold took a long view of the history of commerce and culture—of justice for genius—that reached back centuries before the night that Shanley's first offered cabaret-style entertainment with Victor Herbert songs:

> The only type of economic structure in which government is free and in which the human spirit is free is one in which commerce is free. The Renaissance began with the rebirth of commerce.... Out of commercial civilizations have come not only experiments in industry and production, but experiments in art and literature. Free commercial enterprise breeds free dissemination of ideas.[48]

Arnold issued subpoenas for ASCAP records in the spring of 1940, signaling that a criminal indictment under the Sherman Act was under consideration. It turns out those G-men from the twenty-ninth floor may not have been up to no good after all. Twenty years after receiving its first complaints from the music-using public, the feds were finally ready to take on ASCAP.

BAD MUSIC INSTEAD

Ninety percent of those who listen in on radios prefer the old music and the old songs which are not subject to copyright. So far as I am concerned, when I hear this modern stuff coming in, I promptly close the radio. Jazz, like boasting and bragging and high living, is passing out much more rapidly than you suspect.
—*Senator Josiah W. Bailey (D-NC)*

Sandwiched between the first round of U.S. Supreme Court arguments in the Snide Act cases in January, and the trial of the MultiSuit in March, the twenty-fifth anniversary of the founding of ASCAP in February 1939 passed without public fanfare or ceremony. In September 1939, ASCAP belatedly announced plans to celebrate by offering New York City a week of free Carnegie Hall concerts that spanned the full breadth of ASCAP's catalog, from symphonies to Sousa marches, culminating with a nationally broadcast show devoted to the core popular song repertoire, with Rudy Vallée's orchestra and ASCAP stalwarts Irving Berlin, George M. Cohan, and W. C. Handy on hand to perform their own classics. "We believe that this musical cavalcade of the works of the members of ASCAP," Gene Buck effused, "will be one of the outstanding events in the history of the nation." The German invasion of Poland, just as plans for the gala were being finalized, only added to the momentousness of the occasion. "There's going to be no profiteering on sorrow and anxiety," Mayor Fiorello La Guardia declared, knowing that under the dire exigencies of the moment no one would quibble with the non sequitur that followed: "I know of no better way to get this message across than with music."[1]

The outbreak of war in Europe and the previously unobserved silver jubilee were handy pretexts for ASCAP to launch an urgently needed public relations response to fresh rumblings of trouble on the radio front. From its founding in 1923, the NAB's Holy Grail had been the creation of a viable reservoir of tax-free contemporary music. Its early efforts, amounting to little more than listing services for non-ASCAP members who were willing to waive performance royalties, had been underfunded and little utilized. In the summer of 1939, under the new leadership of President Neville Miller, the NAB announced its intention to organize a full-fledged competitor to ASCAP, Broadcast Music, Inc. (BMI). The plan developed by Sidney Kaye, an attorney for CBS, called for raising several million dollars of initial capital through the sale of stock to member broadcasters, and for BMI to operate as both a music publisher and as a licensor of performing rights. The broadcasters' idea was to "arm themselves" with enough music "to enable them to conduct future negotiations with the society on terms of some equality."[2]

Crucially, BMI had the enthusiastic backing of NBC and CBS. Their interest in reducing the cost of music rights was heightened as expiration of the five-year ASCAP licenses signed after the abortive 1935 antitrust trial neared. ASCAP had come to realize that it had left millions of dollars on the table in those earlier deals by basing the license fees on local station revenues only. In future contracts, it announced, it would also look to collect "at the source" of network programs. *Variety* estimated that under a new formula proposed by ASCAP total radio fees for 1941 would increase from $4.1 million to $7.3 million, with local stations seeing a slight decrease, more than offset by $4 million in new network fees.[3] The networks pressured their affiliates to subscribe to BMI's stock offering, and ordered their on-air talent to begin weaning themselves off of ASCAP music. Thurman Arnold and his staff, then in the midst of their reinvigorated investigation of ASCAP, were watching these developments with mounting alarm, wondering whether this was another music trust in the making.

BMI enticed songwriters to its fold with the promise that performance royalties would be distributed in strict, scientifically measured proportion to the frequency of radio performances, live or recorded, network or local, with no favoritism shown to old boys—all in stark contrast to ASCAP's tradition-bound and highly subjective distribution system. Submissions from amateurs and newcomers, BMI announced, would be welcomed and given careful, unprejudiced consideration. Nathan Burkan's suggestion that the broadcasters make their own arrangements of public domain music was taken up; BMI hired dozens of arrangers to create swing versions of nineteenth-century chestnuts. Publishers with desirable catalogs were either purchased outright or offered multiyear guarantees in exchange for making BMI their licensing agent for performance rights. To make these deals work, shareholder stations were called upon to pledge additional capital almost as soon as their initial subscription checks cleared the bank.

ASCAP's lock on the Broadway crowd forced BMI to search far afield for its inventory, to musical genres and geographic regions that ASCAP, as well as the radio networks, had historically disdained. BMI played the hand that it was dealt brilliantly, covering its rank commercial opportunism with the perfume of cultural populism. On the back page of its early sheet music publications, in place of the traditional advertisements and musical samples, BMI printed a mission statement of breathtaking immodesty:

> To open the road for all who have anything to say in music this company, Broadcast Music, Inc., was organized within the broadcasting industry. Through BMI broadcasters are working to assure equal opportunity and fair compensation to all composers young and old, the newcomer as well as the famous maestro . . . BMI gives to American music a freedom for creative progress that it has never had before.[4]

Whether it was by design or by necessity, it cannot be denied that the founding of BMI set in motion profound changes in the sound of American radio, beginning with the licensing arrangement that it made with Ralph Peer's Southern Music Publishing Company. Peer, while working for Nathaniel Shilkret in the 1920s as a producer in Victor's Race, Hillbilly, and Export departments, had taken recording equipment to remote corners of North and South America, where he discovered authentic vernacular artists quite unlike the ersatz hillbilly stars, such as Vernon Dalhart and Gene Austin, who recorded for Shilkret back east. In just one 1927 session in Tennessee he made the first commercial recordings of both Jimmie Rodgers and the Carter Family. Peer, Shilkret remembered, was "always a soft speaker, but shrewd." He persuaded Victor to finance the creation of a company to publish his finds, "making him president and dividing the profits."[5] When RCA bought out Victor in 1929, David Sarnoff—who had no interest in the down-market music that Peer specialized in—let Peer walk out the door with the largest and most valuable catalog of blues, country, and Hispanic music then extant. Peer's affiliation with BMI, at the very moment that the networks were threatening to replace most of the popular music that had filled the airwaves for twenty years, was a giant leap toward respectability for these genres. Two mambos by Mexican composer Alberto Dominguez, "Perfidia" and "Frenesi," published by Southern, were among BMI's very first big and lasting hits.

BMI signed up foreign and ethnic music of all sorts, including the catalog of Italian publisher G. Ricordi, which featured the Puccini operas. Sholom Secunda struck a deal to give BMI the performing rights to the Society of Jewish Composers' catalog of 2,500 Yiddish theater songs, turning down a chance to make a lucrative arrangement for himself with ASCAP.[6] Large guarantees and advances provided by BMI allowed new publishing companies, especially in the country and western field, to germinate. Testifying before Congress in the late 1950s, by which time Nashville had become "Music City, U.S.A.," Tennessee governor Frank Clement remarked that "ASCAP belonged to New York and California. . . . Not a single music publishing enterprise of even the slightest professional consequence existed in Nashville prior to the organization of BMI."[7]

ASCAP, at first, was dismissive of the upstart. "They have a perfect right to form their own group," Gene Buck told the press when the BMI plan was first announced in 1939, though he "wondered where the new group would find its music."[8] But as the steady drumbeat of accessions to the BMI catalog continued, ASCAP's rhetoric heated up. In a lengthy August 1940 open letter to radio advertisers, Gene Buck sneered at BMI's artistic pretensions:

> It is of course the most utter and puerile nonsense for the proponents of BMI to contend that they are interested in encouraging composers who are barred by ASCAP. It is equally stupid to contend a purpose to contribute to American culture. All camouflage aside, and all speeches to the contrary notwithstanding, the purpose is, if possible, to beat ASCAP's members to their economic knees, and to use their music cheaper than is now available.[9]

Neville Miller, speaking at the NAB convention in San Francisco a few days later, was ready to play Churchill to Buck's Goebbels: "Now is the critical time for broadcasters. We must not fail. Let this convention send out the word that San Francisco is to be no Munich."[10]

The presence of ASCAP music on radio declined steadily throughout 1940. Midnight New Year's Eve—when the existing five-year ASCAP licenses were to expire—would be the zero hour, when a complete radio boycott of ASCAP would begin. "Auld Lang Syne," thankfully, was in the public domain, but if Guy Lombardo intended to use it to usher in 1941 for his national radio audience, he was going to have to find a BMI arrangement.

"Hitherto unsuccessful songwriters, including many amateurs, saw in BMI the open-sesame for recognition at last."[11] Ira B. Arnstein was among their number. No sooner was the NAB's plan announced in 1939 than Arnstein began peppering Neville Miller with letters, first offering to provide dirt on ASCAP, then offering his services to BMI's publishing operation, which needed to assemble a professional music staff from scratch, and finally offering his music, promising Miller "that he alone could write more 'hits' than the entire Tin Pan Alley in a year." All of this before BMI's stock offering was fully subscribed and the Kaye plan was a definite "go." Miller counseled Arnstein to be patient.[12]

By the summer of 1940, BMI was up and running. Arnstein submitted eleven songs, including some unpublished tunes that he had previously peddled to ASCAP members, but also the published and recorded "V'Shomru" and "Soldiers of Zion." Sidney Kaye, now vice president and general counsel of BMI, who knew Arnstein well from having represented CBS in the MultiSuit, assured Arnstein that any music he submitted "will receive the same attention as other manuscripts submitted to us by reputable musicians, and there will be no discrimination against the works whatsoever."[13] Arnstein's chances of success were slim nonetheless. BMI's multi-tiered committee system was reviewing thousands of submissions per week, and recommending less than half of 1 percent for publication—odds only marginally better than he would have had with a publisher who refused to open unsolicited manuscripts at all. Unluckily for Arnstein, even if one of his songs had managed to surmount the committee hurdle, the final arbiter would be BMI's chief music editor, Milton Rettenberg, who for many years had been a close musical associate of Nathaniel Shilkret. Arnstein's songs did not make the cut.

The final weeks of 1940 were eventful and tense, as the long-simmering conflict between ASCAP and radio reached the boiling point. ASCAP's five-year agreements with its member publishers were also expiring at the end of the year, and it was common knowledge that BMI was hoping to poach a few.

In early December, BMI announced that it had lured one major ASCAP publisher to its ranks. To no one's surprise, it was Edward B. Marks. BMI guaranteed Marks $250,000 per year, about three times what he had been receiving from ASCAP. BMI had dangled large sums in front of many other ASCAP members, but Marks, independent in mindset and perennially disgruntled over his treatment by ASCAP, was peculiarly well situated to make the move. Thanks to his long-standing aversion to the care and feeding of the songwriter-auteur, Marks's catalog was light on songs by writers who were affiliated with ASCAP—only about 3,000 out of a total of 20,000 songs. As to those, the deal raised an important, but long dormant, legal issue—was it the publisher or the songwriter who controlled the performing rights? Under ASCAP's bylaws, both publishers and songwriters assigned performing rights to the society and the royalties were divided equally. Up until the Marks defection, both sides had been content to let the matter rest there, preferring "to maintain the entente of equal partnership" in performing rights and leaving the question of their legal ownership to "mental speculation in idle moments."[14] By purporting to transfer songs written by ASCAP writers to BMI, without their consent, Marks was asserting the view that standard songwriter contracts transferred complete control of performing rights to the publisher. Taking this position to its logical conclusion, Marks refused to share any of his BMI lucre with the songwriters, without doubt the most malevolent attack on the rights of songwriters by any publisher since the heyday of Tin Pan Alley. BMI filed suit against ASCAP to obtain a determination of its rights to these songs. John Paine, ASCAP's general manager, characterized it as a situation where "the captain had struck his colors, but the crew refused to surrender."[15]

Marks's ASCAP numbers would remain in a legal limbo for four years. But there was no such cloud over the rights to many of the old, pre-ASCAP favorites that Marks published—standards like "There'll Be a Hot Time in the Old Town Tonight," "Parade of the Wooden Soldiers," and his recent prize acquisition, "Ta-Ra-Ra Boom-Der-É"—nor with respect to his large Cuban and South American holdings. With the addition of the

Marks catalog, BMI was claiming that its repertoire had reached the 250,000-piece milestone.

The broadcasters' negotiating strategy hinged upon the credibility of their threat to take all ASCAP music off the air by New Year's Day. ASCAP had initially been supremely confident that advertisers and bandleaders would prevail upon the broadcasters to stand down. Gene Buck issued this taunt:

> How foolish to instruct orchestra leaders and others that they must abandon their musical signatures or themes, if in the ASCAP repertoire, on January first. Does anyone suppose that Whiteman will abandon "Rhapsody in Blue"—his musical trade-mark? Does anyone imagine that Amos n' Andy will abandon "The Perfect Song"? Will Waring discontinue "Sleep," which he has used for twenty years?[16]

Buck's memory was short—Paul Whiteman had managed without *Rhapsody in Blue* for most of 1936, when Warner Brothers' music publishing subsidiaries had briefly bolted from ASCAP in the hope of striking their own licensing deals, taking with them some 40 percent of the active popular music repertoire, including most Gershwin, Herbert, Kern, and Porter. The radio people took comfort from the precedent of 1936, when they had called Warners Brothers' bluff by successfully removing its music from the airwaves. Broadcasters grew increasingly confident of their ability to replace all ASCAP music as January 1, 1941 approached. In mid-November 1940, *Variety* reported that five of the top seven songs on the air were published by BMI.[17] By Christmas, the networks had completely expunged ASCAP from their sustaining programming. Sponsors were actively making preparations to follow suit. *Amos n' Andy* found a perfectly acceptable replacement for "The Perfect Song" in its public domain inspiration, Gaetano Braga's "Angel's Serenade."

As the clock ticked down, the propaganda war continued to ratchet up, reaching its high-water mark when ASCAP mailed out a circular titled "Watch the Irish Get Their Irish Up!" Referring to BMI's arrangements with Italian and German publishers, the circular asserted that "under the BMI system, Irish music will be replaced by Nazi and Fascist songs through recent deals 'not disapproved' by the Hitler and Mussolini propaganda ministries, which regard music as their most subtle weapon."[18]

An ASCAP circular in 1940 charged that its members had been "blacklisted" by radio and that under BMI "Irish music will be replaced by Nazi and Fascist songs." (*Courtesy ASCAP*)

All of this was taking place against the backdrop of the Justice Department's antitrust investigation of ASCAP. The smart money was betting that negotiations for a consent decree would be completed by New Year's Eve, which would in turn light the path to a lasting music-radio peace, notwithstanding ASCAP's protestations that the two matters were unrelated. But ASCAP's internal divisions undermined the authority of its negotiating team, and a chance confluence of legal setbacks in the few days right before Christmas 1940 had a paralyzing effect—the Supreme Court agreed to review lower court decisions that had sustained ASCAP's challenges to the Nebraska and Florida Snide Acts, while a federal court in the state of Washington refused to enjoin enforcement of the Snide Act there on the ground that ASCAP was an unlawful monopoly. On December 27th, after ASCAP's representatives walked away from the negotiating table, Thurman Arnold put a pox on all sides, announcing that the Justice Department intended to institute criminal antitrust proceedings—"immediately after the first of January"—against not only ASCAP, but against BMI, NBC, and CBS as well. In a press release issued in time for the morning papers, Arnold explained:

> The mutual boycotts already begun will hamper and obstruct the rendition of all copyrighted music over the radio and deprive the public of the privilege of hearing that music except on terms dictated by the victor in the contest. In such a struggle the public is in the position of a neutral caught between two aggressive belligerents. This Department cannot sit by and see ASCAP and the broadcasters engage in a private war at the expense of the public, using violations of law as their weapons in order to fight fire with fire.[19]

Thurman Arnold's blunderbuss attack caught BMI by surprise; Neville Miller claimed that the Justice Department had given it no prior warning at all. This development would require some changes in BMI's carefully laid war plan, but Mr. Arnold's wood-shedding came too late to avert the long-anticipated New Year's showdown.

Until the unruly genre was tamed under the stultifying yoke of *Oklahoma!* and its progeny, no Broadway musical was complete without a patter song or a topical comedy number that could be updated frequently to give a nod and a wink to the day's headlines, a convention that supported a cottage industry for ghostwriters adept at reworking a lyric. In *Pal Joey*, Rodgers and Hart's spoof of Gypsy Rose Lee's "intellectual" recitations *cum* undress, "Zip," all nod-and-wink to begin with, was infinitely adaptable for this purpose. Shortly after the show's opening on Christmas 1940, Lorenz Hart added his own special lyric: *"Zip! On the radio good music is dead/Zip! BMI just means 'Bad Music Instead.'"*[20]

By New Year's Day 1941, ASCAP's patrimony, nearly every well-known popular song published over the preceding thirty years, had disappeared from the network ether. The NBC broadcast booth at the 1941 Rose Bowl was hermetically sealed off from ambient sounds, lest its microphones accidentally capture the University of Nebraska or Stanford marching bands striking up an ASCAP tune. Listeners-in had to take announcer Bill Stern at his word that the 90,000 fans "were having the time of their life," when all they could hear was a sepulchral silence. That night, on Eddie Cantor's show, his latest discovery, Dinah Shore, had to forego her breakout hit, Jack Lawrence's "Yes, My Darling Daughter," in favor of a BMI arrangement of "Listen to the Mockingbird." For his first show of the new year, Rudy Vallée performed Schubert's "Ave Maria," "Frenesi," and songs by the brand new BMI songwriting team of Stanley Cowan and Bobby Worth. So it went for months, original BMI tunes alternating with old public-domain favorites like "Home on the Range," "Polly Wolly Doodle," and songs of Stephen Foster. "Jeanie with the Light Brown Hair," published in 1854, is often said to have been the most performed song on radio in 1941. For some, it was a welcome change:

> Thanks to the banning of ASCAP, lovers of music are relieved, temporarily at least, of the noisy swing blasted out by dance orchestras, and are enjoying a revival of the tuneful, melodious airs that have remained popular because of merit and are not the fulfillment of a conga or rumba impulse of a jitterbug. At least there is some real poetry and sentiment in the old songs and my friends agree they sound pretty good.[21]

The scrubbing of ASCAP's repertoire was remarkably thorough. A number of bandleaders simply gave up their network shows, some because they couldn't eliminate ASCAP music from their repertoire, and others because they wouldn't sign indemnity agreements demanded by the networks, who worried that copyright infringement claims would result if a rogue player were to "suddenly interpolate a few 'hot licks' of an ASCAP tune into an otherwise perfectly safe number."[22] NBC banned Kate Smith from a Four-H Club broadcast, rather than make an exception for "God Bless America." Even "Sharkey," a trained seal act then enjoying a brief vogue, was barred from the air—his signature trick was playing "Where the River Shannon Flows," an ASCAP tune, on a set of horns.

For ASCAP and its members, the events of early 1941 were a stunning comeuppance. "An awful licking," Oscar Hammerstein called it.[23] Besides losing the two-thirds of their ASCAP distributions that came from radio, members saw their mechanical and sheet music royalties plummet as well. The incessant radio play of its small stock of original songs made BMI, temporarily, the top music publisher in the country. Lucky Strike's "Your Hit Parade," one of the most coveted plugs on radio, became the BMI hit parade—seven ASCAP numbers that made the final Hit Parade of December 1940 were gone in the first week of January 1941. Gene Buck mocked it as the "Bit Parade." But the public rebellion that ASCAP anticipated never did materialize. Nor, on the other hand, were there any immediate stirrings of the cultural upheaval promised by BMI. BMI's early hits—such as "I Hear a Rhapsody," its first lasting contribution to the Great American Songbook—were, with few exceptions, cast in the same familiar molds as the ASCAP tunes they displaced.

"Everyone knows that ASCAP is in the hands of racketeers," wrote Ira B. Arnstein back in the fall of 1936, shortly before he left New York in a futile attempt to escape the umbra of ASCAP's pernicious influence. "The United States Government will get them sooner or later."[24] In January 1941, with ASCAP's music off the air, its members losing income, and the Justice Department preparing to indict it, who would have begrudged Arnstein a little schadenfreude as his prophesy finally came to pass? But the catty pleasures of vindication were overshadowed by a sense of foreboding. With its back against the wall, there was no telling what ASCAP might do to silence its most trenchant and persistent critic. ASCAP, he had long feared, "would even go to the extent of removing me from this earth."[25] Despite his heightened state of vigilance, and under circumstances that remain murky, Arnstein did find himself taken out of circulation at that very moment.

On January 14, 1941, two New York City detectives were assigned to investigate a complaint received from an Upper West Side rooming house where Arnstein was residing. It is unclear whether Arnstein had called the police to complain of another burglary by Tin Pan Alley goons, or his landlady had called to complain of Arnstein's threatening behavior in accusing her of complicity in the crime. In either event, no charges were filed against anybody. But under the authority of New York State's Mental Hygiene Law of 1927, Arnstein was taken to the psychopathic ward of Bellevue Hospital for a period of observation. The Mental Hygiene Law, a progressive-sounding rebranding of the "Mental Deficiency" and "Insanity" acts that it had superseded, was widely heralded as an advance in the care and treatment of the mentally ill, but it was no bill of rights for mental patients. It provided little in the way of due process, and no guarantee of access to family, social workers, or public legal advocates. Arnstein's long experience with the civil litigation system was no preparation for the Kafkaesque nightmare he faced under the law of civil commitment.

Convinced that ASCAP had somehow inveigled the police to kidnap him, Arnstein was verbally abusive toward the doctors and hospital staff. Unsurprisingly, his vociferous protestations that he was of sound mind and being detained illegally fell on deaf ears. After six days of observation, he was handed written notice—a "Certificate of Lunacy" in the uneuphemistic statutory language—advising that the medical superintendant of Bellevue had applied for a court order to commit Arnstein to Pilgrim State Hospital. A hearing was scheduled for early the very next morning at the hospital.

At the Pilgrim State of 1941, the paranoid, defiant behaviors Arnstein presented would have indicated a regimen of electro-convulsive or insulin shock therapy. Within a few years, the prefrontal lobotomy would become the treatment of choice. Arnstein averted this grim fate by the narrowest of margins. According to his later account, he managed to smuggle a note through a departing patient to his sister Mae, who appeared at the hearing and agreed "to assume all responsibility on the discharge of the said Ira Arnstein, such discharge being against the advice of the physician in charge." No landlady or other witness appeared to testify at the commitment hearing, and absent any evidence that the patient posed a danger to anyone, the judge ordered Arnstein released. The prognosis, one of the examining psychiatrists noted on the discharge, "is poor."

When Arnstein left the hospital on January 24th, he was under the misapprehension that his release had been conditioned on his refraining from

Arnstein believed that ASCAP had arranged for him to be kidnapped and taken to Bellevue Hospital's psychopathic ward.

"prosecuting any of the suits which he had begun or contemplated against the American Society of Composers and Publishers (ASCAP)."[26] It was a small price to pay for his freedom, especially with ASCAP finally being brought to heel by the government. Besides, it was now BMI that was stealing his songs and turning them into America's biggest hits.

BMI moved quickly to make its separate peace with the Department of Justice. No criminal charges were filed; instead, the government brought a civil action, prepackaged with a negotiated consent decree ready for the court's approval.[27] The gravamen of the complaint was that BMI, along with co-conspirators NAB, CBS, and NBC, had coerced broadcast stations into purchasing BMI stock and BMI licenses, and pressured them to refrain from using non-BMI music. Other allegations—such as improperly restricting the use of certain compositions, or discriminating in price among similarly situated users— had no relation to BMI's actual business practices and seem to have been cribbed from the 1934 ASCAP dissolution petition.

BMI was not inclined to complain about being tarred with the same brush as ASCAP. Quite the contrary, it was eager to enter into a consent decree prohibiting such practices, whether it had been guilty of them or not, because this was a template for what ASCAP would have to agree to as well. (The most important provision in the consent decree, from BMI's perspective, was that it would not be effective until the government had also procured a consent decree or final judgment "by which restraints and requirements in terms substantially identical with those imposed herein shall be imposed upon ASCAP.") The only real concession BMI was forced to make was agreeing to the principle of payment "at the source" for network programs. But by quickly and completely capitulating to the government—the settlement was approved on February 3, 1941—BMI grabbed the upper hand in the public relations war with the dithering ASCAP, and avoided the stigma of criminal prosecution that the officers and directors of ASCAP would have to bear.

Two days later the Justice Department, bypassing the grand jury, filed a criminal information against ASCAP in Milwaukee, a venue chosen for its light docket and for the presence of Judge F. Ryan Duffy, who, in his earlier capacity as a U.S. senator, had not been friendly disposed toward ASCAP. Arraignment was scheduled for March 5th, a deadline that filled ASCAP with a new sense of urgency. Before that date arrived, ASCAP agreed to Thurman Arnold's terms, which included fines, pleas of *nolo contendere* to criminal antitrust violations, and a consent decree that required ASCAP to offer meaningful "per piece" and "per program" alternatives to the blanket license, and prohibited it from acquiring performing rights on an exclusive basis.[28] These provisions gave music users, for the first time, options to tailor their licenses to their actual needs, and created a realistic opening for non-ASCAP music. Internal reforms imposed by the consent decree were equally dramatic. Every ASCAP member was given a vote for directors. Distribution of royalties was to be based on objective criteria, determined "in a fair and non-discriminatory manner." The bar to membership was lowered—anyone with a single published credit was eligible. Although the membership committee insisted it still had discretion to deny applications for good cause, Justice Department oversight deprived ASCAP of the weapon it had wielded most successfully for years to restrict membership, inaction. More than 800 applications were pending when the decree was entered, some for as long as fifteen years. Within two years, the backlog was gone. ASCAP was no longer a private club answerable only to itself; henceforth it would bear public responsibilities analogous to those of common carriers or utilities.

BMI, conceived only two years earlier, had established itself as a performance rights organization on an equal footing with ASCAP. Within days of ASCAP's guilty pleas, BMI was making its first licensing overtures to non-broadcast music users, touting the power of its 700 member radio stations to create hits, and assuring theaters and hotels that they "need no longer pay any price which ASCAP may see fit to ask."[29] BMI had arrived. Further validation came on February 24, 1941, when it was sued for copyright infringement by Ira B. Arnstein.

Of the eleven songs that he had submitted to BMI, Arnstein claimed that BMI had copied eight to create some of the most conspicuous of its early successes. "I Hear a Rhapsody," a passionate love song with lush arpeggios and flexible tempos that have made it a favorite of jazz instrumentalists, he alleged, was copied from his sob ballad, "Sadness Overwhelms My Soul." The dirge-like "V'Shomru" and the martial "Soldiers of Zion" were, per Arnstein, turned into Alberto Dominguez's infectious cha-cha-cha's "Perfidia" and "Frenesi." (Dominguez, as far as Arnstein was concerned, was just a Mexican Emery Deutsch: "He is nothing because he never wrote before and he will never write again outside of the two compositions he has copied from me."[30]) And so on. These were, at first blush, Arnstein's most implausible allegations of similarity to date. Moreover, the evidence that the accused songs predated the submission of Arnstein's to BMI was airtight. BMI's attorneys were understandably incredulous, but out of what may simply have been morbid curiosity, they undertook a detailed and enlightening exploration of Arnstein's theories of similarity. Arnstein obliged with a spirited defense of his ideas. The crazier Arnstein's cases seemed to get, the more fissures in the law they illuminated.

Music copyright law has perpetually been in a state of analytic confusion as to what "similarity" means, how much similarity is required, how it is to be proved, and to whose ears the similarity must be apparent. Two judicial decisions that appeared during the pendency of *Arnstein v. BMI* illustrate the extremes of the spectrum. In *Carew v. RKO Pictures*,[31] Judge Leon Yankwich followed what might be called the holistic approach: "It is not the dissection to which a musical composition might be submitted under the microscopic eye of a musician which is the criterion of similarity, but the impression which the pirated song or phrase would carry to the average ear." Unable to hear any "substantial part" of the accused song "which can be traced to and discerned by the ordinary listener in the composition which it is claimed to infringe," Yankwich did not need to hear from experts for the defense in the case before him—he directed a verdict for the defense at the close of the plaintiff's case.

In *Allen v. Walt Disney Productions*,[32] Judge Edward Conger, whose first exposure to music copyright was presiding over the MultiSuit, took a more analytic approach. Conger carefully parsed the testimony of competing experts, which he found "impossible to reconcile," on alleged similarities in structure, harmony, melody, rhythm, ornamentation, accidentals, and progression. The dissection charts presented by each side also left him at sixes and sevens: "At first, I was much impressed by the charts of the complainant; they did tend to show more similarity than would ordinarily appear by accident. But then, the respondent's charts were produced, and they showed many differences, that is, a similarity but many differences." With the analytic evidence in approximate equipoise, Conger ruled that the plaintiff had not met its burden of proof, only mentioning in passing the evidence of his own ears, with which he heard similarity, but "would not take the one for the other."

Arnstein's approach, to stretch the taxonomy a little further, was hyperanalytic and far outside the legal mainstream as delimited by *Carew* and *Allen*. But he intuited an important nuance that had, thus far, eluded the judges. Similarity was relevant to two separate elements of an infringement case. First, as circumstantial evidence that might justify an inference of copying, and, second, as a measure of the extent of copying, specifically whether sufficient protectable matter had been taken so as to amount to an unlawful appropriation of intellectual property. In both these aspects, Arnstein believed, microscopic dissection from the viewpoint of the musical expert, not the layperson, was appropriate. To look only for similarities that would imply copying to a layperson was to play right into the hands of the willful infringer, who is proficient in disguising his copying by ornamentation or minor changes in sequence. To a musical ear, Arnstein said, "Soldiers of Zion" and "Frenesi" would "sound absolutely alike, but laymen would say there are a lot of notes [in "Frenesi"], which you have not got because he has jazzed it up.... They always add two notes or three notes in order to cover up the identity."[33] Such differences, even if aurally significant, could not negate *copying*. Referring to his own brief, Arnstein told the court, "if the last page be placed before the first, [it] will sound or assume a different meaning, but the person who placed the last page before the first, has not written a word of it."[34]

It would be equally fallacious, Arnstein argued, to require substantial stretches of similarity before finding an unlawful infringement. "The average popular song consists of only eight measures which are constantly repeated. And if they adopt a few measures here and there they have their entire song."[35] He went on:

> Would it be logical or consistent with truth and justice if in a case where the diamond manufacturer submitted his goods to a dealer and the Court stated: "The dealer had only taken a few diamonds here and there from each of the eleven trays; he has not stolen the entire stock and is therefore a good and honest man. . . ." Why must there be substantial stealing in music when only adopting a few measures here and there serves their purpose?[36]

BMI's attorneys, surprisingly, conceded the latter point. If he proved copying by direct evidence, they agreed, then Arnstein "would not have to prove substantial similarity and that the songs sounded alike to the layman's ear. . . . The number of measures copied is unimportant (save as to damages) in a case where there is 'direct proof of copying.'"[37]

After a six-day bench trial, Judge John Bright wasn't ready to break any new ground on the law of similarity. He came down foursquare in Judge Yankwich's holistic camp:

> After all, music is written for that great multitude and not for the few who listen to music either to criticize, or with a critical ear to detect variations from the manuscript, or discords, or some other change which to his or her technical ear may seem a sin. There must be in the last analysis such a substantial appropriation that the general public will detect the same air in the new arrangement.[38]

Again, Arnstein was unable to raise funds to have a transcript of the trial prepared. This time the Second Circuit granted him special dispensation to brief and argue an appeal based on the pleadings and the documentary exhibits alone. But when the appeal was assigned to a panel that included Judges Charles E. Clark and Harrie B. Chase, both of whom had been on the panel that dismissed his appeal of the MultiSuit for lack of a transcript, Arnstein took exception. He moved to have the appeal reassigned on the ground that "judging by the past, Judges Clark and Chase have shown prejudice against plaintiff and he would have not a ghost of a chance if he comes before them."[39] (Notably, Arnstein never sought to disqualify a judge who had previously decided a case against him on the merits; denying him his day in court was quite another matter.)

Clark and Chase did not recuse, but on Clark's suggestion the assignment to author an opinion for the court was given to the third member of the appellate panel, Augustus N. Hand, "the judge who is without fear and beyond reproach so far as the plaintiff is concerned."[40] Judge Hand (Learned Hand's cousin) accepted the thankless task without enthusiasm: "Probably something had better be said as to why the appellant cannot prevail, although it will be certain not to satisfy a man with so profound a sense of grievance."[41] His opinion summarily affirmed the district court without offering any fresh thinking on the legal issues.[42] Still, Arnstein's ever-more bizarre claims were pushing the existing state of the law closer to the breaking point.

A post-apocalyptic cultural historian, searching for the essence of the life we made at the apex of the Age of the Songwriter, would do well to study the "I Got a Gal in Kalamazoo" sequence from the 1942 Twentieth Century–Fox film *Orchestra Wives*. Composer Harry Warren and lyricist Mack Gordon had no lofty aspirations for this number—they were simply looking to crank out a sequel to their earlier hit, "Chattanooga Choo-Choo," and "do a craftsmanlike job in creating a popular song based on an almost sure-fire formula."[43] Filmed in black and white, with unobtrusive cinematography and stripped-down production values appropriate to wartime, "I Got a Gal" makes for an incandescent eight minutes of sight and sound. The song is performed first by Glenn Miller's orchestra and then reprised by the Nicholas Brothers, Harold and Fayard, who execute an exuberant tap dance, unencumbered by a chorus line, tricked-up choreography, or props, except for a pair of discreetly positioned trampolines. And the same score introduced Warren and Gordon's wedding classic, "At Last." *That* is entertainment.

Arnstein v. Twentieth Century–Fox Film Corp. was a minor addition to Arnstein's litigation canon, a sequel to a sequel to an unrelievedly dreary remake on an old formula. "I Got a Gal" was, by his running count, the forty-eighth hit stolen from him; even Arnstein may have been getting a little blasé about the whole business. Arnstein's "Ka-la-ma-zoo," written in 1926 for an abandoned musical revue at New York's Neighborhood Theatre, was a "humorous travesty on grand opera" for vocal quartet. A parody of Wagner's style, it included snippets of the Grand March from *Tannhäuser*, sung to the syllables "Ka-la-ma-zoo." (The inspiration for this oddity was likely none other than Sigmund Spaeth, who had just published a book of such musical confections, *Words and Music*, that included a Wagnerian version of "Jack and Jill," replete with a quote from *Die Walküre*.[44])

Some similarities between the Warren-Gordon song and Arnstein's were obvious—each song spelled out or syllabified "Kalamazoo" with thirteen notes on a single tone, and both employed a "zoo-zoo-zoo" vamp. Arnstein's theory of access had all the familiar elements: Before permanently heading west, Harry Warren frequently came to Arnstein's rooming house to call upon his landlady, a Mrs. Selzer. One day Arnstein played "Ka-la-ma-zoo" for him. A few days later that manuscript and some others mysteriously disappeared from his room. After Arnstein brought the matter to ASCAP's attention, Mrs. Selzer mysteriously disappeared as well, while Harry Warren "went to Hollywood and became a great song writer."[45]

The *Twentieth Century–Fox* case had one new twist. For the first time, Arnstein sought a trial by jury. "For twelve years," he told the court, the infringers "have had a Roman holiday, taking advantage of the fact that judges know little or nothing about music and therefore had to rely on the testimony of a few hired fakers who posed as music experts."[46] Here Arnstein fell victim to a glitch in the law that would not be remedied in his lifetime. Prior to the new Federal Rules of Civil Procedure, he could have brought an "action at law" exclusively for damages, with a right to trial by jury under the Seventh Amendment (which applies only to "suits at common law"), or a "bill in equity" for injunctive relief, as to which there would have been no jury trial right. The Federal Rules abolished the archaic law/equity distinction in favor of a single "civil action" for all available forms of relief. Arnstein's complaint sought damages, but also recited the ancient talismanic language required to make out a claim for an injunction: that he was "without adequate remedy at law." Judge Francis Caffey, in accord with the vast weight of judicial authority at the time, held that by doing so Arnstein had "so framed his complaint as to deprive himself, through the form he adopts, of any right to a jury trial in this case."[47] This was precisely the type of sclerotic formalism the Federal Rules had been intended to eliminate, but it would take a series of Warren Court opinions in the 1960s to ensure the primacy of the Seventh Amendment right to a jury in cases seeking both equitable and legal relief.

The case went to trial in June 1943. For the third time, Arnstein failed a courtroom identification test—this time he was unable to pick out Harry Warren in the crowd of spectators. (Arnstein insisted that he had been tricked by Fox's attorneys, who filled the courtroom with "stooges in various disguises," including one man bandaged like a mummy and another "in a long white robe and blue eyeglasses." Naturally, he could not find Harry Warren amidst "such conglomeration of masqueraders."[48]) After three days of testimony, the case reached the usual denouement. "By ingenious manipulation of his composition the plaintiff attempts to establish similarity . . . he transfers notes from accompaniment in the bass to melody in the treble, he omits and changes notes and the rhythm of some of his phrases, and separates parts of some of his phrases and places them in different parts of his composition," Judge William Bondy wrote. "It has frequently been held that similarity cannot be established in this manner."[49] Arnstein vowed that the next time he would get his jury.

A comprehensive radio-music peace was finalized in November 1941, when NBC and CBS signed nine-year agreements with ASCAP. The radio networks had stalled for months after ASCAP signed its consent decree before beginning serious negotiations toward new license terms, and for many months more before completing deal. The agreement they reached was a severe blow to ASCAP's finances, reducing its take from radio by $1 million compared to 1940, and to a level that was about half of what ASCAP had been seeking under the proposal that triggered the boycott. But coming a few weeks before Pearl Harbor, the deal was done just in time to ensure that morale on the home front would not suffer from underexposure to the indispensable music of Irving Berlin. This was a blessing lost upon Harry Warren. Having spent virtually his entire career working within the Hollywood studio system, Warren was relatively unknown, despite having had more songs on "Your Hit Parade" than Irving Berlin. His resentment was immortalized in his wartime quip: "They bombed the wrong Berlin."[50]

When war came, Sergeant Irving Berlin quickly reported to Camp Upton on Long Island to begin work on an update of his famous World War I all-soldier musical revue, *Yip, Yip, Yaphank*. Before leaving the city he left explicit instructions for his lawyers to structure a business deal in which all profits from his new score—to be called *This Is the Army*—would flow to the

Army Emergency Relief Fund. "These numbers are being exploited and handled a hundred per cent by Army personnel, whose salaries are being paid by the public," he told Francis Gilbert. "Mr. and Mrs. John Doe Public will have just as much of a property right in the *This is the Army* score as a publisher who has spent his money exploiting a songwriter's song."[51] Any hint of personal profit, he warned, would be "playing with dynamite."[52] In accordance with Berlin's wishes, Gilbert advised the NAB that ASCAP would be instructed to license songs from the show "free of charge to all broadcasting stations."[53]

ASCAP, however, was slow to appreciate that with the country at war more than bare minimal compliance with a Justice Department consent decree would be expected of it. ASCAP general manager John Paine was exasperated by the number of requests he was receiving from military bases and morale officers seeking gratis licenses: "Nobody thinks that the patriotic thing to do is to sign a contract and pay authors and composers just the same as they pay everybody else."[54] While it might be Mr. Berlin's desire to license *This Is the Army* songs for radio broadcast free of charge, Paine told his counterparts at the NAB, "the Society must be responsible for its own policies, it cannot always do that which is requested."[55] As Berlin predicted, ASCAP's mercenary attitude was incendiary. On behalf of BMI and the NAB, Sidney Kaye fired off a broadside to Francis Gilbert:

> If the result of this expenditure of the taxpayers' money is to popularize a score which will be available only to the licensees of ASCAP, it constitutes not only a breach of contract, but a public scandal. I intend, unless I receive the appropriate assurances promptly, to take this matter up through the necessary channels. That this will cause embarrassment not only to ASCAP but also to Mr. Irving Berlin personally is something that I regret.[56]

Gradually though, a new, chastened ASCAP emerged. "We used to picture the Society as a great monopoly at the same time that we denied it. We used to believe that it was impossible to get along without our music and, believing that, we based all our thinking on that premise," Paine candidly told his members. "We learned to our great sorrow that our premise was wrong."[57] After suffering the humiliation of having to personally appear before Judge Duffy in Milwaukee to enter their *nolo contendere* pleas, ASCAP's directors decided that a complete makeover of ASCAP's public image was in order. Although the flamboyant, acerbic Gene Buck's popularity with the rank and file membership was undiminished, the board replaced him with Deems Taylor, mild-mannered composer of operas and orchestral music and erudite radio personality. The battle-scarred E. Claude Mills was the next to be "retired." The system of regional, commissioned attorneys, which had engendered so much anti-ASCAP rage from the organization's very beginning, was phased out in favor of local branches under the direct control of the home office. ASCAP sought to reinvent itself as a service organization that would help customers profit from increased use of its repertoire, and this kinder, gentler profile allowed it to reach accords with all the Snide Act states save Nebraska.

Arnstein believed he had set in motion the chain of events that liberated the music industry from the heavy hand of the Music Trust: "ASCAP was investigated by the U.S. Government right after my exposé and was indicted."[58] With ASCAP neutralized for the benefit of all, Arnstein was ready for his next crusade. Though he was reluctant to burden the Roosevelt Administration with his personal travails while total war raged on, once ultimate victory seemed assured in early 1945 he wrote to the First Lady and gingerly broached a subject that would consume much of the remainder of his life: "I know that you are a very busy lady in manifold humanitarian projects, but this is a matter in which all those who believe in building a better world ought to take an interest, because it reflects on our way of life, our system of justice, our free enterprise and free press." He was referring, he went on to explain, to the villainy of just one man—Cole Porter—who had copied all of his hits from Arnstein, blocked Arnstein's music from broadcast, and suppressed all press coverage of Arnstein's allegations.[59]

It was a good thing Arnstein was not accusing Irving Berlin of these un-American activities. Mrs. Roosevelt, who had seen *This Is the Army* three times, might have thought that he was nuts.

GIFT FOR A PRESIDENT TURNED INTO SONG TO A COW

Everybody steals, but you gotta steal classy!
—Leonard Bernstein

Cole Porter, alone among the Age of the Songwriter's major figures, hadn't established himself as one of them by the age of thirty. After one modest Tin Pan Alley hit, the sentimental 1919 ballad, "An Old-Fashioned Garden," Porter spent most of the next decade living fabulously in Europe on his and his wife Linda's family wealth. There he feigned having no more than a dilettante's interest in writing music, while occasionally mailing in a score to a theatrical producer stateside. One night in 1926, when the Porters were summering in Venice, renting the Palazzo Rezzonico, they entertained Richard Rodgers, who at twenty-four was eleven years Cole Porter's junior but already a rising star on Broadway. After playing some of his songs for a duly impressed Rodgers, Porter Delphically remarked that "he had discovered the secret of writing hits . . . 'I'll write Jewish tunes.'"[1]

And so he did. Some of Porter's songs—for example, "My Heart Belongs to Daddy" ("*Da-da/Da-da-da/Da-da-da-ad*" is so Jewish, Alec Wilder found the song vaguely anti-Semitic[2]) or "You'd Be So Nice to Come Home To"

(*"Under stars chilled/by the win-ter/Under an August moon/burn-ing above"*)—
owe such an undisguised debt to the Ashkenazim no musical sophistication
is required to recognize it. Attendance at a few Jewish weddings or a passing
familiarity with *Fiddler on the Roof* will qualify the ear. Dissection of countless other Porter songs turns up phrases, intervals, rhythms, and modula-
tions evocative of Jewish liturgy.[3] With his advanced musical training, Porter
could achieve effects undreamt of even by those of his peers who had been
hearing such sounds since the womb.

To Rodgers it was unfathomable that "the one who has written the most
enduring 'Jewish' music should be an Episcopalian millionaire who was
born on a farm in Peru, Indiana."[4] But the explanation for Porter's sudden
reversal of fortune in the 1930s was all too obvious to Ira B. Arnstein, himself no slouch when it came to employing the synagogue modes: "Ever since
he discovered that any charlatan can become a genius overnight by stealing
Arnstein's themes, he began to 'compose' the greatest song hits in this country."[5] Porter's attempts to "match Arnstein's melodies, mainly written in a
minor key, with his own lyrics which are frivolous, banal, degenerate, and
senseless" showed that he had no intuitive feel for the music he was stealing.
It was, Arnstein said, "like squeezing a fat man's legs into a boy's knee pants."[6]
After Warner Brothers announced in the summer of 1944 that it was planning to produce a musical based on Porter's life story, Arnstein wrote to
Harry Warner with the suggestion that, before beginning production, it
would be prudent to "consult any real musician (such as Schoenberg or
Korngold) and ask his opinion whether all of Cole Porter's songs have not
been copied from my music."[7]

Arnstein proposed a test. Porter was at that moment working on a new
show, Billy Rose's ambitious *Seven Lively Arts*, which was set to open in
December 1944. Now that Arnstein had called out his scam, "Mr. Porter
would not dare copy any more of my music":[8]

> It will be interesting to see whether he'll have any song hit in Billy Rose's
> new show. I doubt it, because his inspiration will vanish as soon as he
> stops pilfering my melodies.[9]

It came to pass as Arnstein predicted. The New York critics panned Porter's *Seven Lively Arts* score. The *World-Telegram* wrote that "Cole Porter
seems to have lost his inspiration. The score is serviceable without being

distinguished or memorable." "Undistinguished and reminiscent," the other papers echoed, "Cole Porter has done nothing at all overpowering in the way of tunes." "The tunes are definitely not his best."[10] (Somehow, the very beautiful, and Jewish-sounding, "Every Time We Say Goodbye"—"*how strange/the change/from major to minor*"—largely went unnoticed at the time.) For the rest of his life, Porter remembered *Seven Lively Arts* as "his unhappiest experience in the theatre,"[11] a "rank turkey."[12]

Warner Brothers' West Coast legal department, unfamiliar with Arnstein, worried that a lawsuit "might create a menace or disturbing element to the exhibition of our picture."[13] The studio had paid Cole Porter $300,000 for the right to use up to thirty-five of his songs. Arnstein's warnings, characteristically, had aimed high, singling out some of the most desirable material, including the title song, "Night and Day." He knew how to stoke a studio executive's anxieties: "If Cole Porter is such great genius," he wrote to Jack Warner, "let him write new songs for the production."[14] Warner's New York-based lawyers, however, were rather more sanguine. Stanleigh Friedman, who had represented the studio in the MultiSuit, counseled resolve:

> The man is a psychopathic case. He has a persecution complex and believes that all music published by Tin Pan Alley is stolen from him. He was rejected by ASCAP and appeared on Sixth Avenue with a huge placard. . . . The court unfortunately never tries to gag him and he makes trouble for everybody whenever he can but has never collected a nickel. Naturally, it is troublesome and expensive to defend these cases but they must be defended at all costs.[15]

Warner's attorneys dithered for several months over how best to put Porter on notice of Arnstein's claims. Fellow composer Arthur Schwartz, the film's producer and an attorney, wouldn't tell Porter.[16] Max Dreyfus, his publisher, "didn't like to worry writers about claims."[17] Matters were further complicated by Porter's health—after the opening of *Seven Lively Arts* he had to undergo further surgery on his legs, shattered seven years earlier in a debilitating equestrian accident, leaving him hospitalized for weeks, in great pain and with both legs in heavy plaster casts. Finally, it was agreed that Friedman, a fellow Yale alumnus, would inform Porter by letter. "I am sufficiently qualified to venture the opinion that these claims are absolutely ridiculous,"

Friedman wrote Porter on December 27, 1944; "on the other hand, if Arnstein follows his usual course, he can become an awful nuisance."[18] Porter's response, Friedman reported back, was curt. He telephoned Friedman to say that he had "discussed the claims with his publishers, Chappell & Co., who advised him that Arnstein was insane and that he had unsuccessfully sued every publisher in the business and that there was nothing to fear from his claims. He therefore did not think it necessary to discuss the matter further with me and the conversation terminated quite abruptly."[19]

Porter's ill-humor was mitigated to some extent when "Don't Fence Me In," his contribution to Warner Brothers' *Hollywood Canteen*, a New Year's Eve 1944 release, became a surprise hit, "the most instantaneous song hit Cole Porter ever had."[20] But on the first business day of 1945, an agitated Arnstein telephoned Warner attorney Joseph Karp, who transcribed Arnstein's message:

> I can't write you a letter because I have to show you something—in the *Hollywood Canteen* you have the biggest song, "Don't Fence Me In." . . . I don't come to fight with you or argue with you. I want to show it to you and you ask anybody that knows music and he will tell you that this is absolutely the same thing, and I wrote that song for the President and I have letters from the President thanking me for writing the song.[21]

Arnstein was referring to "A Modern Messiah," a song that he had dedicated to Franklin Roosevelt and sent to the president on his fifty-third birthday back in 1935. This was the most galling affront of all, Porter turning his gift for the president of the United States "into a song to a cow."[22] This is what prompted Arnstein to bring the Porter situation to the attention of Eleanor Roosevelt. When her secretary wrote back to him, conveying Mrs. Roosevelt's regrets that "there is nothing she can do in cases requiring the decision of courts,"[23] he felt that *Arnstein v. Porter* had been given the green light, by the First Lady of the United States no less.

The complaint that Arnstein filed in February 1945 was, for the most part, the very model of lawyerly civility, a recycling of highfalutin linguistic formalities Arnstein had long since learned to parrot, methodically stating the legal elements of his claim to authorship of seven of Cole Porter's greatest hits: "Night and Day," "Begin the Beguine," "I Love You," "You'd Be So Nice

THE WHITE HOUSE
WASHINGTON

February 15, 1935

My dear Mr. Arnstein:

Your note of January twenty-sixth has
been received. The President asks me to thank
you ever so much for writing and to say that he
appreciates your thoughtfulness in sending him
the song for his birthday. He is also grateful
for the kind birthday greetings which your com-
munication conveys.

Very sincerely yours,

M. A. LeHand
PRIVATE SECRETARY

Ira B. Arnstein, Esq.,
133 West 69th Street,
New York, N. Y.

Missy LeHand's note conveying President Roosevelt's thanks for "A Modern Messiah" was one of Arnstein's treasured possessions. (*Courtesy FDR Library*)

to Come Home To," "My Heart Belongs to Daddy," "What Is This Thing Called Love?," and "Don't Fence Me In." He demanded a jury trial and, to make sure he got it, limited his prayer for relief to money damages—$1 million. Only at the very end did Arnstein allow himself a point of privilege: "For fifteen or twenty years prior to his onslaught on plaintiff's creative work," he alleged, Porter "wrote dozens of songs and numerous musical shows without any marked success and was practically unknown. Due to the wholesale pirating by the defendant of all plaintiff's creative work, he became the most successful and highest paid song writer in the world."[24] Porter succeeded in having this stricken as impertinent and scandalous, without having to suffer the indignity of parsing out any morsels, such as the "dozens of songs and numerous musical shows without any marked success" part, that he would have been forced to admit were true.

Porter turned the defense of the matter over to his personal attorney, John Franklin Wharton, a partner in the firm then known as Cohen, Cole, Weiss & Wharton. Although Wharton was well known for his representation of theatrical producers, the firm was not part of the tight-knit music copyright circle, nor was it known for its litigation practice. (It was not until 1950, when Judge Simon Rifkind, who decided some of the preliminary motions in *Arnstein v. Porter*, joined the renamed Paul, Weiss, Rifkind, Wharton & Garrison, that it was transformed into a litigation powerhouse.) The case was assigned to the firm's only litigation specialist, a recent recruit from the New York City Corporation Counsel's office, Samuel J. Silverman.

Silverman's mission was to get the case disposed of swiftly, with the least possible prejudice to Cole Porter's health and work routine. When Arnstein expressed a desire to take Porter's deposition, Silverman was quick to accommodate him, making sure that it took place before Porter was scheduled to leave New York for a long West Coast stay to oversee the filming of *Night and Day*. The resulting encounter between Cole Porter and Ira B. Arnstein, on April 30, 1945, must surely have been one of the strangest interludes in Porter's pampered, gilded life. Arnstein was whisked to Porter's forty-first-floor apartment at the Waldorf Towers, a plush homoerotic retreat decorated with two grand pianos "placed curve to curve," antique parquet floors imported from a French chateau, and extravagant oriental rugs. In a dialogue worthy of Samuel Beckett, sparse and absurd, Arnstein sought to place Porter—he of the rue Monsieur, the Palazzo Rezzonico, Brentwood, Buxton Hall, and the Waldorf-Astoria—someplace, anyplace, where his hands or ears might have glommed onto the music of Ira B. Arnstein. Was he in Miami Beach in 1936 or 1937? Did he ever rent a room at 18 West 71st Street? Did he know Arnstein's landlady, Mrs. Saffir?

ARNSTEIN: Do you employ a few stooges to follow the plaintiff?
PORTER: I don't know who the plaintiff is.
ARNSTEIN: I am the plaintiff.
PORTER: I beg your pardon. No.
ARNSTEIN: You do not know of any man?
PORTER: I said no.[25]

At his own deposition, which followed immediately afterwards at Silverman's Wall Street office, Arnstein was feisty and expansive, but he stuck to his theoretical guns when it came to the issue of similarity. He consistently deflected any questions as to what resemblances the layman would recognize ("The moronic listener? How should I know what that person would say? Could I tell what the blind man would say when he sees the sun set?"[26]) and defended his methods of analytical dissection:

SILVERMAN: Would the average listener, untrained in music, notice a substantial resemblance between "A Modern Messiah" and "Don't Fence Me In" just as written?

ARNSTEIN: I will answer again as if you compared a long novel with a short story which has been derived from that novel. By omitting about 200 pages of the original, I would say that if you compared the original with the short story, the ordinary layman, who is probably not as ignorant about language as he is about music, would still be fooled and would not be able to tell that both of them are alike. In order to prove the piracy, we would have to cut the novel to the length of the short story and use only the material that the plagiarist has picked.[27]

Arnstein was equally firm, if not nearly as lucid, on questions of access. After eliciting the particulars of rooming house break-ins dating back fifteen years, Silverman asked Arnstein to connect the dots:

SILVERMAN: How do you know that Cole Porter had anything to do with any of these burglaries?

ARNSTEIN: I don't know that he had to do with it but I only know that he could have had. . . . When the songs come out exactly as mine I would say that such person had access, that the stooges were his or else why were his songs similar to mine.[28]

Silverman had to be delighted with the record he had made. He had nailed Arnstein—more accurately, Arnstein had nailed himself—on both access and similarity. Arnstein admittedly had no evidence that Cole Porter had seen or heard his music ("Neither have I evidence," Arnstein added irritably, "that he has seen a copy of Schubert's 'Ave Maria'"[29]), leaving Porter's unequivocal denials uncontroverted. As a matter of principle, Arnstein refused to even attempt to meet the governing legal test for similarity, as stated in *Arnstein v. BMI*, that there was "such a substantial appropriation that the general public will detect the same air in the new arrangement." There was no way, on such facts, that Arnstein could prevail under existing law. Porter's attorneys rightly complained that Arnstein "simply does not agree with this Court's view of the law and therefore he will not stop litigating."[30]

It was a situation seemingly tailor-made for another new procedural tool introduced by the Federal Rules of Civil Procedure, a motion for summary judgment, a device that obviates the need to hold a trial where the documentary record, including pretrial depositions, shows that there is "no genuine dispute as to any material fact" and therefore judgment can be rendered strictly "as a matter of law."[31] In essence, the Federal Rules offered litigants a quid pro quo—a plaintiff need only provide bare notice of the cause of action in the complaint, but after being afforded a greatly liberalized opportunity for pretrial discovery, the case could survive a motion for summary judgment and go to trial only with a showing that there was sufficient evidence to sustain the claim, that the case wouldn't simply "evaporate when proof is made a trial."[32]

Relying principally on Arnstein's deposition testimony, Silverman moved for summary judgment. For good measure, he also submitted recordings of each of the Arnstein and Porter pieces, performed in their entirety on piano, along with the official court files from Arnstein's five previous federal cases. The motion was presented to Judge Francis Caffey, who had stricken Arnstein's jury demand in the *Twentieth Century–Fox* case a few years earlier. Caffey, in what was obviously a cursory, hastily written memorandum, made no mention of the recordings, nor did he address the issue of similarity. The issue of access was dispositive: "My conviction is that access by the defendant to the plaintiff's compositions involved in this action has not been proved. I feel warranted in characterizing as fantastic the story on the subject told in the plaintiff's behalf."[33] Summary judgment granted for Cole Porter.

Silverman had done his job. *Arnstein v. Porter* was out of court before production of *Night and Day* had wrapped. Cole Porter had not been discommoded with a trip to Foley Square, and the vicious trade libel that Arnstein was circulating, that the film was not biography at all, but "a fictitious story of how Cole Porter became a genius"[34] (Arnstein thought that a contemporaneous Bette Davis picture, *A Stolen Life,* had the more appropriate title) had been squelched in its incipiency.

Arnstein had grown accustomed to getting his day in court, saving his most piquant outbursts of indignation not for his losses, but for those few occasions when procedural technicalities had prevented him from getting a full hearing on the merits. Summary judgment was a fresh assault upon his sense of justice. How could a judge simply dismiss his allegations as "fantastic" without taking the trouble to hear all the evidence? "Why is such thing fantastic in a city filled with all kinds of criminals, racketeers, and gangsters? Was Murder, Inc. a fantastic organization?"[35] Arnstein took an appeal to the Second Circuit.

Unlike much of the rest of the world, the United States does not recruit and train a cadre of professional judges. Our federal judges are generalists, plucked from all corners of the legal profession by a combination of happenstance, political connections, and merit, and then called upon to develop, on-the-job, a reasonable level of expertise across not only the vast expanse of federal jurisdiction, but in many areas of state law as well. And under Article III of the Constitution, the judges must confine themselves to deciding actual "cases and controversies" with real-world consequences for the parties that chance to come before them; a federal court cannot reach out to decide contrived legal questions based on its idle interests or prior expertise, or because some area of the law seems to be in need of clarification or improvement.

Seldom will an existentially generated controversy and a randomly selected group of federal judges converge as felicitously as in *Arnstein v. Porter*. The Second Circuit of 1946, "Learned Hand's Court," represented a gold standard, second in influence only to the U.S. Supreme Court, and perhaps more highly respected. The three-judge appellate panel assigned to hear *Arnstein v. Porter*—Learned Hand, Jerome Frank, and Charles Clark—was as illustrious as any that could have been mustered in the United States in 1946 for any case, and it was miraculously well suited to the subject matter of this one. Learned Hand was widely recognized for his seminal contributions to U.S. copyright law. He was also a former trial judge of the old school, that is to say, he believed that the job should entail actually presiding over trials. Clark, while serving as dean of Yale Law School before being appointed to the Second Circuit in 1939, was the principal draftsman of the Federal Rules of Civil Procedure. He, more than anyone, was responsible for the summary judgment procedure being adopted and made available in every kind of civil case. In his early years on the Second Circuit he was a lonely champion of the rule and a frequent dissenter on a court which, he believed, was interpreting it so narrowly, contrary to its words and spirit, as to effectively gut it.

On this, and many other issues, Jerome Frank was Clark's most dependable foil. A widely published polemicist of the legal realist school of thought and an uncompromising liberal provocateur, it is beyond imagining that Frank could serve today as general counsel to an executive branch agency, chairman of the Securities and Exchange Commission, or U.S. Court of Appeals judge—all positions to which he was appointed by Franklin Roosevelt. His appointment to the Second Circuit in 1941 was compared by one contemporary to "the choice of a heretic to be a Bishop of the Church of Rome."[36] From the day Frank took his seat, "the outstanding feature of the court's work," writes Marvin Schick, "was the virtually uninterrupted friction between Judges Clark and Frank." "Each was combative, possessed it seems with inexhaustible energy for prolonging debate and with a comparable capacity and penchant for committing to writing whatever was believed in a particular moment."[37]

All three judges were erudite, articulate, and strong-willed. And all three carefully preserved for posterity the internal memoranda they exchanged as they deliberated over cases, leaving behind a sumptuous feast for lovers of jurisprudence and vitriol.

Arnstein's appellate brief, like most *pro se* efforts, was light on legal analysis. It read more like a closing argument to a jury. That was not a bad approach in the circumstances; these judges hardly needed to be enlightened on the law, nor would they have been likely to rely on Arnstein for enlightenment. Arnstein's brief was not without force in stating a plausibility argument for letting the case go to trial. He described the economics of the popular music industry, in particular its ability to translate a few catchy bars of melody into large profits, which made putting stooges in positions of trust at multiple rooming houses and bribing law enforcement to look the other way perfectly reasonable costs of doing business. He explained how easy it was to conceal signs of copying from the ordinary listener, and how even if similarities between any two songs can be chalked up to coincidence, "two individuals could not conceive seven times the same ideas, plans, or inspirations. Such a thing is incredible, impossible, and against all laws of nature."[38] Who is to say that a jury of his peers would not agree?

The panel heard Arnstein and Silverman orally argue the case on January 10, 1946. Strongly worded memoranda began flying between the judges' chambers shortly thereafter. Frank was first to weigh in, voting to reverse.[39] Ever the legal realist on the alert to police personal biases that might compromise judicial decision making, Frank confronted such factors head-on: "I am opposed, merely because we may think Arnstein is nutty, to creating a bad precedent." He expounded at some length on the fine line between genius and insanity in the arts and sciences. "There have been partly crazy men who have been artistically creative: Nietzsche ended up in a bat-house, and so did Swift. Moreover, there have been cases where men have been treated unfairly as to some particular matter and have then gone nutty." Even a paranoid, Frank seemed to reason, can have enemies. Nor did he think it followed "that because Porter is exceedingly successful financially, and maybe has a touch of genius, he did not plagiarize." Frank had listened to the records submitted by Porter and felt that he heard some "marked resemblances." "So too," he added, "does my secretary, who improvises music." The summary judgment procedure, he thought, had placed Arnstein at an unfair disadvantage. Although he could not afford to make recordings of his own to counter Porter's on summary judgment, at a trial he would be able to "play parts of the compositions so as to emphasize the similarities."

Judge Clark was next to vote.[40] After reviewing Arnstein's "dissection-analysis of the alleged similarities," and listening to the records, he concluded there was nothing remotely actionable. "This conclusion, I might add, was concurred in by my secretary and my law clerk, both of whom have studied music somewhat as I have." But Clark did not stop there. "In order to be quite sure," he wrote, "I spent Sunday afternoon with my friend Professor Luther Noss, Yale University organist, who is not above playing and understanding popular music." He summarized Professor Noss's conclusions as best he could, but assured his colleagues that "I am very confident myself that had you been with me or if you now do the same thing with a really good musician, you will not have the slightest doubt there is nothing to this at all." Reversing the grant of summary judgment in a case like this, Clark feared, would render the procedural reform he had so recently accomplished ineffectual:

There ought to be some way whereby lawyers and litigants can get away from costly trials where there is absolutely nothing whatsoever to the case as here; and if we make useless the carefully worked out procedure for testing the merits by summary judgment, pre-trial, and discovery, which is the heart of the new federal rules, then we naturally will drive trial courts and lawyers back to getting rid of such foolish cases in the old way for want of the better.

"I don't believe one of us thinks for a moment that there is one chance out of a hundred of Arnstein's ever succeeding here," Clark concluded, "and I think we cast doubt on the process of justice and our standing as a court if we simply postpone decision and not have the backbone to stop it when we should."

Frank and Clark continued to exchange increasingly acerbic memoranda, not with any hope of persuading the other, but for the benefit of Learned Hand, who would cast the deciding vote. Frank was particularly appalled by Clark's private consultation with Professor Noss: "I can't see why we should have a trial (and a secret one at that) in an appellate court to show the world that a summary judgment is beneficent reform—because, forsooth, it avoids a trial in a trial court."[41] "A summary judgment, in the hands of a skilled lawyer against a mediocre one," Frank argued, "often leads to the injustice of winning a case on clever pleading tactics," the very result that Clark's reforms were intended to prevent.[42] Clark, in response, accused Frank of shirking the hard analysis of the facts that the case called upon the judges to do. "Jerry makes no answer to the musical analysis, and once the *music itself* is studied, there is none."[43]

Hand finally came down on Frank's side.[44] "This appeal has troubled me more than anything else of the week's batch. . . . I have after much hesitation come to the conclusion that there ought to be a trial." Hand's rationale was straightforward; for him it was a question of invading the province of the jury. The issue of access would ultimately turn on the credibility of Cole Porter. "How can we say that a jury might not be incredulous of his denials if they saw him?" The test for infringement was "the impression made upon the ear of the ordinary hearer, and I cannot think of any issue which should be more exclusively for a jury than that." As the senior judge in the majority, Hand exercised his prerogative to assign the opinion to himself. But after sleeping on it, he changed his mind and gave it to Frank.[45] It was a ticklish position for Frank, who was on record in his judicial and nonjudicial writings as an extreme skeptic of the value of juries in civil cases. But he tackled the assignment with his usual gusto, producing an opinion in which his concern that summary judgment was unfair to the little guy and Hand's reverence for the jury combined to resuscitate Arnstein's case and create a more plaintiff-friendly law of copyright infringement.

The opinions that Frank and Clark released for public consumption barely disguised the backbiting that was percolating behind the scenes, even if (as Frank and other legal realists would have expected) their stated reasoning seems only loosely related to the actual decision-making process. Frank's opinion for the majority and Clark's spirited dissent, together, make for a fascinating symposium on issues of both substance and procedure in copyright cases. For courts, *Arnstein v. Porter*[46] long reigned as the "analytical bedrock of infringement cases."[47] It is one of very few intermediate federal appellate court decisions to retain an enduring place in scholarly treatises and journals, never superseded by a more authoritative Supreme Court pronouncement.

Frank's opinion divides the elements of proof in a copyright infringement case along lines that could, with some effort, be teased out of prior case law, but which surely had not been expressed with the clarity or precision that he imposed upon it. Arnstein, it turned out, had been half right all along. "It is important to avoid confusing two separate elements essential to a plaintiff's case in such a suit," Frank wrote: "(a) that defendant copied from plaintiff's copyrighted work and (b) that the copying (assuming it to be proved) went so far as to constitute improper appropriation." There was copying, and then there was *copying*, the latter being what Frank termed "misappropriation." As to copying, Frank went on, "analysis ('dissection') is relevant, and the testimony of experts may be received." This was a vindication of Arnstein's long-held view that only the minute inspection of a score by someone knowledgeable of music can ferret out the hallmarks of copying that may be cleverly concealed by rhythmic changes, passing notes, and other tricks of the trade. Where there was evidence of "access," Frank went on, little evidence of similarity would be needed to send the issue of copying to the jury. If there was no evidence of access, similarities would not support an inference of copying unless they were "striking."

Where Frank parted company with Arnstein was on the issue of misappropriation. There, Frank came down squarely in line with *Arnstein v. BMI*. The question "is whether defendant took from plaintiff's works so much of what is pleasing to the ears of lay listeners, who comprise the audience for whom such popular music is composed, that defendant wrongfully appropriated something which belongs to the plaintiff." On this, "'dissection' and expert testimony are irrelevant." Frank explained why Arnstein's query, "Is it not theft to take just a few of my diamonds?," was inapposite: "The plaintiff's legally protected interest is not, as such, his reputation as a musician but his interest in the potential financial returns from his compositions which derive from the lay public's approbation of his efforts." Unlike the theft of a few diamonds, the theft of a few musical phrases that can only be detected under an expert's magnifying glass, whatever moral censure it may deserve, deprives the owner of nothing of legally cognizable value.

Working backward from that substantive template, Frank considered whether summary judgment was procedurally appropriate in the case at hand. Based on the recordings, there were similarities between the Porter and Arnstein pieces, not striking, but sufficient to support a finding of copying provided that there was evidence of access. On that, Frank acknowledged, Arnstein's theory was highly improbable, but "we should not overlook the shrewd proverbial admonition that sometimes truth is stranger than fiction." Because "the demeanor of witnesses is recognized as a highly useful, even if not an infallible, method of ascertaining the truth and accuracy of their narratives," the majority held that even though Arnstein had come forward with no evidence contradicting Porter's deposition denials, he could not be deprived of the opportunity to cross-examine Porter in front of a jury. "Plaintiff, or a lawyer on his behalf, on such examination may elicit damaging admissions from defendant; more important, plaintiff may persuade the jury, observing defendant's manner when testifying, that defendant is unworthy of belief."

Misappropriation, the majority held, was strictly a matter of the lay listener's reaction, and therefore an "issue of fact which a jury is peculiarly fitted to determine." (Here Frank inserted a suggestion made by Learned Hand— that the tone deaf should be excluded from the jury.) "At the trial, plaintiff may play, or cause to be played, the pieces in such manner that they may seem to a jury to be inexcusably alike, in terms of the way in which lay listeners of such music would be likely to react." Though Frank could imagine a case in which summary judgment for the defendant would be appropriate ("suppose that Ravel's 'Bolero' or Shostakovich's 'Fifth Symphony' were alleged to infringe 'When Irish Eyes are Smiling'"), here the similarities were not so "trifling."

"I don't think we should jeer this fellow out of court," Judge Jerome Frank wrote, "merely because we think he is a little touched." (*Library of Congress Harris & Ewing Collection*)

It is hard to find a much better example of the fine art of judicial invective than Judge Clark's dissent, in which he decried the "anti-intellectual and book-burning nature" of the majority's ruling. Despite having himself relied on the recordings submitted by Porter and a private demonstration given by Professor Noss, Clark attacked the majority for relying on "the judicial eardrum" to detect similarities. Echoing the views of Sigmund Spaeth, Clark wrote that "sound is important in a case of this kind, but it is not so important as to falsify what the eye reports and the mind teaches." Clark insisted that summary judgment would be proper on the basis of Arnstein's own written dissections of the compositions alone, as they, at best, showed similarities only in "small detached portions here and there, the musical fillers between the better known parts of the melody," never more than five consecutive notes, and in most cases less. To rely instead on ears that may have been "dulled by long usage, possibly artistic repugnance or boredom, or mere distance which causes all sounds to merge" renders the outcome of any case a matter of what Clark termed "adscititious fortuity."

As to Frank's copying-misappropriation distinction, Clark could not find in the cases cited by Frank "any suggestion of two steps in adjudication of this issue, one of finding copying which may be approached with musical intelligence and assistance of experts, and another that of illicit copying which must be approached with complete ignorance. . . . This is a single deduction to be made intelligently, not two with the dominating one to be made blindly." In their private correspondence, Clark was blunter about what he considered Frank's misuse of precedent. "The cases you cite," he told Frank, "show how hard you must grub for not even a faint suggestion of what you have done."[48]

Knowing full well that neither Frank nor Hand believed that Arnstein had any chance of prevailing on the merits, Clark called their ruling "one of those procedural mountains which develop where it is thought that justice must be temporarily sacrificed, lest a mistaken precedent be set at large." Accordingly, he spilled little ink in responding to Frank's speculation as to how Arnstein's case might fare better upon a full trial, other than to point out that the peripatetic Cole Porter might not even show up to be cross-examined, in which case the jury would have nothing but his deposition transcript to work with. Clark attacked the attitudes that he knew had truly animated the majority, "a belief in the efficacy of the jury to settle issues of plagiarism, and a dislike of the rule established by the Supreme Court as to summary judgments." As to the first, Clark could not resist needling Frank. "I am not one to condemn jury trials," he wrote, followed by a string of pinpoint citations to prior writings of Frank doing exactly that. As to the second, Clark argued, a rule of preference for allowing such cases to go to juries invited "clever musical tricks in the hope of getting juries . . . to divide the wealth of Tin Pan Alley."

Arnstein had already sent the three appellate judges a "personal friendly letter" in which he chided them for taking three weeks to rule where "a legal reversal would take no more than ten minutes," and expressed his fear that "a loophole to further injustice is being sought."[49] Fortunately, his letter crossed in the mail with their decision. And he finally had that monkey of "never having collected a nickel" off his back—the court of appeals awarded him $75 in court costs against Cole Porter.

With a million-dollar claim against the well-heeled Cole Porter going to a jury, for the first time in ten years Arnstein could get the attention of the bar. A well-respected commercial law firm, Tenzer Greenblatt, signed on to try the case. With *Night and Day* due to be released in the summer of 1946, Porter's attorneys moved swiftly to get the case on the May 1946 trial calendar of Judge John Knox.

The selection of the jury was completed in a matter of minutes. Arnstein was not satisfied with the results. His idea for implementing the court of appeals' suggestion that the tone deaf should be excluded from the jury— testing whether prospective jurors could distinguish two simple folk tunes—had been rejected. The result, he complained, was a jury that consisted of "several housewives, one janitor, one garage worker," and only one juror who had an ear for music.[50] He was incensed by the inclusion of an actress: "No member of Equity could decide against Cole Porter and ever get a job on Broadway again."[51]

Judge Frank's prediction that a trial in *Arnstein v. Porter* would not be "farcical" proved wide of the mark. There was little that Arnstein's attorneys could do to persuade a jury that "My Heart Belongs to Daddy" took so much of what is pleasing to a layperson's ear in "A Mother's Prayer" as to constitute a wrongful appropriation, although one of Porter's expert witnesses, Richard Rodgers, perhaps influenced by the secret that Porter had confided to him in Venice twenty years earlier, did concede there were similarities.

If anything, Arnstein's theories of similarity had only grown more farfetched and abstruse, and his dissection charts—dense spaghettis of staff lines, notes, ties, annotations, sarcasm, and ink splotches—had come to look as though they'd been faked by Saul Steinberg. ASCAP president Deems Taylor, testifying as an expert for Porter, got straight to the nub of the problem with Arnstein's charts: "You can always yank a given phrase out of its context and put it somewhere else. But music isn't written with scissors."[52]

With Richard Rodgers and Deems Taylor testifying as experts on Porter's behalf, an appearance by Sigmund Spaeth would strike most trial lawyers as overkill. Yet there he was. Pompous, cranky, and long-winded, his demeanor was becoming a liability. And now he handed Arnstein's lawyers a stiletto they could use to stab holes in his credibility.

Naughty but Nice (1939), also called *The Professor Steps Out*, was the last musical that Dick Powell made for Warner Brothers. The screenwriters

Arnstein accused Porter of stealing his somber minor key melodies and adding lyrics that were "frivolous, banal, degenerate, and senseless."

wanted to create comic possibilities by having the boyish Powell play a shy, pedantic character, with surefire high jinks to ensue when he was placed in some incongruous setting. They settled on a promising conceit: Powell would be a very square small-town music professor, Donald Hardwick, who goes to New York City to find a publisher for a symphony he has written, only to become a darling and a dupe of Tin Pan Alley. Harry Warren would be composing the score, so the writers decided to give Professor Hardwick a talent they had seen Warren demonstrate at social gatherings—"taking one of the songs on the Hit Parade and gradually tracing it back to the original source"—a feat which the Hardwick character performs almost reflexively, to the great annoyance of the one-finger songwriters he meets in New York.[53] At the behest of a lady lyricist, Linda McKay, who recognizes Hardwick's genius, publisher Ed Clark (played by Warner's up-and-coming B-movie idol, Ronald Reagan) buys the symphony. But after the professor has returned home, Clark and McKay turn his music into a swing tune, "Hooray for Spinach," which becomes a smash hit.

Hardwick, disgraced in the eyes of his professional peers and family, goes back to New York where he and McKay become the top songwriting team in Tin Pan Alley. After a scheming rival lifts an orchestral movement by the great Ridowski and publishes it as a Hardwick song, the Ridowski estate sues Hardwick. The day is saved when Hardwick's three spinster aunts from back home show up at trial and convince the judge that in music everybody steals, and that even Ridowski's piece copied from earlier works. Hardwick's symphony finally receives a gala premiere.

Arnstein recognized elements of his *Broadway Music* script in *Naughty but Nice*—the noble artist cheated by Tin Pan Alley sharpies, the climactic trial and exoneration, the triumphal symphonic finale. But it was Sigmund Spaeth who brought suit against Warner Brothers, claiming that Professor Hardwick was intended to be identified with him, a representation Spaeth claimed was libelous. Spaeth's theory of libel was odd—it was not that Hardwick is portrayed as a pedant and a naif, but rather that he was portrayed as espousing beliefs diametrically opposed to Spaeth's well-known views, that is, "that contemporary popular music should be held in low esteem and contempt; that all contemporary popular music is plagiarized and stolen from works and music heretofore written and therefore is a fraud upon the public generally; that the study of contemporary popular music is not a fit subject for education but that on the contrary it is degrading and immoral; and that people who appreciate the performance of contemporary popular music are degraded and people of vulgar tastes." Rather than concluding from all this that Professor Hardwick couldn't possibly be a stand-in for Sigmund Spaeth, so the theory went, the audience is led to believe that the real Sigmund Spaeth, when he proselytizes on behalf of popular music, is a hypocrite and a liar.[54]

It was a legal theory as vainglorious and illogical as any Arnstein had ever advanced. When unexpectedly asked about it on the stand, Spaeth initially testified falsely as to the nature of the suit. The case, he said,

> was based upon the fact that I had submitted a scenario to them built out of the Tune Detective idea, which I had been told in Hollywood had a possibility for a feature film. The scenario was never returned to me. . . . The movie was based on my scenario.

Arnstein's attorneys could have let this testimony stand. Sigmund Spaeth seemed to be having the same difficulty with the concept of independent creation for which he had so often pilloried Arnstein. But Spaeth had opened himself up to stinging cross-examination with public court documents bearing his own signature, and cross-examined he was. Spaeth's *Porter* testimony bears the telltale scent of an expert witness nearing the end of his shelf life.

The trial's principal interest is as a previously overlooked fount of prurient Cole Porter minutiae. His witness list included an entourage of former lovers and sexual co-adventurers—actor Monty Woolley, socialite Howard Sturges, architect Ed Tauch—who were present at the creation of various hits and could swear that they had seen Porter labor over them intensively without reference to *any* other music, much less Arnstein's. Woolley was with Porter in a New York hotel room during the composition of "Night and Day," and with him on the S.S. *Franconia* en route to Java while Porter wrote "Begin the Beguine." Sturges was visiting him in Brentwood and, he testified, "happened to be in the house and in the room with him the night that he wrote 'You'd Be So Nice to Come Home To.'" Tauch (purported to be the "you, you, you" of "Night and Day") was a summer houseguest of Porter's at Lido Beach, Long Island, where Porter played "My Heart Belongs to Daddy" for him at "various stages of its composition." What the postwar, pre–Kinsey Report jury of seven men and five women made of the fact that Porter seemed inspired to turn out some of his most smolderingly romantic ballads while sharing luxe accommodations with a male companion, we do not know. Did they consider Albert Sirmay's mention that he was familiar with the 8,000 records Porter had in his bedroom (none of them Arnstein's) a little too much information? Cary Grant and Alexis Smith this was not.

Arnstein had no idea how right he was that *Night and Day* would be "a fictitious story of how Cole Porter became a genius."

The out-of-town tryouts of Porter's next show, a collaboration with Orson Welles based on *Around the World in 80 Days*, kept the defendant occupied and away from the courtroom for most of the trial. He arrived on the final day to take the stand and to once again emphatically deny that he had ever in his life heard the music of Ira B. Arnstein. Arnstein's attorneys came up with a clever, if not all that effectual, line of attack on Porter's credibility. They confronted him with colorful anecdotes that he had told the press about the creation of his songs, which under oath he was constrained to deny. This did succeed in getting the suave Porter more than a bit flustered: "The interview may have said that I said it but I did not say it." It also elicited a rather definitive statement that future Porter biographers, as they sort through the discrepant etiologies of Porter's songs, ought to note: "I am always inspired by scripts. I never have written songs except for librettos or picture scripts, and it was a certain indication on a page . . . that gave me the idea of 'Night and Day.'"

The outcome was never in much doubt. Arnstein's attorneys made the tough call to have Judge Knox give the jury a special instruction that candidly acknowledged the elephant in the room. "Mr. Arnstein has told us certain things," Judge Knox told the jury, "that cause me to look askance upon that portion of his testimony."

> I refer particularly to the assertion that his rooms and trunks were searched at times when he would be absent from his apartment. And also to the effect that his landlady or landlords were in a conspiracy with ASCAP's representatives or other people who were trying to steal his music. . . . He apparently is a man of considerable training in music and he has written some of these compositions here which in some respects are pleasing to the ear, and if he has had those works lifted from him improperly, notwithstanding his delusions or obsessions, he is entitled to be protected.

Judge Knox was in the unenviable position of being the first judge to instruct a jury under the Second Circuit's new copying/misappropriation dichotomy. If the jurors understood the distinction—and Judge Clark had confidently predicted they would not—it was in spite of Judge Knox's charge, which thoroughly and confusingly melded the two, not because of it. Comparing Knox's prolix jury instructions, twenty-three transcript pages long, with Chief Justice Taney's succinct four paragraphs in *Reed v. Carusi* one hundred years earlier, one has to question whether this represented progress.

The jury, pausing only briefly to hear the recordings of "A Modern Messiah" and "Don't Fence Me In" replayed once, deliberated for just two hours before returning a verdict for the defendant. Porter, who once said that a courthouse was the only place he would go without his signature boutonniere, "because a carnation in the buttonhole never helps your case before a jury,"[55] remained in the courtroom and graciously shook hands with each juror before getting back to work on *Around the World in 80 Days*.[56] The show, as Arnstein had expected, was another in Porter's growing string of flops.

The only remaining question was whether Judge Knox would grant Porter's motion for an award of his attorney's fees. Knox, who found in his files letters from Arnstein going back ten years, seemed especially troubled by the notion that "A Mother's Prayer" could have been the source for so many different hit songs. Silverman argued that a substantial award was needed "in the hope that maybe this plaintiff will be discouraged and will realize he has something to lose by bringing these lawsuits and harrying people." Not only had Arnstein recently threatened to sue Richard Rodgers, Silverman told the judge, "he also said that if Rodgers is not careful 'I will punch him in the nose.'" That seemed to seal it. Knox awarded the relatively nominal sum of $2,500. It was not even enough to cover Cohen, Cole, Weiss & Wharton's out-of-pocket costs, but since Arnstein couldn't pay it anyway, the paltry amount scarcely mattered. It was enough to ensure that *Arnstein v. Porter* would be the sixth and last Arnstein case to go to trial in the Southern District of New York.

FOUR LAST SONGS

I am afraid Arnstein is going to be as far from justice as ever—that he is now stopped from beginning to build a better world in the United States courts, and that there is no hope for the human race.
—Judge Charles E. Clark

In private, Judges Charles Clark and Jerome Frank continued lobbing barbs back and forth for several months after their opinions in *Arnstein v. Porter* had been published. "I realize," Clark told Frank, "that you are merciless on any procedural rules that get in your way."[1] In response to Clark's accusation that his opinion had also cavalierly swept aside settled copyright law, Frank pointed out that no less an authority than Learned Hand, the veritable Moses of copyright law, was, "in every sense, the co-author of my *Arnstein* opinion."[2] Their correspondence then devolved into a testy exchange over whether Frank, whom Clark called "the vigorous force in this case from the beginning," had steamrolled an uncharacteristically supine Learned Hand.[3]

Frank and Hand had to have been relieved that Clark was not assigned to sit with their panel in December 1946, when Arnstein's second *pro se* appeal in the Cole Porter case came before the Second Circuit—the "I-told-you-sos" would have been difficult to stomach. In Clark's absence, their internal memoranda show, Frank and Hand assumed the attitude of innocent bystanders whistling past a train wreck, disinclined to draw any attention to the fact that they had been responsible for overriding the stop signal. Hand admitted to harboring some "wicked" thoughts after reading Arnstein's briefs, and expressed his devout hope that he would not be forced to spend too many of his remaining years "engaged in delving through the sinuous aberrations of the mentally unsound" and "trying to arrange in the cadres of sanity the disordered meanderings of the deranged."[4]

Joined by Circuit Judge Harrie B. Chase, Hand and Frank did make sure that the opinion that the court issued, though unsigned and only three sentences long, validated their earlier judgment that the case should go to a jury: "There can be no doubt that the evidence upon the trial presented a disputed issue as to whether the defendant had in fact copied the plaintiff's music; and that it was not so clearly in the plaintiff's favor that the judge could properly have directed a verdict."[5] Privately, the appellate judges recognized that Judge Knox's charge failed to instruct the jury in accordance with the intricate scheme laid out in the first appeal, but because Arnstein's attorney had failed to make an objection they agreed, in Frank's words, that "we needn't flyspeck it."[6] The opinion stated only that the jury charge "fairly presented the questions which the jury had to decide."[7] *Arnstein v. Porter* finally staggered to its desultory, inevitable conclusion when the U.S. Supreme Court denied Arnstein's petition for writ of certiorari in April 1947.[8]

For Arnstein, there was still no justice. Judge Frank's admonition that the tone deaf should be excluded from the jury had been ignored. His lawyer had failed to subpoena his witnesses, had failed to make objections "although the Court did the most terrible things," had spent his evenings fraternizing with attorneys from the other side, and had given a summation amounting to "twenty minutes of mumbled trivialities."[9] Arnstein had suffered another decade's worth of slights, insults, and oppression since he had filed the MultiSuit in 1937. Encouraged by the courts' refusal to protect his rights and punish malefactors, the music business was helping itself to his music more profligately than ever before. These grievances and more became the subject of what *Billboard* aptly called the "Omnibus Suit,"[10] *Arnstein v. Crestview Music Corp. et al.* "When a man suffers so much injustice and undeserved persecution, just because he was gifted by nature with talent," Arnstein declared, "and so many unscrupulous people wish to deny him even the right of earning a living, he must fight back."[11]

Francis Gilbert was scarcely exaggerating when he told Irving Berlin that, along with the two of them, Arnstein had sued "pretty nearly everybody else in the industry."[12] By the time Arnstein had finished amending his complaint, the suit named fifty defendants and sixty songs. One of 1948's biggest hits, Eden Ahbez's "Nature Boy," published by Crestview Music and recorded by Nat King Cole, Sarah Vaughn, and Frank Sinatra, he alleged, had been copied from the ballet section of *The Song of David*. (Arnstein's timing wasn't what it used to be—Herman Yablokoff, a well-known Yiddish theater actor and composer, had beaten Arnstein to the courthouse by a month with a claim that Ahbez's ballad of the "very strange enchanted boy" infringed his "Shvayg Mayn Harts"—"Be Still My Heart"—and he eventually settled for $25,000.[13]) The big hits of the 1940s that Arnstein accused, including "How Are Things in Glocca Mora," "The Woody Woodpecker Song," "White Christmas," and much of Berlin's score from *This Is the Army*, could have filled out several box sets. In addition to his claims for common law copyright infringement of unpublished compositions (having worn out his welcome in the federal court, he filed the case across Foley Square in New York State court) Arnstein asserted claims of fraud and unfair competition against various music industry defendants, for conspiracy against a raft of lawyers, his own and his opponents', and for libel against *Variety*, the *New York Herald Tribune*, and Sigmund Spaeth.

Over the years Spaeth had published more than his share of unflattering references to Arnstein, sometimes insinuating that he was mentally disturbed, at other times that he was bent on extortion. But it was not Spaeth's imputations of unsound mind or criminality, either of which would have constituted libel per se, that were the basis for Arnstein's claim. Arnstein took offense from a magazine article in which Spaeth had made the relatively benign assertion that Arnstein had, by commencing his lawsuit against Cole Porter shortly after Warner Brothers had announced plans for *Night and Day*, had shown a knack for "timing his activities with rare commercial perspicacity."[14]

It took more than a year, but every one of the defendants in the Omnibus Suit won a dismissal, whether because of the statute of limitations or Arnstein's failure to meet the New York requirement to plead "a plain and concise statement of material facts," because the matter had already been the subject of one of his earlier lawsuits and was therefore *res judicata*, because the state court lacked jurisdiction, or, it seems in quite a few instances, because of just plain Arnstein fatigue. Arnstein had finally reached the final destination in the obsessive litigant's Baedeker, where the lawsuits become meta-lawsuits, arising not from events occurring in life as we live it, but out of earlier lawsuits, and where even the most liberal of courts will no longer abide the disordered meanderings of the deranged.

Sigmund Spaeth's golden years were a mix of the mellow and the curmudgeonly, homey comforts and cruel afflictions, professional stumbles and fresh accolades, worthy charitable work and crass commercialism. He was turning sixty as World War II came to an end, and the demographics were favorable to the apostle of "Music for Everybody." The accelerating birth rate, the vast expansion of leisure time, the redirection of wartime energy into community life, and the introduction of the long-playing record all converged to revitalize Spaeth's career. At the height of the baby boom, the childless Spaeth emerged as the Dr. Spock of musical childrearing. He wrote a widely distributed pamphlet for the Selmer musical instrument company, *Your Child Is Musical*, promoting participation in school bands and orchestras. His endorsements and instructional manuals spurred sales of "recreational" instruments—harmonicas, accordions, and autoharps. Although his ideas seemed to be informed mainly by his own experiences growing up in a family of eleven in the late nineteenth century, the son of a Lutheran hymnal author, he tested them out on his two adoring postwar step-granddaughters, and published the results of his experiments in an article and photo spread for *Better Homes and Gardens* entitled "No Musical Prodigies in *My* Family."

The LP put the world's greatest music within reach of everyone, and Dr. Sigmund Spaeth did his part to close the sale. He provided liner notes and recorded commentary for Remington Records' low-priced "Music Plus!" discs, and served as musical adviser to the "Basic Library of the World's Great Music," sold in weekly installments through Grand Union and First National supermarkets, for as little as $1.37 per record. (For these projects, Spaeth said, "I thought of myself as a dietician first and music critic second."[15]) The "extraordinary burst of civic activity"[16] that began after the war and continued into the 1960s replenished the audience pool for the man who promoted himself as "the final answer to a program chairman's prayer."[17] Spaeth embarked upon a leisurely valedictory tour, raising money along the way for such pet causes as the Braille Music Institute and the National Committee for the Musical Arts, judging musical competitions, picking up speaking fees from local chapters of the Knife and Fork and National Dinner Clubs, and graciously accepting cheesy plaques and engraved bric-a-brac from music organizations of every description.

The drudgery of serious musicology and music criticism, never his strong suits to begin with, had long since lost all appeal. Nonetheless, Spaeth devoted a large part of the 1940s to an ambitious project commissioned by Bennett Cerf of Random House, *A History of Popular Music in America*. First published in 1948, it was a genuine effort to produce a comprehensive, well-documented reference work, a sharp departure from the cocksure and thinly sourced style

Sigmund Spaeth in 1958, showing off an award from the American Accordionists Association. (*Library of Congress New York World-Telegram and the Sun Newspaper Photograph Collection*)

of his earlier books on popular music. Spaeth admitted to having struggled with the assignment and to having nearly given up when he reached the 80,000-word mark, his previous endurance record. The book as published, which Spaeth considered still unfinished, was about 200,000 words, quite a lot to prove a thesis that Spaeth described in the first pages as "a commonplace"—that "popular music is an index to the life and history of a nation." Marred overall by Spaeth's habit of tossing in casual asides and peremptory conclusions (the creation of BMI, for example, was a "determined effort to break down copyright law"[18]) and by embarrassing lapses of logic and judgment (blackface minstrelsy was "an enormous though often indirect contribution on the part of the Negro race"[19]), *A History of Popular Music in America* remains a useful, frequently cited reference, albeit one unlikely to find its way on to many recommended reading lists today.

Especially disappointing to Spaeth was the rather icy response that the book received from its most thoroughly and flatteringly covered subject, Irving Berlin. Spaeth was anxious to get Berlin's reaction and nonplussed when Berlin repeatedly begged off, claiming that he was too busy to look at it.[20] Unbeknownst to Spaeth, Berlin had in fact obtained an advance copy, immediately read the passages covering his career, and referred the book to Francis Gilbert. Spaeth had picked at the most scabrous spot on the great man's thin skin. "He said many nice things about my work," Berlin wrote Gilbert, "but a great many of the references to me have the feel of 'when did you stop beating your wife?'"[21] In reference to Berlin's score for *Annie Get Your Gun*, which had been produced by Richard Rodgers and Oscar Hammerstein, Spaeth had written that "there are those who believe they can detect the hand of Rodgers in some of the tunes and that of Hammerstein in the clever lyrics."[22] Spaeth dismissed this notion—"it would be unfair to suggest that Berlin needed any such help"—but Berlin was irritated nonetheless. As far as he knew, "this was the first time anyone had suggested that Rodgers and Hammerstein had anything to do with the writing of the score." Berlin recalled that on several past occasions he had refused Spaeth's requests to participate in various pet projects, and he wondered if there was a connection. "I may be over-sensitive," he told Gilbert, "but I had a strong feeling that there was something not quite kosher in reading all his references to me."[23]

In 1944, the Edward B. Marks Music Corporation celebrated its fiftieth anniversary and the publication of the boss's second book of reminiscences,

They All Had Glamour, with a two-day (and night) open house at its offices in 30 Rockefeller Plaza and a gala dinner, emceed by Sigmund Spaeth, at the Waldorf-Astoria. Reporters covering the festivities uniformly remarked upon the seventy-nine-year-old Edward Marks's youthful appearance and unflagging energy. Contributing to his high spirits was "Paper Doll," another one of his catalog's obscure back numbers, a flop when he first published it in 1922, but suddenly a top wartime seller, helped along by the pin-up girl craze and recordings by the Mills Brothers and Sinatra.

The litigation that grew out of the company's defection to BMI had been wending its way through the New York State courts for three years, with little of substance having been accomplished. It finally landed in the courtroom of State Supreme Court justice Ferdinand Pecora, the "Hellhound of Wall Street," so-named for his aggressive stewardship of the U.S. Senate's investigation into financial shenanigans in the run-up to the Great Depression. He was in possession, at that moment, of the country's most sensitive nose for sniffing out corporate greed and perfidy. The Marks-BMI deal did not pass Pecora's smell test.

Broadcast Music, Inc. & Edward B. Marks Music Corp. v. Deems Taylor, et al. was a declaratory judgment action designed to resolve the long-mooted legal question whether standard songwriter-publisher contracts gave the publisher control of the performing rights to a song. Marks had not given BMI any warranty regarding the performing rights to the 3,000 or so songs in his catalog written by ASCAP members, and under their agreement it was BMI's burden to establish its legal right to license the performing rights to such songs. In initiating and footing the costs of this test case—defending Edward Marks's extreme position that he, and by extension any publisher, could unilaterally reassign the performing rights for an ASCAP member's composition to BMI, without compensation—BMI forfeited its claim to being the downtrodden songwriter's great friend.

Each side could find verbiage in the relevant legal documents to support its position, but Justice Pecora's May 3, 1945 ruling did not dwell at length on niceties of contract law, it went straight to the equities of the dispute.[24] It was not only, or even primarily, the language of the various contracts that mattered, but also the "inherent character" of ASCAP as a joint venture between songwriters and publishers, "expressed and implied in the very structural arrangement of ASCAP itself." Publishers, he found, held title to the copyrights merely as a trustee for the songwriters. To sanction Marks's unilateral action would amount to a ruthless violation of the underlying pact made between publishers and creators when they became members of ASCAP, to divide such compensation equally between them; and it would shock the sense and spirit of equity. Trust responsibility is not a garment to be doffed at the mere pleasure of the wearer.

Having transferred the risk of such a ruling to BMI, Marks may have figured that he had no economic stake in the case. Justice Pecora did not see it that way. Not satisfied to merely declare that ASCAP had retained control of the performing rights to its members' songs when Marks bolted, he went on to grant the ASCAP writers' request for rescission of their contracts with Marks in toto. Pecora observed that Marks's actions had destroyed the "essential object" of the publisher-songwriter contract:

> As a result these songs have not since then been publicly performed as far as known, and their creators have not received any income from their exploitation; nay, not even a cent from the one million dollar consideration paid by BMI under its contract with Marks. . . . The only executive officer of Marks who took the stand testified that his Company did not consider itself obligated to pay any part of that handsome consideration to any of the writers of its songs.

Pecora's ruling was a thunderbolt. Within days, ASCAP writers led by L. Wolfe Gilbert were making preparations to sue Marks for their share of his BMI money. The ASCAP board used the ruling to thwart an effort by publishers to cut the society and its songwriters out of the negotiations to license music's newest frontier, television. For Edward B. Marks—"a big *goniff* disguised as an honorable Victorian gentleman,"[25] Jack Lawrence called him, seventy years after escaping a contract that he had signed with Marks while still a teenager—the idea that publishers owed a "trust responsibility" to songwriters was a bridge too far. A dinosaur who had survived the mass extinction of Tin Pan Alley, so remarkably hale and hearty only a short time earlier, Marks was dead within a few months of Justice Pecora's ruling.

Under the leadership of his son Herbert, the company managed to carry on for another forty years as "one of the few old-line pubberies still owned by a member of the founder's family."[26] In 1983, the family sold it to a group headed up by Freddy Bienstock. Bienstock had established himself as a force in the music business while with Hill and Range Songs, a country and western publisher that had been founded with BMI seed money in the 1940s, "one of the most prominent of the BMI family of upstart young song publishers,"[27] and the publisher of much of Elvis Presley's early repertoire. Bienstock went on to acquire Chappell & Co. in 1984, bringing the outstanding catalogs epitomizing old Tin Pan Alley (Marks) and the Age of the Songwriter (Chappell) together under one roof, in a house that BMI and Elvis had built.

Performing rights, impossible to monetize at the beginning of the twentieth century, were nearly as portable, transferable, and money-good as Federal Reserve notes by the time Bienstock acquired the Marks and Chappell catalogs in the 1980s. ASCAP and BMI, despite their vastly disparate histories and structures, had become generic performing rights organizations, interchangeable within the music industry and all but invisible as far as the public was concerned. Their repertoires were of roughly equal value and variety. By choice or by consent decree they both adhered to "open door" membership policies, allowed writers to move freely between them, paid distributions to new members almost entirely on the basis of scientific performance surveys, and were subject to the regulatory oversight of a "rate court." (The former Society of European Stage Authors & Composers, officially renamed SESAC, had remained a family-owned, niche operation until the early 1990s, when new owners made a splash by luring Bob Dylan and Neil Diamond away from ASCAP, a talent raid that would have been well-nigh impossible in an earlier era.) Publishing firms could no longer exist as exclusively ASCAP, BMI, or SESAC houses. As a consequence of Judge Pecora's ruling, songwriters controlled their performing rights and publishers had to set up multiple subsidiaries to affiliate with different performing rights organizations to accommodate their songwriters' memberships. Periodic rate negotiations with media trade associations were still not easy, the arrival of new technologies still precipitated new rounds of litigation and lobbying, and the lives of licensing representatives on the frontlines were still no bed of roses (a BMI field representative told the New York Times in 2010 that she would not eat at any establishment that she was attempting to license because "God only knows what they might put in your food"[28]) but there never has been a bear market in performing rights. Even in an "age of digital media uncertainty, the predictable fee stream of a homely business like music publishing" can be more highly valued "than an ego-driven trophy asset like music recording."[29]

ASCAP and BMI had pursued markedly different paths to this place of equilibrium, and throughout the 1940s and 1950s they had continued to clash. ASCAP had circumvented the 1941 consent decree through rules and policies that made it difficult for music users to license directly from copyright holders and made alternatives to blanket licenses impracticable, by continuing to apply highly subjective criteria to membership applications, and by locking up catalogs for terms that approached perpetuity. The problem of devising a distribution system that recognized the legacy contributions of its aging "written-out" members, while adequately rewarding the performance activity of current hit-makers, solved in countless hypothetical back-of-the-napkin exercises over cheesecake at Lindy's, proved intractable in the real world. Deliberations that began after the 1941 consent decree finally produced, eight years later, a plan that gave a paltry 20 percent weight to contemporaneous performances. ASCAP lamely argued that if it gave current performances any greater weight, writers would spend too much time plugging performances and "will have neither the incentive nor the time to create new works."[30] Two major revisions to the consent decree, one in 1950 and another in 1960 (which allowed members to elect between a distribution formula based entirely on current performances and one which gave credit for longevity, "quality," and other factors), were necessary before Thurman Arnold's vision of a free market in "energy, entertainment, and ideas" could even be approximated. Notwithstanding ASCAP's feigned concerns, the performance-based system of payment used by BMI did not snuff out the creative impulse. To the contrary, "songwriters were spurred on by the unmistakable returns of employment and cash. New songs flooded the market in great numbers."[31]

"BMI's early investment in country music and rhythm-and-blues paid off handsomely," sociologist John Ryan wrote. "When these two genres melded together in the 1950s into the new genre of rock 'n' roll, BMI was there first."[32] On the *Billboard* charts for December 23, 1957, thirty-six of the top fifty pop songs, forty-five of the top fifty country songs, and forty of the top fifty R&B songs were licensed by BMI. This hadn't occurred because ASCAP had lost its hold on traditional live network radio programming, but rather because the networks were atrophying while independent stations that relied on recordings, were growing by leaps and bounds. "It was the local station that was putting the hits on the air," said Professor Philip Ennis, another sociologist, in his scholarly account of the emergence of rock and roll. "The future of popular music lay in the hands of the disk jockey on the independent stations."[33]

Postwar improvements in recording technology, most notably the introduction of magnetic recording tape, had made it possible to record songs, and get them on the air, anywhere. "There isn't a market in the United States of any size that isn't a place where a song may start," a BMI executive observed in 1958. "I doubt there is a town of any size in this country, certainly a town that has even a 250-watt daytime station with tape, that you can't go in and record."[34] As a result, records and radio play often preceded publication, and disc jockeys became popular music's all-powerful gatekeepers.

These trends triggered the last great conflagration of the ASCAP-broadcasting war. This time ASCAP's songwriter-members were the aggressors, employing the same three-prong strategy of litigation, legislation, and propaganda that Charles Tuttle and the NAB had used against ASCAP to so little effect thirty years earlier. In 1953, a group of ASCAP's elder statesmen, led by Arthur Schwartz and Oscar Hammerstein, instituted a $150 million antitrust suit against BMI and the networks, alleging a conspiracy to keep ASCAP music off the air. The plaintiffs were perplexed by their sudden inability to produce hits, and by the rapidly declining performance activity of the standards that had sustained them over the preceding three decades. "The simultaneous change in our position as writers of songs that could receive exploitation," Schwartz and his cohorts concluded, "could not be coincidence or the result of the atom bomb or the Russian preparation for the next world war. Therefore, it must be somebody's doing, and we concluded that it was the doing of the defendants."[35] Hammerstein portrayed his group of songwriter-auteurs as dispossessed exiles:

> Since the two biggest networks also own the two biggest recording companies their interlocking strength is obvious. Add to this the fact that they are stockholders in BMI, and bear in mind also that the broadcasters are the employers of the disk jockeys in whom lies the power to choose which records are to be played. You may then have an idea how insecure it must feel to be an outsider, a writer whose work is not published by a BMI publisher, but by a publisher who cannot avail himself of the concentration of power of which BMI publishers might avail themselves.[36]

They prevailed upon Florida senator George Smathers to introduce an amendment to the Federal Communications Act of 1934 that would have prohibited broadcast licensees from owning interests in recording and music publishing companies. To obtain passage of this legislation it would not be enough to show that ASCAP songwriters were losing income or feeling insecure. It had to be wrapped in the mantle of the public interest. At Senate Committee hearings held between March and July 1958, the Smathers Bill's proponents attempted to show that BMI and the broadcasters were carrying out a nefarious scheme to foist inferior, even dangerous, music upon the American people.

The songwriters brought in author Vance Packard, whose book *The Hidden Persuaders* was on the best-seller lists, to share the results of his research showing that "the broadcasters have resorted to manipulating the public taste in order to assure themselves that the economically cheap music they wish to purvey will be in public demand."[37]

> The result of all this manipulation has been among other things a gross degradation in the quality of music supplied to the public over the airways. Our airways have been flooded in recent years with whining guitarists, musical riots put to a switchblade beat, obscene lyrics about hugging, squeezing, and rocking all night long.

Packard took particular aim at country and western, which he described as "a neglected lode of cheaply mined music," and rock and roll—"race music modified to stir the animal instinct in modern teenagers, monotony tinged with hysteria."[38]

Many, including Tennessee senator Albert Gore, Sr., came to the defense of country music. But the most eloquent and pointed rejoinder came from singing cowboy Gene Autry, an ASCAP member who had been a major star for a decade before finally being admitted on a "nonparticipating" basis in 1938:

> It is perfectly true that ASCAP by its policy of exclusion and monopoly had reduced the economic aspirations of so-called hillbilly writers to a point where most of them received no economic benefits at all from their music. It now seems strange indeed for them to accuse the very group that they suppressed as being available at a cheap price. . . . Country music is no longer cheap, and, as a matter of fact, is being paid for by BMI at the same rate as all other music.[39]

Defenders of rock and roll were scarce on the committee's witness list; not even Sun Records' Sam Phillips, who testified against the bill in his capacity as a radio station owner, took up the cause. The task was left to George Marek, RCA Victor's general manager, and the author of many books on classical music. Marek rattled off an overwhelming array of statistics belying any BMI bias in his company's repertoire, or any bias by either network favoring the products of their affiliated record companies. Then he turned to the issue of taste. "*Tristan and Isolde*," his peroration began, "was called names that we can apply to rock 'n roll today."

> It was called cat music—the incomprehensible wailings of a madman. In the 19th Century when the waltz came up, it was predicted "this licentious dance would open the sluice gates of immorality and degradation." . . . I don't think that the composers of this music which was popular in 1921 have any right to say that music which is popular today is being forced on the public by illegitimate means. Let's not be hypocrites and pretend that "Yes! We Have No Bananas" is Schubert.[40]

Neither the massive pretrial discovery record compiled in *Schwartz v. BMI*, the fourteen days of committee hearings on the Smathers Bill, nor numerous studies of rock music and juvenile delinquency substantiated any of the charges. The songwriters were never able to provide a compelling motive for the alleged conspiracy, since virtually all broadcasters carried ASCAP blanket licenses, and BMI operated without a profit and paid no dividends to broadcaster-stockholders. Nor could they explain why music programming on the broadcast networks, supposedly the linchpins of the scheme, was still dominated by ASCAP music. It would, however, "take years for the near schizophrenic denunciation of BMI and the simultaneous imitation of its methods to subside."[41]

The worm had surely taken a most dramatic turn. The Age of the Songwriter was over. Musical genius, once again, was being treated unfairly. Query, though, whether the conspiracy theories of the polished and natty ASCAP crowd were demonstrably more sane than the paranoid ravings of the shabby, solitary man who once stood outside their headquarters with sandwich-board signs, or whether their well-financed campaign had any better prospect for success than did Arnstein's one-man guerrilla operation.

Sigmund Spaeth was flabbergasted when he heard about the testimony of George Marek, one of his regular co-panelists on the Metropolitan Opera Quiz. "I don't think he is sincere about it," Spaeth told an interviewer. "He has to say that, because Elvis Presley has made a lot of money for his company. I still can't believe that he approves of the music as such. It isn't music."[42] Spaeth had positioned himself as one of rock and roll's most visible and virulent critics, a highly vocal adherent of Vance Packard's theories of its origins and consequences: "I hold BMI very largely responsible for rock and roll. The whole so-called conspiracy has resulted in rock and roll, and I think this taste has been foisted on the American public."[43] His rants, published and unpublished, drew a straight line from rock and roll to juvenile delinquency and illiteracy:

> It's nothing but a beat. It has absolutely nothing to recommend it, because the beat is a reversion to savagery. The savages did it better in the jungle. It's purely jungle music, and of course it leads to the logical development to which the savages followed it instinctively and without any inhibitions whatever. The logical development of rock and roll is violence of one kind or another, including murder, and sex orgies.[44]

When it was pointed out to Spaeth that he was stepping on a message that he had spent a professional lifetime spreading—that music should, above all, be fun, the opinions of so-called musical experts be damned—he was unapologetic: "There are limits to human tolerance."[45] More and more things were testing the limits of his tolerance; Spaeth had just become grumpier and more irascible as he aged. His growing list of peeves included not only rock and roll, but also country music ("vapid banality"[46]), "song stylists" who did not perform the popular standards as they were written ("the mayhem committed by Ella Fitzgerald on 'Lady Be Good' is really inexcusable"[47]), recording technology ("the engineers have become more important than the artists"[48]), television ("too stilted, patronizing and snobbish" in presenting classical music[49]), and, for reasons utterly mystifying to his loved ones, song-and-dance man Gene Kelly. "Sig Spaeth," Larry Rothe notes with sadness, "stopped being a man of his time."[50]

Spaeth's last original book of any note, *Dedication: The Love Story of Robert and Clara Schuman*, a dewy narrative woven from their youthful letters and diaries, was published in 1950. From then on, Spaeth's principal writing outlets were short magazine articles and a weekly syndicated newspaper column that appeared, at its peak, in a few dozen midsized markets. These pieces liberally recycled ideas, enthusiasms, criticisms, and anecdotes mined from his past oeuvre. His writing was geared strictly, as one reviewer noted, to "these kinds of people: musical novices; Saturday morning music clubbers; beginning teachers; Reader's Digest, Time Magazine enthusiasts."[51]

Katherine Lane Spaeth had struggled for some time with alcoholism, and by the early 1950s had largely withdrawn from involvement in Spaeth's professional and social life. After nearly drowning in shallow waters near their summer home on Long Island Sound in 1954, and suffering a massive stroke, she was confined to a nursing home. Spaeth remained attentive to her until the end of her life, curtailing his own travels and taking a salaried job for the first time since the late 1920s—editing *Music Journal*, a magazine for music educators.

Meanwhile, the years were taking their toll on him physically. The delicate wire-framed glasses that Spaeth had worn since at least his days at the *Evening Mail* gave way to thick, bifocal Coke bottles. Leg ailments and infections led to frequent hospitalizations and ended his racquet sport playing days. The waist of his pants migrated northward to mid-torso as his once athletic build sagged under the weight of too many banquets and testimonial dinners, too many second helpings of dessert, too many Manhattans, and too many maraschino cherries filched from his companions' Manhattans. He relied upon a cane to get about. The deterioration must have been apparent and alarming to his many friends and colleagues who contributed to a sixty-page festschrift published by the *Music Journal* in the spring of 1959. "I believe such unique ability," publisher Al Vann wrote in an introductory essay, "should receive its due while the man is still with us."[52]

Examples are legion of great-but-long-fallow artists who, near the end of their lives, experience remarkable creative revivals. Frank Lloyd Wright, considered passé with the ascendency of the International Style, rallied back with his Guggenheim Museum, living just long enough to see it constructed. After suffering from writer's block for sixty years following the publication of his transcendent first novel, *Call It Sleep*, Henry Roth finished three-quarters of a projected hexalogy, *Mercy of a Rude Stream*, before dying at age eighty-nine. Richard Strauss, his reputation sullied by his dalliance with the Nazis, found a measure of redemption with his haunting *Four Last Songs*. Ira

B. Arnstein had his four last songs as well—"Come Along with Me," "I Love Paris," "C'est Magnifique," and "Allez-Vous-En, Go Away." Like so many others over the years, they were published under the name "Cole Porter." "Cole Porter," *Variety*'s headline writers snickered, "Is Just a Guy Named Arnstein."[53]

Arnstein's bleak old age was devoted to eking out such subsistence as he could manage from odd jobs, public relief, and handouts from sister Mae. His last commercial musical enterprise came in 1948. Inspired by Israel's declaration of independence and the outbreak of the first Arab-Israeli war, Arnstein published "Soldiers of Israel," a new version of the "Jewish national anthem" he had written for Yossele Rosenblatt thirty years earlier, with English and Hebrew lyrics loosely reminiscent of Morris Rosenfeld's original Yiddish poem. A contemporary photo of armed kibbutz combatants and a dedication to the "Valiant Army of Israel" graced the cover, a package designed to appeal to the patriotic instincts of the Jewish musicians and American Zionist *machers* that Arnstein distributed copies to, but there were no takers.

As Arnstein expected, after being exonerated by the courts Cole Porter had reverted to his old habits and produced his first hit show in years—*Kiss Me Kate*—which opened in December 1948. "Mr. Cole Porter is 'tops' again," Arnstein wrote. "After five years of continuous flops, he took the bull by the horns and in desperation swiped again Arnstein's 'I Love You Madly' and turned it into 'So in Love.'" Porter, he added, "is a very loyal man. He lives and sticks by Arnstein."[54] But it was Porter's penultimate Broadway score, 1953's *Can-Can*, that prompted Arnstein to end a five-year litigation hiatus and return to the federal courthouse. His complaint urged the court to have "a few prominent musicians (not defendants' stooges or tune detectives, who are retained by them for no other purpose but deny the truth and whitewash the culprits) advise this Court on the merits."[55] The *New York Morning Telegraph* marked Arnstein's comeback with a nostalgic retrospective, "Arnstein Still Suing 'Em":

> Mr. Arnstein had established his unique musical and legal reputation long before this reporter began chronicling the didoes of the music world for the Billboard 17 years ago. . . .
>
> Ira Arnstein's persistence is an amazing thing. While other amateur tunesmiths come and go, suing the writers of this or that smash hit en route, Arnstein is like ol' man river (over which he probably sued Kern at

some time or other) and just keeps rolling along tossing infringement claims at all and sundry, and especially at the biggest boys in the cleffing league. So far he's batting .000, but judges, like umpires, can be wrong, of course.[56]

Porter's lawyers moved quickly to make sure that Arnstein wouldn't be calling on their client again at the Waldorf Towers, where he was at work on

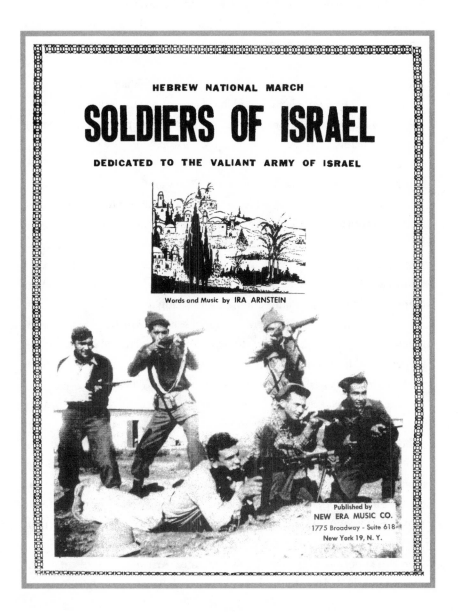

the score for his final show, *Silk Stockings*, and where Linda Porter lay dying of emphysema. Their trump card was the unpaid $2,500 award of legal fees from the earlier case. They moved to have the court impose a stay on the new case until Arnstein put up an equal amount as security for costs in the new case—a requirement that all involved knew he would never be able to meet. Arnstein argued that as between "a pauper being deprived of a day in court" and "an affluent defendant claimed to have reached such affluence by the labor and art of plaintiff," the equities favored the poor plaintiff.[57] Arnstein, however, had drawn from the well of "justice for rich and poor alike" one time too many. The court granted the stay:

> For plaintiff to have another try against the same defendant as to different music would be a pure luxury. If plaintiff cannot pay for it, it is no more unjust to require him to forego that luxury than to require him to forego any other luxury for which he cannot pay.[58]

He could not pay, and in December 1955 the *Can-Can* case was dismissed for lack of prosecution, ending with a whimper a scourge of litigation that had stretched across four decades. A few weeks later, Arnstein lost his last lifeline when his elder sister Mae died suddenly during a New Year's Day game of bridge. For some younger family members, the only lasting memory of their eccentric uncle—the black sheep they knew only as a bachelor musician who was involved in a lot of lawsuits and had something to do with Sigmund Spaeth—was the scene he caused at Mae's burial service. Arnstein berated Mae's son Joseph, the "beloved nephew" to whom he had dedicated one of his earliest published pieces fifty-five years earlier, for not knowing the customary Jewish doxology recited at graveside, the Mourner's *Kaddish*.

Arnstein was last seen alive on the afternoon of September 9, 1956, a few hours before Elvis Presley's first appearance on the *Ed Sullivan Show*, the symbolic coda to the Age of the Songwriter, the moment when records and performers irrevocably asserted dominance over songs and their writers. On September 11th, a registered letter addressed to Arnstein (possibly from Cole Porter's attorneys, who had succeeded in having a receiver appointed to take ownership of Arnstein's copyrights) arrived at the last of his innumerable Upper West Side addresses, a fifth-floor walk-up apartment on 77th Street. When the superintendent was unable to roust Arnstein to sign for it, the police were called. They found his cold dead body sitting upright in an old armchair, fully dressed, legs crossed. The cause of death was given as "gene-ralized arteriosclerosis" and the medical examiner estimated his age as eighty—probably five years too high. Nephew Joseph, his nearest surviving kin, claimed the body and arranged for cremation and interment of the ashes in an unmarked, infant-size plot, a short stroll from the site of their altercation over Mae's grave at Mount Lebanon Cemetery, part of a vast necropolis in the highlands that straddle the Queens-Brooklyn border.

It was a finale not worth a doxology. But Arnstein's hilltop resting place had a view to die for, overlooking Manhattan's Midtown East in the distance, the Promised Land where many of his erstwhile nemeses still resided, aged, infirm, and struggling to maintain their relevancy in the era of rock and roll.

Sigmund Spaeth was living out his years alone in a spacious Turtle Bay apartment on East 48th Street, digging in his heels to the point of self-parody over the "festering sore" and "abysmal worthlessness" of rock and roll.[59] By 1959, he had begun to speak of it in the past tense: "Perhaps it did reflect a spirit of our times, but even the kids are dropping it."[60] "If rock 'n' roll needs a final kick to assure it complete extinction," he wrote with misplaced opti-mism a year later, "its administration may be credited to Broadway's new musical smash, *Bye, Bye Birdie*."[61]

Spaeth's reputation as a courtroom tune detective took a final hit in 1961, with the publication of Louis Nizer's memoir, *My Life in Court*. Nizer recounted in forensic and loving detail his 1947 confrontation with Spaeth in a celebrated music plagiarism involving comedian Morey Amsterdam's wartime hit, "Rum and Coca-Cola." Nizer astutely recognized that Spaeth was at heart "an entertainer" who sought to compensate for lack of analytic rigor with an attitude of "over-zealousness and truculence."[62] Over several days of hostile cross-examination, Nizer confronted Spaeth with more than twenty-five years' worth of his own contradictory statements in print, skill-fully exploited Spaeth's preening vanity and verbal "tells," and systematically demolished his shoddy courtroom scholarship. "No one was more grateful for Dr. Spaeth's prolific pen than I was,"[63] Nizer wrote. "I had become his most studious reader." The trial judge, Simon Rifkind, was vexed by Spaeth's attitude: "I want to learn from the expert, but this expert would make a won-derful virtuous girl, he has such great reluctance to saying 'Yes.'"[64]

Spaeth lived long enough to be treated to a second round of *inter vivos* eulogies in the spring of 1965, when the confluence of his eightieth birthday, his twenty-fifth anniversary on Metropolitan Opera Quiz, and his tenth anniversary with *Music Journal* was marked with printed tributes and public celebrations. Katherine Lane Spaeth died in July 1965, and Sigmund followed in November. The cause was esophageal varices, a condition commonly associated with alcohol abuse. In one of his final interviews, he took a parting shot at the Beatles as "mere primitive noisemaking."[65]

Cole Porter accepted the country's changing tastes with comparative grace. He agreed to write a rock and roll song for the 1957 movie version of *Silk Stockings*. The result, sung by Fred Astaire in the film, was "The Ritz Rock-and-Roll," a sporting if campy crossover effort by two paragons of the bygone culture of elegance. It was one of Porter's last songs. After the amputation of his right leg in early 1958 he never wrote again. When not hospitalized, he lived as a virtual shut-in, though by no means a recluse, entertaining guests at the Waldorf Towers until his death in 1964.

The recording companies had climbed to the top of the music business hierarchy ("Stereophonic Sound" was another song Porter wrote for *Silk Stockings*), but Nat Shilkret of East 73rd Street, a seminal figure in its history, no longer had any place in it. To his distant successors at RCA Victor, George Marek and others, he was a footnote at best. After the war his recording activities were limited to making electronic transcriptions for SESAC—polkas, characteristic pieces, and other oddities from its repertoire mixed with public domain classics. (Providing such canned material to small radio stations was SESAC's principal business for several decades after BMI had come along and offered a more lucrative platform for the types of musical outcasts that SESAC had originally served.) Shilkret retired in 1958 and moved in with his son's family on Long Island, where he lived until his death in 1982. Though he regretted the decline of live musicianship, a decline that his pioneering work in the recording industry helped make possible, the memoir he wrote in the mid-1960s (published posthumously in 2005) ended on an upbeat: "With so many young people singing and striving for expression, some new form of art may develop."[66]

Irving Berlin, 17 Beekman Place, wasn't losing any sleep over rock and roll either. He had seen the pendulum swing many times over his fifty years in music. "Twenty years from now we will be laughing at most of rock n' roll," he told *Variety* in 1956, "but some of it will last."[67] (Only when Elvis dared to record "White Christmas," a rendition that Berlin considered sacrilegious, did he seriously object.) He assumed that the country would always yearn for an old-fashioned Berlin ballad. Eventually, though, the market passed him by. After his final recording and movie projects were shelved by new-generation industry chieftains who were chasing the "youth market" in the late 1960s, Berlin threw in the towel. He shipped his transposing piano off to the Smithsonian in 1972,[68] and was a cantankerous and stingy curator of his own musical legacy until his death at age 101 in 1989.

"*Arnstein* is dead but not buried,"[69] one legal commentator declared, prematurely, in 1984. Another, writing four years later, insisted that, to the contrary, "the copyright infringement principles of *Arnstein* have endured."[70] Both were referring, of course, to the case of *Arnstein v. Porter*, not the eponymous music teacher, composer of "A Mother's Prayer," and serial plaintiff, long since dead, cremated, *and* buried. The *Porter* case, the crowning achievement of Ira B. Arnstein's strange and litigious career, has proved remarkably resilient, leading one treatise author to remark recently that *Arnstein v. Porter*, "even though it has been distinguished, ignored and disapproved, still rises like a phoenix."[71] In the second decade of the twenty-first century, leading copyright law casebooks used in law schools excerpt at least Jerome Frank's majority opinion, and some include Charles Clark's dissent as well, and not simply as historical curiosities. Clark's warning that the decision issued an "invitation to the strike suit par excellence" continues to resonate, amped up to be heard over the din of a post-9/11 world; now it is said to give "carte blanche to potential musical terrorists."[72] There is always a federal judge or an academician, somewhere, grappling with *Arnstein*'s framework of analysis, not only in music cases, but in literary, visual art, and architectural cases as well. "It is within American jurisprudence and not popular music that the name of Ira B. Arnstein reverberates."[73]

Arnstein departed this vale of tears without a dime to show for his contribution to the life of the law. The assumption that he was a strike suit artist, a musical terrorist, does not ring true, not when the entire corpus of his work is considered. He pursued his claims long past the point where there was any prospect of either victory or settlement. His theories displayed more intellectual consistency—albeit "warped in some respects"—than "commercial perspicacity." The deeply jazz-influenced Harold Arlen and Hoagy Carmichael, to name just two examples, were hit machines during the years of Arnstein's most conspicuous activity. There was money to be made there, but Arnstein didn't bite. Why would he invent a wholly fantastic claim to authorship of "My Wishing Song" when it would be just as easy to shake down

"Stormy Weather" or "Skylark"? Because he couldn't—an Arnstein song just doesn't go like that.

There is no doubt that he was delusional and more than a little paranoid, but that is hardly a full or satisfactory diagnosis. Most folks who think they are being persecuted don't spend thirty years of their life fighting in court over it. A small body of psychiatric literature discusses a behavior disorder— "morbid querulousness"—characterized by the pursuit of personal vindication "in a manner seriously damaging to the individual's economic, social, and personal interests, and disruptive to the functioning of the courts." For more than a century researchers have noted consistent patterns in the writings of these "unusually persistent complainants"—"invective," "curious formatting," "unusual methods of emphasis," and "copious marginal notes." They tend to be "individuals who have cloaked themselves in an intellectual superiority that negates the potentially moderating influence" of family, friends, and professionals.[74] What Baron Münchausen was to mendacity, Ira B. Arnstein was to querulousness. Arnstein's tragedy was that he sought artistic validation in a forum that could never deliver it. Courts are designed to award compensation for harm, not recognitions and honors for achievement. His litigation mania doomed him to a life of personal and professional isolation, and a level of poverty more abject than that of the starving artist he was always meant to be.

Others following in Arnstein's precedential footsteps, however, have often done very well indeed. If only he could have collected a royalty on the case law that bears his name.

NOTES

Due to space limitations, notes are limited to direct quotations, legal citations, references to primary source materials, and certain other secondary references deemed likely to be useful. A general source note is provided for each chapter, and further documentation may be obtained from the author at grosen@logarpc.com.

ABBREVIATIONS

Archival Materials

ASCAP	Legal Files, American Society of Composers, Authors, and Publishers
CCR	Central Committee for the Relief of Jews Suffering through the War, Yeshiva University
CEC	Charles E. Clark Papers, Yale University
COHP	Columbia Oral History Project, Columbia University
CRC	Charles R. Crane Papers, Columbia University
DOJ	U.S. Department of Justice Antitrust Div. File, No. 60-22-5, National Archives, College Park, MD
EBC	Edmund B. Craney Papers, Montana Historical Society
FDR	Franklin D. Roosevelt Presidential Library
FTP	Federal Theatre Project Collection, National Archives, College Park, MD
IB	Irving Berlin Collection, Library of Congress
JNF	Jerome N. Frank Papers, Yale University
LH	Learned Hand Papers, Harvard University
MA	Milken Archive of Jewish Music
MO	Metropolitan Opera Archives
MR	Morrie Ryskind Papers, New York Public Library
NS	Nathaniel Shilkret Archives, c/o Niel Shell, 632 Smith Street, Franklin Square, NY 11010
NYPL	New York Public Library for Performing Arts, Clippings Files
RCMH	Radio City Music Hall Archives
SPW	Samuel P. Warren Collection, Library of Congress

SS   Sholom Secunda Papers, New York University
WB   Warner Brothers Pictures Archive, University of Southern
                   California

Court Records

ASCAP	*United States v. ASCAP* (S.D.N.Y. 78-388)
Arnstein	*In re Arnstein* (Sup. Ct. N.Y. No. 8233 1941)
Baron	*Baron v. Leo Feist, Inc.* (2d Cir. No. 30-112)
Berlin	*Arnstein v. Irving Berlin, Inc.* (N.Y. Sup. Ct. No. 7758 1928)
BMI I	*Arnstein v. Broadcast Music, Inc.* (S.D.N.Y. No. 12-79)
BMI II	*Arnstein v. Broadcast Music, Inc.* (2d Cir. No. 18645)
Crestview	*Arnstein v. Crestview Music Corp.* (N.Y. Sup. Ct. No. 1948–16737)
Marks	*Arnstein v. E. B. Marks Music Corp.* (2d Cir. No. 14417)
MultiSuit	*Arnstein v. ASCAP* (S.D.N.Y. No. E-86-78)
Porter I	*Arnstein v. Porter* (S.D.N.Y. No. 29-754)
Porter II	*Arnstein v. Porter* (2d Cir. No. 169 1945)
Porter III	*Arnstein v. Porter* (2d Cir. No. 20386)
Porter IV	*Arnstein v. Porter* (S.D.N.Y. No. 91-169)
Reed	*Reed v. Carusi* (D. Md. 1845)
Shilkret I	*United States v. Shilkret* (S.D.N.Y. No. C-65-299)
Shilkret II	*Arnstein v. Shilkret* (S.D.N.Y. No. 65-83)
Spaeth	*Spaeth v. Warner Brothers Pictures* (S.D.N.Y. No. 9-49)
Twentieth Century	*Arnstein v. Twentieth Century–Fox Film Corp.* (S.D.N.Y. No. 20-161)
Wilkie	*Wilkie v. Santly Brothers* (S.D.N.Y. No. E-70-232)

"S.D.N.Y." and "2d Cir." cases are available through the National Archives and Record Administration, Northeast Region, New York City. "N.Y. Sup. Ct." cases are available through the County Clerk, New York State Supreme Court, Manhattan. Reed v. Carusi is available at the National Archives and Record Administration, Mid-Atlantic Region, Philadelphia.

Legislative History

1924 Hearings	To Amend the Copyright Act, Hearings before a Subcommittee of the Committee on Patents, U.S. Senate, 68th Cong., 1st Sess. (1924).
1926 Hearings	To Amend the Copyright Act, Joint Hearings before the Committee on Patents, 69th Cong., 1st Sess. (1926).
1958 Hearings	Amendment to Communications Act of 1934, Hearings before the Subcommittee on Communications of the Committee on Interstate and Foreign Commerce, U.S. Senate, 85th Cong., 2d Sess. (1958).

Periodicals

BE	*Brooklyn Eagle*
CH	*Chicago Herald*

CP	*Chicago Evening Post*
CT	*Chicago Tribune*
LAT	*Los Angeles Times*
MJ	*Music Journal*
MTR	*Music Trade Review*
NYA	*New York American*
NYHT	*New York Tribune/New York Herald Tribune*
NYJ	*New York Journal/New York Journal American*
NYLJ	*New York Law Journal*
NYM	*New York Evening Mail*
NYP	*New York Post*
NYRB	*New York Review of Books*
NYS	*New York Sun*
NYT	*New York Times*
NYWT	*New York Evening Telegram/New York World Telegram*
OT	*Oakland Tribune*
TNY	*The New Yorker*
WP	*Washington Post*

Other periodicals are identified by their full names. Periodical citations without page numbers refer to articles found in clipping files or online databases.

PROLOGUE

1. Francis Gilbert to Irving Berlin, 9/14/1948, IB (Box 379/Folder 8).
2. Irving Berlin to Francis Gilbert, 9/15/1948, IB (Box 379/Folder 8).
3. *Three Boys Music Corp. v. Bolton*, 212 F.3d 477 (9th Cir. 2000); *ABKCO Music, Inc. v. Harrisongs Music, Ltd.*, 722 F.2d 988 (2d Cir. 1983).
4. *Gaste v. Kaiserman*, 863 F.2d 1061 (2d Cir. 1988).
5. Post-Trial Conference, 10, 6/3/1946, *Arnstein I*.
6. Charles Rosen, "Playing Music: The Lost Freedom," *NYRB* 47 (11/3/2005).
7. Lessig, *Future of Ideas*, 6.
8. John Anderson, "Weathering a Scandal and Now a Movie," *NYT* (*Arts & Leisure*) 8 (7/10/2011).
9. Seldes, *Seven Lively Arts*, 347.
10. Sandage, *Born Losers*, 263.

CHAPTER 1. LOONY TUNES, SCHMALTZY MELODIES

Valuable accounts of the popular music business in the late nineteenth and early twentieth centuries relied upon include Ennis, *Seventh Stream*; Ewen, *Life and Death*; Furia, *Poets of Tin Pan Alley*; Marks, *They All Sang*; Meyer, *Gold in Tin Pan Alley*; Sanjek, *Pennies from Heaven*; Suisman, *Selling Sounds*; and Witmark and Goldberg, *Ragtime to Swingtime*.

1. Sacks, *Musicophilia*, 344.
2. *Variety* 1 (8/23/1932).
3. Interview of Jack Yellen, 16, COHP.

4. Cantor, *Caught Short!*, 37.
5. *NYT* 28 (10/25/1929).
6. Interview of Jack Yellen, 16, COHP.
7. Barnet, Nemerov, and Taylor, *Story Behind the Song*, 85–86.
8. Alter, *Defining Moment*, 107–8.
9. Neal, *Happy Days Are Here Again*, 253.
10. Shana Alexander, "'Call Me Al'? 'I'm a Dole Man'?," *NYT (Sunday Magazine)* 92 (11/3/1996).
11. James A. Kieran, "He Is 'Ready for Action,'" *NYT* 1 (7/2/1932).
12. Walt Strony, Paul van der Molen, and John Shanahan, Chicago Area Theatre Organ Enthusiasts, e-mail messages to author, 1/12/2008.
13. *NYT* 16 (6/14/1932); Elmer Davis, "Mr. Gloom Stirred by Dickinson's Art," *NYT* 11 (6/15/1932); Elmer Davis, "Walsh Condoled by Godfrey Gloom," *NYT* 17 (6/29/1932).
14. *NYT* 19 (10/5/1932).
15. Ben Bornstein to "Dear Friend," 2/28/1933, DOJ (Box 223).
16. "Nat Shilkret Audition," 1/26/1933, MR (Box 5/Folder 6).
17. John S. Wilson, "Cabaret: 'The Street Singer' Returns," *NYT* 56 (2/28/1982).
18. Dickstein, *Dancing in the Dark*, 408.
19. John Black, "Story of the Depression Is Told in Song," *NYT (Sunday Magazine)* 20 (2/25/1934).
20. *NYT* 27 (12/15/1930).
21. *Variety* 49 (2/14/1933).
22. Suisman, *Selling Sounds*, 21.
23. Ennis, *Seventh Stream*, 42.
24. Rodgers, *Musical Stages*, 45.
25. Hamm, *Irving Berlin*, 9–10.
26. Dreiser, *Twelve Men*, 97.
27. *M. Witmark & Sons v. Peters*, 164 A.D. 366, 149 N.Y.S. 642 (App. Div. 1914).
28. Gill, *Here at the New Yorker*, 319.
29. Marks, Jr., *Still Counting*, 11.
30. Marks, *They All Sang*, 3.
31. Ibid., 62–63.
32. Mooney, *All Join in the Chorus*, 124.
33. Furia, *Poets of Tin Pan Alley*, 41.
34. *White-Smith Music Publishing Co. v. Apollo Co.*, 209 U.S. 1 (1908).
35. *1926 Hearings*, 355.
36. John Chapman, "By Special Permission," *Elks Magazine* 12 (4/1932).
37. *Herbert v. Shanley Co.*, 242 U.S. 591 (1917).
38. Marks, *They All Sang*, 216.
39. Jerry Hoffman, "Westward the Course of Tin Pan Alley," *Photoplay* (9/29), reprinted in Kreuger, *Movie Musical*, 56.
40. Jeff Smith, "Banking on Film Music: Structural Interactions of the Film and Record Industries," in Dickinson, ed., *Movie Music*, 63–81.
41. ASCAP, *How the Public Gets Its New Music*, 7–8 (1933); *NYT* 20 (7/19/1933).
42. *1924 Hearings*, 163.

43. Meyer, *Gold in Tin Pan Alley*, 60.

44. *1924 Hearings*, 116 (Minutes of Conference Held at Offices of ASCAP, 9/20/1922).

45. "The Murder of Music," *Broadcasting* (8/1/1933).

46. Telegrams, ASCAP to WKY, Oklahoma City (5/11/1933); ASCAP to WDAY, Fargo, ND (3/28/1934); ASCAP to WDAY, Fargo, ND (2/2/1934)—DOJ (Box 224).

47. E. C. Mills to All Licensed Broadcasting Stations, 3/29/1932, DOJ (Box 222); *NYT* X10 (5/15/1932).

48. A. E. Garmaize to E. C. Mills, 12/17/1932, DOJ (Box 223).

49. *Variety* 43 (6/19/1935).

50. *RCA Mfg. Co. v. Whiteman*, 114 F.2d 86 (2d Cir. 1940).

51. Rudy Vallée to Learned Hand, 6/5/59, LH (Box 97/Folder 35).

52. Sheed, *House That George Built*, 53.

53. Wilder, *American Popular Song*, 97–98.

54. ASCAP Payments to Members, 1921–1934, DOJ.

55. Kenneth Clark, "Why Our Popular Songs Don't Last," *Forum and Century* 168, 171 (3/1934).

56. Gilbert, *Lost Chords*, 344.

57. Sheed, *House That George Built*, 26.

58. S. N. Behrman, "Accoucheur," *TNY* 20 (2/6/1932).

59. Ewen, *Life and Death*, 296–297.

60. Goldmark, *Tunes for 'Toons*, 17–18.

61. Edward B. Marks to B. R. Sprague, 11/10/1938, EBC (Box 8/Folder 6).

62. Edward B. Marks to Ralph Story, 4/9/1936 and 9/16/1936, FTP.

63. Marks, *They All Sang*, 108 and 211; H. I. Brock, "Tin Pan Alley Is Always in Tune," *NYT (Sunday Magazine)* 14 (2/13/1944).

64. Marks, *They All Sang*, 219.

65. *NYT* C22 (3/19/1982).

66. ASCAP Payments to Members, 1921–1934, DOJ; *Variety* 47 (12/27/1932).

67. *Variety* 56 (9/24/1952).

68. Paul Jonas to "Dear Friend," 9/16/1932, DOJ (Box 223).

69. Arnstein to Emery Deutsch, Def. Ex. D, 9/22/1932, *Marks*.

70. Trial Transcript, 155–56, 6/4/1935, *Marks*.

CHAPTER 2. A MOTHER'S PRAYER

The Chicago newspapers provided blanket coverage of the World's Columbian Exposition. The *New York Times* and *Music Trade Review* covered Scharwenka's time in the United States extensively. Thomas, *Musical Autobiography*, and Scharwenka, *Notes from My Life*, provided very useful background. Arenstein family genealogical information was provided by Jeanne Weston and Ginny Brill, which supplemented information obtained from the New York City Department of Records. Professor James O. Bailey generously shared his expertise on Eugeniia Papritz-Lineva. Gino Francesconi, Carnegie Hall's archivist, provided a wealth of information.

1. Adams, *Education*, 343.

2. Ibid., 339.

3. Nicolai Ouroussof, "An Epoch Locks Its Doors," *NYT (Week in Review)* 1 (10/25/2009).

4. Jenks, *Century World's Fair Book*, 18–19.

5. Mueller, *American Symphony Orchestra*, 34.

6. Schabas, *Theodore Thomas*, 78–81.

7. Crawford, *America's Musical Life*, 311.

8. Mueller, *American Symphony Orchestra*, 22.

9. Thomas, *Musical Autobiography*, vol. 1, 194–95.

10. *Harpers Weekly* 419 (5/6/1893).

11. White and Igleheart, *World's Columbian Exposition*, 413.

12. Frolova-Walker, *Russian Music*, 230–35; James Bailey, "A Collection of Translations of Russian Folk Songs: E. E. Lineva's Visit to America (1892–1896)," *SEEFA J.* 4 (1999): 24–34; *CT* 26 (10/1/1893).

13. Letter from Frederic Engels to Eugenie Papritz (6/26/1884), reprinted in 47 *Marx & Engels Collected Works*, Letters: April 1883–December 1886 (Progress 1976); Evgeniya Taratua, *Our Friend Ethel Lilian Boole/Voynich* 45–46 (S. O'Coigligh trans. 2008) (http://www.corkcitylibrary.ie/media/SOCoiglighweb-version172.pdf) (accessed 10/2/2011).

14. P. J. Popoff, "Russian Folk Songs," *Frank Leslie's Popular Monthly* 420, 423 (9/1893).

15. E. Lineff to Charles R. Crane, 12/31/1892, CRC (Box 1/Folder 8).

16. *NYT* 4 (12/22/1892); *NYHT* 6 (12/22/1892); *Harper's Weekly* 1218 (12/17/1982).

17. Lineff, *Peasant Songs*, 2d ser., x.

18. E. Lineff to Charles R. Crane, 5/25/1893, CRC (Box 1/Folder 10); A. Lineff to Crane, 6/16/1893, CRC (Box 1/Folder 11); A. Lineff to Charles R. Crane, 6/19/1893, CRC (Box 1/Folder 11).

19. *CT* 26 (6/11/1893).

20. *CT* 3 (6/6/1893).

21. *CP* 12 (6/11/1893).

22. Ibid.

23. A. Lineff to Charles R. Crane, 6/16/1893, CRC (Box 1/Folder 10).

24. *CH* 25 (6/4/1893).

25. *CT* 6 (10/25/1893).

26. *CT* 3 (10/4/1893).

27. *CP* 9 (10/14/1893).

28. Lineff, *Russian Folk Songs*.

29. Upton, *Musical Memories*, 299.

30. *CT* 26 (6/11/1893); *CH* 9 (6/6/1893).

31. *Musical Observer* 16 (6/1907).

32. Chapin and Weinstock, *Road from Letichev*, 1–6.

33. Kriwaczek, *Yiddish Civilization*, 255.

34. Heskes, *Passport*, 118.

35. Howe, *World of Our Fathers*, 6.

36. Ibid., 62.

37. Ibid., 82.

38. Chapin and Weinstock, *Road from Letichev*, 110–15.

39. *BE* 5 (2/4/1894).

40. *Outlook* 239 (2/3/1894).
41. *Collier's Once a Week* 9–10 (12/9/1893); *NYT* 2 (12/16/1893); *NYHT* 11 (11/29/1893).
42. *NYT* 3 (1/17/1894).
43. Quoted in Taruskin, *Stravinsky and the Russian Traditions*, 727.
44. Olmstead, *Juilliard*, 8.
45. Carnegie, *Triumphant Democracy*, 226–27.
46. *NYT* D27 (12/15/1968).
47. Alan Rich, "Whatever Happened to Jan Sibelius?" *New York* 80 (6/9/1975).
48. Fay, *Music-Study in Germany*, 167–68.
49. F. W. Reisberg, "Xaver Scharwenka: A Few Personal Reminiscences," *Buffalo Morning Express* 12 (2/21/1891).
50. *WP* 4 (8/23/1890).
51. *BE* 2 (8/19/1890).
52. Scharenka, *Sounds from My Life*, 99.
53. *BE* 2 (8/19/1890).
54. H. E. Krehbiel, "Xaver Scharwenka," *Harper's Weekly* 68 (1/24/1891).
55. *Boston Globe* 6 (4/1/1891).
56. *WP* 4 (4/4/1891).
57. *Syracuse (N.Y.) Daily Standard* (2/28/1893).
58. *CT* 30 (2/1/1891).
59. *MTR* 76 (9/20/1891).
60. *Atlanta Constitution* 7 (2/14/1892).
61. *Scharwenka Conservatory of Music, Season 1896–97*, 3, SPW (Box 34).
62. *MTR* 277 (2/5/1891).
63. Miles, *Orpheus in the Wilderness*, 230.
64. *CT* 5 (3/8/1899).
65. *LAT* 22 (3/26/1899).
66. Mihalyo, *Life and Keyboard Works*, 32.
67. The recording (Victor 68366) can be heard on the Library of Congress National Jukebox (http://www.loc.gov/jukebox/recordings/detail/id/3092) (accessed 10/2/2011).
68. Shealy, ed., *World's Favorite Piano Solos*, 11.

CHAPTER 3. SOLDIERS OF ZION

The biography of Cantor Rosenblatt written by his son Samuel is relied upon extensively here, albeit with a healthy dose of skepticism. The account of Robyn's career is largely drawn from a remarkable oral history that he sat for at the age of one hundred for the Milken Archive of American Jewish Music, and an article by T. Brooks, "William Robyn: A Recording Artist in the 1920s," published in two parts in the *ARSC Journal* in the spring and fall 1992 issues. The New York Public Library for the Performing Arts has useful clipping files for both Rosenblatt and Robyn. I am grateful for information and family documents provided by Theodore Arison's son, Byron. Esther Sloan and Robert Freedman shared their expertise in Yiddish and *Yiddishkeit*.

1. Roth, *Mercy of a Rude Stream*, 20.
2. Gurock, *When Harlem Was Jewish*, 161.
3. Rosenblatt, *Yossele Rosenblatt*, 100.
4. Oring, *Jokes of Sigmund Freud*, 91.
5. Henry Pachter, "Marx and the Jews," *Dissent* 26 (1979) 450, 454.
6. Kaplan and Bernays, *Language of Names*, 58.
7. *Musical Observer* 16 (6/1907).
8. *NYWT* (11/20/1913).
9. *Miami Daily News*, 10-A (12/13/1936).
10. *MTR* 52 (11/15/1919).
11. *MTR* 29 (1/4/1913).
12. Leavy, *Sandy Koufax*, 169–70.
13. *Boston Evening Transcript* (12/2/1918).
14. Rosenblatt, *Yossele Rosenblatt*, 112.
15. Samuel Rosenblatt, "Yossele Rosenblatt," *Cantor's Voice* 6 (6/1958).
16. *NYT* XX2 (4/24/1932).
17. *Boston Evening Transcript* (12/2/1918).
18. Resolution of the Central Committee for the Relief of Jews Suffering through the War, 3/16/1917, CCR (Box 26/Folder 13).
19. M. H. Hanson to Bernard Horwich, 4/17/1917; M. H. Hanson to J. Abend, 4/18/1917; Stanley Bero to M. Finkelstein, 1/15/1918—CCR (Box 26/Folder 13).
20. M. H. Hanson to Mrs. Samuel Untermyer, 4/18/1917, CCR (Box 26/Folder 13).
21. *NYT* 9 (5/7/1917).
22. *CT* 4 (3/18/1918).
23. Resolution of the Central Committee for the Relief of Jews Suffering through the War, 3/16/1917, CCR (Box 26/Folder 13).
24. *NYWT* (5/18/1919).
25. Pitts Sanborn, "Some Extraordinary Singing by Cantor Rosenblatt," *New York Globe*, reprinted in *Musical Courier* 13 (5/30/1918).
26. *Toledo News Bee* (5/8/1919).
27. Sigmund Spaeth, *New York Mail*, "Tenor in First Carnegie Hall Recital," reprinted in *Musical Courier* 13 (5/30/1918).
28. Rosenblatt, *Yossele Rosenblatt*, 198.
29. Shandler, *Jews, God, and Videotape*, 31.
30. Regarding Rosenblatt's participation in *The Jazz Singer* generally, see Jeffrey Knapp, "Sacred Songs Popular Prices," *Critical Inquiry* 34 (2008) 313, 322–23.
31. Lee, *Gypsy: A Memoir*, 81–87.
32. Edna Nahshon, "The Yiddish Theatre in America: A Brief Historical Overview," in Baker, *Lawrence Marwick Collection*, xvii.
33. Ravitz, *Imitations of Life*, 54.
34. Rosenblatt, *Yossele Rosenblatt*, 182.
35. The recording (Columbia E4030) can be heard on Florida Atlantic University's Judaica Sound Archives (http://faujsa.fau.edu/jsa/discography.php?jsa_num=504184-A) (accessed 10/2/2011).
36. Okrent, *Great Fortune*, 206–9.

37. http://overautomatedlibrarian.wordpress.com/2010/04/12/cataloging-the-blues ("I have to wonder, was somebody chasing this guy all the way from Latvia?") (accessed 10/2/2011).
38. Interview of Cantor William Robyn, 30, 5/28/1995, MA.
39. The recording (Victor 73378-B) can be heard on Florida Atlantic University's Judaica Sound Archives (http://faujsa.fau.edu/jsa/discography.php?jsa_num=504181-B) (accessed 10/2/2011), as can Shloimele Rothstein's recording (Columbia E5235) (http://faujsa.fau.edu/jsa/discography.php?jsa_num=500152-A) (accessed 10/2/2011).
40. *Musical America* (5/23/1925).
41. *NYWT* 8 (5/18/1925).
42. *NYT* 12 (5/18/1925).
43. *NYHT* 11 (5/18/1925); *NYWT* 8 (5/18/1925); *Musical America* (5/23/1925).
44. Hipsher, *American Opera*, 71.
45. *Who's Who in American Jewry*, 26 (New York: Jewish Biographical Bureau, 1926).

CHAPTER 4. UNMOVED MOVER OF MELODY

Irving Berlin's papers at the Library of Congress provide a fascinating glimpse of this elusive genius and of the Age of the Songwriter generally. Lesley Schoenfeld of the Harvard Law School Library was an immensely helpful guide to Learned Hand's papers, which provide a fascinating glimpse into that very different genius.

1. Green, *Inside Stuff*, 35.
2. Ibid., 24.
3. Ibid., 29.
4. Woollcott, *Story of Irving Berlin*, 79.
5. Furia, *Poets of Tin Pan Alley*, 45.
6. Marks, *They All Sang*, 208.
7. *Twentieth Century Music Corp. v. Aiken*, 422 U.S. 151, 156 (1975).
8. *Feist Publications v. Rural Telephone Service Co.*, 499 U.S. 340, 345 (1991).
9. Goldstein, *Copyright's Highway*, 12.
10. http://cip.law.ucla.edu/Pages/default.aspx (accessed 10/2/2011).
11. Marks, *They All Sang*, 172.
12. *Fred Fisher, Inc. v. Dillingham*, 298 F. 145, 152 (S.D.N.Y. 1924).
13. *Stern v. Jerome H. Remick & Co.*, 175 F. 282 (S.D.N.Y. 1910).
14. *Boosey v. Empire Music Co.*, 224 F. 446 (S.D.N.Y. 1915).
15. *Edward B. Marks, Inc. v. Leo Feist, Inc.*, No. 147-16 (S.D.N.Y. 10/16/1922) (unpublished order), aff'd, 290 F. 959 (2d Cir. 1923), LH (Box 147/Folder 16).
16. *Haas v. Leo Feist, Inc.*, 234 F. 105 (S.D.N.Y. 1916).
17. *Fred Fisher, Inc. v. Dillingham*, 298 F. 145 (S.D.N.Y. 1924). For an account of the trial, see Boardman, *Jerome Kern*, 240–43.
18. Banfield, *Jerome Kern*, 120–22.
19. *Haas v. Leo Feist, Inc.*, 234 F. 105, 106 (S.D.N.Y. 1916).
20. *Fred Fisher, Inc. v. Dillingham*, 298 F. 145, 152 (S.D.N.Y. 1924).
21. Forte, *American Popular Ballad*, 265.
22. Wilder, *American Popular Song*, 91–121.
23. Ibid., 76 (Author's Note) and 91.

24. Bergreen, *As Thousands Cheer*, 562–66.

25. Wilder, *American Popular Song*, 93.

26. Sheed, *House That George Built*, 17.

27. *Smith v. Berlin*, 207 Misc. 862, 868, 141 N.Y.S. 2d 110, 116 (Sup Ct. 1955).

28. Helmy Kresa to Irving Berlin, 12/28/1937, IB (Box 378/Folder 2).

29. Irving Berlin to Francis Gilbert, 1/10/1938, IB (Box 378/Folder 2).

30. Bergreen, *As Thousands Cheer*, 521.

31. *NYT* 29 (3/31/1955); *NYT* 18 (4/1/1955).

32. Woollcott, *Story of Irving Berlin*, 82–83.

33. Irving Berlin to Francis Gilbert, 4/30/1931, IB (Box 378/Folder 2).

34. Irving Berlin to Francis Gilbert, 1/10/1938, IB (Box 378/Folder 2).

35. Orrin Dunlap, "Harmonies Galore," *NYT* X11 (10/8/1933).

36. Complaint, ¶ 6, 2/14/1928 *Berlin*.

37. Complaint, ¶ 3, 2/14/1928, *Berlin*.

38. Amended Complaint, ¶ 4, 3/26/1928, *Berlin*.

39. Irving Berlin to Francis Gilbert, 10/6/1936, IB (Box 378/Folder 2).

40. Lindey, *Plagiarism and Originality*, 194.

CHAPTER 5. ARRANGER ON A TRAIN

Important sources on Nathaniel Shilkret's career include his posthumously published memoir, *Sixty Years in the Music Business*, his grandson Niel Shell's "Nathaniel Shilkret: A Most Prolific and Diverse Creator of Recorded Sound," *ARSC Journal* 80 (Vol. XXX–IX, No. 1 Spring 2008), and Gracyk, *Popular American Recording*. The Encyclopedic Discography of Victor Recordings (http://victor.library.ucsb.edu/index.php) contains literally thousands of entries for Shilkret, and newspapers throughout the United States reported on his activities regularly during the 1920s. Charles Tuttle's political activities and tenure as United States Attorney were covered in detail by *The New York Times*. Vernon Dalhart's biographer, Jack Palmer, shared his mother lode of information about "The Prisoner's Song."

1. Shilkret, *Sixty Years*, 37.

2. Interview of Cantor William Robyn, 31, 5/28/95, MA.

3. Jim Walsh, "Favorite Pioneer Recording Artists," *Hobbies* (8/1960).

4. Palmer and Olson, *Vernon Dalhart*, chap. 7; Cazden, Haufrecht, and Studer, *Folk Songs*, 371–76.

5. Niel Shell, e-mail message to author, 6/22/05; *Time* (10/5/1936).

6. Gordon Whyte, "Nat Shilkret, Radio's Favorite Musician," *Metronome* 24, 25 (1/1/1927).

7. *Variety* 49 (2/14/1933).

8. *Variety* 26C (12/31/1924).

9. *Variety* 40 (1/7/1925).

10. Gordon Whyte, "Nat Shilkret, Radio's Favorite Musician," *Metronome* 24 (1/1/1927).

11. Hilmes, *Radio Voices*, 114.

12. Barrios, *Song in the Dark*, 18.

13. Mordaunt Hall, "The Screen," *NYT* 25 (3/23/1929).

14. Marks, *They All Sang*, 213–16.

15. ABA, Standards Relating to the Administration of Criminal Justice 3-1.2(c) (1974).

16. 29 Stat. 481–482 chap. 4 (54th Cong., 2d sess. 1897).

17. Vaidhyanathan, *Copyrights and Copywrongs*, 35–37.

18. Act of 4 March 1909, sec. 28 (emphasis added).

19. *TNY* 1 (3/21/1925).

20. Alva Johnston, "Saint in Politics," *TNY* 23 (3/23/1929).

21. *Tyson & Brother-United Theatre Ticket Offices v. Banton*, 273 U.S. 418 (1927).

22. *NYT* 1 (7/7/1927).

23. Complainant's Trial Memorandum, 1–4, 12/1933, *Shilkret II*.

24. Nathaniel Shilkret to I. E. Lambert, 7/22/1929, NS.

25. *NYT (Arts and Leisure)* 120 (4/6/1930); Hays, *City Lawyer*, 135.

26. *Fendler v. Morosco*, 253 N.Y. 281, 171 N.E. 56 (1930); Tuttle, *Life Stories*, 59–60.

27. *NYT* 11 (4/19/1924).

28. J. C. Rosenthal to Nathaniel Shilkret, 7/1/1929, NS.

29. Nathaniel Shilkret to I. E. Lambert, 1/28/1932, NS.

30. ASCAP Payments to Members, 1921–1934, DOJ.

31. Nolle Prosequi, 6/4/1931, *Shilkret I*.

32. *Marx v. United States*, 96 F.2d 204 (9th Cir. 1938); *NYT* 40 (10/31/1937); *NYT* 32 (11/2/1937).

33. I. E. Lambert to Nathaniel Shilkret, 7/17/1931, NS.

34. Nathaniel Shilkret to I. E. Lambert, 1/28/1932, NS.

35. *NYS* 16 (4/28/1930).

36. *Musical America* (5/10/1930).

37. *NYT* 29 (4/27/1930).

38. Memorandum to Arnstein Legal File, 4, 1/20/1939, ASCAP; Marks, *They All Sang*, 249.

39. *BE* (10/18/1931); *NYT* X10 (9/20/1931) (advertisement); Deposition of Vyschslaw Mamonoff, 1–5, 2/23/1939, *MultiSuit*; *NYT* 13 (4/2/1932) (advertisement).

40. Hays, *City Lawyer*, 227.

41. Arthur Garfield Hays to Arnstein, 8/3/1931, *MultiSuit*.

42. Record of New Operas Submitted to the Metropolitan Opera, 1917–1950, 102, MO.

43. Arthur Garfield Hays to Arnstein, 3/23/1933, *MultiSuit*.

44. Affidavit of Arnstein, 1-2, 2/20/42, *BMI I*.

45. Memorandum Opinion, 3–4, 12/20/1933, *Shilkret II*.

46. Ibid., 5–6.

47. Affidavit of Arnstein, 1, 2/20/1942, *BMI I*.

48. Sigmund Spaeth to Nathaniel Shilkret, 12/31/1933, NS.

CHAPTER 6. THE TUNE DETECTIVE

For a figure so little known today, it is remarkable how thoroughly documented Sigmund Spaeth's life was in the popular press of his day. Much of the biographical information about Spaeth is drawn from newspapers throughout the country, as well as detailed interviews he gave to the Columbia University Oral History project in 1951 and 1958. A representative sample of his radio work lives on in the NBC Collection at the Library of Congress. Diane Joust, the archivist at Radio City Music Hall, provided details about the Tune Detective's appearance there.

1. Woollcott, *Story of Irving Berlin*, 159.
2. *WP* 1 (7/29/1923).
3. *Atlanta Constitution* 4 (8/27/1923).
4. *NYT* 3 (12/31/1923).
5. *NYT (Book Review)* 8 (8/12/1923).
6. W. Rogers, "Slipping the Lariat Over," *NYT* XX2 (8/12/1923).
7. Interview of Sigmund Spaeth (1951), 3, COHP.
8. Interview of Sigmund Spaeth (1958), 1, COHP.
9. Interview of Sigmund Spaeth (1951), 7, COHP.
10. Spaeth, *Milton's Knowledge of Music*, 69.
11. Interview of Sigmund Spaeth (1958), 31–33, COHP.
12. *NYM* 8 (10/28/1915).
13. *NYM* 6 (8/8/1916).
14. *NYM* 4 (9/12/1916).
15. *NYM* 6 (8/1/1916).
16. *NYM* 12 (8/24/1916).
17. *NYM* 6 (9/28/1916).
18. *NYM* 4 (8/17/1916).
19. Philip Brett and Elizabeth Wood, "Lesbian and Gay Music," in Brett, Wood, and Thomas, eds., *Queering the Pitch*, 375.
20. *NYT* 11 (7/10/1918).
21. Allison Danzig, "Memories of the Old Times," *MJ* 154 (4/1959).
22. Betty Brainerd, "How My Wife Helped Me," *Portsmouth Daily Times* 10 (6/22/1927).
23. Interview of Sigmund Spaeth (1951), 45, COHP.
24. Ibid., 56.
25. Ibid.
26. Spaeth, *Common Sense of Music*, 13.
27. *The (Monessen, PA) Daily Independent* 2 (10/24/1921).
28. Lewis, *Babbitt*, 261.
29. Spaeth, *Common Sense of Music*, 32.
30. Korsyn, *Decentering Music*, 97–99.
31. Gilbert, *Lost Chords*, 335.
32. Spaeth, *Words and Music*, 35.
33. *Oswego Daily Palladium* (7/31/1923).
34. *Variety* 2 (6/14/1923).
35. *Atlanta Constitution* 15 (5/2/1924); *Ogden Standard-Examiner* 10 (11/25/1923).
36. *MTR* 9 (1/19/1924).
37. Spaeth, *Common Sense of Music*, 31.
38. Sigmund Spaeth, "Art Grows Democratic," *Bridgeport Telegram* (8/27/1925).
39. *CT* 25 (5/22/1925).
40. *The Rotarian* 16, 19 (10/1936).
41. Bennett, *Anxiety of Appreciation*, 51–73.

42. *LAT* A3 (4/20/1927).
43. Interview of Sigmund Spaeth (1951), 81, COHP.
44. Ibid., 83.
45. Hilmes, *Radio Voices*, 58.
46. *Miami Herald* 5-A (1/20/1937).
47. *Time* (8/22/1932).
48. Script and Program, 8/24/1933, RCMH.
49. *Wilkie v. Santly Brothers*, 13 F. Supp. 136 (S.D.N.Y. 1935), *aff'd*, 91 F.2d 978 (2d Cir. 1937).
50. Petition of Defendants for Rehearing, 4-5, 12/23/1935, *Wilkie*.
51. *New York Amsterdam Star-News* 17 (2/28/1942); *Chicago Defender* 20 (3/7/1942).
52. Notes of Testimony, Sigmund Spaeth, 23, 5/16/1946, *Porter I*.

CHAPTER 7. SONG-LIFTING TRIAL GOES INTO AGITATO

The account of the trial in *Arnstein v. Edward B. Marks Music Corporation* is drawn from the official court record (*Marks*) and contemporaneous press accounts. Transcripts of testimony have been edited lightly for readability and flow. All headlines actually appeared in New York City newspapers. The late Jack Lawrence, who died in 2009 at the age of ninety-six, was generous with his time and his memories.

1. Gilbert, *Without Rhyme or Reason*, 166.
2. Green, *Inside Stuff*, 9.
3. Caroline Moseley, "'The Old Arm Chair': A Study in Popular Musical Taste," *J. of American Culture* 4 (1981): 177–82. A performance of "The Old Arm Chair" by Moseley is available at http://utc.iath.virginia.edu/sentimnt/armchairf.html (accessed 10/2/2011).
4. John Morse, "Letters of Charles Dickens, 1842," in Massachusetts Historical Society, *Proceedings*, 150; Vaidhyanathan, *Copyrights and Copywrongs*, 51.
5. Spaeth, *History of Popular Music*, 78-79.
6. Complaint, *Reed*. Regarding *Reed v. Carusi* generally, see Frank McCormick, "George P. Reed v. Samuel Carusi: A Nineteenth Century Jury Trial Pursuant to the 1831 Copyright Act" (available for download at http://digitalcommons.law.umaryland.edu/mlh_pubs/4/) (accessed 10/2/2011).
7. *Reed v. Carusi*, 20 F. Cas. 431 (C.C. Md. 1845).
8. Tyler, *Memoir of Roger Brooke Taney*, 312–14.
9. National Archives, *Copies of Presidential Pardons and Remissions, 1794–1893 (Vol. 5)* 342 (1965).
10. Memorandum to Arnstein Legal File, 11, 1/30/1939, ASCAP.
11. Arnstein, *Broadway Music*, 7.
12. Lawrence, *They All Sang My Songs*, 99; "Play, Fiddle, Play: The Story Behind the Song," http://www.jacklawrencesongwriter.com/songs/play_fiddle_play.html (accessed 10/2/2011).
13. *NYA* 3 (6/7/1935).
14. *Radio City Music Hall Program Magazine* 15, 5/9/1935; Radio City Music Hall Music Card No. 2907-E—RCMH.
15. John P. Chandler to Arnstein, 2/17/1933, *MultiSuit*.

16. Leonard Liebling to Arnstein, 4/18/1935, *MultiSuit*.

17. Arnstein to Emery Deutsch, Def. Ex. E, 1/15/1933, *Marks*.

18. *NYP* 2 (6/5/1935).

19. *NYT* 26 (6/4/1935).

20. *NYJ* 3 (6/4/1935).

21. "Play, Fiddle, Play: The Story Behind the Song," http://www.jacklawrencesongwriter.
com/songs/play_fiddle_play.html (accessed 10/2/2011).

22. *NYP* 2 (6/5/1935).

23. Ibid.

24. *NYWT* 3 (6/5/1935).

25. *NYA* 3 (6/7/1935).

26. Affidavit of Arnstein, 3, 9/29/1936, *Marks*.

27. *NYT* 24 (6/6/1935).

28. *NYWT* 3 (6/5/1935).

29. *NYP* 2 (6/5/1935).

30. "Play, Fiddle, Play: The Story Behind the Song," http://www.jacklawrencesongwriter.
com/songs/play_fiddle_play.html (accessed 10/2/2011).

31. *NYS* 10 (6/5/1935).

32. Lawrence, *They All Sang My Songs*, 102.

33. Marks, *They All Sang*, 133–35.

34. Suisman, *Selling Sounds*, 84

35. *NYP* 2 (6/5/1935).

36. *Arnstein v. Edward B. Marks Music Corp.*, 82 F.2d 275, 276 (2d Cir. 1936).

37. *NYA* 3 (6/7/1935).

38. *NYS* 19 (6/6/1935).

39. Ibid.

40. T. Scott Buhrman, "New York and the Cinema," in H. Westerby, ed., *The Complete
Organ Recitalist* 347 (1927).

41. *NYS* 19 (6/6/1935).

42. *NYP* (6/6/1935).

43. *NYWT* 4 (6/6/1935).

44. *NYA* 3 (6/7/1935).

45. Ibid.

46. Martha Neumark, "Lights of New York," *The Sentinel* 24 (6/27/1935).

47. *Arnstein v. Edward B. Marks Music Corp.*, 11 F. Supp. 535 (S.D.N.Y. 1935).

48. Theodore B. Richter to Arthur Altman, Def. Ex. J, *Marks*.

49. Jack Lawrence, e-mail message to author, 6/21/2005; memorandum to Arnstein
Legal File, 8, 1/30/1939, ASCAP.

50. Harrie B. Chase to Learned Hand and Thomas Swan, ca. 1/1936, LH (Box 195/
Folder 22).

51. 183 F. 107 (2d Cir. 1910).

52. *Edward B. Marks, Inc. v. Leo Feist, Inc.*, No. 147-16 (S.D.N.Y. October 16, 1922)
(unpublished order), *aff'd*, 290 F. 959 (2d Cir. 1923), LH (Box 147/Folder 16).

53. Learned Hand to Harrie B. Chase and Thomas Swan, 1/20/1936, LH (Box 195/
Folder 22).

54. Ibid.

55. *Arnstein v. Edward B. Marks Music Corp.*, 82 F.2d 275 (2d Cir. 1936).
56. John C. Paine to Manuel Neufield, 8/13/1935, *MultiSuit*.

CHAPTER 8. JUSTICE FOR GENIUS

The account of ASCAP's early history, and in particular its early encounters with the theater operators and broadcasters, draws heavily on the Department of Justice's antitrust investigation file (DOJ), including a report by Special Agent J. A. Brann, "Summary Report: ASCAP Alleged Violation of Sherman Anti-Trust Act" (6/2/25) ("Brann Report"), and congressional hearings (*1924 Hearings* and *1926 Hearings*). Richard Reimer and Jim Steinblatt of ASCAP provided access to its Arnstein file. Arnstein's unpublished and unproduced script, *Broadway Music*, is deposited with the Copyright Office (D-38076).

1. Meeting of ASCAP, Beverly Wilshire Hotel, 13, 9/9/1942, DOJ.
2. *1926 Hearings*, 56–57.
3. *1924 Hearings*, 109 (Minutes of Conference Held at Offices of ASCAP, 9/20/1922).
4. Brann Report, 41–42 and 180; J. C. Rosenthal, "The A.S.C.A.P.," *Variety* 30 (10/1/1934).
5. E. C. Mills to Louis Bernstein, 1/31/1925, DOJ (Box 219); *Variety* 7 (11/18/1925).
6. *1924 Hearings*, 60.
7. Brann Report, 36.
8. Brann Report, 46.
9. Brann Report, 57.
10. *Harms v. Cohen*, 279 F. 276 (E.D. Pa. 1922); J. C. Rosenthal to Sydney S. Cohen, 3/29/1922, DOJ (Box 219); *NYT* 7 (7/18/1924).
11. Russell F. Brown to MPTOA, 4/20/1922, DOJ (Box 219).
12. *NYT* 40 (7/9/1925).
13. *1924 Hearings*, 53.
14. F. J. Rembusch to Sen. Harry S. New, 2/18/1922, DOJ (Box 219).
15. Ray A. Grombacher to MPTOA, 1/26/1923, DOJ (Box 219).
16. P. K. Peters to MPTOA, 10/27/1922, DOJ (Box 219).
17. Brann Report, 74
18. ASCAP Payments to Members, 1921–1934, DOJ.
19. "5,000,000 Songs," *Fortune* 27, 32 (1/1933).
20. *1926 Hearings*, 145–46.
21. J. C. Rosenthal to Radio Broadcasting Stations, 5/24/1922, DOJ (Box 219).
22. David Sarnoff to William Brown, 9/11/1922, DOJ (Box 219).
23. I. J. Adams to David Sarnoff, 3/3/1922, DOJ (Box 219).
24. I. J. Adams to David Sarnoff, 9/14/1922, DOJ (Box 219).
25. *NYT* E3 (3/25/1923).
26. Frankel and Frankel to E. H. Jones, 3, 11/25/1925, DOJ (Box 219).
27. *CT* 14 (2/7/1924).
28. *1926 Hearings*, 147.
29. *1924 Hearings*, 5.
30. Quoted in *1926 Hearings*, 337.
31. *1924 Hearings*, 9.

32. Ibid., 11–12.
33. Ibid., 14.
34. Ibid., 52.
35. Ibid., 74.
36. Ibid., 61.
37. Henry Waterson to Paul B. Klugh, 2/5/1924, DOJ (Box 219).
38. *1924 Hearings*, 27.
39. Ibid., 248.
40. H.R. Rep. No. 60-2222, at 7 (1909).
41. *1924 Hearings*, 33–34.
42. Ibid., 5–6.
43. *1926 Hearings*, 246–47.
44. Ibid., 145.
45. *Jerome H. Remick & Co. v. American Automobile Accessories Co.*, 298 F. 628, 631 (S.D. Oh. 1924), *rev'd*, 5 F.2d 411 (6th Cir. 1925).
46. Litman, *Digital Copyright*, 52.
47. *1926 Hearings*, 329.
48. Memorandum from G. Stanley Thompson to Colonel Donovan, 4/22/1926, DOJ (Box 219).
49. *Federal Baseball Club of Baltimore v. National League of Professional Baseball Clubs*, 259 U.S. 200 (1922).
50. Kevin McDonald, "Antitrust and Baseball: Stealing Holmes," *J. of Supreme Court History* 2 (1998): 89–128.
51. *Variety* 1 (11/10/1926).
52. ASCAP Payments to Members, 1921–1934, DOJ.
53. *Variety* 46 (7/24/1935).
54. Ryan, *Production of Culture*, 80.
55. Ennis, *Seventh Stream*, 47.
56. *Variety* 51 (3/18/1925).
57. *1926 Hearings*, 57.
58. Articles of Association of the American Society of Composers, Authors and Publishers, as in effect 1935, art. 3, sec. 1, Def. Ex. B-5, *MultiSuit*
59. Ryan, *Production of Culture*, 53.
60. Memorandum to Arnstein Legal File, 1–3, 1/30/1939, ASCAP.
61. Ibid., 3.
62. Ibid., 6.
63. Ibid., 11–12.
64. Ibid., 13–15.
65. Federal Trade Commission Field Report, NYA-3337, 1-3, 7/25/1933, DOJ (Box 224).
66. *1926 Hearings*, 196–97.
67. Arnstein to Learned Hand, 7/13/1936, LH (Box 48/Folder 3); Affidavit of Arnstein, ¶¶ 6–7, 9/29/1936, *Marks*.
68. Learned Hand to Arnstein, 7/15/1936, LH (Box 48/Folder 3).
69. Affidavit of Arnstein, 6, 9/29/1936, *Marks*.
70. Affidavit of Arnstein, 1, 10/3/1936, *Marks*.
71. Report of Special Master, 10/29/1936, *Marks*.

72. Oliver W. Nicoll to Hallie Flanagan, 2/13/1936; J. Howard Miler to Hallie Flanagan, 3/19/1936; Munsell to Nicolai Sokoloff and Hallie Flanagan, 3/23/1936—FTP.
73. Arnstein to Homer S. Cummings, 9/9/1934, DOJ (Box 227).
74. Harold M. Stephens to Arnstein, 9/13/1934, DOJ (Box 227).
75. Memorandum for the Division Files, 12/1/1936, DOJ (Box 227).
76. *Miami Daily News*, 10-A (12/13/1936).
77. Dickens, *Sketches of Boz*, 202.
78. Sandage, *Born Losers*, 255.
79. Memorandum to Arnstein Legal File, 15, 1/30/1939, ASCAP.
80. Sigmund Spaeth, "A Tune Detective Testifies," *'47: The Magazine of the Year* 143, 145 (3/47).
81. Lawrence, *They All Sang My Songs*, 98.
82. Shilkret, *Sixty Years*, 158.
83. *Variety* 47 (8/11/1937).
84. Complaint, ¶ 6–8, 17, 18, 25, and 40, 11/24/1937, *MultiSuit*.

CHAPTER 9. MY BEER IS A SHAME

The account of the MultiSuit trial is drawn from the official court record (*MultiSuit*), material from the Warner Brothers Archive (WB), and contemporaneous press accounts. Transcripts of testimony have been edited lightly for readability and flow.

1. Interview with Mr. Sammy Cahn, Re: Arnstein v. Harms, Inc. and Warner Bros., 1, 2/2/1939, WB.
2. Letters from Sholom Secunda to Betty Secunda, July–August 1937, SS (Series XIX/Box 101); Interview with Sholom Secunda, Re: Arnstein v. Harms, Inc. and Warner Bros., 1/31/1939, WB; Arthur Gelb, "Author Regains 'Bei Mir Bist du Schoen,'" *NYT* 22 (2/17/1961).
3. Interview with Mr. Sammy Cahn, Re: Arnstein v. Harms, Inc. and Warner Bros., 1-2, 2/2/1939, WB.
4. Michel Mok, "Composer of 'Bei Mir' Tells How He Had to Split $30 Fee," *Camden Courier-Post* (1/26/1938).
5. Opinion re Motions of National Broadcasting Company and Columbia Broadcasting Company to Dismiss the Bill as to Themselves, *Arnstein v. ASCAP*, 1/6/1938, WB.
6. Memorandum of District Judge Conger Deciding Motion of Defendant Broadway Music Publishing Corp. to Dismiss Complaint, *Arnstein v. ASCAP*, 11/10/1938, WB.
7. Clark, *Handbook*, 12–13.
8. Ibid., 57–58.
9. *Conley v. Gibson*, 355 U.S. 41, 45-46 (1957), overruled, *Bell Atlantic Corp. v. Twombly*, 550 U.S. 544 (2007).
10. Richard Marcus, "The Revival of Fact Pleading under the Federal Rules of Civil Procedure," *Colum. L. Rev.* 86 (1986): 433–94.
11. Bulletin issued by National Association of Broadcasters, 8/27/1932, DOJ (Box 223); Resolution Adopted by the National Association of Broadcasters at the Annual Convention Held in St. Louis, Missouri, November 14–16, 1932, DOJ (Box 223).
12. Petition, 20-21, 8/30/1934, *ASCAP*.
13. 288 U.S. 344, 360 (1933).

14. Transcript, 210, 6/11/1935, *ASCAP*.
15. *Variety* 63 (6/19/1935).
16. Transcript, 636, 6/17/1935, and 719, 6/18/1935, *ASCAP*.
17. *Variety* 49 (6/26/1935).
18. *Variety* 53 (7/10/1935).
19. John C. Paine to Rene Jeanne, 8/27/1937, DOJ.
20. A. M. Wattenberg to Robert Perkins, 12/9/1937, WB.
21. *NYT* 25 (3/7/1939).
22. *NYHT* 15 (3/7/1939).
23. Additional Interview with Sholom Secunda, Re: Arnstein v. Harms, Inc. and Warner Bros., 3/1/1939, WB.
24. Sigmund Spaeth Expert Report, ca. 2/1939, WB.
25. *Arnstein v. ASCAP*, 29 F. Supp. 388, 399 (S.D.N.Y. 1939).
26. Kenneth Clark Expert Report, ca. 2/1939, WB.
27. *NYWT* (3/7/1939).
28. Dunning, *On the Air*, 341.
29. Golenpaul, ed., *Information, Please!* 28, 37, and 44.
30. Levant, *Memoirs of an Amnesiac*, 158.
31. Kashner and Schoenberger, *Talent for Genius*, 214.
32. Ibid., 219.
33. Levant, *Smattering of Ignorance*, 252–53.
34. Kieran, *Not under Oath*, 66.
35. Interview of Sigmund Spaeth (1951), 97–98, COHP.
36. Spaeth, *Great Program Music*, ix.
37. John Rockwell, "Saturday Critic," *OT* 25-E (4/19/1969); Larry Rothe, "Sigmund Spaeth, Someone You Should Know," in Steinberg and Rothe, *For the Love of Music* 187, 191–93.
38. 29 F. Supp. at 392.
39. Ibid.
40. Ibid. at 391.
41. Memorandum signed by Milton L. Gould, ca. 11/15/1938; Affidavit of Nat Nevins, 11/18/1938, *MultiSuit*.
42. Arnstein to Harry Warner, 7/23/1938, WB.
43. Enclosure to letter from Arnstein to Hon. Roy E. Ayers, Governor of Montana, 2/24/1940, EBC (Box 11/Folder 14).
44. 29 F. Supp. at 393.
45. *Gibbs v. Buck*, 307 U.S. 66 (1939).
46. 307 U.S. at 82.
47. *Buck v. Gallagher*, 36 F. Supp. 405 (W.D. Wash. 1940).
48. Arnold, *Bottlenecks of Business*, 283.

CHAPTER 10. BAD MUSIC INSTEAD

The ASCAP-BMI war was covered in-depth by the *New York Times*, *Variety*, and other periodicals. This chapter draws upon that contemporaneous reporting as well as later histories, in particular Ennis, *Seventh Stream*; Meyer, *Gold in Tin Pan Alley*; Ryan,

Production of Culture; and Sanjek, *Pennies from Heaven*. The NBC Collection at the Library of Congress contains numerous recordings from 1941 evidencing the effects of the ASCAP boycott.

1. *NYT* 1, 48 (9/10/1939).
2. *NYT* 11 (8/4/1939).
3. *Variety* 31 (12/11/1940).
4. "BMI: Something New in American Music," in George Fragos, Jack Baker, and Dick Gasparre, "I Hear a Rhapsody" (New York, BMI: 1940), 6.
5. Shilkret, *Sixty Years*, 72.
6. Secunda, *Bei Mir*, 157–59; *Variety* 47, 50 (10/2/1940).
7. *1958 Hearings*, 482.
8. *NYT* 24 (9/16/1939).
9. Gene Buck to All Advertisers, 7, 8/1/1940, NYPL (Clippings—ASCAP).
10. *NYT* 21 (8/6/1940).
11. Meyer, *Gold in Tin Pan Alley*, 99.
12. Affidavit of Neville Miller, 1–2, 3/7/1942, *BMI I*.
13. Deposition of Sidney Kaye, 1, 2/7/1942, *BMI I*.
14. Ben Bodec, "Marks' Desertion of ASCAP May Push Untested Publisher Status on Copyrights to Adjudication," *Variety* 29 (12/11/1940).
15. *NYT* 20 (12/10/1940).
16. Gene Buck to All Advertisers, 8, 8/1/1940, NYPL (Clippings—ASCAP).
17. *Variety* 42 (11/27/1940).
18. *Variety* 25 (12/18/1940).
19. U.S. Department of Justice Press Release, 2–3, 12/27/1940, *ASCAP*.
20. *NYT* 20 (12/31/1940).
21. *NYT* X10 (1/26/1941).
22. *NYHT* (1/3/1941).
23. *1958 Hearings*, 22.
24. Affidavit of Arnstein, 3, 10/3/1936, *Marks*.
25. Ibid.
26. Affidavit of Russell Lord Tarbox, 4/18/1941, *Arnstein*.
27. Complaint and Consent Decree, *United States v. BMI*, 2/3/1941 (E.D. Wis. No. 459), DOJ.
28. *United States v. ASCAP*, 1941 Trade Cas. (CCH) ¶ 56,104 (S.D.N.Y. 1941).
29. *Variety* 39 (3/19/1941).
30. Deposition of Arnstein, 40, 3/11/1942, *BMI I*.
31. *Carew v. RKO Pictures*, 43 F. Supp. 199 (S.D. Cal. 1942).
32. *Allen v. Walt Disney Productions*, 41 F. Supp. 134 (S.D.N.Y. 1941)
33. Deposition of Arnstein, 42–43, 3/11/1942, *BMI I*.
34. Plaintiff's Motion for New Trial, 6, 7/14/1942, *BMI I*.
35. Ibid.
36. Ibid.
37. Affidavit of Stuart Sprague in Opposition to Plaintiff's Motion for a New Trial, 6–7, 7/17/1942, *BMI I*.
38. *Arnstein v. BMI*, 46 F. Supp. 379, 381 (S.D.N.Y. 1942).
39. Affidavit of Arnstein, 4/13/1943, *BMI II*.

40. Memorandum of Charles E. Clark, 4/15/1943, CEC (Box 31/Folder 57).
41. Memorandum of Augustus N. Hand, 4/21/1943, CEC (Box 31/Folder 57).
42. *Arnstein v. BMI*, 137 F.2d 410 (2d Cir. 1943).
43. Deposition of Mack Gordon, 7, 5/5/1943; Deposition of Harry Warren, 5–6, 5/5/1943, *20th Century*.
44. Spaeth, *Words and Music*, 26–28.
45. Complaint, ¶¶ 8B & 9, 12/28/1942; Affidavit of Arnstein, 4/27/1943, *20th Century*.
46. Plaintiff's Opposition to Motion to Strike Jury Demand, 2/5/1943, *20th Century*.
47. *Arnstein v. Twentieth Century–Fox Film Corp.*, 3 F.R.D. 58, 59 (S.D.N.Y. 1943).
48. Third Amended Complaint, ¶ 58, 2/11/1949, *Crestview*.
49. *Arnstein v. Twentieth Century–Fox Film Corp.*, 52 F. Supp. 114, 115 (S.D.N.Y. 1943).
50. Sheed, *House That George Built*, 201.
51. Irving Berlin to Francis Gilbert, 4/4/1942, IB (Box 378/Folder 5).
52. Irving Berlin to Francis Gilbert, 5/29/1942, IB (Box 378/Folder 5).
53. Francis Gilbert to Sydney M. Kaye, 6/15/1942, IB (Box 378/Folder 5).
54. Meeting of ASCAP, Beverly Wilshire Hotel, 30–31, 9/9/1942, DOJ.
55. John C. Paine to Neville Miller, 7/3/1942, IB (Box 378/File 5).
56. Sydney M. Kaye to Francis Gilbert, 7/8/1942, IB (Box 378/File 5).
57. Meeting of ASCAP, Beverly Wilshire Hotel, 32, 9/9/1942, DOJ.
58. Arnstein to Arthur Schwartz, 10/15/1944, WB.
59. Arnstein to Eleanor Roosevelt, 2/2/1945, FDR (White House Papers of Eleanor Roosevelt).

CHAPTER 11 GIFT FOR A PRESIDENT TURNED
INTO SONG TO A COW

The principal sources for this chapter are the official court records of the U.S. District Court for the Southern District of New York (*Porter I & IV, Spaeth*) and U.S. Court of Appeals for the Second Circuit (*Porter II & III*), the Warner Brothers Archives (WB), and the papers of Judge Hand (Harvard) and Judges Clark and Frank (Yale). Eells, *Life That Late He Led*, and McBrien, *Cole Porter*, were especially useful sources for Cole Porter background.

1. Rodgers, *Musical Stages*, 88.
2. Wilder, *American Popular Song*, 246.
3. Gottlieb, *Funny, It Doesn't Sound Jewish*, 98–99, 186–91.
4. Rodgers, *Musical Stages*, 88.
5. Arnstein to Warner Brothers Legal Department, 11/19/1944, WB.
6. Complaint, 2/16/1954, *Porter IV*.
7. Arnstein to Harry Warner, 9/10/1944, WB.
8. Arnstein to R. W. Perkins, 1/14/1945, WB.
9. Arnstein to Warner Brothers Legal Department, 11/19/1944, WB.
10. Clippings attached to Letter from Arnstein to Warner Brothers Legal Department, 1/14/1945, WB.
11. Eells, *Life That Late He Led*, 216.
12. Hubler, *Cole Porter Story*, 44.
13. Roy J. Orbinger to Morris Ebenstein, 9/20/1944, WB.

14. Arnstein to Jack Warner, 8/26/1945, WB.
15. Stanleigh P. Freedman to Roy J. Orbinger, 10/2/1944, WB.
16. Roy J. Orbinger to Stanleigh Friedman, 11/17/1944, WB.
17. Memorandum to S. P. Friedman, 1/5/1945, WB.
18. Stanleigh P. Friedman to Cole Porter, 12/27/1944, WB.
19. Stanleigh P. Friedman to Roy J. Orbinger, 1/3/1945, WB.
20. Eells, *Life That Late He Led*, 218 (quoting columnist Sidney Skolsky).
21. Transcript of Conversation, Arnstein and Joseph Karp, 1/2/1945, WB.
22. Complaint, Exh. A-2, 2/21/1945, *Porter I*.
23. Secretary to Eleanor Roosevelt to Arnstein, 2/12/1945, FDR (White House Papers of Eleanor Roosevelt).
24. Complaint, ¶¶ 62-63, 2/21/1945, *Porter I*.
25. Deposition of Cole Porter, 5, 4/30/1945, *Porter I*.
26. Deposition of Arnstein, 22, 4/30/1945, *Porter I*.
27. Ibid., 23.
28. Ibid., 5–6.
29. Ibid., 7.
30. Memorandum in Support of Motion for Summary Judgment, Dismissal for Vexatiousness and Other Relief, 25, 7/18/1945, *Porter I*.
31. Fed. R. Civ. P. 56.
32. James and Hazard, *Civil Procedure*, 220.
33. Memorandum, 4, 7/26/1945, *Porter I*.
34. Arnstein to Jack Warner, 8/26/1945, WB.
35. Affidavit and Memorandum Opposing the Dismissal of Suit before Trial, 7, 10/7/1945, *Porter I*.
36. Book Review, "If Men Were Angels," *Virginia Law Rev.* 29 (1943): 664.
37. Schick, *Learned Hand's Court*, 219–46.
38. Plaintiff Appellant's Brief, 9, 12/5/1945, *Porter II*.
39. Memorandum of Jerome N. Frank, 1/11/1946, CEC (Box 33/Folder 75).
40. Memorandum of Charles E. Clark, 1/14/1946, CEC (Box 33/Folder 75).
41. Reply Memorandum of Jerome N. Frank, 1/15/1946, CEC (Box 33/Folder 75).
42. Supplemental Memorandum of Jerome N. Frank, 1/15/1946, CEC (Box 33/Folder 75).
43. Supplemental Memorandum of Charles E. Clark, 1/15/1946, CEC (Box 33/Folder 75) (emphasis in original).
44. Memorandum of Learned Hand, 1/18/1946, CEC (Box 33/Folder 75).
45. Jerome N. Frank to Charles E. Clark, 4/3/1946, CEC (Box 33/Folder 75).
46. 154 F.2d 464 (2d Cir. 1946).
47. Alan Latman, "'Probative Similarity' as Proof of Copying: Toward Dispelling Some Myths in Copyright Infringement," *Colum. L. Rev.* 90 (1990): 1187, 1191.
48. Charles E. Clark to Jerome N. Frank, 4/2/1946, CEC (Box 33/Folder 75).
49. Arnstein to Judges Hand, Clark, and Frank, 1/31/1946, LH (Box 66/Folder 20).
50. Statement of Points, 1, undated, *Porter III*.
51. Petition for Rehearing, 7, 1/7/1947, *Porter III*.
52. Notes of Testimony, Deems Taylor, 5, 5/21/1946, *Porter I*.
53. Depositions of Jerry Wald and Richard McCaulay, 5/2/1941, *Spaeth*.

54. Complaint, ¶ 9, 3/13/1940, *Spaeth.*
55. Schwartz, *Cole Porter,* 221.
56. *Peru Republican* 1 (6/7/1946).

CHAPTER 12. FOUR LAST SONGS

Information about the later days of Ira B. Arnstein, Sigmund Spaeth, and Nathaniel Shilkret was provided by Jeanne Weston, Robert Cumming, Connie Lane Duckel, and Niel Shell. Justice Jacqueline W. Silberman, formerly of the New York State Supreme Court, provided assistance in locating the "lost" *Crestview* file.

1. Charles E. Clark to Jerome N. Frank, 3/21/1946, JNF. (Box 97/Folder 852).
2. Jerome N. Frank to Charles E. Clark, 3/22/1946, JNF (Box 97/Folder 852).
3. Jerome N. Frank to Charles E. Clark, 4/2/1946, JNF (Box 97/Folder 852); Jerome N. Frank to Charles E. Clark, 4/3/1946, JNF (Box 97/Folder 852).
4. Memorandum of Learned Hand, 12/10/1946, LH (Box 209/Folder 1).
5. *Arnstein v. Porter,* 158 F.2d 795 (2d Cir. 1946).
6. Memorandum of Jerome N. Frank, 12/12/1946, LH (Box 209/Folder 1).
7. *Arnstein v. Porter,* 158 F.2d 795 (2d Cir. 1946).
8. *Arnstein v. Porter,* 330 U.S. 851, 67 S. Ct. 1096, *rehearing denied,* 331 U.S. 867, 67 S. Ct. 1529 (1947).
9. Third Amended Complaint, ¶¶ 70–82, 2/11/1949, *Crestview.*
10. *Billboard* 20 (10/23/1948).
11. Arnstein to R. W. Perkins, 3/24/1949, WB.
12. Francis Gilbert to Irving Berlin, 9/14/1948, IB (Box 379/Folder 8).
13. Charles Davis, "'Nature Boy' Needs Gold Mine to Pay Off," *Chicago Defender* 9 (7/10/1948); Gene Homel, "Nature Boy," *Outlook* 11 (7/2008); *Billboard* 18 (7/3/1948).
14. Sigmund Spaeth, "A Tune Detective Testifies," '47 143 (3/1947); Second Amended Complaint, ¶ 57, 10/8/1948; *Crestview.*
15. Leonard Lyons, "Lyons Den," *Chicago Defender* 5 (6/11/1956).
16. Putnam, *Bowling Alone,* 268.
17. Brochure, "Sigmund Spaeth: America's Most Popular Speaker and Writer on Music," ca. 1952, NYPL (Clippings—Sigmund Spaeth).
18. Spaeth, *History of Popular Music,* 526.
19. Ibid., 92.
20. Sigmund Spaeth to Irving Berlin, 12/2/1948; Irving Berlin to Sigmund Spaeth, 12/13/1948; Sigmund Spaeth to Irving Berlin, 4/11/1949; Irving Berlin to Sigmund Spaeth, 4/18/1949—IB (Box 358/Folder 32).
21. Irving Berlin to Francis Gilbert, 10/4/1948, IB (Box 378/Folder 6).
22. Spaeth, *History of Popular Music,* 462.
23. Irving Berlin to Francis Gilbert, 10/4/1948, IB (Box 378/Folder 6).
24. *BMI v. Taylor,* 106 Misc.2d 9, 20, 55 N.Y.S.2d 94 (N.Y. Sup. Ct. 1945).
25. Jack Lawrence, in discussion with author, 4/2005.
26. *Variety* 123 (3/9/1983).
27. Guralnick, *Last Train to Memphis.*

28. John Bowe, "The Copyright Enforcers," *NYT* (*Sunday Magazine*) 38, 40 (8/8/2010).
29. Andrew Ross Sorkin, "Raising a Glass to 2011," *NYT* B1, B5 (1/3/2012).
30. Writers Classification Committee of ASCAP, Memorandum for Department of Justice: Proposed Revision of Classification, 3, 5/26/1949, DOJ.
31. Ennis, *Seventh Stream*, 108.
32. Ryan, *Production of Culture*, 113.
33. Ennis, *Seventh Stream*, 167.
34. *1958 Hearings*, 764.
35. Ibid., 401.
36. Ibid., 4.
37. Ibid., 107.
38. Ibid., 136.
39. Ibid., 450.
40. Ibid., 917–18.
41. Ennis, *Seventh Stream*, 165.
42. Interview of Sigmund Spaeth (1958), 17, COHP.
43. Ibid., 31.
44. Ibid., 21.
45. Hal Boyle, "50-Year Champion of Music Draws Line at Rock-'n'Roll," *Berkshire Eagle* 9 (9/5/1958).
46. Sigmund Spaeth, "Musical Illiteracy Widespread," *OT* B-7 (9/9/1956).
47. Sigmund Spaeth, "Music for Everybody," *OT* 8-C (12/6/1959).
48. Sigmund Spaeth, "Science Substitutes for Singing Ability," *OT* 2-C (7/19/1959).
49. *Variety* 34 (7/22/1953).
50. Larry Rothe, "Sigmund Spaeth, Someone You Should Know," in Steinberg and Rothe, *For the Love of Music*, 187, 194.
51. Max Ervin, "The Importance of Music," *Music Educators Journal* 51 (1964): 127.
52. Al Vann, "A Message from the Publisher," *MJ* 127 (4/1959).
53. *Variety* 41 (4/24/1954).
54. Enclosure to Letter from Arnstein to R. W. Perkins, 3/24/1949, WB.
55. Complaint, 3, 2/16/1954, *Porter IV*.
56. Dan Richman, "Arnstein Still Suing 'Em," *New York Morning Telegraph*, ca. 2/1954, NYPL (Clippings—Ira B. Arnstein).
57. Affidavit in Support of Plaintiff's Motion, ¶ 9, 5/14/1954, *Porter IV*.
58. Memorandum, 7/15/54, *Porter IV*.
59. Spaeth, *Importance of Music*, 200–201.
60. *Berkshire Eagle* 14 (4/22/1959).
61. Sigmund Spaeth, "Music for Everybody," *OT* 3 (4/30/60).
62. Memorandum on Behalf of Plaintiff, 50, 12/15/1947, *Baron*.
63. Nizer, *My Life in Court*, 275.
64. Transcript, 846, *Baron*.
65. Robert Peterson, "Music Master Is Near 80," *Valley Independent* 16 (3/22/1965).
66. Shilkret, *Sixty Years*, 218.
67. *Variety* 43 (5/16/1956).
68. Berlin to Roland A. Hoover, 11/9/1972, IB (Box 358/Folder 13).

69. Alan Hartnick, "Summary Judgment in Copyright: From Cole Porter to Superman," *Cardozo Arts and Entertainment Law Journal* 3 (1984): 53, 70.

70. Note, "The Role of the Expert Witness in Music Copyright Infringement Cases," *Fordham L. Rev.* 57 (1988): 127, 134.

71. Rosen, *Music and Copyright*, 208.

72. Mark Avsec, "'Nonconventional' Musical Analysis and 'Disguised' Infringement: Clever Musical Tricks to Divide the Wealth of Tin Pan Alley," *Clev. St. L. Rev.* 52 (2005): 339, 342.

73. Note, "Finding the Fact of Familiarity: Assessing Judicial Similarity Tests in Copyright Infringement Actions," *Drake L. Rev.* 49 (2001): 489, 494.

74. Paul E. Mullen and Grant Lester, "Vexatious Litigants and Unusually Persistent Complainants and Petitioners: From Querulous Paranoia to Querulous Behavior," *Behavioral Science and the Law* 24 (2006): 333–49; Grant Lester et al., "Unusually Persistent Complainants," *British Journal of Psychiatry* 184 (2004): 352–56.

BIBLIOGRAPHY

Periodicals, scholarly journal articles, oral histories, archival materials, and interviews and correspondence with the author are cited in full in the notes.

Adams, Henry. *The Education of Henry Adams*. Boston: Houghton Mifflin, 1973.

Alter, Jonathan. *The Defining Moment: FDR's Hundred Days and the Triumph of Hope*. New York: Simon & Schuster, 2006.

Arnold, Thurman. *The Bottlenecks of Business*. New York: Reynal & Hitchcock, 1940.

Arnstein, Ira B. *Broadway Music*. Unpublished manuscript deposited with U.S. Copyright Office (D-38076), 1935.

ASCAP. *The ASCAP Biographical Dictionary of Composers, Authors, and Publishers*. New York: Thomas Y. Crowell, 1948.

———. *How the Public Gets Its New Music*. New York: ASCAP, 1933.

Baker, Zachary. *The Lawrence Marwick Collection of Copyrighted Yiddish Plays at the Library of Congress: An Annotated Bibliography*. Washington, DC: Library of Congress, 2004.

Banfield, Stephen. *Jerome Kern*. New Haven, CT: Yale University Press, 2006.

Barnet, Richard D., Bruce Nemerov, and Mayo R. Taylor. *The Story Behind the Song: 150 Songs That Chronicle the 20th Century*. Westport, CT: Greenwood, 2004.

Barnett, Andrew. *Sibelius*. New Haven, CT: Yale University Press, 2007.

Barrett, Mary Ellin. *Irving Berlin: A Daughter's Memoir*. New York: Simon & Schuster, 1994.

Barrios, Richard. *A Song in the Dark: The Birth of the Musical Film*. New York: Oxford University Press, 1995.

Bennett, Rebecca. *The Anxiety of Appreciation: Virgil Thomson Wrestles with a "Racket."* Ph.D. diss., Northwestern University, 2009.

Bergreen, Laurence. *As Thousands Cheer: The Life of Irving Berlin*. New York: Penguin, 1990.

Boardman, Gerald. *Jerome Kern*. New York: Oxford University Press, 1980.

Bradley, Edwin. *The First Hollywood Musicals: A Critical Filmography of 171 Features, 1927 through 1932*. Jefferson, NC: McFarland & Co., 1996.

Brett, Philip, Elizabeth Wood, and Gary C. Thomas, eds. *Queering the Pitch: The New Gay and Lesbian Musicology, 2nd Edition*. New York: Routledge, 2006.

Brothers, Thomas, ed. *Louis Armstrong in His Own Words: Selected Writings* New York: Oxford University Press, 1999.

Brown, Anthony Cave. *Wild Bill Donovan: The Last Hero.* New York: Times Books, 1982.

Cahn, Sammy. *I Should Care: The Sammy Cahn Story.* New York: Arbor House, 1974.

Cantor, Eddie. *Caught Short! A Saga of Wailing Wall Street.* New York: Simon & Schuster, 1929.

Carnegie, Andrew. *Triumphant Democracy: 60 Years' March of the Republic,* rev. ed. New York: Scribner's, 1893.

Cazden, Norman, Herbert Haufrecht, and Norman Studer. *Folk Songs of the Catskills.* Albany: SUNY Press, 1982.

Chapin, David, and Ben Weinstock. *The Road from Letichev: The History and Culture of a Forgotten Jewish Community in Eastern Europe.* San Jose, CA: Writer's Showcase, 2000.

Clark, Charles. *Handbook of the Law of Code Pleading.* St. Paul, MN: West, 1947.

Crawford, Richard. *America's Musical Life: A History.* New York: Norton, 2001.

Dickens, Charles. *Sketches of Boz.* London: Baudry, 1839.

Dickinson, Kay, ed. *Movie Music: The Film Reader.* New York: Routledge, 2003.

Dickstein, Morris. *Dancing in the Dark: A Cultural History of the Great Depression.* New York: Norton, 2009.

Dreher, Carl. *Sarnoff: An American Success.* New York: Quadrangle, 1977.

Dreiser, Theodore. *Twelve Men.* New York: Boni & Liveright, 1919.

Dunning, John. *On the Air: The Encyclopedia of Old Time Radio.* New York: Oxford, 1998.

Eells, George. *The Life That Late He Led.* New York: Putnam, 1967.

English, Timothy. *Sounds Like Teen Spirit: Stolen Melodies, Ripped-Off Riffs, and the Secret History of Rock and Roll.* New York: iUniverse, 2006.

Ennis, Philip. *The Seventh Stream: The Emergence of Rocknroll in American Popular Music.* Middletown, CT: Wesleyan, 1992.

Ewen, David. *The Life and Death of Tin Pan Alley: The Golden Age of American Popular Music.* New York: Funk & Wagnalls, 1964.

Fay, Alice. *Music-Study in Germany.* London: Macmillan & Co., 1886.

Feinstein, Michael. *Nice Work If You Can Get It.* New York: Hyperion, 1995.

Ferber, Edna, and George S. Kaufman. *Dinner at Eight.* New York: Doubleday, 1932.

Forte, Allen. *The American Popular Ballad of the Golden Era.* Princeton, NJ: Princeton University Press, 1995.

Frank, Jerome. *Law and the Modern Mind.* New York: Brentano's, 1930.

Frankel, Noralee. *Stripping Gypsy.* New York: Oxford University Press, 2009.

Friedwald, Will. *Stardust Memories: A Biography of Twelve of America's Most Popular Songs.* New York: Pantheon, 2002.

Frolova-Walker, Marina. *Russian Music and Nationalism: From Glinka to Stalin.* New Haven, CT: Yale University Press, 2007.

Furia, Philip. *The Poets of Tin Pan Alley.* New York: Oxford University Press, 1990.

Gabler, Neal. *An Empire of Their Own: How the Jews Invented Hollywood.* New York: Anchor, 1988.

———. *Walt Disney: The Triumph of the American Imagination.* New York: Knopf, 2006.

Gilbert, Douglas. *Lost Chords: The Diverting Story of American Popular Songs.* New York: Doubleday, 1942.

Gilbert, L. Wolfe. *Without Rhyme or Reason*. New York: Vantage, 1956.

Gill, Brendan. *Here at the New Yorker*. New York: Random House, 1975.

Goldmark, Daniel. *Tunes for 'Toons: Music and the Hollywood Cartoon*. Berkeley: University of California Press, 2005.

Goldstein, Paul. *Copyright's Highway: The Law and Lore of Copyright from Gutenberg to the Celestial Jukebox*. New York: Hill and Wang, 1994.

Golenpaul, Dan, ed. *Information, Please!* New York: Random House, 1941.

Goodman, Peter. *Morton Gould: American Salute*. Portland, OR: Amadeus, 2000.

Gottlieb, Jack. *Funny, It Doesn't Sound Jewish*. Albany: SUNY Press, 2004.

Gracyk, Tim. *Popular American Recording Pioneers 1895–1925*. New York: Haworth, 2000.

Grams, Martin Jr. *Information, Please*. Albany, GA: BearManor, 2003.

Green, Abel. *Inside Stuff on How to Write Popular Songs*. New York: Paul Whiteman, 1927.

Green, Abel, and Joe Laurie. *Show Biz: From Vaude to Video as Seen by Variety*. New York: Permabooks, 1953.

Gunther, Gerald. *Learned Hand*. New York: Knopf, 1994.

Guralnick, Peter. *Last Train to Memphis: The Rise of Elvis Presley*. Boston: Little, Brown, 1994.

Gurock, Jeffrey. *When Harlem Was Jewish*. New York: Columbia University Press, 1979.

Hamm, Charles. *Irving Berlin: Songs from the Melting Pot: The Formative Years 1907–1914*. New York: Oxford University Press, 1997.

Hart, H. L. A. *The Concept of Law*. Oxford: Clarendon, 1961.

Hays, Arthur Garfield. *City Lawyer: The Autobiography of a Law Practice*. New York: Simon & Schuster, 1942.

Hazard, Geoffrey, Colin Tait, William Fletcher, and Stephen Bundy. *Pleading and Procedure State and Federal*, 9th ed. New York: Foundation Press, 2005.

Heskes, Irene. *Passport to Jewish Music*. Westport, CT: Greenwood, 1994.

———. *Yiddish American Popular Songs: 1895–1950*. Washington, DC: Library of Congress, 1992.

Heyworth, Peter. *Otto Klemperer: His Life and Times*, vol. 1. Cambridge: Cambridge University Press, 1983.

Hilmes, Michelle. *Radio Voices: American Broadcasting, 1922–1952*. Minneapolis: University of Minnesota Press, 1997.

Hipsher, Edward E. *American Opera and Its Composers*. Philadelphia: Theodore Presser Co., 1934.

Howard, John T. *Stephen Foster: America's Troubadour*. New York: Thomas Y. Crowell, 1934.

Howe, Irving. *World of Our Fathers*. New York: Touchstone, 1977.

Hubler, Richard. *The Cole Porter Story*. Cleveland, OH: World, 1965.

Hurst, Fannie. *Humoresque*. Whitefish, MT: Kessinger, 1997.

Isacoff, Stuart. *Temperament: How Music Became a Battleground for the Great Minds of Western Civilization*. New York: Vintage, 2003.

Jablonski, Edward. *Irving Berlin: American Troubadour*. New York: Holt, 1999.

James, Fleming Jr. and Geoffrey C. Hazard Jr. *Civil Procedure*, 2d ed. Boston: Little, Brown and Co., 1977.

Jasen, David. *Tin Pan Alley*. New York: Donald I. Fine, 1980.

Jenks, Tudor. *The Century World's Fair Book for Boys and Girls*. New York: The Century Co., 1893.

Kanfer, Stefan. *Stardust Lost: The Triumph, Tragedy, and Mishugas of the Yiddish Theatre in America*. New York: Vintage, 2006.

Kantor, Kenneth. *The Jews of Tin Pan Alley: The Jewish Contribution to Popular Music*. Jersey City, NJ: Ktav, 1982.

Kaplan, Justin, and Anne Bernays. *The Language of Names*. New York: Simon & Schuster, 1997.

Kashner, Sam, and Nancy Schoenberger. *A Talent for Genius: The Life and Times of Oscar Levant*. New York: Villard, 1994.

Kieran, John. *Not under Oath: Recollections and Reflections*. Boston: Houghton Mifflin, 1964.

Kimball, Robert, and Linda Emmet, eds. *The Complete Lyrics of Irving Berlin*. New York: Knopf, 2000.

Korsyn, Kevin. *Decentering Music: A Critique of Contemporary Musical Research*. New York: Oxford, 2003.

Kreuger, Miles. *The Movie Musical from Vitaphone to 42nd Street as Reported in Great Fan Magazine*. New York: Dover, 1975.

Kriwaczek, Paul. *Yiddish Civilization: The Rise and Fall of a Forgotten Nation*. New York: Knopf, 2005.

Labov, William. *The Social Stratification of English in New York City*. Washington, DC: Center for Applied Linguistics, 1966.

Larson, Erik. *The Devil in the White City*. New York: Vintage, 2003.

Lawrence, Jack. *They All Sang My Songs*. Fort Lee, NJ: Barricade, 2004.

Leavy, Jane. *Sandy Koufax: A Lefty's Legacy*. New York: HarperCollins, 2002.

Lee, Gypsy Rose. *Gypsy: A Memoir*. New York: Harper, 1957.

Lessig, Lawrence. *The Future of Ideas*. New York: Random House, 2001.

Levant, Oscar. *The Memoirs of an Amnesiac*. New York: Putnam, 1965.

———. *A Smattering of Ignorance*. New York: Doubleday, 1940.

Lewis, Sinclair. *Babbitt*. New York: Harcourt, Brace, 1922.

Lewis, Tom. *Empires of the Air: The Men Who Made Radio*. New York: HarperCollins, 1991.

Lindey, Alexander. *Plagiarism and Originality*. New York: Harper & Bros., 1952.

Lineff, Eugeniia. *Peasant Songs of Great Russia as They Are in the Folk's Harmonizations*, 2d ser. Moscow: Imperial Academy of Science, 1911.

———. *Russian Folk Songs as Sung by the People and Peasant Wedding Ceremonies Customary in Northern and Central Russia*. Chicago: Summy, 1893.

Litman, Jessica. *Digital Copyright*. New York: Prometheus, 2006.

Loncraine, Rebecca. *The Real Wizard of Oz: The Life and Times of L. Frank Baum*. New York: Gotham, 2009.

Marcus, Richard, Martin Redish, Edward Sherman, and James Pfander. *Civil Procedure: A Modern Approach*, 5th ed. St. Paul, MN: West, 2009.

Marks, Edward B. *They All Had Glamour: From the Swedish Nightingale to the Naked Lady*. New York: Messner, 1944.

Marks, Edward B. *They All Sang: From Tony Pastor to Rudy Vallée*. New York: Viking, 1934.

Marks, Edward Jr. *Still Counting: Achievements and Follies of a Nonagenarian.* Lanham, MD: Hamilton, 2005.

Massachusetts Historical Society. *Proceedings, October 1920–June 1921.* Cambridge, MA: University Press, 1922.

McBrien, William. *Cole Porter.* New York: Knopf, 1998.

McLeod, Kembrew. *Freedom of Expression®: Overzealous Copyright Bozos and Other Enemies of Creativity.* New York: Doubleday, 2005.

Meyer, Hazel. *The Gold in Tin Pan Alley.* Philadelphia: Lippincott, 1958.

Mihalyo, Michael. *The Life and Keyboard Works of (Franz) Xaver Scharwenka.* Ph.D. diss., West Virginia University, 2002.

Miles, Henry. *Orpheus in the Wilderness: A History of Music in Denver 1860–1925.* Denver: Colorado Historical Society, 2006.

Miller, Marc. *Representing the Immigrant Experience: Morris Rosenfeld and the Emergence of Yiddish Literature in America.* Syracuse, NY: Syracuse University Press, 2007.

Mooney, Matthew. *All Join in the Chorus: Sheet Music, Vaudeville, and the Formation of American Cinema, 1904–1914.* Ph.D. diss., University of California, Irvine, 2006.

Mueller, John. *The American Symphony Orchestra.* Bloomington: Indiana University Press, 1951.

Neal, Steve. *Happy Days Are Here Again: The 1932 Democratic Convention, the Emergence of FDR—and How America Was Changed Forever.* New York: Wm. Morrow, 2004.

Nemtsov, Jascha. *Der Zionismus in der Musik.* Wiesbaden: Harrassowitz, 2009.

New York Landmarks Preservation Commission. *West End—Collegiate Historic District Designation Report.* 1984.

Nimmo, Harry. *The Andrews Sisters: A Biography and Career Record.* Jefferson, NC: McFarland & Co., 2004.

Nizer, Louis. *My Life in Court.* New York: Doubleday, 1961.

Okrent, Daniel. *Great Fortune: The Epic of Rockefeller Center.* New York: Viking, 2003.

———. *Last Call: The Rise and Fall of Prohibition.* New York: Scribner, 2010.

Olmstead, Andrea. *Juilliard: A History.* Champaign: University of Illinois Press, 2002.

Oring, Elliot. *The Jokes of Sigmund Freud.* Philadelphia: University of Pennsylvania Press, 1984.

Palmer, Jack, and Robert Olson. *Vernon Dalhart: The First Star of Country Music.* Denver, CO: Mainspring, 2005.

Pegolotti, James. *Deems Taylor: A Biography.* Boston: Northeastern University Press, 2003.

Perino, Michael. *The Hellhound of Wall Street: How Ferdinand Pecora's Investigation of the Great Crash Forever Changed American Finance.* New York: Penguin, 2010.

Pressman, Jack. *Last Resort: Psychosurgery and the Limits of Medicine.* Cambridge: Cambridge University Press, 1998.

Putnam, Robert. *Bowling Alone.* New York: Simon & Schuster, 2000.

Ravitz, Abe. *Imitations of Life: Fannie Hurst's Gaslight Sonatas.* Carbondale: Southern Illinois University Press, 1997.

Reich, Howard, and William Gaines. *Jelly's Blues: The Life, Music, and Redemption of Jelly Roll Morton.* Cambridge, MA: DeCapo Press, 2003.

Rodgers, Richard. *Musical Stages.* New York: Random House, 1975.

Rosen, Ronald. *Music and Copyright.* New York: Oxford University Press, 2008.

Rosenberg, Chaim. *America at the Fair: Chicago's 1893 World's Columbian Exposition*. Charleston, SC: Arcadia, 2008.

Rosenblatt, Samuel. *Yossele Rosenblatt: The Story of His Life as Told by His Son*. New York: Farrar, 1954.

Roth, Henry. *Mercy of a Rude Stream*. New York: St. Martin's, 1994.

Rubin, Ruth. *Voices of a People: The Story of Yiddish Folksong*. Chicago: University of Illinois Press, 2000.

Ryan, John. *The Production of Culture in the Music Industry*. Lanham, MD: University Press of America, 1985.

Rybczynksi, Witold. *A Clearing in the Distance*. New York: Knopf, 1999.

Sacks, Oliver. *Musicophilia: Tales of Music and the Brain*. New York: Knopf, 2007.

Sandage, Scott. *Born Losers: A History of Failure in America*. Cambridge, MA: Harvard University Press, 2005.

Sanjek, Russell. *Pennies from Heaven: The American Popular Music Business in the Twentieth Century*. Cambridge, MA: DeCapo Press, 1996.

Sanjek, Russell, and David Sanjek. *American Popular Music in the 20th Century*. New York: Oxford University Press, 1991.

Schabas, Ezra. *Theodore Thomas: America's Conductor and Builder of Orchestras*. Urbana: University of Illinois Press, 1989.

Scharwenka, Xaver. *Sounds from My Life: Reminiscences of a Musician*. Lanham, MD: Scarecrow Press, 2007.

Schick, Marvin. *Learned Hand's Court*. Baltimore: Johns Hopkins Press, 1970.

Schwartz, Charles. *Cole Porter: A Biography*. Cambridge, MA: DeCapo Press, 1979.

Secunda, Victoria. *Bei Mir Bist Du Schön*. Bozeman, MT: Magic Circle, 1981.

Seldes, Gilbert. *The Seven Lively Arts*. New York: Dover, 2001.

Shandler, Jeffrey. *Jews, God, and Videotape: Religion and Media in America*. New York: New York University Press, 2009.

Shaw, Arnold. *The Jazz Age: Popular Music in the 1920s*. New York: Oxford University Press, 1987.

Shealy, Alexander, ed. *World's Favorite Piano Solos*. Carlstadt, NJ: Ashley Publications, 1968.

Sheed, Wilfred. *The House That George Built*. New York: Random House, 2007.

Shemel, Sidney, and M. William Krasilovsky. *The Business of Music*. New York: Billboard, 1964.

Shilkret, Nathaniel. *Sixty Years in the Music Business*. Lanham, MD: Scarecrow Press, 2005.

Slonimsky, Nicolas. *Lexicon of Musical Invective*. New York: Coleman-Ross Co., 1965.

Spaeth, Sigmund. *The Common Sense of Music*. New York: Garden City, 1924.

———. *The Facts of Life in Popular Song*. New York: Whittlesey House, 1935.

———. *Great Program Music: How to Enjoy and Remember It*. New York: Garden City, 1940.

———. *Great Symphonies: How to Recognize and Remember Them*. New York: Garden City, 1936.

———. *A History of Popular Music in America*. New York: Random House, 1948.

———. *The Importance of Music*. New York: Fleet, 1963.

———. *Milton's Knowledge of Music*. Ann Arbor: University of Michigan Press, 1963.

————. *Read 'Em and Weep: The Songs You Forgot to Remember*. New York: Arco, 1959.

————. *Words and Music: A Book of Burlesques*. New York: Simon & Schuster, 1926.

Steinberg, Michael, and Larry Rothe. *For the Love of Music: Invitations to Listening*. New York: Oxford University Press, 2006.

Suisman, David. *Selling Sounds: The Commercial Revolution in American Music*. Cambridge, MA: Harvard University Press, 2009.

Taruskin, Richard. *Stravinsky and the Russian Traditions*. Berkeley: University of California Press, 1996.

Thomas, Theodore. *A Musical Autobiography*. Chicago: McClurg, 1905.

Tuttle, Charles H. *Life Stories of a Celebrated Lawyer in New York and Lake George*. Clinton Corners, NY: College Avenue, 2002.

Tyler, Samuel. *Memoir of Roger Brooke Taney, LL.D*. Baltimore: Murphy & Co., 1872.

Upton, George. *Musical Memories*. Chicago: McClurg, 1908.

Vaidhyanathan, Siva. *Copyrights and Copywrongs: The Rise of Intellectual Property and How It Threatens Creativity*. New York: New York University Press, 2001.

White, Trumbull, and William Igleheart. *The World's Columbian Exposition, Chicago, 1893*. Philadelphia: P. W. Ziegler & Co., 1893.

Whitehead, John. *A Life in Leadership: From D-Day to Ground Zero*. New York: Basic, 2005.

Wilder, Alec. *American Popular Song: The Great Innovators*. New York: Oxford University Press, 1990.

Witmark, Isadore, and Isaac Goldberg. *From Ragtime to Swingtime: The Story of the House of Witmark*. New York: Lee Furman, 1939.

Woollcott, Alexander. *The Story of Irving Berlin*. Cambridge, MA: DeCapo Press, 1983.

Wright, Charles. *Law of Federal Courts*, 4th ed. St. Paul, MN: West, 1983.

Zinsser, William. *Easy to Remember: The Great American Songwriters and Their Songs*. New York: David R. Godine, 2001.

INDEX

"President Cleveland's Wedding March"
(Witmark), 6
Presley, Elvis, xiii, 184, 245, 250, 254,
256
Princeton University, 104–7
"Prisoner's Song, The" (Shilkret/
Massey), 84–85
Producers, The, 91
Prohibition, 3, 21, 89–91, 100, 112, 125,
152
Proust, Marcel, 3, 28
Puccini, Giacomo, 196

Rachmaninoff, Sergei, 44, 110
Radio broadcasting. *See* ASCAP; BMI;
CBS; National Association of
Broadcasters; NBC; Sarnoff,
David; Shilkret, Nathaniel
Radio Corporation of America. *See* RCA
Ragtime, 12, 32
"Ramona" (Gilbert), 96, 120
Ramona (movie), 120
Random House, 241
Rapée, Ernö, 67, 150
Rathbone, Basil, 186
Ravel, Maurice, 187, 228
RCA (Radio Corporation of America),
93, 95, 153, 155, 160, 196, 249,
256
Reader's Digest, 251
Reagan, Ronald, 233
Recording industry, 5, 18–20, 67, 83–86,
240, 246–47, 256
Reed v. Carusi, 122–25, 142, 236
Reed, George P., 122–25
Rehfeld, Fabian, 55
Remick, Jerome (Jerome H. Remick &
Co.), 10, 74
Remington Records, 240
Republic Pictures, 117
Rettenberg, Milton, 197
Rhapsody in Blue (Gershwin), 85, 199
Rhythm and blues (race music), xii, 246
Richter, Theodore B., 127, 130–35,
139–42, 165
Ricordi, G., 196
Rifkind, Simon, 220, 255

"Ritz Rock-and-Roll, The" (Porter), 256
RKO (Radio-Keith-Orpheum) Pictures,
87
Robeson, Paul, 33
Robison, Carson, 84
Robyn, William "Wee Willie," 67–68, 84,
88
Rock and roll, xii, 21–23, 247–50,
255–56
Rockwell, John, 187–88
Rodgers, Jimmie, 195
Rodgers, Richard, 10, 76, 215, 231, 236,
242
Rogers, Ginger, 78
Rogers, Will, 3–4, 17, 21, 102
Romberg, Sigmund, 138
Roosevelt, Franklin D., 3–6, 90–91, 94,
114, 148, 214, 218–19, 224
Roosevelt, Eleanor, 214, 218
Rose, Billy, 99, 216
Rosenblatt, Josef ("Yossele"), xv, 51,
56–65, 67, 69, 74, 84, 252
Rosenfeld, Morris, 65, 252
Rosenthal, J. C., 93
Rotarian, The, 112
Roth, Henry, 51, 251
Rothafel, Samuel ("Roxy"), 67–68, 114,
140
Rothe, Larry, 188, 250
Rothstein, Shloimele, 67
"Row, Row, Row with Roosevelt"
(Coots/Dowling), 4
Rubinoff, David, 8
"Rum and Coca-Cola" (Amsterdam), 255
Rumshinsky, Joseph, 50, 163
Russell, Henry, 123
"Russian Peasant Wedding, The," 37–40
Ryan, John, 246
Ryskind, Morrie, 6

Sacco (Ferdinando) and Vanzetti
(Bartolomeo), 98
SACEM (Société des Auteurs,
Compositeurs et Éditeurs de
Musique), 148
Sackler, Harry, 69
Samson and Delilah, 69